A RARE BOOK SAGA

Photo by Karsh, Ottawa

A RARE BOOK SAGA

The Autobiography of
H. P. KRAUS

G.P. Putnam's Sons · New York

Copyright © 1978 by H. P. Kraus
All rights reserved. This book or parts thereof must
not be reproduced in any form without permission.
Published simultaneously in Canada by Longman Canada
Limited, Toronto.

SBN: 399-12064-5
Library of Congress Cataloging in Publication Data

Kraus, Hans Peter, 1907–
   A rare book saga.

   Includes index.
   1. Kraus, Hans Peter, 1907–   2. Antiquarian booksellers—United States—Biography.   I. Title.
Z473.K74K7   658.8'09'0705730924 [B]   77-28643

PRINTED IN THE UNITED STATES OF AMERICA

*TO MY BELOVED
WIFE AND PARTNER*

Contents

	Introduction	xi
	Preface	xiii

PART I

1.	"In the Beginning . . ."	1
2.	A Boy Hunts Treasures	12
3.	Working for $4.20 a Month	20
4.	On the Road as a Salesman	26
5.	A Salesman Becomes a Rare Book Dealer	35
6.	Competing in the Rare Book Trade	45
7.	I Am a Survivor	56
8.	A New Life Begins	73
9.	The Ideal Partner Found	79
10.	Business During the War	83
11.	16 East 46th Street	98
12.	Europe Revisited	104
13.	H. P. K.'s Family	112

PART II

14.	Success at Jenkintown	117
15.	Five Significant Failures	127
16.	Unsold for Twenty Years	139
17.	The Buenos Aires Ghost	143
18.	An Old Noble Family Sells	151
19.	Clandestine Literature	157
20.	Three Gourmets	166

21.	Walking Up the Main Staircase	168
22.	Joint Ventures	171
23.	Discoveries Celebrated by Postage Stamps	180
24.	Some Bibliomaniacs	183
25.	Finding the Hours of Catherine of Cleves	191
26.	A Lucky Purchase	196
27.	From the Victorian Past	201
28.	My Greatest Disappointment	205
29.	A Book-Collecting Banker	211
30.	There Was No Silver Lining	215
31.	The Most Mysterious Manuscript	218
32.	The Obsessed	223
33.	The Cradle of Printing	227
34.	The First Printer of England	244
35.	Window Shopping in Florence	251
36.	The Battles of Three Auctions	257
37.	The Collector *Par Excellence*	271
38.	In Noble Company	289
39.	Yale and Beinecke	295
40.	The Great Collector of Aachen	302
41.	The Bibliophile of Schweinfurt	308
42.	Three Generations of Collectors	313
43.	One Manuscript for $750,000	319
44.	A Constitution Bought, a Declaration Lost	324
45.	Bestiaries	329
46.	My Lifelong Romance with Cartography	335
47.	I Am Also a Collector	343
48.	Why I Will Be Remembered	351
49.	The Elegant Bookman	358
50.	Thank You, Uncle Sam	361
51.	The Great Transaction	367
	Epilogue	373
	Index	377

Figures

1.	Mercator Atlas, 1595	15
2.	Postcards from Concentration Camps	61
3.	Giant Bible of Mainz	124
4.	Pfister "Ghost" Book	145
5.	Rabelais Source Book	155
6.	Communist Manifesto	161
7.	Haymarket meeting	162
8.	Doctrina Christiana, Philippine stamp	181
8a.	"Roger Bacon" Cypher Manuscript	220
9.	First Phillipps catalogue	225
10.	Constance Missal	232
11.	Gutenberg Bible	239
12.	Chaucer, *The Canterbury Tales*	247
13.	Caxton's *Recuyell of the Historyes of Troye*	249
14.	Printer's device of Caxton	250
15.	Some newspaper clippings	256
16.	Lea & Perrins label	267
17.	Four famous firsts from Bodmer	285
18.	Clark collection bookplate	300
19.	Basel Planetenbuch	311
20.	The 1457 Psalter	315
21.	The 1459 Psalter	315
22.	Declaration of Independence	326
23.	English Bestiary	331
24.	Waldseemüller, globe gores, 1507	339
25.	Title pages from H.P.K. Collection	345
26.	J. F. A. Kraus, Celebration of 300 years of printing	346
27.	First American Type Specimen Book	347
28.	Some H.P.K. catalogues	354–355
29.	Congressional Record 1970	362
30.	*New York Times* front page	364
31.	*Amoretti Codex*	365

Introduction

THESE MEMOIRS TELL the most extraordinary story of dealing in rare books and manuscripts that I have ever read. Extraordinary stories are not uncommon in the world of books: the tales of Sir Thomas Phillipps and his collections or of the Boswell Papers would be branded outrageous fiction if they were not fully documented as fact. The following narrative of the life of my friend Hans P. Kraus is no less incredible, and no less true.

Having been a book collector for more than fifty years and a librarian for more than thirty, I have known, with varying degrees of intimacy, almost all the collectors, librarians, and dealers of the period. I have seen their collections and listened often to their anecdotes, sometimes in the manner of the Persians, of whom Herodotus tells us that they debated important matters once drunk and once sober. Much that is told of rare books gains greatly in the telling, and another noted book dealer wisely printed in his catalogues a passage from Proverbs: "It is naught, it is naught, saith the buyer; but when he is gone his way, then he boasteth."

There is nothing of such amiable fiction in what follows. If all the books and manuscripts that have passed through the hands of Hans Kraus (and those still in his hands) could be assembled in one place, they would form a collection such as has never been seen in a dealer's hands.

There is vanity in all memoirs and these are no exception. But what there is of it here rests on justified pride in accomplishment. To have pursued, secured, and purveyed a legion of the greatest books and manuscripts, the precious possessions of emperors and princes for which the rich and powerful eagerly compete, is an attainment all the greater because of its humble beginning. It is a history of the success of hard work, knowledge, skill, cunning, patience, and a great deal of good luck in dealing with some of the most valuable, most beautiful, and most significant objects created by man. It is a treasure hunter's story.

Happily, Hans's memory is sharp and his records are very full, so that the long parade of riches can be passed before our eyes and the unknown stories behind them can be related. Take this book to your favorite chair, arm yourself with the beverage of your choice, and read. Scheherazade herself never told better tales, and these have the virtue of being authentic. I have never believed of any book, including this one, the claim that it cannot be put down, but I know this is a book that I will always pick up with pleasure.

Herman W. Liebert
New Haven, Connecticut
June 1977

Preface

THERE IS NOTHING HEROIC in the story of my life. Still I could not resist calling it a saga—"A Rare Book Saga."

There were drastic ups and downs during the tumultuous period of history I have lived in. I was part of a generation beset by war and economic chaos but, at the same time, marked by unparalleled advances in science, medicine, and technology. It has been a privilege to live during these years as well as a satisfaction to overcome their difficulties. Thinking back over the various large and small personal dramas, and reflecting on the fact that everything turned out successfully, often when success appeared impossible, I believe I am justified in calling my life a saga. I hope my readers will agree.

Dealing in old and rare books may sound like a scholarly, dull pursuit. For anyone passionate about books it can be exciting, suspenseful, and dramatic; but it can also be nerve-wracking; and each day's events are often unpredictable.

Antiquarian bookselling involves detective work, research carrying one back through all of recorded history, across the globe, and into just about every human activity.

Romance occurs in ample doses, with the discovery of 500-year-old works in attics and cellars, and the rescue of valuable books and manuscripts considered trash by their owners. About 1840 an Englishman making a purchase at a shop in Boulogne found that it was wrapped in a fragment of a letter written and signed by James Boswell. The shopkeeper told him she had bought the paper from a wastepaper dealer and had some more. He was able to buy 97 autograph letters from Boswell to his lifelong friend and confidant, the Reverend William Johnson Temple. These letters were published in 1856.

The rare book business has its battlefield: the auction room. No combatants ever faced each other with more determination, or more fight-to-the-death spirit, than bidders competing to buy the same book. The fever of the auction room is contagious and paying record prices can become an obsession.

The players in this bookish drama are often colorful: the present-day counterparts of collectors like Morgan and Huntington, who may buy a hundred-thousand-dollar book with as little deliberation as one buys a magazine from a news dealer, speculators who hope to realize large profits by investing in rare books, scholar-collectors whose work and discoveries are often based on their private libraries (Wilberforce Eames slept in a hammock with piles of books beneath it). There are vellomaniacs like Sir Thomas Phillipps, a species by no means extinct, who delight in anything written or printed on parchment. There are even some not interested in the book as a whole but only in a certain part of it: the binding, the illustrations, or the size. You have the obsessed, too, like Henry C. Folger, founder of the great Folger Library, who spent the better part of his life buying multiple copies of the Four Folios of Shakespeare and anything else by or about him.

The writing of memoirs by an antiquarian bookseller is no unique undertaking. Henry Stevens published his *Recollections*, a fascinating volume. More recently, reminiscences have been compiled by many other dealers. Adding a further volume to the group, with no purpose other than recording another bookseller's life—stringing together a collection of anecdotes—might be looked on as pure vanity. Every major bookseller, like successful people in other professions, has a good story to tell. But this book is much more than an account of my life; essentially it serves as a record of some of the most important transactions of rare books and manuscripts during the past forty-five years.

Many of the dramatic purchases and sales detailed here are of historic interest. A number made international headlines. Still, the full inside stories have never been told. Even well-informed persons in the trade knew little of the particulars. They wondered how I was able to buy the Washington-Rochambeau papers, and where they came from; they marveled at the emergence of the legendary *Constance Missal* on the market, when I sold my copy to the Morgan Library. And they expressed amazement at my other exploits, in particular my ability to buy from collectors who refused to sell to others, and my luring of ancient manuscripts out of the monasteries which had housed them for centuries.

This book presents numerous records of prices, even into seven figures. But it shows at the same time that capital alone does not make a great bookseller. Most of my memorable acquisitions could not have happened without a thorough knowledge both of books and of human nature; also essential was a belief in the values of rare books and manuscripts, a conviction about books as artistic and historical objects, and a willingness to gamble—because no matter how great the book, the eventual fate of a purchase is never certain.

People often ask me, "What was your greatest book, the one supreme book among all that you've bought and sold?"
That depends on one's definition of greatness. In monetary terms my most expensive purchase was the Shuckburgh-Houghton Gutenberg Bible, acquired in 1970 in a transaction involving a seven figure amount for a single book—which still stands, after nearly a decade, as a record price. But to get things in proper perspective—and this applies to all statements of prices throughout this work—you must realize that yesterday's sale prices are irrelevant today. In a market where the commodity is in very limited supply, and the number of buyers is constantly increasing, prices can and often do rise sharply. Books which seemed expensive ten or even five years ago are seldom found at yesteryear's prices. A glance through my old catalogues bears this out. For some books that appeared in my early catalogues I would gladly pay many times the price today. Just one example: in my catalogue 75, issued in 1956, a splendid large copy in magnificent French morocco of the *Nuremberg Chronicle*, 1493, is listed at $875. This is now a $10,000 to $17,000 book in such condition.

Shakespeare's name is readily mentioned in connection with greatness. My personal choice for a great Shakespearean book, aside from the Four Folios, is a first edition (1608) of *King Lear* printed on paper different from that of the six recorded complete copies. I purchased this volume as part of my largest overall acquisition, when during a period of several years in the early 1970s I bought many great treasures from the library of the late Dr. Martin Bodmer of Geneva. *King Lear* went to the Beinecke Rare Book and Manuscript Library at Yale in 1974 for $140,000.

With the Bicentennial just behind us, the first printing of the Declaration of Independence comes to mind. Unsuccessful in my first two attempts to buy a copy (the first was when a Texan spent $404,000 to outbid me, in a heavily publicized sale), I succeeded in 1975.

Manuscripts, each being unique, belong in a separate class. I think I can safely state that few booksellers of this century have handled so many significant manuscripts of all varieties: Books of Hours, early Bibles, Arab and Coptic texts, Korans, Greek and Latin classics, papyri. While others bought manuscripts occasionally, I made bids at every important sale and bought for stock. The amounts tied up in this fashion were staggering. But my fondness for manuscripts would have prompted me to buy in any event, as a collector, even without prospects for resale

The *St. Albans Apocalypse* might well be called one of my greatest manuscripts. Bought in 1959 from the Dyson Perrins collection, it gave me international TV and press publicity, the first in my career.

But, frankly, my own choices for the "greatest" books and manuscripts include none of these.

My nomination, among printed books, is the first to be set from moveable type in the English language: LeFèvre, *Recuyell of the Historyes of Troye*, printed at Bruges, Flanders (now Belgium), by William Caxton in 1473–74. It could hardly be termed physically beautiful, but this is the book which brought printing to the English language and—almost as important, to bibliophiles—launched Caxton's career after his apprenticeship at Cologne.

My greatest manuscript was, in my opinion, a hitherto unknown 13th-century *Apocalypse*—not the St. Albans—containing seventy-two large illuminations in a fresh original style. It appeared in a sale along with eleven other illuminated manuscripts at Paris on June 24, 1968, and was sold by me to the Metropolitan Museum. Its story, too, is told at greater length in these reminiscences.

As you will see, a reversal of earlier trends occurred during the 1950s. Precious books and manuscripts started to migrate back to Europe into the great private collections in Geneva, Aachen, Schweinfurt, as well as many other places.

I do not want to give readers the impression that I deal only in great and expensive books and manuscripts. This would be contrary to my temperament. Such opportunities occur infrequently, and I like not only quality but also quantity—both in buying and in selling.

In fact I deal in all fields, in books by the thousands and at moderate prices. To keep up-to-date I have even started to handle early photographs, in which there is rising interest.

My catalogues of bibliographies and reference works have always been very successful.

Many books sell for between $20 and $100, even items of the 16th to the 18th century. This is my bread-and-butter business which I consider a service to libraries and to scholars.

PREFACE

My chief handicap in writing these memoirs has been my shortcoming in the English language. When I arrived in America in 1939, my vocabulary was poor, as well as my grammar, and even today I do not write or speak English as if it were my native tongue. Encouragement came from my old friend Herman (Fritz) Liebert. For his help, and that of others, I owe a large debt of gratitude.

The principal assistance came however from my dear wife Hanni. Without her energy and spirit I would never have accomplished this monumental task. During the last few months, when our publisher impatiently asked us for the finished manuscript, she worked literally day and night, contributing new ideas and correcting mistakes.

Since our marriage she has been a full partner in the business and has lived most of these adventures with me. Her uncanny memory vividly brought back many of these stories and the details surrounding them. When in this book I use the first person, my readers will understand that "we" is often intended.

The book is divided into two parts, a more or less chronological biography covering my boyhood and early days as a bookseller, emigration to America, and establishing a business in New York; and then accounts of individual reminiscences.

I hope my reader will understand my feelings. As one gets on in years and tends to look back on the old days, one recaptures old emotions, remembers old friends, and revels in past glories.

H.P.K.
December, 1977

PART I

CHAPTER 1

"In the Beginning . . ."

THE LITTLE BOY rolled his hoop down the sunny sidewalk of Vienna's Volksgarten with all the careless abandon of a five-year-old.
It was 1912 and this was old Vienna, the imperial capital, with music of Strauss in the air and the prospect of war as distant as a flight to the moon. Life was a ball, a waltz.

The hoop had ideas of its own and rolled into the cobblestoned street, into an oncoming carriage's path. In an instant the hoop was crushed to splinters beneath its wheels.

The boy began to howl.

His governess stared in blank amazement.

This was no ordinary carriage but a stately, well-known one. In it sat an equally stately looking old gentleman with long, flowing white sideburns and stern expression. The breast of his military uniform bore medals upon medals, gleaming in the midday sun. On his head was a green-feathered military hat.

Rapidly a crowd began gathering.

A young officer riding with the old man climbed down and pressed a coin into the governess's hand, to buy a new hoop.

The boy continued wailing, but now his misery mixed with wonder. Cheering went up on all sides. Police appeared. "Remove your hat," someone told the boy, pushing him forward. "And make a bow."

He did so, and the old man responded with an imperial wave of the hand.

That was how I met Franz Joseph, Emperor of Austria and King of

Hungary. Within four years he was dead and old prewar Europe with him.

I was born October 12, 1907, into a Vienna that was one of the great cultural, intellectual, and scientific capitals of Europe. Paris turned out more painters, perhaps, but no city could equal Vienna's output of composers, musicians, sculptors, philosophers, inventors, scientists, or great physicians. Vienna could support multitudes of medical doctors because patients came to them from all parts of the country, not to mention other countries of Europe. Both my father, Emil, and his father, Ignatius Kraus, were doctors.

Grandfather Kraus had his share of noble bearing and could easily be mistaken for one of the royal family. Tall and dashing, he had a medical practice at the Karlsbad spa, in a palatial house called "The Duke of Brabant." There he ministered to old dowagers and their spouses, who came each summer to "take the waters" and go back revived to face another English or Dutch winter. Sometimes they took him along, to continue the treatments. Once, while he was staying at London's Savoy Hotel, a letter arrived for him, forwarded from Karlsbad. Seeing the address, "The Duke of Brabant," the hotel manager thereafter addressed grandfather as "Your Grace" and promised that his real identity would not be revealed to anyone. Why a Flemish nobleman would masquerade as a doctor seemed a bit puzzling, though.

My uncle and cousin were also physicians, so it was assumed that I would enter the medical profession. But medicine, secure and comfortable a career though it was, held no charms for me. This was disappointing for the family, but my father, a man of scholarly pursuits and an amateur antiquarian, found my interest in books not entirely displeasing. Had I chosen the bar, or an acting career, this would have been totally foreign to him. Collecting he could understand, even if my mother and the rest of the family could not. He collected stamps ardently, filling over a hundred albums, mostly with issues of Austria-Hungary. In addition he collected paintings, bronzes, porcelain, textiles, antique furniture, and general bric-a-brac. For all these, early 20th-century Vienna was a happy hunting ground indeed. Three centuries of furnishings, made for homes of aristocrats and near-aristocrats, could be bought in the marketplaces, often selling for less than newly manufactured pieces.

My great-grandfather on my mother's side, Dr. Adalbert Rix, was also a physician. He practiced in Budapest. One notable break with medicine came in the person of Anton Rix, my mother's father, who started out as a doctor but became a merchant. He died young. Afterward his widow,

Hermine, ran the business, in addition to ruling the family. She was the matriarch in our family tree.

My mother, Hilda Rix, and my father were married in 1904 and I was their only child.

Vienna was an ideal place in which to be a child before the war, with its parks where you were taken every afternoon by a nanny. As an only child, I probably received more than my share of pampering. In 1913, the year after my encounter with the Emperor, I was enrolled in school. I was six years old. Vienna had comparatively few public schools, as many families retained private tutors for their children or sent them to boarding schools. It happened that the nearest public school was beyond walking distance for my young legs. So I went to a nearby private school: a girls' school. End of pampering.

The teacher, a well-disposed old woman, was willing to endure me. Her class had other feelings. A lone boy in the midst of several dozen female students fares no better than the other way round. No matter where I sat, my head served as target for flying balls of paper and paper airplanes sailed into my lap. At recess my classmates showered even more attentions and debris on me. It was more than tender young emotions could endure. How could I fight back against girls?

During the next period, I decided to make my escape.

I raised my hand for bathroom leave (which brought another wave of giggles, confirming my decision to go A.W.O.L.), and bolted out to the street. Without looking back, I kept walking.

I would go home, explain the indignities I had suffered, and of course mother and father would not expect me ever to return.

There was just one slight problem. In my haste I turned a wrong corner and was now on an unfamiliar street.

After an hour of walking I realized that I was lost. Luckily this was not the forest, with nobody around. As always, strollers filled the streets. So I did what any six-year-old does under such circumstances, I began to cry bitterly, until a policeman came to my aid, asked my address, and brought me home.

There I found, instead of a lynching party, a weeping mother and an hysterical teacher, both certain I had met with foul play.

Next day I was back at class, but in a suddenly more decorous atmosphere. My little escapade had served its purpose. In fact I was treated by the girls as something of a hero: the first student who had enough courage to walk out.

Later that semester I came down with scarlet fever, a common ailment in those days, and spent three months at home. By the time I recovered, school was recessed for the summer.

All sorts of recollections come back to me about those years. There was the *Stellwagen*, the horse-drawn streetcar that ran on tracks like a trolley but far surpassed a trolley for thrills. Though it was not very elegant, children delighted in watching the *Stellwagen* rumble along. Never did I tire of watching it, racing to the window as hoofbeats and clattering signaled its approach. On my birthday I was allowed to ride the entire route.

Yes, we had autos on the streets, but not many in prewar days. Carriages outnumbered them, for tradition died hard in old Vienna. Some noble families, disdaining gas-guzzling cars but not wanting to be considered too old-fashioned, moved sedately in electric automobiles. Why the odorless, quiet, nonpolluting electric car failed to catch hold is beyond me.

Vienna and its way of life still belonged to the 19th century. Then, in one afternoon, everything changed.

St. Wolfgang, a mediaeval village where the Kraus family usually spent its summers, had been built in the 15th century. Still intact was the town's pride and joy, the church of St. Wolfgang with its famous altar carved by Michael Pacher and paintings by Friedrich Pacher.

On June 28, 1914, I was strolling with grandmother along the lakefront. My father came running along the road. I knew it must be urgent news of some kind; he was not the sort to run without provocation.

Archduke Franz Ferdinand had been shot . . . yes, it was sure . . . in his car while passing through the streets . . . where? . . . the place was called Sarajevo.

Sarajevo meant nothing to me at the time, nor to most of the world. Later it would be on everyone's lips. It would become synonymous with assassination.

A month later Austria declared war on Serbia and my father was called into service.

Still, many people continued to live in a sort of dreamworld, sitting peacefully at sidewalk cafés, joking about all the fuss over one little assassination. Within a month it would be all over, they confidently predicted. Austrian armies would triumph, then return in grand parade to join the civilians in a victory celebration. Just an annoyance, this war. Mostly a political thing. Nothing to worry about. And they sang and danced and made merry, while the foundations of old imperial Austria quaked beneath them.

War was exciting, for those not on the battlefield. Back home there was general mobilization, with some factories working 24 hours to produce military supplies. Long columns of flag-bearing troops marched smartly and loudly along the boulevards, singing, "We'll be home by Christmas." Then, gradually, the realities set in. It would not be a short war. Austria's very survival hung in the balance. Shortages began. Prices rose. There was black marketeering. More and more men were called up.

For a child it was baffling. We had been taught to love our neighbors. Now the reverse was being drummed into us: Hate the Serbs, kill the Serbs. In school we learned to sing *Serbien muss sterbien*—Serbia must die—as if it were the national anthem.

If anyone asked why Serbia must die, he received this answer: "Because the Serbs killed Franz Ferdinand, heir to the throne."

Yes, the sins of a single man had washed over all his countrymen. It seemed incredible. But there was no point in carrying the questions any further. A war was going on, and Austria's people had to unite in the effort.

With all the talk of war, children began playing war games on the streets and in the parks. I played with my mates in the Volksgarten ("People's Park") before the House of Parliament and the Hofburg. It seemed an ideal setting, where so much history had been made. We chose sides. One side consisted of imperial forces, the other of "bad Serbs." The script was always the same. After half an hour of fierce fighting—more in good weather—the bad Serbs were put to rout or massacred. If some of the "imperial forces" took things too seriously, it could go very badly for the unlucky boys playing Serbs. One small tyke, persuaded by blandishments of candy to play Serb, could withstand the pummeling no longer and beat a retreat, despite his promise to stay and be "killed."

My father, upon his call-up, abandoned his practice in Vienna and our apartment there, despite warnings from everybody that this was hasty since the war should end in a few months.

He was sent to Baden, which, considering the places one might be sent, was a stroke of good fortune. No fighting went on at Baden. It was, in fact, only 17 miles south of Vienna. As a popular resort it ranked second to none in the whole country, with its curative springs visited by the lame, the palsied, and the arthritic since Roman times.

The Austrian army established its Supreme Headquarters at Baden (because, it was jokingly said, so many of the generals were old relics in need of the springs). The generals Hindenburg and Ludendorff were seen frequently on the streets. The place buzzed with activity. Soldiers were everywhere, in the shops, in the cafés. Later in the war young Karl, the last Emperor, was often at Baden to discuss strategy. Karl's official residence was the nearby Laxenburg castle but most of his days were spent at the Kaiserhaus in Baden, a two-story townhouse bought by Franz Joseph before the war. Here the business of state went on, generals were consulted, foreign dignitaries received. Among the guests was Wilhelm II, the German Emperor. One of Karl's children was born at the Kaiserhaus and my father assisted at the birth.

My father was given the rank of captain, because of his profession. Like other Austrian doctors he had no military experience (the nation had not been at war for more than a generation). He was assigned to work at an army hospital. Mother worked there too, as a nurse. Back in Vienna father had been an obstetrician, but obstetricians quickly became general practitioners during the war. Never, to my knowledge, had he amputated an arm or a leg. Now he was performing twenty such operations daily, and speeding them along to make room for new arrivals. The inflow of casualties from the battle fronts was constant, and most required major surgery. Some died before any treatment could be given. The hospital was poorly supplied: only morphine as a pain-killer, ether as an anesthetic. Often there was no time to disinfect instruments properly, and gangrene would ensue. The fatality rate from infections—from bullet wounds and from unclean hospital instruments—ran high.

After ten or twelve hours of utter chaos, trying to deal with these poor maimed soldiers and at the same time coping with inadequate equipment, father would return exhausted. "I wonder how many survived today," he would sigh. He never knew. It was like an assembly line. When patients left him they went on to another part of the hospital—or to the morgue.

Though it wasn't the most pleasant place on earth, I went to the hospital each day to eat with my parents during their lunch break. After the wards had filled up, men on stretchers—the new arrivals—were lined up in the halls. They had to be stepped over. At first I recoiled. Then, after a few weeks, even the goriest sights became routine.

The hospital's activity depended on the battlefield's. A lull in the fighting gave doctors a chance to mend the wounded, as far as was possible, and send home those who could be released. Then the corridors might be empty for a while. When news came of a major battle, it was sure to be followed by arrivals of wagon-loads of casualties. Then father would work day and night, suturing wounds, digging out rifle balls and shrapnel, setting broken bones.

During periods of calm he tried to spend as much time with me as possible. Anything approaching a normal life was out of the question. Still, Baden and the surrounding areas had places of escape, where you could walk in the woods and the war seemed very far away. The forest remained as always: nonpolitical, unspoiled by wars.

The odor of pine trees contrasted sharply with ether.

"Hans," said my father, "take a deep breath, so your body can absorb some of that beauty."

The war brought my father and me even closer than we had been, which was true of many families. We were in this struggle together; we each knew the other was hurting and needed moral support.

My father underwent a kind of transformation at Baden.

No longer in private medical practice, he turned more and more attention to his hobbies, his stamp collection, his paintings, antiquities, and objets d'art. Capable a physician though he was, one could not help feeling that art and antiques were his real calling. He delighted in them. Such was his interest in them—call it passion—that in the darkest days of war he could relax for hours with his stamp collection. When the time came to put his albums away, real life resumed. Until then, he lived in another world, and a much more pleasant one. This is one sure mark of a genuine collector: the ability to be totally immersed in the subject and oblivious of all else.

His stamp collection became a family project. Each evening, when he was not at the hospital, albums were spread about the dining-room table, along with loose stamps on bits of envelopes that needed soaking and drying. That was my job. Into a little tub of warm water I placed each specimen, handling it as carefully as a British Guiana one-penny magenta. In a few minutes it floated free, under my watchful eye, and I placed it upside-down on a sheet of newspaper or a blotter. Meanwhile, father riffled through reference books trying to identify color or shade varieties, or gazed attentively at his stamps through a magnifying glass.

He was a scientific philatelist, specializing in the stamps of Austria-Hungary and trying, so far as was possible, to collect cancellations from every town and village in the empire. Most of the stamps had little monetary value. Even today, many Austria-Hungary stamps dating before 1900 sell under $1. But together, as a collection, there was probably not another in the country quite like it. I have no idea of its market value. Maybe one should not always think in terms of cash. It was a marvelous collection, he and I derived great enjoyment from it, and it helped, in its way, to pull us through those miserable days.

Stamps could pass some time for me, but my enjoyment of them really came through my father: I enjoyed *his* enjoyment. Left to myself, I felt I could not get excited about a stamp collection.

My chief hobby during the war was natural history specimens: butterflies, insects, flowers, fossils, and minerals. Seldom, while hiking in the woodland, was I without full paraphernalia: a butterfly net, botanical box, and a geologist's pick for taking specimens of minerals and fossils. With Baden's richness in such specimens, free for the taking, a fine collection could be assembled without much trouble.

Many important Austrian families moved to Baden during the war to be near Supreme Headquarters and, later, the Emperor Karl. The belief (true or not I cannot say) was that it had the best defenses of any Austrian city—but on the other hand it might also be a select target of the enemy. In any case this influx of aristocrats, business executives, and assorted nobility gave Baden something of the taste of prewar Vienna. Without troops constantly on the march, without daily delivery of the sick and wounded, without reports of raging battles, it might have been grand.

In the fall of 1914 I returned to school, not in Vienna but in Baden. As classmates I had children of many important persons. Our *ordinarius* (home-room teacher) was a Jesuit priest, Father Hlavatin, who considered seven- and eight-year-olds not too young for a dose of *Gewissenserforschung* (conscience-searching). This, a forerunner of Zen, taught one to review the good and evil of each day's actions. It became so ingrained that I still find myself practicing it, to avoid repeating my mistakes.

To aid the war effort, young students went to the rail depots with loaves of bread and pitchers of water for the wounded returnees. Scarcities of food and materials became noticeable during the first winter of the war (1914–15). Unless you "knew somebody," a grocer or baker who could be bribed, there was no butter or bread. When such things could be obtained, they had to be whisked home in secrecy. Mother got some milk from a farmer and brought the bottle home under her skirt, on a bicycle. Ration cards did little good. The favored few who "knew somebody" still got, and the rest did not. There was also a brisk trade in the sale of ration cards.

Days dragged on without much encouragement. The local newspapers reported only victories of the Central Powers, like the English papers during the American war of independence, but we heard otherwise from more reliable sources. Returning soldiers told of the enemy's massive air power, and of poison gas used on the Italian front that turned faces blue. More and more casualties coming to the hospital were victims of gas.

Accurate information was always mixed with wild rumor, and nobody—I think not even the generals—knew exactly what was happening. Reports kept coming of Russian advances. The Russians, it was said, were at Austria's door, pouring arsenic down the drinking wells and raping the women. Little did we know that, at the same time, Londoners and Parisians heard the same rumors about German troops in Belgium.

Militarily, things became bleak indeed. Or so we feared. Yet our way of life remained more or less as it had been when we first came to Baden nearly a year earlier. In the summer of 1915, despite great activity on the battlefields, my father succeeded in getting a vacation leave. We made the most of it, going each day to the Wienerwald to explore the ruined castles of the 13th and 14th centuries. Ordinarily they might be crowded with tourists, but nobody could travel during the war. So I clambered for hours over walls and through arches, where knights and heralds must have passed. With my geological hammer I tested for hollows behind masonry in which some mediaeval baron might have stashed a few gold pieces. I had read a story of a boy who fell into a hole in a castle and discovered a strongbox brimming with coins. It was a well-known fact that kings and princes would try to hide their valuables upon the approach of an enemy, or if the castle had to be vacated because of plague or other reason. Certainly, some of the old treasure lodes must still be in place. Why couldn't I be the one to find them?

Now, looking back, I can see that this early quest for treasure was not very different from the questing done by an antiquarian bookseller. Many times when I've found a great book or beautiful manuscript in a monastery library I have thought of the little boy tapping with his hammer.

Never did I succeed in finding walled-up castle treasures, but that summer of 1915 did result in quite a "find." Going through the streets of nearby Mödling we passed a watchmaker's shop. In the window was a glass jar filled with coins, some of glistening silver, others fat bronze with green patina. The edges were irregular and they looked very different from the Austrian coins with which I was familiar.

After only slight begging, because my father was interested too, we entered the shop.

Taking the jar from the window, the watchmaker poured its contents on a cloth for our examination. Then he told us the story. They were Roman coins, dating from the time when Vienna (Vindobona, as the Romans called it, and as it still appears in books of the 15th and 16th centuries) served as a Roman garrison town. Marcus Aurelius was said to have died there in A.D. 180. Mödling, like Baden—and Bath in England—had been a summer resort for vacationing well-to-do Romans. All the coins turned up in a foundation niche of a neighboring house, during excavations for a new building. There they had slumbered, salted away by a miser 18 centuries earlier.

I was wild with excitement. So was my father, whose antiquarian blood was now fully ablaze. He bought the coins for me, and they marked the beginning of a new hobby.

Step by step, I was getting closer to collecting.

Our life changed drastically in early 1917. Father was transferred to a hospital at Dervent, Bosnia (now Yugoslavia), more than 400 miles south of Baden, where we could not follow. To save money, mother and I moved to a small room, giving up our comfortable apartment. Here we faced hardships of no electricity, no heat, little food, and had no idea how long we must go on like this. The war seemed stalemated, yet heavy casualties continued.

The burning of firewood from the forest kept us warm, but my school fared poorly in that department. Often it was closed for lack of heat. The ration cards no longer bought anything; there was nothing to be had, unless you could pay black-market prices.

Our life went from one of comparative luxury before the war to bitter poverty.

Somehow we managed.

News of the war grew less and less encouraging. By the fall of 1918 there was no denying that all had been lost. It was a bitter blow, after so much sacrifice and the loss of millions of lives—10 million combatants. Dejectedly the soldiers, many of whom had seen three or four years of battle, began returning from the front, shell-shocked, dazed, many of them emaciated, defeat etched on their faces. By sardine-packed trainloads they came, day after day, bearded, soot-blackened, wearing lice-infested clothing. They wandered about the streets, not knowing where to go, unable to find their families, unaware whether any relatives were still alive. Not like starched-uniformed soldiers on leave they wandered the streets, but like derelicts, homeless, unfed for days, glancing nervously at the skies for enemy aircraft as if still on the battlefield. They collapsed, fell into doorways. Some were picked up and cared for by kindly people, until they could be reestablished. Others had no such luck.

In November, 1918, Emperor Karl retired from government but chose not to abdicate. At age 31, he felt there was sufficient time for the Empire to rise again. After staying briefly at Eckartsau near Baden, he was obliged to flee to Switzerland. A short time later he tried to return and was exiled to Madeira, where he died in 1922.

As soon as the war ended we waited anxiously for word of father. Not having heard from him in weeks, we were unsure of his whereabouts and safety. Though not an active combatant, he could have fallen victim to the atrocities committed by occupation forces. When time passed with no news we began to fear the worst.

One morning before I left for class, the doorbell rang. I hoped it was the postman bringing news. Instead a man dressed in rags stood at the door. Thinking he was a beggar I shut the door and waited several minutes before going on to school, to make certain he had left. When I opened the door again he was sprawled on the step outside. I called to mother.

She looked at the beggar's face and cried, "It's your father!"

Never did I feel such emotion, seeing my beloved father lying unconscious on the floor in a most pitiful condition. Tears streamed down my face. Fortunately he was alive. We put him to bed, with pneumonia and a raging fever. Later he told us of riding for two weeks in a cattle-car filled with sick and dying soldiers, from whom he might have contracted any number of diseases. The car was unheated and its occupants went mostly unfed. Such was the fate of the defeated. Next day he was placed in the hospital, the same hospital where he had worked during the war's early years. He was seriously ill but, strong of constitution and of body, recovered fully within a few weeks.

The family was together again, though the future looked anything but rosy.

CHAPTER 2

A Boy Hunts Treasures

SLOWLY WE PICKED UP the pieces and tried to resume life as before the war. We returned to Vienna, to my grandmother's house in the Praterstrasse. It was as elegant as ever with its crystal chandeliers and hand-rubbed wood paneling. But Vienna was a broken city, morally and spiritually if not physically. The old AEIOU motto, "Austria erit in orbe ultima" (Austria shall be supreme in the world), now seemed hollow, just a bitter reminder of old times. Even in peace, wartime conditions lingered on: soaring inflation, a scarcity of everything, no fuel, and little transportation.

In this not-too-encouraging atmosphere I resumed my studies, enrolling in the third grade of the *Realgymnasium* (high school) near our home.

I also went back to coin collecting, based on the Roman specimens from Mödling. Nearby in the Stubenbastei was an old man, Dr. Walla, who operated a coin business from the parlor of his apartment. The house was old, as was the street; the Stubenbastei had been part of the mediaeval fortifications. We got on famously together. My interest in ancient coins pleased Dr. Walla, and his knowledge—not to mention his array of coins—enthralled me. Past 70, he was tall but bent with age, had a leathery wrinkled face, a white goatee, and spoke with a marked Hungarian accent. He wore thick glasses, but behind them his eyes sparkled, especially when he was examining coins. I spent every Saturday afternoon at Dr. Walla's, seated in a corner with coins spread about on a table. I was now 12, but my finances had not improved much. My father had no means; in a gush of patriotism he had invested all his money in war bonds, which now had no more value than waste paper. Mrs. Walla thought it foolish for her husband to show coins to a boy who could not afford to buy them.

"Let him sit here and look at the coins," he would reply. "He loves them, and he does not disturb me. Someday he may become an important collector."

My goal was to complete a set of the Roman emperors—that is, to own at least one coin depicting each emperor from Augustus Caesar to the fall of Rome in A.D. 476. That was 500 years worth of emperors, some with brief reigns and few appearances on coinage. On a tight budget it was an impossible task, but I succeeded in building a run of more than fifty, mostly the big bronzes.

Rarity meant little to me. Even design and artistic quality influenced me only slightly. My chief fascination was with the emperors' portraits and their names. Reading legends on Roman coins helped sharpen my Latin. Here was Latin at the source, from its days as a spoken language. Yet on coins it could be very difficult to decipher. Faced with lengthy inscriptions and limited space in which to work, coin designers abbreviated unmercifully. Dr. Walla was there to help me over the rough spots. I was indebted to him. Vienna's two other coin dealers would not even allow me to inspect their stock. "Come back when you've grown up," they said, regarding me as a nuisance. I suppose I was, considering the time I spent browsing through trays of coins and the little I bought. But good Dr. Walla never complained. I felt I was letting him down when I switched to books.

Vienna, one of Europe's gourmet headquarters before the war, could no longer feed its own inhabitants in 1919. Food was critically short. A bread line for children was set up by the American relief agency in the Augarten. Thousands flocked there each day, receiving little but looking upon it as manna from above. I went there after school with a tin cup. The choice was bread, canned milk, canned beans, or oatmeal. Like most Viennese youths I lost weight, contracted a mild case of tuberculosis, and was unable to continue school that year. As better food was available in the countryside, mother took me there for two months. After steady doses of fresh milk, bread, meat, and vegetables, I regained strength.

Incurable collectors will collect no matter what the circumstances. This was true of both my father and myself. The war had brought (along with chaos, suffering, and food shortages) unparalleled opportunities to collect. Owners of collector's items found themselves forced to sell at a fraction of the values. Contents of noble households were sold almost daily.

Seldom in this century have antiquarians enjoyed a more bounteous harvest, except that only a few had the money to take full advantage of it. My father was among the majority of collectors who might have filled warehouses with art objects but could not afford buying in quantity.

A treasure hunter at heart, he wondered what might be available in the small villages. Often he took me on his excursions. Chiefly we visited old farmhouses, most of which are about two or three times as old as American farmhouses. They date from the 16th and 17th centuries. Unlike Americans, Austrians are not discarders by nature. They store things away in their attics and have been doing so through many generations. Browsers in a Maine or Vermont attic, no matter how many delights meet their eye, encounter tame fare compared to the finds we made. Furniture, pottery, glassware, pictures, and the like—articles of little or no value originally—were transformed into collector's items with the passing of time. Some very fine pieces came from those attics, storerooms, cellars, and wherever we were allowed to rummage. Even much of what we dismissed as junk, by standards of the time, would be worth a good deal of money today. Anything of interest could be bought cheaply; owners were only too glad to raise some cash.

We became such confirmed scavengers that even to this day I look longingly at any old house I pass on the street, wondering what surprises it might contain. In certain parts of Europe there are even now attics untouched for centuries.

But I might not be so partial to attic-hunting, had I not discovered my first rare book in that fashion.

The owner of this particular house, a confectioner, gave us permission to poke about under the building's eaves. As usual there was no telling what awaited us, but the house seemed very old and promising. When no good antiques turned up, father was disappointed. We had apparently wasted time and put a thick coating of grime on our clothing for nothing. Then I noticed a vellum-bound book of folio size, propped up at an angle against the wall. This was something new for us; we had not collected books, but it bore all the appearance of a handsome antique. Inside we found engraved maps, showing old but nearly accurate delineations of the Mediterranean and not-quite-so-accurate ones of other parts of the world.

How old were they?

We searched for a date and I succeeded in finding one: MDXCV.

A bit more searching revealed the cartographer's identity: Gerard Mercator, the celebrated Flemish mapmaker. (See Fig. 1.)

Never had I handled such an old book. I begged father to buy it. He was willing but the owner hesitated. He looked at me quizzically, then at

Fig. 1. Mercator Atlas 1595. Title page. My first rare book.

father, then turned the pages slowly. The maps I considered so beautiful, filled with sea serpents and ships, struck him as quite the reverse.

"No, no," he said. "Everything in this atlas is wrong. Your son will get poor marks in geography if he uses it."

He thought we wanted it to aid in my schoolwork!

To mention that such a volume might have antiquarian value was not the right approach. So we explained that, even with its inaccuracies, the maps had some appeal for us because of the attractive engraving.

He weakened and gave in. "Take it and keep it," he said to me. "I don't want money for this outdated old thing."

I was elated, thanked him profusely and we left as quickly as possible, fearing he might have a change of heart.

Incidentally, the book *did* help my grades. It increased my interest in geography as never before and, at the same time, improved my grasp of Latin. Only much later did I learn the book's real value.

The Mercator atlas was the first great book I owned. Little could I suspect then, that I would be acquiring other copies in later years, from the libraries of princely collectors. But not as gifts! The value today is $6,000 to $8,000.

It also ushered me into the world of rare book dealing.

In the spring of 1925 I was 17 years old and passed the *Matura* or final school examination at the Academy of Commerce. It was then customary for parents to offer the graduate a *Matura-Reise,* or graduation trip abroad, as a reward. "Abroad" meant the sunny south of Europe, where one could dine exotically, swim, or, if inclined in that direction as I was, visit old and famous churches and museums. Alas, my father had no money for such a trip. I was disappointed, having looked forward to seeing Italy and trying out my phrasebook Italian on the natives. For weeks I had been putting penciled crosses in my Baedeker's Italy, to chart my course. I went through art books, planning which galleries to visit. I even consulted Mercator's maps of Italy.

While bemoaning my fate, a thought struck me. That old atlas, so precious to me, might be equally precious to a dealer in rare books.

Could it raise enough to finance my trip?

I felt the book might be valuable monetarily, but how valuable or salable I had not the slightest idea. My only experience as a "bookseller" was occasionally buying first editions of 19th-century German literature from antique shops, where they could be picked up for a song as library furniture, then reselling them at a modest profit in secondhand bookshops.

Before offering the Mercator for sale I had to get some information on its value. I knew nothing about *Book Auction Records* nor even the procedures for collating a book. Putting it under my arm I headed for Vienna's National Library. The immensity of this institution did little to instill confidence. Walking down the long marble hallways, past rooms of documents and catalogues and newspapers, I became more and more nervous. Upon reaching the map curator's door I froze.

Finally I summoned enough courage to knock and was received amiably.

The curator leafed through my book with interest.

"Yes, it's a first edition," he exclaimed, confirming my fondest hopes. "And apparently complete."

The "apparently" called for investigation.

"How can I find out more about it by myself?" I asked.

He showed me how to use a reference work, to determine if all the maps were present. As he stood by beaming, I collated the book from cover to cover—the first book I had ever collated. Yes, it was complete. My hopes soared.

"I see that you love to handle a beautiful old book," he said. "Some day you may become a good bookman. I am much older than you, and I never grow tired of old books. There is always something new to learn about them and from them. Every time I look through one I learn something new."

I then popped the question: What was the book worth in cash?

He regretted that he could not, as a public librarian, give valuations. For this I must seek the advice of an experienced collector, an appraiser, or possibly an auction house.

But I considered the trip a great success. I had learned that the book was complete and, as I had collated it in the presence of the National Library's map curator, nobody could tell me otherwise. The next step was to sell it, or try to.

I knew that no dealer would make an offer, but ask instead how much I wanted. If I asked too much it might end any hope of a sale. I would be dismissed without a chance to lower my price. On the other hand I wished, like every seller, to get as much as the book was worth and not give it to the purchaser. I knew how much I would need for my Italian trip and that was what I hoped to get.

Rather than the secondhand booksellers with whom I had slight acquaintance, I took it to Gilhofer & Ranschburg, Vienna's foremost rare book specialists, confident they would appreciate its value and be in a better position to give a good price. Again I felt very nervous. But gradually I was overcoming my reticence, as I found that people to whom I showed the atlas took an interest in it.

The man at Gilhofer & Ranschburg examined it attentively, flipping from one map to another, peering so close that his nose almost touched the leaves.

My heart was in my mouth. "It belongs to a friend of mine who wants . . . who wants . . ."—I finally blurted it out—"one thousand schillings."

This seemed to me an astronomical sum for a book, but a thousand schillings would cover my trip. Little did I realize that the shelves round the room contained books considerably more valuable.

I expected him to collapse on the floor, or erupt into laughter. He did neither. Instead he asked calmly, "Who is your friend?"

"My father."

I brought my father to the shop, he confirmed my ownership of the book, and a check was put in my hands for 1,000 schillings!

Thanks, Great Mercator! You bought me a trip to Italy!

You also gave me a sufficient taste of bookselling to know, there and then, that I must make a career of it. The only sadness was in parting with the book.

I had never been in a foreign country. I knew about Italian culture from books and the schoolroom, but its language remained a mystery. Except for a random phrase or two, I was at the Italians' mercy in restaurants, railroad stations, shops and on the streets. Like most novice tourists, I carried a dictionary and tried to make conversation from it, but with mixed results at best. In Verona I asked the name of a church:

"Quanto costa questa chiesa?"

"Our churches are not for sale," came the indignant reply.

But Italy was hospitable, all things considered. Just a few years earlier, Italy and Austria had been enemies, but the memories of war were fading. I traveled first through the Dolomites, site of bitter fighting between Austrians and Italians. Here and there one saw grim reminders: vast cemeteries at the scenes of battle, where soldiers from both sides had been buried alongside each other. They included battle casualties as well as thousands who died of disease. I thought of the schoolroom teaching, that they died "for God, Emperor, and Fatherland," but the columns of bleak crosses dotting mountainside after mountainside looked anything but heroic. They suggested nothing but the uselessness and stupidity of war.

Grey and foggy skies in the Dolomites added to the depression and made me count the miles to the sunny south, unravaged by war. I thought of Goethe's moving sentiment, which expresses the feeling of most German-speaking visitors to Italy: *Kennst Du das Land, wo die Zitronen blühn?*

Plentiful though it was to my slender purse, the Mercator money would not last forever. I found prices in Italy higher than expected and had to economize on everything. I rented the cheapest rooms in no-star hotels, ate starchy foods that would fill my stomach and keep hunger away, traveled by bus or third-class train or (whenever possible) by foot. From sunrise until late at night I ran through the streets, into and out of churches, museums, libraries, parks, and other points of interest, flipping the pages of my Baedeker as I went.

I got my 1,000 schillings worth. A month later I was back in Vienna and back to reality.

CHAPTER 3

Working for $4.20 a Month

KNOWING I HAD NO LOVE of the medical profession, father did not urge me in that direction. In fact he bent over backward to show that I had not disappointed him. "I don't want you to sit and wait for patients," he would say. Not to mention the fact that a physician's career meant years of further study at the university. I had had my fill of schoolwork, and more than my fill of the leftist propaganda that ran rife among postwar college students. Most of them came from wealthy families but, in spite of that, preached the overthrow of capitalism and imperialism. They blamed the war and every other evil on the rich and said we should follow Russia's example, taking estates away from landowners, farms from farmers, and so on, for equal distribution among the people. Ironically at this same time the great masses of poor Austrian citizenry, who stood to profit by socialism if anyone did, wanted only a chance to get jobs and make money. Seldom did one hear any talk of revolution from them.

Though I did not exactly come from a poor family, my political philosophy tended toward democracy and free enterprise. I wanted to make money, and the making of it meant a great deal to me. I had met wealthy patients of father's and saw, in Italy, the luxury that wealth could buy. But I must not, I resolved, follow the errors of so many people who take any well-paying job without regard to their tastes or future. I felt that a person must enjoy his work, otherwise there is no enthusiasm and it becomes drudgery. Drudgery even at a good price was not appealing.

Bookselling appealed to me more than anything else. Whether there was much money to be made in it, I did not know. But I could, as a successful bookseller, be independent, perhaps travel, and—no small inducement—acquire books for my own library along the way. Handling books all day, talking about them, and making a living by doing so was the life for me.

But Rome was not to be built in a day. Most Americans are unaware that as recently as 50 years ago Austrian trade regulations still followed the mediaeval "guild" system. Everything was closely regulated to prevent "unfair competition" with existing businesses, as well as to maintain professional standards. Today anyone can open a bookshop if he has the funds, or can work in one if the proprietor will hire him. There are no formalities, no red tape, no government bureaucrats to answer to. In Austria in 1925, becoming a bookseller was hardly less arduous than going into law or teaching. Upon deciding to become a bookseller you first served an apprenticeship of three years in an already established bookshop, just like a cabinetmaker or goldsmith. You watched how the business was operated, saw what was expected of a bookseller and the profession's rewards and demands. As for the former, you received few of them in apprenticeship, only a bit of pocket money, to pay carfare and keep you from starving. At the same time you were obliged to attend a special class for apprentice booksellers. The Austrian guild had a booksellers' school, just as in other trades. To graduate one had to pass a searching examination administered by a guild member, involving questions related to various aspects of the business. If you passed, you became a *Gehilfe* or assistant. Only then did you begin receiving a monthly pay check. But the guild set up still more hurdles to be cleared.

After getting a dose of working as bookshop assistant you went abroad, which was called the *Wanderjahre.* This consisted of working for a few months, not at very good pay, in bookshops in different European countries. It could take as long as four years. Then you returned to being an employee or, if you had some capital, you could request permission from the guild to open a shop. If your apprenticeship had been satisfactorily concluded, the guild made no objection to your opening a shop. However it would not allow you to locate too near an existing shop and possibly draw customers from it.

I did not like the guild system, to put it mildly, but it eventually worked to my advantage. In 1932, when I opened my own shop, no "unrestricted" locations could be had except in very unpromising areas far from the central city. When I used upstairs rooms as an office, the guild forbade any nameplate near the door, to let passersby know of the business. They considered that unfair to booksellers paying rent on shops. This made it impossible to get customers from the street, so I had to issue catalogues and do some advertising. In this way I got in touch with collectors, librarians, and other dealers around the world, most of whom would never have strolled along the Praterstrasse and never have known about me, even if I had a sign twelve feet high. I have partly to thank the guild's old-fashioned regulations for my success.

So far as apprentice positions went, they were hard to find. Thanks to a good word on my behalf from an uncle, I was accepted as an apprentice at Lechner's University Booksellers and Publishers, a large, prestigious shop. My salary was 30 schillings per month, then about $4.20, but my academy degree, which few apprentices had, reduced the apprenticeship period from three years to two.

Lechner's was a once-stately old shop dating from a much more prosperous age, located in the center of town, near St. Stephen's Cathedral. Books on shelves or piled on the floor made browsing difficult. I surveyed the scene with awe.

While not expecting to be in charge of things on my first day at work, I had hoped for more meaningful duties than were assigned to me.

I catalogued no books. I spoke to no customers. Instead I was given a broom and told to sweep the floor. Then a cloth for dusting the bookcase windows. Then commands from the office staff to fetch coffee. It hardly seemed right to subject a young, well-bred, academy-educated gentleman to menial labor. After all, I had written poetry and plays. Unpublished, true, but three years of literary effort should count for something. I was indignant. Both pride and person cried out.

After two weeks of it, with no improvement in sight, I protested that I was an apprentice and should be learning about books.

"Very well," said my boss. "You will learn about books."

He meant it.

To say I started at the bottom would be strictly accurate. Beneath the shop was a huge basement which seemed to stretch half the city's length. This is not much of an exaggeration. Corridors connected it to the catacombs of St. Stephen's Cathedral. Here were stacked, in solid walls of books reaching almost to the ceiling, unsold remainders of every title Lechner had published since its founding in the 19th century, as well as stocks from other publishers.

I was to take a complete inventory, grouping together all copies of the same book and making note of the quantities. Someday, the proprietors had obviously said to each other, an eager-beaver young man will come here, and we'll give him this job.

Compared to this, floor-sweeping looked not only good but clean. These books, untouched for two generations, sent up billows of black dust when moved. One risked coal miner's disease by spending just a few minutes in such an environment. There was not a single window, no source of fresh air. I came up each day covered with dust and grime, wheezing, choking, certain that every breath was my last.

Lechner's thought I'd learn a lesson. Maybe I did. But I surprised them by completing the entire assignment in a few weeks. I felt like Hercules after cleaning the Augean stables. So well had I performed that I was given another task involving sorting. It was still in the cellar but in a cleaner, better-lighted area, one where several other clerks also worked. This, I discovered, was the children's book department. With Christmas approaching, when most juvenile books are sold, Lechner's wanted to get its stock in order, after a year's disarrangement.

"They must all be filed in a single alphabet, by author," I was told.

At first glance this seemed impossible, with volumes stacked on the floor in absolutely no order. How could they be alphabetized in a short time?

"It's really not that difficult," one of my veteran co-workers explained, then demonstrated a tried-and-true bookshop trick that had proved effective since the time of Aldus Manutius.

Four piles were made, with authors whose names had initials A–G, H–K, L–R, and S–Z. After making these piles it was just a matter of making smaller piles, grouping authors whose names began with A, B, C, and so on. Finally we alphabetized within each letter.

Again I worked hastily, too hastily to suit my fellow workers. Lechner's was not geared to that kind of enthusiasm on the part of employees.

"Look, son," our foreman said, taking me aside, "if we all work so fast we'll be finished in two days. That's antisocial. The boss would learn he could run the business with a smaller staff. He'd fire some of us, and where would we find work in times like these?"

This I was not expecting.

"Slow down," he advised. "This job should take two weeks."

"But how can I stretch two days' work into two weeks?"

"Easy. It just takes a little experience. Hide behind the shelves. Do a little reading each day, or take a nap on an empty shelf. We can hear anyone coming down the metal staircase."

There was no choice. I was outnumbered. I converted an empty shelf into a desk, on which I read books (no shortage to choose from) or wrote poetry. It furthered my education and nobody came to check on us in the entire two weeks. I began to feel that no one knew we existed, that we had been banished to a sort of nether world like disfavored gods.

I had learned my first lesson as an apprentice bookseller: Never leave employees alone and presume they're working.

Within a few months I knew the ins and outs of retailing books: how to wrap packages, how to tie them with the bookseller's knot, how to pack books in shipping cartons, and how to order new books without dealing with their publishers. Lechner's ordered all its new books from a central agent in Leipzig, received one shipment per week and paid for it with one check, making for a minimum of headaches and paperwork. When a customer wanted an out-of-stock book we could promise it within one or two weeks and not risk disappointment.

In time I was allowed to wait on customers, which had been my ambition all along. Playing the role of book expert, I recommended books as gifts for grandchildren, books for people who just had their appendix removed, racy French novels for undergraduates, somber scholarly works for professors. Until then I hadn't realized how few people come into a bookshop knowing what they want. This still holds true today, even on 46th Street. Most new customers have only a vague notion of what interests them.

Every imaginable type found its way to Lechner's. One day it was a stylishly dressed Polish prince passing through Vienna. He needed a carload of books to fill the shelves of his newly built castle in Galicia. Could we help? Indeed we could, and we were flattered that he bypassed the Warsaw booksellers in our favor. Within ten days the shipment was on its way.

I enjoyed selling, as I knew I would. It tested one's powers to judge human nature. What sort of book does this individual *really* want? Can I interest him in several works by the same author? Will he object to the price? I got on well with the staff, too. I had a good memory and lost no opportunity to display it. When somebody misplaced a book, I usually recalled where I had seen it.

Since Lechner's eschewed rare books, it made no headlines with auction purchases. But it did get into the newspapers on one notable occasion during my employment.

Like many large bookshops in those days, Lechner's held exhibitions of drawings, prints, and watercolors. These were generally tame affairs geared to the Saturday afternoon browsers. When we exhibited works of the now-famous Egon Schiele (1890–1918), browsers turned into tigers. A virtual unknown outside his native land in those days, Schiele was not fully appreciated and his erotic subject matter drew protests. One morally outraged woman clouted a particularly titillating picture with her umbrella. Next day the incident was written up in the papers. I liked the exhibition very much, especially the drawings which were selling at about $20.00 each. Now each would have a value of $5,000 to $10,000. The newspaper article brought throngs of people. Never did we have such a turnout. The shop was jammed. Then further protests erupted and the exhibition had to be shut down.

My apprenticeship drew to a close. I was eligible to become a full-fledged assistant with regular wages. But it was not to be. As soon as my apprenticeship expired, Lechner's announced that they no longer required my services.

I seemed to be back where I started.

It was a critical time for the family.

Father's practice had not flourished. He realized some income by selling antiques and duplicates from his stamp collection, but he was too much a collector at heart to become a full-time dealer. If he had, I believe he could have made a success of it. The family was in a bad way financially. Then father fell ill, and we learned he was suffering from terminal cancer. He lived just six weeks after the diagnosis, the most agonizing weeks of my life. Mother and I felt helpless. There was nothing we could do for him. So we put all our efforts into feeding him and making him comfortable; I read books to him, told jokes, struggled to keep a cheerful face.

Having neglected myself during this period, I suffered a recurrence of my tuberculosis of five years before. After the funeral I was sent to a sanatorium at Semmering, about 40 miles south of Vienna, where patients slept in the open air, drank gallons of milk, and spent most of the day having their temperatures taken. Many of the patients were my age and one in particular was quite pretty. I looked upon my stay as a vacation. After two months I returned to Vienna, fully recovered and ready to tackle the world.

CHAPTER 4

On the Road as a Salesman

I FOUND A NEW JOB at the same place I lost the old one: at Lechner's. Everybody concerned with bookselling in Vienna passed through Lechner's, buying, selling, or catching up on gossip. Among them were salesmen for every major publishing house. They arrived all day long, going in and out with bulging valises full of lists and sample books. One happened to be a representative of Wasmuth Verlag of Berlin, a large publisher of German-language art books. Wasmuth, he told me, was opening a branch office in Vienna to handle its growing trade there and was in the process of putting together a staff.

I applied for a job and got it.

Because of my Academy of Commerce degree I was given the position of bookkeeper, in which I would handle the accounts of several salesmen. The fact that I had no bookkeeping experience was never considered. Any academy graduate certainly knew the job's fundamentals and the rest could be learned, or so it was presumed. Shortly thereafter, the folly of this presumption became evident. So thoroughly did I scramble up Wasmuth's ledgers that a professional accountant had to be called in.

Another turning point had been reached. Without any doubt, my days as bookkeeper at Wasmuth were numbered, but maybe I could serve them in some other way rather than getting the dreaded pink slip and leaving. I looked around me. Bookkeeping was dull work at best, nothing but figures and eight hours of sitting on a hard wooden chair each day. You didn't even handle any books, except those in which the accounts were kept. And it paid miserably. Successful salesmen, on the other hand, had the world by a string. Wasmuth's salesmen made good money, from 10 to 30 percent commission on sales, and received attractive fringe benefits, including expense accounts for travel and lodging. They visited romantic places and had the time of their lives on Wasmuth's money. I envied them as they came and went, fashionably dressed, their deep tans contrasting with the pallor of bookkeepers' cheeks, always going somewhere or just returning.

I decided to become one of them.

The salesmen working out of Vienna covered central and eastern Europe. Western Europe and the south were handled from the main office in Berlin. They sold the Wasmuth publications door-to-door on the installment plan, mostly books on architecture and related arts, to bookshops, architects, libraries, museums, and institutions, as well as the set known as *Orbis Terrarum*. These were topographical albums with views of towns of various European countries in photographs by excellent masters like Kurt Hielscher and Martin Hürlimann.

In the manager's office hung a large map of Europe and the Middle East, such as army generals have on their walls, dotted with a forest of pins. Each pin denoted the location of a Wasmuth salesman. Judging by the number of pins, not much territory remained.

"Everything's taken, my boy," said the boss, with a gesture toward the map. "Everything. Even Roumania, Bulgaria, and . . ."—he paused for a moment—". . . Serbia."

If you had a salesman in Serbia, the implication clearly was, you had one everywhere.

"But not Egypt," I countered.

After the shock waves subsided he looked at me quizzically. "It's yours. But at your own risk and expense."

My own risk and expense meant, first of all, that the company would not gamble an expense account in such a remote part of the world. For all they knew, the Egyptians were still reading papyrus scrolls. Trying to sell them the same books read in Germany, Holland, and Switzerland seemed like a losing proposition. Also, Wasmuth was not about to pick up the tab for medical expenses if I contracted any exotic Middle Eastern disease. I could go on my own, with Wasmuth's blessing, but it had to be just that: on my own. If I succeeded, well and good. I would receive the standard commissions. If not, tough luck.

That was fine with me. It gave me just what I wanted, my own territory and a chance to make good. Here was a land of 20 million souls, untouched by Wasmuth representatives.

With a sort of Horatio Alger enthusiasm I made preparations. I would need money, of which I had none, so the hat was passed round to my mother, grandmother, and uncles. It seemed to them, as it should have to me, a ridiculous job to take, but they contributed. When not busy fund-raising I brushed up my schoolboy French, believing that most Egyptians understood French.

Never had I been so far from home, nor in a land or among a people so utterly foreign. It was just a little frightening, especially when friends started warning against the drinking water and the wicked women. Still, with the prospect of riches before me, I was prepared to endure all hardships. The route was all laid out. First I would go to Bucharest and then to Istanbul by rail, from there to Alexandria by sea, loaded down with my cornucopia of *Musterbände*—sample volumes.

As usual I went the cheapest way. A third-class train ride from Vienna to Bucharest in the 1920s was an experience not soon forgotten. Most of my fellow-passengers were swarthy Arab types on their way home to Turkey or Persia. They puffed vile-smelling tobacco and carried their food in canisters, or paper bags. I counted the minutes until we arrived.

After 48 hours we pulled into the Roumanian capital.

Bucharest might have been a highly enjoyable city under other circumstances. It looked more inviting than I had expected. I could have been comfortable there on a holiday, visiting the public squares and those great stone-walled old orthodox churches. Lugging 20 or 30 pounds of books and facing an uncertain fate, I did not feel its charms. But it did hold out a glimmer of opportunity. Wasmuth's salesman in Bucharest had fallen ill, so I decided to stay overnight and pinch-hit for him next day. I could ring doorbells as well as anybody.

It was worth a try.

The following morning I copied the names and addresses of a few architects from the phone directory and ventured forth to show them my wares.

As Robert Burns said of the best-laid plans, it failed miserably.

Having neglected to group my calls geographically, I drove from one part of the city to another, going round in circles and wasting valuable time. To make matters worse I couldn't afford a taxi and had to go by droshky, or horse-drawn carriage, not the fastest means of transportation. When I finally did reach an architect's address, maids and doormen greeted my halting French with total lack of comprehension. Nor could the droshky-driver understand me.

I could not accept defeat that lightly. Given a few more days and better organization my fortunes would certainly improve. So I stayed in Bucharest, hired a Jewish droshky-driver and was able to communicate with him, thanks to the similiarity of Yiddish and German.

After ten days of wandering about and knocking on doors and talking to unresponsive people I still had not made a sale. By now my going-to-Egypt money was nearly gone, spent on hotel bills and endless droshky rides. I was marooned in Bucharest with no way to continue my journey and no way to stay in Roumania either, without some cash.

I had to raise money in a hurry, and it obviously wasn't going to be from sales commissions.

I telegraphed mother for money.

Her answer was "Come home."

I was crushed. Going home meant admitting I had been a fool. Everyone would say, "I told you so." Even worse, what would Wasmuth say? I had already shown myself to be an inefficient bookkeeper. If I failed at being a salesman, too, they would be finished with me.

I was in a panic. Night had fallen when mother's wire arrived at the hotel desk. Rather than going to my room I sat in the dim, shabby lobby, my big bag of *Musterbände* at my feet, and cried. The world was at an end.

The night concierge, an elderly Polish Jew, asked what the matter was.

I told him the whole story, pouring out every detail, though I hardly expected he could be of any help. Just a sympathetic ear at that moment was welcome.

"What business are you in?" he asked kindly.

"I am trying to sell architectural books."

A smile crossed his weathered face. He wrote out and handed me a slip of paper. "Tomorrow you will take all your books to this address in the main street, the Alleja Kissilev. It is the office of Bucharest's most famous architect, who works for the royal family. My son is a draughtsman there. He will try to introduce you."

Next morning found me at the address at 9 o'clock sharp. The concierge's son met me, took me to a conference room, and told me to spread my books on a table. Carefully I laid them out in the empty room. Then I waited, an experience not new to me.

Around one in the afternoon the architect entered, an elegant-looking man in his mid-40s. He ignored me but attentively inspected my books, opening one after another. I remained silent, afraid to speak. He left without a word.

Later the concierge's son returned. "Leave all your books here," he instructed, "and come back tomorrow morning."

After a sleepless night I was back, knowing that my fate hung in the balance.

I soon received the good news: "The boss wants everything. In two copies."

I was saved! Delirious though I was, I managed to retain enough composure to get the order signed. I promised the concierge's son a share of my commission, which would far exceed travel expenses. A wire went off to Wasmuth in Vienna:

SOLD BOOKS FOR 20,000 MARKS. REQUEST PERMISSION TO CONTINUE WORK HERE. WIRE 2,000 MARKS.

That was showing them!

All bedlam must have broken loose at the office. Wasmuth's regular Bucharest salesman, whoever he was, probably hadn't sold that many books in months. Certainly not in a single day with a single order.

An enthusiastic reply was received, along with the money.

From then on I got much warmer receptions. Whenever prospective customers heard that the royal architect was buying Wasmuth's publications they suddenly became more attentive. I started making my calls in style, too, befitting the royal architect's bookseller. Instead of a droshky I went by taxi. No longer did I entertain thoughts of Egypt. Bucharest was the place for me!

Within three weeks I had sold plenty of books and earned a small fortune in commissions. For my triumphal return I would ride in a first-class berth on the luxurious Orient Express, a striking contrast to my mode of arrival. I felt like a victorious Roman general coming home from the provinces. But because of my Polycrates complex, the fear of good luck, or rather of the consequences of too much good luck, I could not enjoy the well-appointed sleeping car. At Belgrade it was moved to the end of the train, where I did not fancy riding, certain that fate had a collision in store and that the last car would be the worst damaged. Riding in the middle cars I stood a better chance of survival. When the train pulled into Vienna I emerged from the third-class section. My boss, waiting at the station to greet the prodigal, congratulated me on my thrift.

Some apprehensive moments have arisen out of my Polycrates complex. After every success I am haunted by fear that it must be followed by retribution. The inevitable question, "What will I have to pay to the gods for this?" interferes with my enjoyment of every fortunate experience.

Its source is an old myth which is retold in Friedrich Schiller's poem, *Der Ring des Polykrates*, that every German schoolboy learned by heart. It tells of Polycrates, ruler of the island of Samos, who boasts to his guest, the King of Egypt, that everything he undertakes turns out well. The King warns Polycrates of the envy of the gods:

"So much good fortune must lead to disaster. It is dangerous to be too lucky. You will pay dearly for it."

This worries Polycrates and, in an attempt to placate the gods, he throws one of his most precious possessions, a beautiful ring, into the sea. The next evening a large fish is served at dinner. When it is carved before Polycrates, his ring is found in its stomach.

The King of Egypt rises from his place in horror:

"The gods have rejected your offering. Disaster is near."

The King of Egypt hurriedly departs from Samos. The next day Samos is captured by the Persians and Polycrates is killed. So runs the legend. In fact, the pirate and tyrant Polycrates was lured, on a pretext, from Samos to the mainland, where he was crucified by Oroetes, Persian governor of Lydia, about 515 B.C.

After my Roumanian trip more doors began to open.

In 1929 Wasmuth sent me to Poland, to sell the same line of architectural books. Compared to Roumania this was for me the Promised Land. Nearly everybody spoke German.

At the beautiful town of Lemberg (Lwów) I made friends with Rudolf Kotula, Librarian at the University, who bought one copy of every book I could show. I lived at the Hotel Warszaski. Resolving to keep down expenses, I avoided the city's more fashionable hotels but hardly bargained for the living conditions in this one. The sheets were ironed once a week, but changed only every three weeks. Among the permanent residents of each room were colonies of bedbugs, as bold in their nocturnal ramblings as the girls who strolled the hotel's corridors. But the less said about the Warszaski the better.

To economize further I traveled not by taxi but streetcar. This presented the problem of not knowing where to get off, until I became familiar with Lemberg's streets.

One day I asked, in German, a kindly-looking man where I should disembark for the Polytechnic Institute.

"Follow me," he replied. "I am going there."

He introduced himself as Professor Bartel. As we walked along he asked what I was doing. "Selling books? Fine. Come to see me."

I went to his office, showed him Wasmuth's publications, and he bought several. He also invited me to his home that evening. There he told me of his background; he had been an officer in the Austrian army and Prime Minister in the short-lived Polish provisional government of 1926.

"A young man has to be helped," he said. Then he gave me a letter of introduction to Stefan Demby, Chief Librarian of the new Bibliotheka Narodowa, the National Library at Warsaw.

Though prospects at Lemberg remained bright—I was making steady sales and getting good commissions from them—I lost no time going to Warsaw and calling upon Mr. Demby.

Warsaw delighted me. Next to Vienna it was the most beautiful city I had seen, spacious, clean, appealing old architecture, many of the streets unchanged for centuries, 18th-century palaces dotting the city, and a main square of mediaeval houses gaily painted in bright colors. Then there were the people: warm, friendly, good-natured. More than a million of them. Warsaw was an immensely big city. It would probably have grown to three million or more in population but for the war.

Once again, good fortune found me in the right place at the right time. Old Wawel Castle, destroyed in World War I, was being rebuilt according to the original plans, undoubtedly the most exciting cultural project in Poland at the time, into which huge sums of money were being poured. The castle had possessed a notable library, which had perished along with its other contents. To stock it, thousands of volumes would be needed.

Mr. Demby proved an even more valued customer than I had hoped. He introduced me to the Minister of Education, a priest who happened to be very much in a book-buying mood. They bought multiple copies of everything and asked me to act as agent in getting other books from England, France, and Germany. I was to fill the National Library apparently single-handed! It was a bookseller's dream come true.

As bookseller to the Ministry of Education I became welcome at all the libraries in Warsaw, of which the city had many, whose staffs comprised knowledgeable, amiable people. At the National Library I met Kazimierz Piekarski, its chief bibliographer and compiler of a number of scholarly works. His current project was a study of Hieronymus Vietor, early 16th-century printer who was active in Vienna and Crakow. For some time Piekarski had been buying (for the Library) every Vietor imprint that turned up. Later I was able to locate some in Vienna for him, to his great satisfaction.

My style of living in Warsaw far surpassed Lemberg. The plush Hotel Europejski was my home. I ate at the best restaurants and spent my evenings in fashionable cafés. The expense was small compared to my earnings. Checks now arrived regularly from Vienna, while Wasmuth's shipping department sent off cartons of books to my customers. Warsaw could not have been more profitable. It had pretty girls, too, and as a bachelor living alone my mind was not permanently on books. But unlike Boswell and most other young gentlemen on the Grand Tour, I ignored their blandishments. For better or worse, father had put the fear of syphilis into me. It was not so easily treated in those pre-wonder-drug days. But I was not in the Polish capital long before finding another object of affection—a mistress of another kind, safer and more exciting, who has been with me all my life. I bought my first expensive and important rare book.

Much of my free time was spent in the antiquarian booksellers' quarter. Warsaw never had world-famous dealers in rare books but a kind of 4th-Avenue trade of secondhand, used, and sometimes (if you persisted) rare books, all jumbled together. Mostly the shops were clustered together on a street called the Święto Krszyska. They were more or less untouched by western European bibliophiles; compared to bookshops in other countries they were little frequented by collectors or dealers. They stocked primarily Russian and Polish books, which in those days nobody outside Eastern Europe was buying. But there was no telling, really, what might turn up with some exploration of these age-old shops.

The best store was run by a man named Fiszler. Upon learning that I was interested in early printing, he disappeared into a corner and returned lugging an immense folio. My knowledge of incunabula at this time was slight. I had never owned any and had read very little about them. This volume contained, in addition to a profusion of woodcuts, a map of Europe dated 1493. That was a century earlier than the Mercator and only a single year after Columbus' first voyage. It was, of course, the huge *Nuremberg Chronicle* of Hartmann Schedel, printed by Anton Koberger. I knew nothing about the *Nuremberg Chronicle,* but its beauty impressed me, and I felt that any incunabulum so lavishly and handsomely illustrated must be fairly valuable. I was unaware that this is one of the commonest 15th-century books. Koberger, who ran the biggest publishing operation of the whole incunabula age, issued German and Latin editions and sold copies all over Europe. The total number printed was around 2,000, very large for those times, of which a considerable quantity has been preserved.

I felt the same about it as about the Mercator a decade earlier. I must have it.

"Well, how much?" I asked.

"Twelve hundred zloty."

That amounted to about $135. I had no way of knowing if the price was fair, but I could afford it and decided to buy, after a bit of bargaining. In this kind of shop it was unsporting, as well as highly detrimental to future transactions, to pay the asking price.

I made a counter-offer. We thrusted and parried. Finally the price came down to 800 zlotys, which probably was twice what my friend Fiszler hoped to get. Even so, there were no handshakes or kind words. We viewed each other with open suspicion.

"Give me the money so I can count it," said Fiszler in a sinister tone.

"Give me the book," I countered, holding tight to my eight 100-zloty notes. I was not about to hand over the money without having the book in my possession. I had heard tales of Polish booksellers refusing to hand over the merchandise after receiving payment. By the same token, he had doubts about my paying, once I had the book.

So we agreed on a compromise. The book was placed on a table, untouched by me, and I counted out the banknotes beside it, untouched by him. Upon completing the count we looked at each other and said in unison, "ONE, TWO, THREE, GO." He scooped up the money, I the book, and we went our separate ways.

Later examination proved the book not so irresistible. Several leaves were missing, which reduced the value considerably. When many complete copies of a book exist, as with the *Nuremberg Chronicle,* collectors take a dim view of an imperfect one. I lost money reselling it, though, of course, it would be worth many times the purchase price today.

In any case it marked a milestone, the first incunabulum I had owned, and anybody starting out with a *Nuremberg Chronicle* is starting in a big way. And I also learned a good lesson: collate a book before paying for it.

CHAPTER 5

A Salesman Becomes a Rare Book Dealer

For the rest of 1929 I stayed on as Wasmuth's agent for Poland, traveling back and forth from Vienna to Warsaw. I was becoming one of their most successful salesmen and, for the first time in my life, financially independent. I was enjoying myself, being on my own, making money, taking in the delights of foreign travel. Any thoughts of slowing down never entered my mind. Life is uncertain. I would make as much money as I could, while I could.

If Wasmuth had wanted to keep me in Poland I would not have objected. But, since I had demonstrated my selling ability to their satisfaction, they decided to use me where there were more (and presumably wealthier) book buyers. Early in 1930 I transferred to the firm's Berlin headquarters and was given a contract calling for nine months of travel per year. I went everywhere in Europe. I crossed the continent from Scandinavia to the Balkans, went to England, France, and Italy, always lugging my *Musterbände*, not always speaking the native language well but bringing in orders. Four weeks here, five there, checking into and out of hotels, riding trains and taxis, taxis and trains. Everywhere I went, I managed to sell.

For the next two years I lived like a prince, or the way I thought a prince lived. I vacationed at St. Wolfgang, which had not lost its boyhood appeal for me, bought a sailboat and a car, and saw that mother was well provided for. I took my vacations seriously. It was the time to regain energy for the work which I loved. It was exciting. I went to it with gusto.

Push on, hit hard, follow through. That was my philosophy of success in business. It still is.

I had Wasmuth's to thank for my first romance, too. While at St. Wolfgang in 1930 I met another vacationer, a pretty blonde from Berlin who worked there part-time in a nightclub. Berlin nightlife of this era was of the Blue Angel variety, gay, loud, with a sinful reputation. The clubs catered to patrons from all parts of Europe; there were many Americans too. Berlin had a cosmopolitan flavor. For a young man on the loose, few cities could equal it. It was livelier by far than Vienna or Warsaw. When my girl was not working, and I wasn't on the road, I arranged my day to be with her. I slept until midnight, donned a dinner jacket, and met her for dinner around two in the morning. This was early by Berlin standards. Escorting a girl of her looks brought me more than passing attention. Heads turned, and the question was invariably asked, "Who's that man she's with?"

Menacing storm clouds blew over central Europe. As my financial picture brightened, that of the continent darkened. The American stock-market crash of 1929 was felt immediately in Europe. Even before that there were danger signals, some with political overtones. In Austria we had riots between left-wing reformers and the army, with the threat of all-out revolution, then a general strike bringing the country to a standstill. With a reorganized government and a faltering economy, this was serious. Things looked bleak indeed when the Kredit-Anstalt, the largest Austrian bank, followed the path of many in America and went bankrupt.

Many book buyers were forced out of the market. Moreover, nobody cared to be burdened with long installment plans for sets, not knowing what the future might bring. University libraries went on buying, but private people did not. Even worse, many customers from whom I had obtained orders weren't paying, and I, caught in the middle, did not receive commission payments by Wasmuth. The situation very quickly deteriorated so that I was doing less selling and receiving less money for the selling I did.

Not anxious to share one of its more productive salesmen with a rival, but realizing that salesmen must eat like everybody else, Wasmuth gave me permission to represent also Karl W. Hiersemann, one of the top firms of Leipzig. Once again, as at several times in my life, an ill wind brought me good. With Wasmuth I might have remained a book salesman forever, living well perhaps, but not becoming a rare book man. Hiersemann's trade was like Wasmuth's but it also maintained a large antiquarian department. Hiersemann was for years, in fact, the most important rare book dealer in Leipzig. As early as the 1880s he was issuing important catalogues offering incunabula, literature of European countries, fine bindings, and manuscripts. He also published excellent catalogues of rare Spanish books which were purchased en bloc by Archer Huntington and formed the nucleus of the library of the Hispanic Society of America in New York. His stock was one of the country's best, matched at that time only by Jacques Rosenthal of Munich and Joseph Baer of Frankfurt. By reading Hiersemann's catalogues I started to acquire a good education in rare books, not just about their significance but also about their value.

In 1930 my travels took me to Czernowitz (Cernauti) in Roumania. The country looked much better than on my earlier stay in Bucharest. I was desperate then and fairly self-assured now. Moreover it seemed a good place to sell books, not having been hit too hard in the recession. Czernowitz suggested a miniature Vienna. Everybody spoke German; many were Jewish.

Living was inexpensive in Czernowitz. Not just surviving, as I did in Bucharest, but living in style. Food was especially cheap and as palatable as one could ask. I wondered why gourmets failed to discover this city. On the streets, wherever one looked, were suntanned, blue-eyed, blonde, delectable-looking girls. Had I been Napoleon, this would be my choice of a place for exile.

Rather than indulging myself in the luxury of a taxi, I hired a droshky and made my rounds in it. I now drew up my route in advance, calling on any architects, librarians, or booksellers who might be found in a particular neighborhood. Next day I went to another neighborhood. I rode up front with the driver, a talkative Jew. My bags of samples filled the back seat.

After two days of small talk, during which he asked many questions about the bookselling business, my droshky-driver made me a proposition. We should become partners. Instead of charging me for transportation he would take a percentage of my commissions. When I declined (I would gladly have accepted such an offer earlier in Bucharest), he had another proposal, much more to my liking. Whenever I made a call, he would keep the fingers of both hands crossed until my return. For this spiritual or supernatural aid I was to pay one leu for every order up to 100 marks. Up to 200 marks the fee increased to two leu. I wasn't in too deep: A leu equaled .006 of a cent, while a single mark was 24 cents. It was worth that much, just on the slim chance that his crossed fingers *did* carry some magical powers. On each return to the droshky I laughed to see his gnarled hands held high, fingers tightly embracing each other. Not one to take a partner's word, he carefully inspected the signed orders and figured up his cut.

He was a simple, kindly, down-to-earth old rustic. I was sorry we had to part. We had become something like a Don Quixote and Sancho Panza. But, like all salesmen, I had to move on.

On the day before I left the city he became serious for the first time. "I'd like to speak with you privately," he said. We went to my hotel room. He took a rumpled photo of a young woman from his pocket and displayed it with pride.

"This is my daughter," he announced. "I want you to marry her."

I was amazed.

"If you do," he went on, "I will give her one cow and a set of bed linen. She will make fine healthy children for you in Vienna."

I politely declined, but he was determined to convince me. He, too, knew something about salesmanship. She was beautiful; she could cook, sing, sew; knew Hebrew; had learned the Talmud.

When I remained unmoved at this long list of wifely qualifications he delivered what he believed to be the clincher:

"Come home with me for dinner tonight, sleep with her, and I promise you will never want to sleep with another woman."

Still I declined.

He drove me to the railroad station, disappointed, with tears in his eyes when we parted. I will always remember that kind man who was fond of me in his own primitive way and wanted to give me his daughter, his only treasure. I wonder what became of them.

In 1932 I went back to Vienna, not just because of political conditions in Berlin but to open my own book business.

Wasmuth found itself unable to pay my commissions, amounting to a sizable sum, so I suggested taking it out in merchandise. They agreed to this, having, like most booksellers then, far more books than cash. These would serve as the basis of a stock, which could be added to and expanded. Of course I planned to make antiquarian books my main trade, but gathering a stock of them would take time. Meanwhile I could sell Wasmuth's publications and establish a clientele.

As explained earlier, I could not rent a street-level shop in a good neighborhood, so I opened up my first office in a room of grandmother's house on the Praterstrasse, No. 16. It was small but so was my stock. My mother was my first employee. She was glad to help and continued working with me until 1969, at age 86.

As business improved and the workload became heavy, I hired Alfred Wolf, an experienced bookman, from Koehler's Antiquarium in Leipzig. I could get a work permit for him (as a German alien) only by guaranteeing his political integrity, that he was neither a Nazi nor a Communist. As we shall see, my trust in this man was to prove unjustified.

Wolf seemed a very satisfactory worker. His knowledge of the day-to-day operations of a bookshop proved valuable. With his aid we got better organized and were able to expand. Fortunately an office was available directly across the street at No. 17, a handsome 19th-century building used as a townhouse by Count Bellegarde. Its oak-paneled rooms, warm and spacious, provided an ideal setting for a stock of rare books. The rent was ridiculously low: 700 schillings (about $98) per month. I christened it the *Mohrenschloss* or Moor's Castle, as the courtyard led to a street called Lane of the Moors.

Wolf became head of my department of scientific books and periodicals. Next to join the staff was Gerd Rosen, former manager of Wertheim's rare book department. Dr. Wertheim, part owner of Berlin's largest department store, had a reputation as a notable collector specializing in maps and geography books. He had founded the magazine *Imago Mundi*. With Wolf and Rosen I had experienced people and could deal with safety in books on most subjects. Within two years I had ten employees, including a pair of apprentices to whom I returned the favor of paying the same minimal wages I had received at Lechner's.

My stock of rare books continually grew. Rarities in all classes—medicine, the arts, literature, early printing, fine bindings—could then be bought at very low prices. The abundance of incunabula and other rare books can be seen in catalogues of the time: Weiss and Halle of Munich, Gilhofer & Ranschburg of Vienna, Olschki of Florence, and Hiersemann of Leipzig offered 300 to 400 incunabula in a single catalogue. But I preferred not to specialize, despite the opportunities. I had my reasons.

I had no extensive knowledge of rare books. To deal effectively one must be expert or nearly expert. This came later, though I have never become specialized to the degree of some of my colleagues. I handle good books in all fields, so long as they show the chance for profit. When I smell a profit I take a chance. Over the years my sense of smell has improved considerably.

Catalogues were issued regularly from the Moor's Castle, ancestors of the larger, more opulent ones that followed in New York. Still they were good catalogues, well prepared, with informative notes and plenty of attractive buys. Some of them carried illustrations. Like my current catalogues, they were mailed to buyers all over the world.

A routine was established for cataloguing all incoming books. For this we collected a reference library, modest compared to my present one, with bibliographies, dealer and auction catalogues, and other tools of the trade. We also set up an efficient system of bookkeeping, a phase of the business of which I was wary since my Wasmuth experience.

In those first years in the Moor's Castle I worked up to 16 hours a day. At the rate at which orders and incoming stock arrived, work piled up no matter how many people I hired or how hard we worked. It was gratifying. I had become, almost overnight, one of the leading booksellers in Vienna.

Not all my time was spent in the Moor's Castle. Leaving my employees in charge, I would travel all over the continent buying and selling. My philosophy in buying a library was to count the books and to buy them if the cost worked out at 5 cents per volume or less. Silly as this sounds today, many a good library was sold for under 5 cents per volume. Buying a thousand books at that price, one might get 500 of mediocre quality, maybe more; but if just half a dozen important items turned up, the percentage was profitable. The only trouble with this kind of buying was that it consumed all our storage space. In one day, thousands of books might be purchased, but selling them could take years and they had to be stored in the meantime. Space was not limitless and an over-cluttered stock is unattractive. I had to have a warehouse, some place for the stream of incoming books to prevent them from inundating us. Warehouse space was not easy to get, but I succeeded in renting a loft in a neighboring building, which served for a while.

Not only private libraries reached the market. One of the largest to be sold belonged to the Kredit-Anstalt. When I learned in 1932 that it was selling part of its library I hurried there at once. The Kredit-Anstalt had for many years been collecting runs of periodicals. These were much in demand by university libraries and the booksellers who supplied libraries. An en-bloc purchase at a low price was a chance not to be missed.

It was too late. Unaware that any dealer was interested in its books, the Kredit-Anstalt had called in a waste-paper merchant and sold them by the pound. Thousands upon thousands of dollars worth of Europe's foremost periodicals going to pulp!

Luckily the transaction had just taken place. I got the paper mill's address and arrived within minutes. Bound volumes of periodicals, as well as other books, stood in stacks like bales of hay. Usually it's difficult to buy anything from paper or junk dealers; any display of interest prompts them to ask outrageous prices. Conditions being what they were (the recession put many newspapers and magazines out of business, hurting the paper industry), I was able to complete a satisfactory deal. I paid double their cost price. It was easily my biggest coup up to then. But there was a catch: I had to remove all the books immediately. I agreed.

Tons of volumes were involved. I had to engage a moving company, and the warehouse space I had just rented came in very handy. The books were taken there—with no small effort, since it had no elevator. My staff and I worked on them, sometimes long into the night, sorting and checking. To collate each volume page by page I hired a group of housewives from the neighborhood and paid them about 60 cents a day. Though hardly equipped to collate early books or manuscripts, I felt they could work on periodicals as well as anybody. They enjoyed it and enjoyed the money, a scarce commodity in their lives, even more. I got more applicants than I could employ.

Despite the problem of storage and the disruptions it caused, the Kredit-Anstalt purchase has to rank as the foremost of my early years. It was by far the most profitable. At twice the waste-paper value, each volume had cost about five cents. I priced them at $3 to $5, which was very reasonable, and in a few months the whole collection was gone. It amounted to about 15,000 volumes. Most sales were made to American libraries, which bought despite the depression. Another result of the Kredit-Anstalt purchase was to make my name well known in the U.S. among acquisitions librarians. I built up a reputation as a bookseller with "connections," and my future catalogues were read more attentively.

It was not my last purchase from a paper mill. Books gravitated to mills regularly. I bought the excellent library of the Austrian Ministry of War from a waste-paper merchant. About a thousand of its volumes came originally from the collection of the Austrian Archduke Karl, who administered Napoleon's first defeat in the battle of Aspern in 1809. What better customer for Ministry of War books than another Ministry of War library? They went on to Prague at $1 per volume. Periodicals in the lot found other homes, in American libraries.

In 1933 it was no longer possible to remain optimistic about central Europe. One was now asking, how bad would things get? And how long would that take?

At an auction in Lucerne, Switzerland, I met a friend, Dr. Karl E. Bloch. An attorney, he had seen at first hand the work of the new party in Germany. We talked of dangers to Jews in Germany and, if the Nazis' power should spread, in neighboring countries. It was hard, even at this time, to think of the daily incidents as more than overt acts of anti-Semitism by zealots or fanatics, people who had been anti-Semitic all their lives but now felt free to express their hatred physically and violently. I had experienced anti-Semitism in my travels, even in Vienna, where many of the most distinguished citizens were Jewish. Only a few months earlier my mother and I had been on holiday on the Dachstein, a beautiful mountain about 10,000 feet high, near St. Wolfgang, and saw a Jewish-looking tourist dragged from the mountain hut and forced to spend the night in a woodshed.

No one knew what to think. Hitler's plans had been clearly spelled out in *Mein Kampf*, but were taken as so much bluster.

I felt it unwise to lie back and do nothing. Preparations of some kind were advisable in the event of emergency. With Dr. Bloch's help I formed a corporation in neutral Switzerland, the Philobiblon A.G. of Lucerne, taking the name from the famous book of Richard de Bury. To it I transferred a number of my more valuable books and some gold coins. Should the Nazis come to power in Austria I would have this Swiss reserve to fall back upon. Most of my books would probably be lost but I could rebuild the business in safety abroad. Or so I thought at the time.

Lucerne was then the scene of a noteworthy auction, the sale of the Dr. Figdor collection. Though the name is unknown to Americans today, his was one of the first-rate collections, including outstanding manuscripts. Prominent dealers from all parts of the continent attended. Their presence, and that of a number of wealthy collectors, tempted me beyond my resistance. Here was a chance to sell some of the better books I had been acquiring over the past year to buyers who appreciated quality.

I set up a table in the hotel lobby and spread on it a selection of books from my suitcase.

Martin Breslauer, dean of the rare book trade, took one look and turned livid.

"Young man," he bellowed, "you are a disgrace to the book trade. This is not a fair for peddlers."

After a chorus of chuckles from onlookers, I replied: "Mr. Breslauer, I guess I can look at my books wherever I want to."

That brought even louder laughs. Later, we got on better terms.

Lucerne also prompts another memory. Whenever booksellers gathered in that city they dined at a restaurant called "Der Wilde Mann." Here worked a pretty waitress named Louise, to whom I took a fancy. I invited her out for dinner, she accepted, and my expectations ran high.

This was obviously a poor working girl who rarely got a decent meal. She would eat heartily, drink heartily, and, well, who knows?

Once again, appearances proved deceiving. She lived not in the modest apartment I had imagined but in a handsome villa. I was admitted by a servant, taken to a drawing room, and introduced to a distinguished-looking gentleman.

"I am so glad you are taking Louise out," he said. "She works so hard during the week."

The perplexity written on my face told him he ought to explain. It isn't at all unusual, he told me, for Swiss girls from well-to-do families to work briefly as waitresses prior to taking responsible jobs in the hotel business.

Her appetite lived up to my expectations but beyond that she maintained a cool reserve. I went back to my hotel room with a greatly altered opinion of Swiss waitresses.

One more anecdote about Lucerne. The following year a portion of the Prince Dietrichstein library came up for auction there. A good solid collection with strength in early theology, European history, and miscellaneous subjects, as well as in bindings, it contained one item that greatly roused my interest. The catalogue described it, rather curtly, as a 13th-century manuscript Bible in Polish. Though not an authority on Polish books, I had spent enough time in that country and spoken to enough of its librarians to know that mediaeval Polish Bibles were rare. Manuscript Bibles were usually in Latin or Greek. Only occasionally was a native or vernacular language used. A Bible in Polish from the 13th century would be most unusual.

My friend Piekarski of the Warsaw National Library was equally excited when I reached him by long-distance phone.

"Buy it," he instructed, "and bring it here on the next flight. It must be the earliest Bible in Polish."

This was my first important auction. It was vital that I should succeed. Each day before the sale I paced about the gallery, taking note of everyone who examined the Bible and wondering how tough an adversary he would be. Because the sale was not in London or New York, there was a chance some potential buyers might be unaware of it.

An hour before the sale a Munich dealer approached me.

"Kraus, there's a Polish manuscript Bible in this sale," he said, as if I had not known, "very early and worth a fortune. You can surely sell it to one of your Polish customers. Let's buy it together."

That meant splitting my profit but I was in no position to refuse. If I turned down his proposal he would undoubtedly bid against me. Together we could surely overcome any competition. The Bible realized a surprisingly low price, which we ought to have taken as a danger signal but ascribed it instead to bookman's luck.

I immediately telephoned Piekarski. He was exuberant.

Upon my arrival at the Warsaw airport I was met by a delegation from the library, not only Piekarski but Stefan Demby, a representative from the Polish Ministry of Education, and a pair of policemen. Whisked into waiting autos, we rode to the library with sirens blaring. I carried the precious volume in a suitcase.

There it was laid ceremoniously upon a table and I stepped back while the triumvirate of experts went to work. They had not, of course, seen it before, nor had any knowledge of it from bibliographical literature. Excitedly they chattered in Polish. Soon their tones changed from elation to disappointment. Though I understood none of their words, it was obvious something had gone wrong.

A visibly shaken Mr. Demby came forward and gave me the bad news: "I'm sorry, Kraus. This is a Czech Bible."

He explained that Polish and Czech texts of the 13th century were nearly identical except for little details like the endings of certain words. In Polish the genitive case was "-ego" while the Czechs wrote it "-eho." My Bible had "-eho" genitives throughout.

It was nothing to be ashamed of, Mr. Demby pointed out. One had to be an expert on mediaeval Polish grammar to make the identification. Apparently that was the reason for the low price. Bidders did not trust their (or the auctioneer's) expertise in so esoteric a field.

The book was afterward sold to the University Library at Prague for a modest sum, less than it had brought at auction. I at least had the consolation of sharing the loss with the Munich dealer.

CHAPTER 6

Competing in the Rare Book Trade

ONE OF THE MOST remarkable individuals in the rare book business is Helmuth Domizlaff of Munich. Most dealers live by their catalogues. Domizlaff has never, after more than 50 years in the trade, issued a single one. Consequently he does little selling by mail and, in fact, little selling at all so far as his best material is concerned.

I first met Domizlaff as I met most others in the trade, quite by accident, without formal introduction. It was 1933. I had gone to Lienz in the Austrian Alps to buy books from the estate of an old bookseller, Rohracher. Domizlaff was there to do the same. We were both young and I was new to the business. Yet Domizlaff was already a connoisseur and a very canny buyer. He surveyed the shelves very carefully and bought after two days work one single book, a rare early work on coffee. That, to him, was a successful venture. As usual I bought a carload full and had to hire a truck to take them away. They included twenty folio atlases of the 17th and 18th centuries, all incomplete and perfect for "breaking" and selling to decorators.

A year later our paths crossed again, when the Thun-Hohenstein Library came up for sale in Prague.

During the thirties, library after library fell victim to the economic or political situation. The Thun-Hohensteins suffered a particularly degrading fate. It was an old collection, begun in the 16th century by the noble family whose name it bore and added to continuously through the ages. Not a single prominent bibliophile appeared in the Thun-Hohenstein line, certainly none of the stature of Hoym or Duke Eugene of

Savoy. But over 10,000 volumes were accumulated in those 400 years, many books in the vernacular purchased as reading matter. Even if bought for a few pfennigs originally, a large number of the books had become rare and valuable.

All had been stored in the picturesque family castle in Cieszyn (formerly Tetschen) near the Czech-Polish border. The family was prominent in Austro-Hungarian politics for centuries, and very wealthy, but none of its members had reputations as intellectuals. The story is told of one member who studied law at the University of Prague under Dr. Alois Zucker, my wife's great-uncle, in the late 19th century. It was expected that a young nobleman and especially a member of this family should breeze through examinations. Quite the reverse was true in this case, for Dr. Zucker would not allow himself to be influenced by rank. "I cannot prevent it, dear Count," he admonished his illustrious pupil, "that you will one day be governor of Bohemia, but I can prevent you from becoming a doctor of law of this university."

After four centuries as private property, the castle was taken over in 1933 by the military to quarter troops, since tensions along the Czech-Polish border threatened imminent warfare. The Count was evicted, along with all his personal belongings, including his library. While his castle was being requisitioned he was merrily stalking the African veldt on a big game safari, oblivious of the whole thing. He could not be reached and the War Ministry had no intention of waiting until his return. Loaded onto army convoys, the books went to Prague and were sold at a pitiful fraction of their value to an antique dealer named Hořeys. The book world knew nothing of what was happening; it learned of the transaction only later.

Hořeys had no idea what to do with this windfall. Knowing next to nothing about rare books and having no book experts on his staff, he could not issue a catalogue. Nor could he count upon his clients to buy, as he had clients not for books but for bronzes, Meissen, and objets d'art. So with the help of Karel Zink, a bookdealer, he selected a few hundred of what were believed to be the best books and put them up for auction in Prague on April 10, 1933. The sale attracted considerable attention as well as curiosity. Nobody was quite sure what the library contained. The high spot was the 1492 Venice edition of Boccaccio's *Decamerone*, the first illustrated edition, bought by Otto Ranschburg, then of Gilhofer & Ranschburg, for 8,000 Czech crowns ($240) and resold by him to the Italian government. This book was so rare that no copy could be found in any Italian library. In 1970 I owned a copy which I offered for sale in my catalogue 131 (no. 41) at $85,000. This price seemed to be reasonable, because I received two orders.

The remaining books, about 9,000 volumes, were kept in a cellar, shelved by size and priced that way too. Octavos were five crowns, at three American cents to the crown. Quartos went for ten crowns, while 50 crowns bought any folio, regardless of author, subject, age, binding, illustrations, condition, or rarity. Such was an antique dealer's approach to bookselling.

Hořeys ran the equivalent of a garage sale. Doors opened at an appointed hour, throngs of customers descended into the cellar and during the day chaos reigned. The buyers were all dealers and all very eager for their share of the spoils. At Hořeys' prices there was no danger of over-spending. Instead of deliberating over purchases, the dealers went frantically from shelf to shelf trying to find the most valuable items before a rival discovered them. The "cellar of Hořeys" became the biggest treasure-hunt for rare books since Napoleon's troops looted the Italian libraries.

Skirmishes broke out repeatedly. One dealer would pick up a book, only to have three others protest it was theirs. As the participants came from all parts of Europe, threats and swearing in various languages filled the air. Finally a contingent of German dealers offered a peace proposal: divide the cellar into sections, assign one section to each dealer and give him first crack at it. Anything he chose not to buy in his section was then available to the rest if they wanted it. This was adopted, though everyone believed he had drawn the leanest shelves.

Though the French dealers came with appetites as ravenous as their fellows, they were interested only in French first editions. Any non-French volumes were passed over, no matter how rare or significant. The German dealers took a little bit of everything, or a lot of everything: early printing, literature, voyages and travels. Everyone was making snap "buy" or "no buy" decisions. But minds changed. Many books that had been passed over were later bought by those who hesitated the first time. Never did brains or fingers move faster.

There was also a good deal of business between dealers, right there on the spot. Every time someone hooked a big catch, three or four of his competitors offered him a profit for it. It took on all appearances of an auction, with dealers trying to outbid each other and everyone thoroughly confused about what was going on. Martin Breslauer saw I had selected the original watercolor drawing of Montresor's 1766 plan of New York and wanted to buy it from me. When I refused to place a price on it, because I wasn't sure of the value, he fumed. We both imagined it to be worth a great deal, and were both wrong. I put it up for sale at Sotheby's a few months later and saw it fetch, to my great disappointment, £30 (about $150). But I was in no position to complain, having bought it for the equivalent of a few cents.

Domizlaff, as expected, went only for the higher-karat jewels, several first editions of Ronsard in contemporary vellum, snatched away from the French dealers.

Not having so much experience with rare books as most of my competitors, I was at a disadvantage. They could pick up any book and gauge its market value within seconds, having handled copies in the past. But I noticed that few took the trouble to scale ladders and survey the upper shelves. Here, being young and agile, I might have an edge over them. So, while they rummaged near the floor and at eye level, I took to the upper shelves and pulled "sleeper" after "sleeper" down. One shelf, already searched by the noted French dealer Lucien Scheler, still contained a first edition of LaFontaine's *Les Amours de Psiche et de Cupidon*, Paris, 1669, in beautiful condition and sumptuous binding, proving that even a super-sleuth can sometimes lose the trail. Scheler immediately bought it from me and almost as immediately resold it to Jean-Louis Barthou, French premier, foreign minister, and book collector extraordinaire. A year later Barthou was assassinated at Marseilles with King Alexander of Yugoslavia.

As dusk settled and the weary multitude, covered with grime and perspiration, began leaving with their books, I decided to purchase most of what they left behind. How could I go wrong, I figured, at those prices? One hundred and fifty packing cases of Thun-Hohenstein books went from Prague to Vienna.

Going through those cases after their arrival was like opening Christmas presents. Excitement reigned for weeks at the Moor's Castle.

All told, I had done better with that library than the dealers who picked and chose. I also learned something else as the result of that purchase: lengthy runs of serials could be turned over quickly and profitably. The others who bought from Hořeys' cellar bypassed serials as being too cumbersome. Actually they turned out to be better purchases than most of those rare first editions over which their finders gloated. Among the ones I bought were complete sets, up to that time, of the *Monumenta Germaniae Historica*, Martens' *Recueil des Traités*, and publications of the Academies of Vienna, Prague, and Munich.

Values of such sets had been rising steadily. To avoid selling them too low I fixed what seemed enormous prices and sent quotes to the leading dealers of periodicals, Gustav Fock and Koehler's Antiquarium of Leipzig. If they failed to express interest, I would know that my prices were too high and could lower them gradually until a buyer was found. Much to my shock, they both sent telegrams to order the sets.

Here was a pickle!

I had made the mistake of not quoting "subject to prior sale," and each demanded delivery, in default of which they would sue for damages. Of course I could fill only one order, not having duplicates in stock or any way of getting any. Bitter rivals that they were, neither would consent to withdraw. Aside from lawsuits there was also the not very bright prospect that, if I sold the set to one, the other would never do further business with me.

Next morning found me on a train for Leipzig.

I called on Koehler and then Fock, explained the situation, apologized profusely, and trusted to their compassion. Apparently it was a stellar performance, as they decided to split the merchandise between them. "If you could have heard yourself," Dr. Leo Jolowicz, the owner of Fock, told me later, "you would have cried." Rather than alienating these firms, the incident put me on friendlier terms with Jolowicz than I otherwise might have been. Koehler continued as a customer too. But from then on I made liberal use of "All offers are subject to prior sale."

Selling the sets—miles of them, it seemed, and all of massive proportions—provided me with shelf space for other books from the lot. Not that I needed it. When word got around about my bulk purchase, dealers descended on the shop in hopes of getting bargains from the young, inexperienced bookman. Actually I was glad to sell the Thun-Hohenstein books at what amounted to wholesale prices. I was making large profits and it seemed sensible to sell when buyers wanted to buy rather than to sit, wait, catalogue, and perhaps not sell. It was also a good advertisement for me, as everybody knew these books came from my shop and it made them curious about what else might be found there. To give an idea of my profit margin, I sold a first edition of Grimm's *Tales*, 1812-15, in original wrappers, uncut, to another dealer, Julius Hess of Munich, for 600 marks (about $140). I had paid two marks for it. But Hess did well too. He resold it to Dr. Martin Bodmer of Geneva, later to become a customer of mine and one of the greatest collectors, for 2,000 marks. Recently a copy in less good condition realized 19,500 marks. Not many articles within the realm of commerce have risen over nine thousand times in price in less than 50 years.

Another profitable purchase in Prague was the library of a music school. Founded by Josef Proksch, teacher of the composer Frederich Smetena, it had been carried on by his son. No catalogue had ever been published of this collection. Judging by the school's reputation and age, I supposed there might be a fair number of important music volumes. The library was one of many sold in breakneck haste. The school's lease was up, and its books had to be moved without delay.

They languished in 40 packing crates when I arrived, a total of several thousand volumes. At that time I knew hardly anything about music literature but this made little difference as there was no opportunity to examine the books. They had to be bought "blind." But the price was low and, as with the Thun-Hohenstein volumes, the odds were in my favor. The crates were full of agreeable surprises, first editions of scores by Mozart and Beethoven, 18th-century chamber music, all the works of Smetana (probably presented by him to Proksch), and important manuscript scores. At one blow I became owner of the finest music stock in central Europe. This called for a special catalogue, in which I ran photos of the salesrooms at the Moor's Castle as well. It was only my second catalogue. It could not have been greeted with more enthusiastic response. Unfortunately for most of those who ordered, many items were sold before the catalogue arrived from the printers. Another valuable lesson learned: Don't be afraid of buying a specialized library on a subject in which you aren't an expert.

We worked at a feverish pace, my staff and I. Despite adding new people from time to time we were understaffed for the volume of turnover we did. They worked 60 hours a week, ten hours for six days, while I often continued working at night after everyone had left. I was still young, not yet 30, and the work agreed with me. My only respite, and it was a busman's holiday, came in summer when I took six weeks off. Rather than lolling about beaches I usually made a tour of the Austrian monasteries, not as a tourist but as a willing buyer of any worthwhile books they wished to sell. My old passion, mountain climbing, could easily be combined with these visits. Most of the Austrian monasteries are in secluded locations between mountains and woods.

What could be bought from monasteries in my time bore little resemblance to the treasures mined earlier, during the first waves of selling. Many of the illuminated manuscripts handled by dealers in the early part of the 20th century came from monasteries. St. Paul's and Melk Abbey had already exchanged their Gutenberg Bibles for currency. Librarians, dealers, and scouts in a steady stream had passed through most monastic libraries. But there was still some hope of making discoveries. Many of the previous buyers had been looking only for certain kinds of books and did not trouble to examine everything on every shelf. Incunabula might be gone but what of fine atlases or first editions?

I experienced fair success buying from monastery libraries. On several occasions I bought items of importance as well as making many acquisitions of less significant but readily salable books. I bought from the Benedictine Abbey of Göttweig near Krems, founded in 1072, and the not-much-younger Abbey of St. Peter in Salzburg (1131). In upper Austria there was a small and not well-known monastery, Wilhering, about whose library I knew little. It proved more formidable than I imagined, many thousands of volumes. How large it was before assaults by other dealers I cannot speculate. For two days I examined its collection, not under the best of conditions. Having probably been victimized earlier by thefts, the monastic librarian stood by and watched me carefully every minute. To work quickly I adopted certain shortcuts. I excluded from consideration all religious texts except Bibles and any books of octavo size and smaller. Mostly I concentrated on the upper shelves, which I hoped my predecessors had been too lazy to explore. But, to my disappointment, this library had been picked very clean by people who knew what they were about. What remained was little more than a hotchpotch of 16th- to 18th-century religious texts.

I found absolutely nothing to buy.

About to leave, I saw a hefty book-shaped parcel on the librarian's desk. It looked more promising, even from the outside, than the volumes I had been inspecting.

I asked what it was.

"Oh, this is an old atlas," I was told. "We had sold it, but the dealer returned it because the title page is missing."

That sounded good. I had not seen an atlas in the whole library. He unwrapped it, and it proved to be a volume of 16th-century maps. I bought it for 200 schillings ($28).

Still smarting from the defective *Nuremberg Chronicle* sold to me in Warsaw, I collated this purchase carefully. I found the atlas in a bibliography; it was the earliest edition of a series of maps by Antoine Lafreri, a French engraver and publisher who worked chiefly at Rome. Only the later editions had a title page, and my copy contained what few others do, Giacomo Gastaldi's celebrated wall maps in separately printed sections (designed to be assembled, being too large to print in one piece).

The dealer who turned it down because the title page was "lacking" displayed his ignorance. I knew his identity, because the parcel carried a return address.

The next year I went to London, as I did periodically, and took the atlas along. Erwin Rosenthal, son of the Munich dealer Jacques Rosenthal and (as in Rosenthal family tradition for nearly 75 years) himself proprietor of a bookshop in Zurich, took one look and asked the price.

"Seven hundred," I replied.

"That's a terrible price. May I have the trade discount of ten percent?"

I agreed, we shook hands, and I started for the door.

"Send me your bill for 630 pounds," he called out.

Six hundred and thirty pounds! No wonder he thought the price was terrible. I had fixed the sum in Austrian schillings, of which 700 amounted to $100. Six hundred and thirty pounds equaled more than $3,000. I couldn't believe my ears. For £700 you could buy a Caxton in those recession-plagued days. It was by far the highest price I had ever gotten for a book. Though I did not lack courage or confidence in book values, I could never have found the nerve to ask that much.

"Well, yes, I'll do that," I said, trying to maintain composure.

Back at my hotel room I began to worry. Was he serious? Did he really intend to pay £630? Should I send the bill?

It was getting to me. Rather than go down for dinner in that mood I went back to see him.

"What do you want?" he declared in an ill-tempered tone, not expecting me so soon. "You got a damned good price. Go away and be satisfied."

"I'm short of money," I managed to say after several tongue-tied moments. "Could I have something on account?"

Without hesitation he wrote out a check for £630. My hand trembled when I took it.

"One has to be kind to young colleagues," he said. The tough talk was just play-acting.

The book found a perfect home, in the National Maritime Museum, Greenwich, England, one of the finest collections of nautical memorabilia and literature in the world.

A very notable transaction took place with the Abbey of Admont. Like many of its sister institutions it felt the pinch of inflation and dwindling revenues. In a desperate effort to keep functioning it decided to sell its most valuable possession, the famous "Giant Bible." A 12th-century manuscript of atlas folio size, it contained 46 large miniatures and 117 initials of various sizes, some of them also quite large. Potential buyers had admired it for several generations but without any hope of persuading the monastery to sell.

Rather than going to a dealer and negotiating, Admont made its intentions public. An offer, which it deemed acceptable, was received from an American library, but Austria had laws prohibiting the export of national treasures. Only with permission of the Fine Arts Commission could the manuscript leave the country. After pleadings and arguments, it was decided to grant permission for export only if the National Library failed to match the offer by a given date. The British Museum had succeeded in raising close to £100,000 by public contribution to buy the *Codex Sinaiticus* from Soviet Russia, but hope seemed dim for the National Library to come up with enough money.

When I learned of the situation I decided to present a proposal. Like most of my countrymen I wanted the "Giant Bible" to remain on native soil. At the same time I saw an opportunity to make some money.

With the greatest of trepidation I called upon the august General Director, Dr. Anton Bick, at the National Library. I still get nervous visiting people of such rank.

My plan was as follows. Some years earlier the library had acquired, through expropriation, the Emperor's private book collection, the Fidei-Kommiss-Bibliothek, containing many volumes of high value which duplicated titles already owned by the National Library. Why not sell the more valuable duplicates and use the proceeds to buy the Giant Bible?

He was interested.

By no coincidence, I had already prepared a list of 25 of the most desirable titles. The library needed only to choose which copy of each it wished to keep: its own or the Emperor's. Naturally, Dr. Bick wanted to retain those in the best condition. He jotted down, on my list, the net price he expected for each duplicate. Anything I could realize above this was to be my profit.

A more stupendous lot of books could not be easily found. They consisted mainly of incunabula printed on vellum, collected by Prince Eugene of Savoy (1663-1736), who fought beside Marlborough at Blenheim and Malplaquet. The library was begun in 1712. The prince had agents in Paris, Nicolas Lenget and Pierre Mariette, who were mainly responsible for building his collection. Typically French, they concentrated only on superb, impeccable copies, mostly de luxe editions.

Combined in Prince Eugene were the two indispensable ingredients of a great collector, refined taste and enormous wealth. Prices paid by the Prince must have turned contemporary bibliophiles green with envy: 30,000 talers in 1736 for a Blaeu atlas extended to 46 volumes. That sum would equal perhaps a quarter-million dollars today. The famous *Tabula Peutingeriana*, included in a collection of 290 large folios with engravings, cost half a million talers. The library, with 15,000 printed books and 273 manuscripts, was housed in Vienna's Belvedere Palace, now an art museum. An estimate of 150,000 gulden was placed on the Prince's books. Charles VI later bought the collection privately for himself. After expropriation in 1918 the books were incorporated into the National Library. All the world's adjectives could not do it justice. Even the bindings, morocco by the Parisian master Luc-Antoine Boyet with the Savoy arms on the covers, were something to behold. The colors were chosen by subject: blue for theology and law, yellow for sciences, red for classical literature and history.

Time being of the essence, I called on one of my best friends in the business, William H. Schab of Gilhofer & Ranschburg. Schab was delighted to join me in the venture, all the more because not a cent of capital had to be posted. I had the books "on consignment," and anything unsold had only to be returned. There was no way we could lose.

We took them to London. There one heard no talk of wars or invasions. But England, like the U.S., had economic woes, which made selling expensive books no easy task. All the dealers wanted to buy. They had never, or seldom at any rate, had such copies offered to them, but could not write out checks to cover their purchases. They asked for long-term credit, which would not help the National Library. We had to say no.

After two weeks in London we returned to Vienna with most of the books. We had raised some money but not enough, and Dr. Bick was growing restive as the deadline approached. Then a thought struck me: What about periodicals? The library owned long runs of duplicate serials, just the ticket for Fock and Koehler, who had jumped so eagerly at my offers of periodicals from the Thun-Hohenstein collection. Dr. Bick consented, I returned the unsold Prince of Savoy books, and a batch of periodicals was soon on the way to Leipzig. The whole sum was raised and the "Giant Bible" could remain in Austria the rest of its days.

Dr. Bick credited me with saving the "Giant Bible" and thereafter became both a close friend and a good customer. A bookman's bookman, he was also a professor of Greek and president of the arch-Catholic Leo Society. The Nazis put him in a concentration camp.

Another monastery from which I bought was Göttweig. It sold very readily just about anything one wanted to buy from it, but I was a little perturbed at being unable to find any rarities. This I blamed on the predecessor of the present abbot, a man named Fuchs, who used to say of himself, "I am not only called Fox, I am a fox." Fuchs was said to have almost emptied Göttweig of its valuable books, selling them to dealer after dealer. Still I could not be convinced that, in the thousands of volumes remaining, there was nothing of much value. Finally I started going through the library's handwritten catalogue, prepared long ago. Among the listings was the first edition, 1628, of William Harvey's *De motu cordis*, containing his theories on the circulation of the blood. This cornerstone medical work, already bringing stiff prices 40 years ago, would be a great find if the library still possessed it. In vain I searched the shelves for the book, then concluded it must have been liquidated by the "sly fox."

Not at all, said the abbot. He had a list of everything sold and the Harvey was not on it. He would check and let me know. I thanked him for his trouble and dismissed the matter from my mind.

A few weeks later a postcard arrived, informing me that the book was found.

Next day I was in Göttweig.

Yes, it had been found, and not without some difficulty. It lay hidden, bound in a volume with other pamphlets. I bought it for a very low price and sold it to Fock of Leipzig for 20,000 marks ($4,800). Small books had come into demand among collectors, as they could be transported more easily if one had to take sudden flight from the Nazis.

Later I handled two other copies of this book, which may be a record for a dealer. The second I bought from Domizlaff, who seemed to have sources of supply that existed only for him, while the third came in a more or less mediocre collection of medical books bought in the south of France. I paid little for this collection and was unaware it contained a Harvey. It too was bound in a volume of pamphlets and, not being the first item in the volume, had been overlooked by everybody. Any beginning bookman would do well to learn this lesson: no matter what sort of old book you examine, flip through to the end. Two or more volumes may be bound together, perhaps a dozen, and not necessarily related. This third copy went to Dr. Bodmer, from whom I repurchased it in 1971. It has now returned to France, as part of a distinguished private collection.

CHAPTER 7

I Am a Survivor

Life in pre-world war II Austria was a sort of waiting game, with Hitler's forces prepared to march in at any time. I stayed in Vienna, carrying on my business, until the end: March 1938. Alas, I stayed too long.

After 40 years I am just beginning to discuss openly my life in those horrible times. The memories of Nazi prisons, of ordeals in two notorious concentration camps, are still vivid and, until recently, too painful to recount. The passing of time has a way of healing wounds, physical and spiritual, and the safe knowledge that such a menace no longer exists makes the past bearable. Only lately have I realized that I am one of the relatively few survivors of captivity by the Gestapo in two of the most infamous concentration camps, Dachau and Buchenwald. That I came through without permanent harm to mind and body is a miracle; that I survived is more than miraculous.

The nightmare during the 18 months that followed does not belong to this story of books and manuscripts, but to complete the account of my life for the record, I feel that I should say something about these dreadful events.

Now I find it possible to write without distress about those days, omitting the atrocities I saw. The past is shrouded in a protective mist and what remain are the facts of almost unbelievable events.

It was my intent to remain as long as Austria was free. When and if it fell to the Nazis (which was not inevitable), there would be no choice but to go. What I and many of my countrymen failed to anticipate was the rapidity of Hitler's takeover, giving only a few the chance to escape.

On March 12, 1938, when I was 30 years of age and had been for six years the proprietor of my own book business, Hitler's armies marched into Austria uncontested and forced our Chancellor, Kurt Schuschnigg, to resign. For nearly five years this day had been expected. Many non-Jewish Austrians supported Hitler. Jubilation reigned in Vienna's streets when the news came. Crowds gathered, toasts were drunk, fires lighted, music played, there was singing and shouting and the smashing of glass. Less than 24 hours after the takeover, Jewish shops were already being looted. The mood was that of August 1914, except that now we, the Jews, rather than the Serbs, were the enemy.

In stunned, grim silence we sat that evening in mother's apartment on the Praterstrasse in the dark, listening to the tumult outside and knowing that our world had come to an end. We hoped our dark windows would give the impression we were away, in case the mob should want to break in. It seemed incredible. These were Vienna's citizens, our neighbors, the people who sold us goods and services, rode the streetcar with us and fought alongside us in World War I, suddenly turned into marauders.

Schuschnigg's voice came over the radio, a farewell to his countrymen. He was totally beaten.

"People of Austria," he said, "I am yielding to a superior power. Resistance is useless. God bless and protect my Austria."

That was the entire message.

A recording of Beethoven's *Third Leonora Overture* followed. It was dramatic.

Suddenly the radio clicked and Beethoven was replaced by the *Brandenburg March*. The Nazis had occupied the studio. From then on they controlled all broadcasts and every other aspect of Viennese life.

We got no sleep that night, with the crowds chanting until morning and the very real possibility that our door would be kicked in.

Many Viennese Jews spent the night packing, heading for trains the next morning. I went to my office across the street. All was quiet now, though debris lay everywhere and some people still milled about.

The sight which greeted my eyes at my office proved an even greater shock than events of the previous day.

There was Alfred Wolf, my oldest employee in terms of service, a man in whom I placed full trust and who served me for six years, dressed in an SA (*Sturmabteilung*: storm trooper) uniform, giving me the Hitler salute. He was, he proudly announced, commanding officer for Vienna's second district. All the while, since I had hired him from Koehler's in Leipzig, I had been harboring a Nazi official in my shop! He had worked there, taking my money, just as a "cover."

A few days later we were visited by a Nazi officer. I trembled and thought that this is the end of my free life. Fortunately I was mistaken. He brought greetings from Baldur von Schirach, the Reichsjugendführer (leader of the Nazi Youth). Baldur's wife, Helene von Schirach, was one of our best clients. She built up a remarkable collection of German literature of the 15th and 16th centuries. She was the daughter of Hitler's official photographer, Hoffmann, and had means enough to buy even very expensive German incunabula. The officer left the telephone number of Mrs. Schirach and instructions to offer whatever we had in her field. Schirach himself was also a bibliophile: he collected books on bees; his great-grandfather was the founder of apiculture. After this visit Wolf became friendlier.

The Gestapo began their activities in Vienna soon after that day, rounding up Social Democrats, Communists, Free Masons, and Jews, but I doubt if they would have paid such an early call on my shop without Wolf's tip. They arrived a couple of weeks later and were greeted by Wolf like invited guests. He showed them proudly around, pointed out "evidence" along the way. When they saw among our manuscripts letters of famous Russian writers, they were convinced.

I was taken by car to the Gestapo's freshly requisitioned headquarters, the Hotel Metropol, and questioned for an hour about my past, my associates, love life, and financial resources. Finally I was released and allowed to go home, but with a warning not to leave town. I would hear from them again.

For a month I waited for the ax to fall. Every sound of footsteps on the stairs, every knock on the door, every ringing of the phone, sent me into a frenzy. My mother went to the Gestapo and asked what the charge was against me. She was told only that I would have to wait.

I was in the Moor's Castle when a pair of SS (*Schutzstaffel*, the dreaded Nazi elite military organization) rushed in and placed me in handcuffs. One of them handcuffed me to himself.

On the way to the car a crowd, not unused to watching the arrest of Jews, jeered. I tried to keep calm. The agent to whom I was cuffed seemed more nervous than I. "Unlock them," I said. "I won't run away."

To my surprise he complied, but drew a pistol and kept it trained on me during the journey. He said nothing and would not answer questions or give information. I had to keep silent and await developments.

We came to a halt outside the familiar Rossauerlände building, the big armory Hitler had turned into a prison. From the building's size, I presumed each inmate would have a cell to himself, but I had far underestimated the number of persons arrested. I was ushered to a cell crowded with 45 others. There was standing room only. My companions came not only from the ranks of the newly arrested, but old criminals from the Schuschnigg regime, officials of the Social Democratic and Communist parties, radical journalists, and the like. Then there were Jewish businessmen, doctors, professors, and other prominent Jews. We made odd bedfellows. The veteran inmates, accustomed to prison life, resented the newcomers. We—those unfamiliar with prison—found ourselves very uneasy in such close quarters with murderers and thieves.

The Jewish prisoners tried to be optimistic. We pretended our arrest was nothing but a show of force by the Nazis, or that, in an effort to purge the old government, they had mistakenly trapped innocent persons in their nets. Surely this would be straightened out in a few days. In the meantime, so I was notified, my business had been taken over by Wolf.

New prisoners arrived every day, to be wedged in with us. We assumed that the same must be happening all over Austria. Still, many clung to the belief that it was all a mistake and regretted the time lost from jobs or other duties.

After a couple of weeks I was taken away, whether for better or worse I had no idea. Upon hearing I was leaving, my fellow inmates gave me messages for friends, relatives, and business associates on the outside. Instinct told me they would not be delivered.

From the Rossauerlände I was driven to the main Vienna prison, Landesgericht. This, the equivalent of an American federal penitentiary, was where convicted criminals used to serve their sentences. Apparently it had been emptied of its usual residents, as all inmates with whom I came into contact were recently interned Jews. Consequently the atmosphere was far more amiable. Instead of felons I shared my cell with respectable business and professional people. There was also more room. We had only nine to a cell and the food was quite good for prison food. Every day we were permitted a half-hour of exercise in the courtyard, where I met several friends from other parts of the prison whom I had known before. We were able to receive mail and even parcels from home. Mother sent me fresh underwear, a suit, soap, toothbrush, chocolate. None of Landesgericht's inmates complained of mistreatment.

After about another two weeks I again received word to gather up my belongings and prepare to leave. The same scene was repeated. I was congratulated and given messages to deliver. Led to a large auditorium,

I found about a hundred other prisoners already assembled with their luggage. We were evidently to leave together, but whether to freedom, another prison, or some other fate, nobody knew. The SS guards walked about scowling, saying nothing.

We were marched outside and herded into a fleet of police vans, pushed and squeezed together with no room even to raise one's arm or breathe deeply. The SS treated us like olives in a jar. Looking from the Black Maria's tiny windows, I could determine our route: we were heading to the western railroad station, the Westbahnhof. There was no doubting any longer. Our ultimate destination was a concentration camp.

In 1938 very little was known about concentration camps. The network of them which dotted central Europe during the war was just beginning to be set up, using the labor of the inmates to build them. Nothing was suspected of gas chambers, starvation, medical experiments, or other horrors. Jews taken prisoner in the early days of Hitler's takeover of Austria thought of the camps, or "KZ" (Konzentrations Lager), as labor camps, like prison work yards. We were being optimistic again. There would be fresh air, exercise, perhaps not everyone would have to work hard.

At the station we were told to move to waiting cars.

"Run to the train as fast as you can," we were told. "Stragglers might not make it."

At first I had no idea what this meant. Then it became clear. A line of SS stood on each side of the platform, forming an aisle about 150 yards long leading to the train. As we ran by they slapped at us, whipping us on like cattle. They screamed, punched, kicked us with their boots. Though the race to the train took only one or two minutes, many men suffered serious injuries. Nearly all were cut and bleeding.

No sanctuary was offered on the train. SS men, no more compassionate than those at the station, filled its corridors. They too brandished weapons and used them with glee. "Sit with your heads on your knees," we were ordered. Periodically during the night they went from compartment to compartment, lashing out with whips or fists. We were beaten despite obeying their orders.

At daybreak, as a greyish sun washed over the fields, the train pulled into Dachau. The name struck no terror. It was known only as a work camp. Not a hand was laid on us leaving the train; we were now within sight of superior officers. Instead we received barked military commands. We were told to fall into a column and march through a gate—the camp's entrance—inscribed *Arbeit macht frei* ("Work makes you free"). Awaiting us was a panorama of human misery, a huge square filled with about 8,000 prisoners of every age, many of them with the

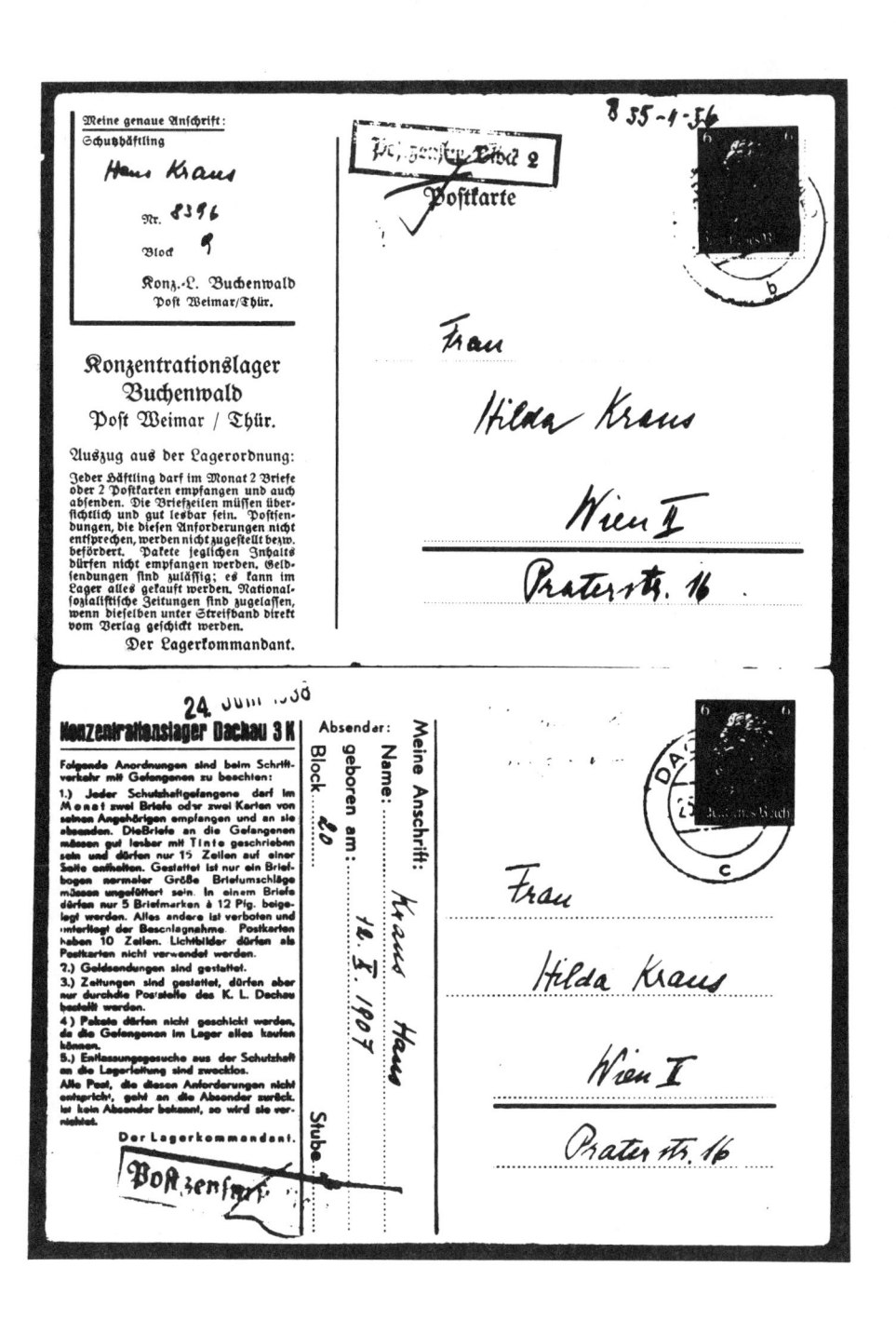

Fig. 2. Postcards from Dachau and Buchenwald.

look of living skeletons, wearing ragged army uniforms of the 19th century, colored patches on the jackets and trousers (these, I learned later, distinguished the different classes of prisoners). They milled around in total disorder.

Not a single SS man was to be seen. But the SS was always there, seen or not.

A loudspeaker suddenly roared: " *Arbeitskommandos antreten.*" ("Work units, line up.")

At this the crowd moved faster but it seemed just as aimlessly. Then miraculously, within minutes, complete order was established. Neatly arranged companies assembled to be counted, and then filed toward the gate where we, the newcomers waited. As the Kommandos went by they sang loudly and lustily. An impressive spectacle but not a very encouraging one.

Later we were "processed." I was measured, weighed, bathed, and my head was shaved. All my clothes and possessions except my toothbrush were taken away. I walked, completely naked, to the clothing station, where older prisoners gave me grey trousers and an old police jacket with tails (pre-World War I, at least), fisherman's shoes, much-darned woollen socks, and underwear. In another room I was assigned my serial number 16376 (later in Buchenwald my number was 8396; neither of them as easily remembered as Oscar Wilde's C.3.3). After 1941, when I was luckily no longer a prisoner, such numbers were tattooed on the arm.

Again in a different room, identification badges to be sewn to the front of the jacket and the left trouser leg were issued. Red cloth triangles (of which I was given one) meant political prisoners like Communists, Social Democrats, but also monarchists and priests; green badges meant criminals; black, antisocial people such as Gypsies; violet, Jehovah's Witnesses; and pink, upright rectangles, homosexuals. A yellow triangle superimposed on any of these badges indicated a Jew.

"Kapos" supervised the work crews, mostly old political prisoners to whom the Nazis extended special favors. They were not above accepting bribes from other prisoners. If you had the right Kapo and paid him something, you could enjoy many privileges. A black market thrived in camp just as on the outside. Things were constantly smuggled in and out. Some inmates boasted of being able to obtain anything.

I got ten marks a week from mother, for use in buying whatever the black market had to offer. After the Kapos' cut I was lucky to have four or five.

Aussenkommando or "outside detail" was more than slave labor. It was a special kind of torture designed not just to get trenches dug or land cleared but to break the workers in mind and body. It consisted of pushing barrows of earth, moving rocks, splitting stones. We were enlarging the camp. Few of us had ever done heavy manual labor and were not physically equipped for it, especially not under camp conditions. There was no training period. A crew was marched into a ravine or field and told at gunpoint what to do. Any display of weakness, exhaustion, or just confusion (of which there was much) brought violence. Workers who fainted, which happened frequently even to the strongest of us, were beaten as malingerers. They were so badly beaten that often they could not walk back to their barracks. Anyone who violated the rule of keeping 30 feet away from the nearest SS man was shot on the spot, in cold blood and as a matter of routine. To this day the sound of gunfire, even a firecracker, jangles my nerves and brings back memories of the camp.

There was no water to drink for "outside detail" workers. Thirst had to be endured. Work began at seven in the morning, rain or shine, hot or cold, with no protection from the elements. The first period lasted until noon, when we received the day's only comfort, a half-hour rest, in which to consume a cup of soup and a piece of bread. Had the SS not needed this break for their own meal, we might have continued nonstop. Work resumed at 12:30 and continued until six. So weak and tired were many prisoners that they used the precious half hour to sleep rather than to eat. The camp commanders made no effort to keep us in fit condition to work; there were more where we came from, arriving daily. The camp was overcrowded and apparently the herd needed thinning out.

Few, except for the hardened old-timers, could survive Aussenkommando long. The only hope for a field-gang member was transfer to an inside detail. In the camp itself there were no SS, no machine guns trained at your head, and work that was, if not appreciably easier, at least physically bearable. Inside workers repaired things, cooked, laundered, washed floors, painted walls, installed plumbing. Any work performed inside a building was called Stubendienst—dormitory duty.

Every concentration-camp inmate aimed for such duty. Few got their wish.

Jobs calling for trade skills, as much dormitory duty did, went to prisoners who as civilians had been carpenters, glaziers, tool-and-die workers, and the like. No apprenticeships were offered. Washing and cleaning duties fell mostly to the elderly and infirm, who were unfit for hard labor. It was next to impossible for a field worker to find a job on the inside, no matter what he was willing to do.

The strong spring sun, so welcome at St. Wolfgang, now became my tormentor. It beat down mercilessly on my shaved head. After two days my face was covered with blisters. "You're lucky," said my barracks commander. "They'll have to excuse you from work."

What he meant, of course, was *outside* work. No prisoner was allowed to remain idle, regardless of injury or illness.

Next day I was completely blinded by the swollen blisters. My eyes looked like a prize fighter's after a hard bout. Nobody could deny that I was sick, as sufferers of non-visible ills were told. I was taken to the *Revier* (sickbay), examined, and placed on inside detail for one week. I took it as the greatest blessing of my prison life. For one whole week I would not be scorched by the sun, not have to touch a shovel or drag 100-pound boulders. But a week was not enough. I had to devise a plan for staying on inside detail.

As soon as my eyes improved, which they did almost immediately, I was put on a window-washing crew and advised by the Kapos always to look busy. This was strictly a make-work assignment, washing already clean windows, letting them dry and washing them again. But inside Kapos were not like the hard-boiled ones in the fields. And with no SS in the dormitories, they could be talked to.

Fritz Müller, one of the Kapos, had been a roofer in Ulm and was doing the same work here, supervising a small crew. He was past 60 but carried his age well. Before his arrest he was a leading propagandist for Communism all over Europe and in Australia and expected to receive harsh treatment. Apparently the Nazis' need for an experienced roofer outweighed other considerations. He was left to himself, fed tolerably well, and in want of nothing but money.

I offered to share with him the 10 weekly marks sent by mother if he would help me to get assigned inside.

He agreed, but to be authorized for inside duty I had to prove myself unfit for heavy labor. There could be no faking or bribing, nor was a temporary ailment sufficient.

"They like broken bones," Müller observed. Many inmates intentionally broke arms or legs. Four months earlier I had broken a few ribs in a skiing accident. They were satisfactorily healed but sometimes ached at night. I decided to try rebreaking them. For several days I flung myself against the corner of a table. My chest was bruised and pained terribly but I could not tell whether the ribs were broken.

One of my fellow prisoners, a doctor of medicine and a bone specialist, saw what I was up to.

"You should report terrible pains and *possible* broken ribs," he advised. "Your chest is now all bruised. Since you really had broken ribs recently, a crack may show in the X rays. Ribs get broken here all the time, thanks to the SS. They won't think it's so unusual. But don't mention the SS. Say you fell on a rock."

I did as he suggested. Next morning I reported to the hospital, where I was handcuffed and brought by ambulance to Munich for X-rays. A pretty blonde nurse brought me the news: "You have broken ribs." I was overjoyed.

Back in my barracks at Dachau I became something of a celebrity: the man who outwitted the Nazi doctors. Others contemplated following my example, until they realized that an outbreak of injured ribs might be suspicious.

Müller congratulated me, but one more hurdle remained. Until then no Jew had been employed as a specialist inside the camp. "You must get rid of the yellow triangle," he said.

"I can't risk the consequences."

"There's no regulation against covering it."

So I was fitted with a black chimney sweep's overalls and joined the roofing brigade.

For nearly three months I was an assistant roof inspector at Dachau. The job consisted of sweeping down roofs, looking for damage and making repairs. Since there was not nearly enough work to keep busy each day, the roofers went from building to building pretending to be on inspection but really making small holes which later could be repaired.

From the roofs one saw the whole panorama of Dachau. The landscape was breathtaking. In the distance snowcapped mountains could be seen. From the thick brush a few deer came each morning to graze, just at sunrise. They came always to the same meadow.

One day I heard a beautiful voice singing Schubert's *Frühlingstraum*. I cried aloud but luckily no SS were there to hear. The singer was a homosexual from the Stubendienst, who had been a professional singer. Brutalities were also witnessed from the roofs. Certain prisoners were marked for extra-harsh treatment. Judge Osio, who sentenced the murderers of Chancellor Dollfuss of Austria a few years earlier, was forced to push a barrow of stones up a hill while an SS man jabbed at him with a bayonet. Past 60, he could have dropped at any moment. The Nazis rated him high on the list of persons to be liquidated. This was their technique, rather than guns or the electric chair. He said, "I hope to be sportsman enough to endure this hell. After a few days they might forget me."

A week later he was gone.

After a while you no longer saw or felt anything. Brutality became a way of life. So did the disappearance of friends. Inmates would vanish without a trace, leaving only rumors about the fate they met. We always hoped they had escaped, but escaping from Dachau was almost impossible.

Gradually Dachau took on the appearance of a thriving community. It was becoming a "show" camp. Colorful flowers were planted along some of the streets, and looked ironically gay. On the side of the assembly square a few shops opened, where out-of-uniform SS men sold candies, cigarettes, newspapers, and shaving gear—even eau de cologne.

Just after we had received new blue-grey uniforms we were reviewed by Himmler and other high-ranking officers, many wearing uniforms of foreign armies. They asked some prisoners about mistreatment. Nobody dared to complain.

Things fell into a pattern. We knew what to expect, whom to trust, when to talk and when to keep quiet. Then without warning, one September day after the 6 A.M. reveille the usual work call was omitted. We stood for an hour in anticipation. Then the order came for certain units to be dismissed. Eight thousand men returned to their dormitories. I was not among them. A few minutes later my barracks was called to report to the uniform depot.

Uniform depot! This could mean the reissue of civilian clothes for returning home.

Instead we were given, in exchange for our new uniforms, old army fatigues to wear again. Within a few minutes we looked like tramps. Then we were assembled into groups in the main square, still not having the slightest idea what was going to happen.

"March!" barked the voice on the loudspeaker. We filed out smartly through the gate and left Dachau. I glanced back and there, astride one of his roofs, stood Müller, his grey head silhouetted against the sky, waving his hat and making a gesture of blessing. I felt I had lost a father.

Once again a train was taking us to some unknown destination. We were only the Austrian prisoners; Germans remained behind. The reason for this I could not comprehend, but I was beyond caring.

I was accustomed by now to riding Nazi prison trains. When you were not beaten it was a good ride. This time there were no beatings. As usual the cars were packed to overcrowding. We were instructed to lean forward and sleep with our heads on the shoulders of those sitting opposite, and so the night was passed. Next morning we reached our destination. It was Weimar, the town of Goethe and Schiller, site of another camp: Buchenwald. It too bore a slogan over the gate: *Recht oder Unrecht mein Vaterland* ("My country, right or wrong"). Considered from the Nazi point of view, it sounded ominous.

Buchenwald was unknown in 1938. The camp was just being laid out, and its name meant nothing. Rather than frightening, it looked seedy compared to Dachau, which had a certain feeling of community; it was inhabitable. Buchenwald was nothing but low mountains and forests of beech trees. A fence had been put up to enclose it, with wooden gun towers equipped with searchlights. Beyond this, not much had been done. The central square, almost elegant at Dachau, was here choked with weeds and grass. Roads were unleveled. A few barracks had been built for the camp's population of 3,000 prisoners.

All work was devoted to building the camp: cutting down trees, removing stumps, digging foundations. The Kapos seemed to operate totally without plan, spending most of their time bumbling around. They were handicapped in part by the impossibility of keeping watch over all the workers, because of the camp's hundreds of acres. Paul Kapper of Linz, a fellow prisoner and newly made friend, joined me in carrying a tree branch up and down the side of a mountain. We appeared to be working and nobody bothered us. Buchenwald provided all sorts of opportunities to escape work. Its brush was dense enough to hide in, and with all the confusion there was little chance that a temporary absence would be noticed. Faces were not recognized. We found wild strawberries in the woods.

The nights were less enjoyable. Buchenwald provided no beds for its guests, not even straw mattresses, no blankets (autumn was coming on), no washbasins or showers, no toilets. We slept where space could be found, wedging between each other, fighting for a few inches of floor.

Unable to shave or wash, we could not maintain the reasonably neat appearances we had at Dachau. After a few weeks we resembled full-fledged tramps. But as we declined, the camp grew and multiplied. New buildings sprang up rapidly. Every day trees disappeared, fresh foundations were laid in their place. New prisoners arrived in a steady stream. The rule at Buchenwald was that newcomers got the least habitable quarters, so when we acquired seniority we moved to barracks with bunks and toilets.

While work went on furiously, Paul and I continued carrying our branch up and down the mountain and got away with it. A Kapo named Schneider, who was on to our game, took a liking to us and agreed to keep quiet in exchange for a weekly payoff. Schneider had the look of an elegant Prussian officer. He was ingenious and insatiably greedy. The SS liked men with those qualities.

Buchenwald's inhabitants swelled to over 10,000 (and later to 18,000). After a broiling summer the rains came, and they kept coming. All during November deluges struck the camp. Not yet paved, the streets turned to mud, then to a thin soup through which walking became impossible. Sometimes we sank up to our knees. Our only consolation was that the SS sank in too.

Nothing is more distressing than to get up at 4 A.M. in cold barracks and to get dressed in wet, cold clothes and shoes, and then to stand over an hour on the Appellplatz. One was happy to march to work. In winter, especially with snow, this was a wet, cold hell.

Here Kapo Schneider was an angel from heaven. He sometimes took me and Paul to the delousing barracks where we stayed comfortable and warm the whole day. I did not feel any pity seeing through the window the other prisoners with blue faces, stamping half frozen through the snow. I became callous to the suffering of my friends. Indeed I felt proud to have avoided their fate. I believe that the instinct of self-preservation numbs most of our noble feelings. To survive is what counts.

Variety only occasionally relieved camp routine. Roedel, our SS Commander, organized a songfest. A tough-talking Bavarian who shouted obscenities over the address system, Roedel had a soft spot for music. A contest was held for the best song; it was named the *Buchenwaldlied*, composed by the well-known Viennese singer Hermann Leopoldi. Early in November, twice a day, 18,000 of us sang it in chorus, accompanied by a band of about 100 pieces, loud and rousing if not always in key. In the mornings the band blared out marches, in the evenings more classical fare. Floodlights were always turned on us at evening assembly, making an impressive sight.

Twice I was called for questioning, but not about anything that occurred at camp. The Nazis had found out about my collection of gold coins in Switzerland and were curious about it. Both interrogations concerned it, but came to nothing.

In April 1939, my eighth month at Buchenwald, my number was called over the loudspeaker at breakfast. I was summoned to the camp gate and told to bring my belongings. "You will be released," said those at the table. Eleven others received the same instructions. Together we marched to the clothing depot, carrying messages to deliver from other prisoners.

This time we got our clothes back. Passing the gate, we heard the *Buchenwaldlied* for the last time. An army truck brought us to the rail station at Weimar. Were we going back to Dachau? Would we be left at the depot to catch trains for home?

The SS turned us over to the police, who handcuffed us.

"You won't need tickets," said a policeman. "You'll have a free ride in one of our cars."

"A ride to where?"

"Sorry, we don't know."

The prison car contained a bank of cages with wire-mesh compartments and tiny windows overhead. We were thrown in, two to a compartment, and our handcuffs removed. Each compartment had two small chairs but no room to lie down. Nightfall found us still traveling. Through the windows nothing could be seen but the darkening sky and an occasional bird. There was no way to tell where we were, or even in what direction we were going. It seemed we had covered several hundred miles. During the next day, after nearly 24 hours, we arrived at Munich.

Handcuffed again, we walked to the police station. It was my first glimpse of a city street in a year. People stared at us. Inside there were other prisoners, some of whom I recognized from Dachau, though they were now considerably thinner. None knew why they were brought here. While waiting we swapped stories and news of old friends. Müller the roofer, my saviour at Dachau, I was told, was still alive.

All during the night we waited nervously, excitedly, for something to happen. In the morning we were sorted out. The Austrians went by train to Salzburg. At the German side, heavily armed police took us from the cars and escorted us to Austrian soil. There we were delivered to a waiting force of Austrian police.

We stood in line as an elderly senior officer greeted us:

"Söhne Österreichs, seid willkommen im Vaterland." (Sons of Austria, welcome to your fatherland.)

There were tears in his eyes, and in ours.

He removed our handcuffs and went to each man, shaking his hand. At this moment the last act of *Fidelio* came vividly to my mind. Now I could understand what Beethoven's message meant.

Within minutes we were loaded aboard another train, bound for Vienna. It arrived late at night. Never had the city looked so beautiful. I was home.

From the train, vans took us to the Rossauerlände, where I had been brought after my first arrest. Another waiting game. Several weeks later a policeman came up to me.

"Kraus, pack up!"

The order to pack up was always dreaded. Now, so near home, I became hysterical. "Where am I going?" I cried.

As usual, he gave no information. "Just do as I say," he replied.

At the property desk I was given back all my personal belongings, which had been taken away at Dachau and miraculously preserved for me. I had had no hope of seeing them again, as if it made any difference. A perfect example, I could not help but think, of Nazi mentality: carefully keeping watch over combs, underwear, and keychains while beating and murdering their owners.

A young man asked, "Are you Kraus?"

I said I was.

"Gestapo. Come along."

I was certain now that I would be going to another prison or concentration camp. But this time I was not handcuffed.

He took me through streets I had walked a thousand times. Life was going on as usual: shoppers lugged their parcels, children played, paper-readers lounged in the cafés. It looked like anything but an occupied city.

I was brought to the Hotel Metropol (SS headquarters), taken in through a rear door, and given a paper to sign.

"You are free," announced my escort. "But you must leave Austria within two months. This is a declaration of emigration."

"What happens if I can't get a visa to emigrate to another country?" I blurted out in stunned reaction.

"Back to Dachau for good."

I left the building a free man.

I hurried to the Praterstrasse, not looking back, not truly convinced I wasn't watched or followed. There was no way of knowing what I'd find at mother's house. Things happened fast under the new regime.

I rang the bell and got no answer. "Arrested" was my first thought. The place must be empty. But downstairs our faithful housekeeper, Frau Pulkert, who served the family 50 years, allayed my fears.

"Your mother is out shopping."

It was joyful news. I got rid of my prison clothes, had a hot bath—my first since Buchenwald's delousing station—shaved and dressed. Mother could not believe her eyes when she found me in the house. We both cried.

I had two months to get out of the country. The book business already had been taken over by Wolf. No Jew could take more than the tiny sum of ten Reichmarks out of Austria, plus the clothes on his back and one change of clothing—nothing else. The only way to take money out was to convert it into diamonds and to swallow them. When emigration officials caught on to this, they began to use X rays.

I had applied for an American visa but it would not come through for four months. Making frantic inquiries and filling out reams of forms, I finally was able to get an interim visa for Sweden. After paying a fortune in taxes and bribes, I finally got my passport.

I went by train to Warnemünde, where I was to board ship for Sweden. The German emigration people put me through their paces. After X rays and searching, my pockets were emptied. Among their contents was a pocketknife. I had carried it since Buchenwald, when a rumor went round that every prisoner was to be killed at the outbreak of war. Knives were distributed by the underground to some of the more trustworthy of us, and we hoped to have an opportunity to kill a few SS men before we died. To deceive the authorities the knives were engraved "Zur Erinnerung" (In Memory) making them appear to be some kind of family memento. I considered this knife to be my most precious possession.

The officer studied it intently, then handed it back. "Don't kill anyone," he said. I was relieved that this last barrier was passed.

I was never so happy as when I stood on deck watching the sun setting slowly over the receding German coastline. "What a wonderful country!" said a voice from beside me. There stood a pretty girl with tears in her eyes.

"That is an illusion. It is only the sun that makes things beautiful." She looked at me curiously, not understanding.

That night, on board ship, I slept soundly for the first time in longer than I could remember.

I felt like an exile in Sweden, but it was an excellent place in which to be exiled. A middle-class boarding house served as my temporary home, where I was fed well and given clothes (I had brought along one spare suit, all that was permitted).

Among the good friends I met was Dr. Isaak Collijn, Librarian of the Royal Library. A year and a half earlier the library had purchased, from one of my catalogues, an Indulgence printed by Fust and Schoeffer at Mainz in 1462. This was in fact in my last Vienna catalogue, No. 18, issued not long before Hitler's takeover. I had found it entirely by accident, pasted into the binding of a book I purchased from St. Peter's monastery in Salzburg. Dr. Collijn wrote a report on it, published in the 1940 *Gutenberg-Jahrbuch*. When I needed the Swedish visa I wrote to this kind man. He made every effort to help and I really believe I would not have succeeded otherwise. Now he extended further aid, giving me a table to work at in the Royal Library. Here I studied many fundamental bibliographies, so important for a rare book dealer.

We talked about my ultimate goal of entering the book trade in America. He was encouraging, but my situation seemed unpromising. All I had taken out of Austria after six years of successful bookselling was a name and reputation, both of them known better in Europe than in the U.S. I would be arriving in America with little money and almost bookless. After owning a stock of 100,000 or more volumes, many of them rare and valuable, I had nothing. I had left a handful of rare books, including the slim, easily concealed but very expensive Columbus Letter of 1494, with Dr. Bloch in Switzerland. He also had some of my collection of gold coins, which he had not declared.

In Vienna, the most lucrative part of my business had been in periodicals and scholarly monographs. For trade of this kind, one needs ready cash with which to buy large collections or whole libraries, as well as warehouse space for storage, and a staff to attend to collation, cataloguing, and shipping. In the New World, I knew, I could not afford any of these; I should have to deal, at least to begin with, in individual rare books which I could manage with my modest capital and my bibliographical knowledge.

On the last day of August, 1939, Dr. Collijn greeted me with the news that Germany was about to invade Poland, and that France and England would then declare war. It was no rumor. Dr. Collijn, an intimate of high government officials, was privy to the latest developments.

"My mother is still in Vienna," I cried. "Can you help me to get her to Sweden?"

"I could request the Ministry for a visa," he replied. "But that has to go through channels. It takes weeks, and that will be too late." Then, after a pause: "But I believe the telephone still works."

He asked a friend in the government to call the Swedish embassy in Vienna and arranged for mother to collect her visa there and buy a ticket for Stockholm. Two days later she arrived. The following day Europe was at war.

CHAPTER 8

A New Life Begins

MY VISA CAME THROUGH in September and I sailed for New York on the SS Kungsholm one week later. We arrived on October 12, 1939, Columbus Day and my 32nd birthday, and this I took to be a good omen. I was bringing with me a memento of America's discoverer, a copy of the rare Columbus Letter of 1494, the Verardus edition, one of my few salvaged possessions, sent to me from Switzerland to Sweden.

The crossing had not been uneventful, and I was thankful that it did not become more so. Hoping to avoid difficulties, the ship did not follow a direct east-west route but sailed along the romantic Norwegian fjords, then across to Greenland and southwest. I'm not sure whether the prospect of icebergs or of German warships disturbed me more. We encountered none of the former but did get stopped by a Nazi U-boat. This was a chilling experience for me. I feared rearrest, even though my documents were in order. For several hours I hid in my bunk under a blanket. But the ship was not searched—we were small game for the Nazis, I suppose—and finally its engines started up again to signal a resumption of our journey.

As for my fellow passengers, most avoided me after learning of my confinement in concentration camps. "He must have done something wrong," I overheard someone remark. "Nobody is jailed unless he has committed some crime." From that moment I spoke no more of my experiences and rarely do so even now.

Still, my spirits remained high. I was beginning a new life, the chaos of central Europe behind me, separated by 3,000 miles of ocean. Lack of money was only a minor discouragement. I had comparatively little when I began to deal in books in Vienna and within two or three years built a thriving business. Surely in America opportunities would be just as great if not greater. I wept at seeing the Statue of Liberty come into view, as have millions of others. I was indeed one of the "poor and homeless" and could feel a close kinship with Irish, Italian, Russian, and other immigrants seeking a better life. Looking back to the day I stepped ashore in 1939, I find it hard to believe that the nearly penniless refugee was to become one of the world's leading dealers in rare books, manuscripts, periodicals, and reprints; a happy husband; father of five children; and a wealthy man.

America would be lucky for me, I could not help but feel.

My luck was instantaneous. On disembarking I was approached by a ship-news reporter. In those days of luxury liners, newspapers kept reporters permanently assigned to the big New York port to interview and photograph celebrities. In the absence of celebrities they photographed pretty girls perched on ship railings or, failing that, tried to get some sort of human-interest story from the passengers. I said I was a rare book dealer and that elicited some curiosity. I told him of the Columbus Letter and this aroused even more interest. Newspapers are partial to topical items and this happened to be Columbus Day.

He had never heard of the book, which did not surprise me, but when I mentioned its place of printing he had not heard of Basel either. Switzerland he seemed to know about, but I would have been happy, at that point, to sketch a map of the European continent if necessary.

"How much is it worth?" he wanted to know.

"It is of fabulous value," I replied. He pressed me for a figure; news items of this sort go better with a price. "I have not decided yet," I told him, which was the truth. I had no way of knowing, as yet, what I might be able to sell it for in America. I went on to say that it was my birthday and that I was the happiest man in the world to land in America on that day.

This little scene was observed with rapt attention by a few of my fellow passengers, in whose eyes my stock suddenly rose. "I knew he was somebody important," one said.

I was not without familiar faces to greet me at the pier. William H. Schab, who had immigrated earlier, was there with his family. So was my cousin, Lily Rona, a sculptor who put up the bond for my immigration permit. I felt at home in their company. The first thing to do was to find a place to live. In view of my financial condition I imagined myself doomed to the most abominable hotel, living a really Spartan existence.

Soon I found that New York's second-class hotels offered luxuries lacking in even some of Europe's better ones. My room, in the west 70s, was cheap but had a private bath. In my travels around Europe I had never stayed in a hotel room with private bath. Even at home in Vienna, hot water did not come from the tap, but had to be specially heated.

That evening I strolled along Broadway, as wide-eyed and fascinated as a country boy getting his first glimpse of the "big city." Amid the skyscrapers, neon signs, movie and vaudeville houses on almost every corner were sights and sounds reminiscent of home: kosher butchershops and dairies, clusters of people chatting in Yiddish or German as well as English. I expected the shops to close by six as in Europe, but most remained open until much later. Nor did the sidewalk chatterers disappear after nightfall. They increased in numbers, lounging on benches, eating, puffing cigars, gossiping. To live in such peace seemed unbelievable after my experiences. I returned to my hotel in a happy daze.

Next morning I went to a lawyer for advice on going into business, since I knew nothing of the legal requirements.

"I want to open a bookshop," I announced.

"So? What's the problem?"

"Must I register at City Hall, show my apprenticeship papers, my identity card, references, give a statement of my assets . . ."

He chuckled.

"Look, nobody needs that stuff here. This is America. Free enterprise."

"Well, then, what do I do?"

"Rent an office, hire a painter to paint you a sign, hang it outside, and you're all set. That's all it takes."

"Where do I register to pay taxes?"

"Taxes? Don't worry about taxes yet. Make some money, then pay taxes after the end of the year."

"Don't I have to register with the booksellers' guild?"

He looked at me as a relic from the Middle Ages. "We don't have booksellers' guilds here."

It was the most enlightening five minutes I had spent in a long while.

Nothing stood in my way now, except little details like renting a place of business and stocking it.

That evening I picked up a newspaper and read the following headline:

IMMIGRANT BRINGS COLUMBUS LETTER
TO AMERICA ON COLUMBUS DAY

There, in dramatic style, was the story of my arrival based on what I had said to the dockside newsman. I got my first American publicity before I had been in the country 24 hours, and without sending out a press release or making a single phone call. I had just one regret. My address failed to appear in the story, because I had none when the interview took place. I wondered how many readers might want to buy the Columbus Letter and be unable to reach me.

There are times when one has to be content starting at the bottom and working up. I did that in Vienna and was resigned to do so again. Offices were not hard to find in prewar New York. They could be rented for modest prices, which surprised me. I expected everything to be terribly expensive; instead it proved to be quite the opposite. Food, lodging, public transportation, clothing, and just about everything else—including books, I was to discover—sold cheaper here than anywhere in Europe and for much less than in Vienna. America's economic depression was partly responsible. Prices had been high ten years earlier but had plummeted. There was plenty of office space: businesses had shut down, and rents had been lowered to attract tenants.

As far as neighborhoods were concerned, I tried to learn enough about the city to choose intelligently. The New York headquarters of the antiquarian book trade was then on lower 4th Avenue and surrounding streets, most of whose shops (Schulte's, Stammer's, Dauber and Pine, and more than a dozen others) dealt in all kinds of secondhand books. In appearance they closely resembled the bookshops of Warsaw. The more prestigious dealers, of which the city had its share (but fewer than London or Paris), seemed to be mostly in midtown. This was "where the money was," I soon learned—near the major public and institutional libraries. Dr. A. S. W. Rosenbach, riding not quite so high as in the 1920s because of the nation's economic ills, but still America's foremost bookman, had his establishment across the street from St. Patrick's Cathedral. Just a few blocks away at Madison Avenue and 57th Street was the city's new and very successful auction house, Parke-Bernet Galleries. Now a part of the international firm of Sotheby's in London with branch offices everywhere, it was then just beginning. Otto Parke and Hiram Bernet, a pair of former employees of Mitchell Kennerley's American Art Association, went into partnership to compete against their old boss, who not long after committed suicide. They started with a bang, with the libraries of two noted American collectors, Morris L. Parrish and John A. Spoor, in their first year. It appeared that this was indeed where the action would be, and I was not mistaken. Just two years later, Parke-Bernet sold the A. Edward Newton library and has since handled virtually every important book and manuscript collection to come up for auction in this country. I felt I could not go far wrong locating nearby.

A NEW LIFE BEGINS

I took a small furnished apartment on the fourth floor of 21 East 57th Street at $50 per month. It seemed inexpensive until I heard that unfurnished apartments in some other parts of the city rented for under $20. But I was not displeased. For a bookseller it was a perfect spot. I was directly across the street from Parke-Bernet and could attend every sale regardless of weather. With any luck, some of its clients might call on me. To alert them of my presence I did what the Viennese booksellers' guild had prevented me from doing at home: I put out a sign at the street door reading "H.P. KRAUS, RARE BOOKS."

I used the living room as my library and lived in the other rooms: bedroom, kitchen and bath. Space meant nothing at that point. I had only a few books and manuscripts and could have kept them anywhere. I had space around the room for a number of bookcases, enough to hold several hundred volumes.

I was in business, though I doubted if anyone knew it.

The steady stream of customers that I envisioned never materialized. Still, in solitude there was opportunity. I had the chance to work on bringing out my first American catalogue, to prepare advertisements for the press, to make phone calls. A catalogue was essential to getting established. Even though I had few books to offer, they were of good quality and I felt confident that a catalogue containing them would be well received. After making some sales and getting badly needed capital I could build up my stock. Good books, especially good continental books, were selling at what seemed to be bargain prices. Scientific and medical works drew no bidding to speak of. Only institutional libraries were buying and even they made no effort to take full advantage of the opportunities. The same was true of scholarly serials. This was the type of material in which I had experience as a dealer. With a few thousand dollars I could have acquired enough books to run a thriving business, but I had no cash at all.

Another obstacle in my path was the language barrier. I couldn't speak much English, though I understood it pretty well. In Europe the lack of one language is seldom a severe handicap since most people, and certainly most educated people, understand several. Without a good command of English I felt lost. When I told someone my name he spelled it Kaus or Karous or something worse. My guttural "R" helped matters not at all. After futile efforts at making myself understood I would blush, stutter, and go away feeling embarrassed. Even today I have a fear of being misunderstood. When phoning someone I don't know, I have my secretary get the party and announce who is calling.

My first sale in America was a good one, both in price and prestige. For $300 the New York Public Library bought a manuscript of the early 16th century of the *Speculum Orbis* of Gualther Ludd. He was a schoolmaster of St. Dié (Vosges), working at the same school where Martin Waldseemüller was teaching geography and had mistakenly applied in 1507 the name "America" to the New World, after Amerigo Vespucci who had sailed to the Western hemisphere following Columbus and was thought by Martin Waldseemüller to be its discoverer. This money was a fortune to me, under the circumstances, and quite a stiff figure at that time.

I had a conviction about values and my policy has been, from the early days of my career until now, to price a book at what I believe it to be worth. If a book is worth $500 I price it at that figure, whether I paid $40 or $400. This has drawn some criticism but I consider it the only fair way. Customers want me sometimes to pass my bargains on to them, to let them buy at half its value a book I acquired for quarter value. I refuse to do this. My good fortune, or lack of it, is not relevant. If I find a dollar bill on the street I do not sell it for 50 cents.

The first sale I attended at Parke-Bernet was the library of an architect and comprised a wealth of 16th- and 17th-century illustrated books. Lot after lot fetched less than the usual selling prices in Europe. I bought several and might have purchased more if I had had the money. Most of the best items went to my friend and competitor William H. Schab. Otto Ranschburg, now of Lathrop C. Harper, also bought extensively. I do not flatter us by saying that we three were the only people in the room able to appreciate books of that kind. We had bought and sold them many times in Europe and looked upon them as more than "breakers" for print dealers and interior designers. The native-born American dealers had made no effort to study them or cultivate any interest in them on the part of their clients. It could not be long, we felt, before prices and interest rose. Even if one had to sit on such books for a while, they made good sitting.

CHAPTER 9

The Ideal Partner Found

TWO WEEKS AFTER ARRIVING in New York I met a girl from Vienna, fell in love with her, and about a year later we were married. It was the luckiest thing that ever happened to me. We became not just husband and wife, and parents of five children, but business partners. More than that, we have been partners in adventure, sharing in the dramas of the auction room, celebrating together after an important purchase, preparing catalogues, tracking down rare books, negotiating purchases and sales, entertaining clients.

To do all this alone would be unthinkable. A great share of my accomplishments I owe to my wife. She also restrained me, when it was necessary in the early part of my career, from buying an expensive book I wanted badly but had no immediate prospect of selling.

We consider it much more exciting to spend a few hours debating the pros and cons of a business venture than to go to a movie or a nightclub. I doubt that there have been any husband-and-wife teams in the rare book business so successful and happy as we. Dr. Rosenbach, when asked why he never married, used to say he didn't want a wife meddling in his business affairs. He never realized that a wife can definitely be an asset. Even among the great collectors, only a handful have received any encouragement or help from their wives. Most have been rebuked for cluttering up the house with books or spending too much money.

We worked together even before marriage, spending evenings at Columbia University's Butler Library doing research about the books in my stock so that I could put out a catalogue. Having lost my reference library in Vienna, I had to depend upon Columbia's until I could assemble a new one.

Hanni's father, Herbert Zucker, was a wealthy industrialist. At that time he rented a house in the Riverdale section of the Bronx, very countrylike in those days. To Herbert Zucker it seemed not quite proper that a prospective son-in-law should be struggling along with a barely solvent business. After I had courted Hanni for several months, with the knowledge of her parents, her father paid me a surprise visit.

He had to see for himself.

There he stood, in my living-room office, worried and embarrassed. The array of books stacked here and there was not impressive. But he was a kind and gentle man, and he did not say (as many another would have in those circumstances), "How on earth do you expect me to allow my daughter to marry somebody whose future looks so unpromising?" He knew we were in love and that there was nothing to be accomplished by standing in the way. Yet he could not hide his amazement.

"Young man," he said, "with this little business, will you ever earn enough to support a family?"

"Yes," I replied, bubbling with confidence.

He left, shaking his head.

In Europe, Herbert Zucker had been the chairman of a textile empire with factories in many countries. The headquarters were at Strakonice in Bohemia. Its chief product was the fez, the headgear of Islamic nations. From Vienna the family moved to France in 1937 and received French citizenship a few days before the outbreak of war.

In late October 1939 the Zucker family arrived in New York to visit the World's Fair. This was a case of good fortune because quite soon all Europe was engulfed in war and they were unable to return to France. There was one problem, however. The Zuckers were in the U.S. only on a visitor's visa. Fortunately, Herbert Zucker was able to get around this. An enterprising businessman, he possessed a strong will to survive and a talent for making friends. Wasting no time, he bought a furniture factory in Vermont. It had been operated for more than a hundred years by a family called Hale and in deference to that he added the name to his own, becoming Herbert Zucker-Hale. With the help of the Senator from Vermont, Warren R. Austin, whom he had come to know well, a private bill was passed by Congress, permitting the family to change its visitor's visa to immigration and later to become American citizens. This piece of legislation, known to us as Lex Zucker, was signed by President Roosevelt and Cordell Hull.

Hanni and I had a plan. My first American catalogue (to be numbered 19 in continuation of the Vienna series) would, we hoped, take the book world by storm, my finances would improve, and I could ask for her hand in marriage as a successful businessman. Alas for matrimonial hopes.

The catalogue was less than a smashing success. In fact, it proved a total failure. Not a single item sold. Anxiously I packed my suitcase with books and went to call on librarians. But few were in a buying mood. Europe's situation, the economy here, and a general feeling among business leaders of "too much Roosevelt" hurt the book trade, not only for beginners like myself but for seasoned dealers. Things got so bad that Hanni and I contemplated giving up books and taking jobs as servants on Park Avenue, where there was always demand for butlers and maids with European backgrounds.

Then a strange thing happened. At a cocktail party Hanni, a nondrinker by nature, downed three martinis and promptly fainted. Her cousin, who was present, went to Mr. Zucker and advised him that Hanni ought to be married before her pregnancy became too obvious. That had the desired effect. Not long thereafter Mr. Zucker came up behind us, as we sat on a bench in the family garden, placed his arms around our shoulders and said softly, "Don't you think, my children, it is time for you to get married?"

He was not thinking in terms of my continuing as a bookseller. Surely, he reasoned, I could be persuaded into quitting that nonsense. The next day he took me aside.

"Hans," he said in a fatherly tone, "since I have no son, I presume you will give up your playing with books and come to work with me in the factory."

It was a tempting proposition. As an assistant to Mr. Zucker I would someday inherit the business. I knew that I ought to accept and be thankful and Hanni knew it too. But still I clung to my seemingly impossible dream of a career in the rare book trade. No matter what I did or how much money I made, I could not have the same satisfaction as in bookselling. Knowing my mind, Hanni counseled me against accepting her father's offer, and that gave me enough strength to say no.

Herbert Zucker died in 1960 and was able to see some of my early big successes, notably the Dyson Perrins purchases. He was so proud to see a picture of Hanni and me in the New York papers. Unfortunately he passed away too soon to witness our further achievements.

The years 1939 and 1940 could not have been more unfavorable for a beginner in the antiquarian book trade. With old, established dealers doing badly, their sales falling off and profits diminishing, a newcomer stood hardly any chance. It was a buyer's market, not a seller's. But nobody bought. Only small sales could be made, not sufficient to support a family. By the summer of 1940 things looked dismal. The European crisis intensified and moved closer, politically if not geographically, to America. Books, new or old, seemed superfluous in a world where the survival of so many human beings was at stake.

Despite her cousin's fears Hanni was not pregnant, but we did plan on raising a family. For this we needed a steady income. My in-laws gave us a monthly allowance of $140, but this was hardly enough to live on, even without children. Mr. Zucker would not consider subsidizing us any further; I could get more, he reminded me, by coming to work with him. Still I refused, but no longer with quite so firm a conviction that I was doing the right thing.

We were married at City Hall on August 27, 1940. It was a typical New York late summer day, swelteringly hot and humid, very unromantic, and City Hall had no air-conditioning. My best man was Otto Ranschburg. We stood in line with Hanni and her father while twenty other couples were married ahead of us. The ceremony, when we finally reached the judge's chambers, lasted only a few minutes. Afterwards Mr. Zucker took us to a drugstore to celebrate in a fashion befitting my financial standing, with hamburgers and ice cream sodas. When I unthinkingly hailed a taxi he waved the cab away and admonished me: "Young man, have you earned enough money this week to afford a taxi? The subway costs only five cents."

Next day there was a reception for us at Riverdale, with family and friends. After cake-cutting and photo-snapping, Hanni and I drove off (in a car lent by the Zuckers) for a honeymoon in New Hampshire.

I had always been something of a gourmet and my wedding gift to myself had been a jar of caviar. Hanni had assured me that she did not like caviar, never having tasted any, but as it turned out that evening she begged me to let her taste some. You don't refuse your new bride any wish. Not only did she taste it, she ate more than half the jar and loved it. What a way to start married life.

For several years thereafter, whenever we made a clear profit of $1,000 or more, we celebrated with caviar.

CHAPTER 10

Business During the War

WHEN WE RETURNED from our honeymoon, we lived in my furnished apartment and office on 57th Street. After almost a year as a bachelor flat it sorely needed a woman's touch to put it in order. The few books with which I started had burgeoned to several hundred. To avoid expenses, I had not bought bookcases but kept books piled in stacks around the room. It made an appalling sight. New furniture was beyond reach, but we discovered the Salvation Army and bought three bookcases—not masterpieces of craftsmanship but strong and durable—for $3 each, delivery included. "Now the place looks like a bookshop," we told each other. "It has bookshelves, books, everything but customers." It also had a secretary-bookkeeper, whom I hired at the extravagant sum of $15 per week. This was a necessary expenditure, because of the filing and correspondence. But some weeks I barely took in enough money to meet his salary.

When it became obvious that we could not live and carry on a business in two rooms, we took a duplex apartment in a brownstone two blocks away, at 64 East 55th Street. Here there was more space and we could set aside one level for business and the other for living quarters. The rent of $100 per month seems unbelievable today for such a location, but in our circumstances it was a huge amount. We could meet it only if business improved, and that was a gamble. It showed no signs of doing so. I really did not believe it when I told myself that the new address would attract new customers.

With Mr. Zucker still offering me a job, which I still refused, we were grateful to accept a modest sum from him to furnish our new apartment. Back we went to the Salvation Army. In addition to our purchases there we were able to buy miscellaneous furnishings from other immigrants equally down on their luck, who had to sell whatever they owned. In this way we acquired rugs, antiques, bronzes, and accessories. Gradually the place attained some aura of elegance. I grew very fond of the apartment, so fond that I used a photograph of it as a frontispiece to my Catalogue 20 (History of Science and Medicine), published early in 1941. Nobody could know that we had bought like scavengers and paid very little for each piece. Though a poor substitute for the Moor's Castle in Vienna, the place had the proper atmosphere for a rare book business.

By now I owned a relatively large stock. But still we lacked customers and, as one of Thomas Hardy's characters remarks in *Jude the Obscure*, "you can't eat books." The Science and Medicine Catalogue, a sure success in Vienna earlier or in New York after the war, met the fate of its predecessor. The books were good, the prices fair, the timing wrong. There was no way to sell rare books profitably in 1941, not even the kind of rare books that American collectors had a reputation for buying. A. Edward Newton's renowned library was sold that year, with the finest array of English literature since Jerome Kern's in 1929 (though not in such good condition). It ought to have created a sensation. Instead, lot after lot sold disappointingly. Even the great books of which Newton wrote so charmingly in his essays, the Johnsons and Blakes and Burnses, foundered under the gavel. Most of the dealers who bought, including Newton's old friends Rosenbach and Gabriel Wells, did so not because they felt the books could be profitably sold but to protect the values of copies they already had in stock for which they had paid more.

Under such circumstances one might normally turn to selling abroad, but of course things were even worse in Europe. Without knowing how long the war would last or what its outcome might be, one faced not merely a question of surviving a temporary hardship but of reevaluating the whole future. Many refugees who had held important positions in their old country took jobs washing dishes, bellhopping, waiting upon tables in restaurants. Some Viennese couples made pastry and sold it to bakeries, if they could not afford to open bakeries of their own. Proud men washed windows and shoveled snow, doing anything to earn money and not questioning whether it fitted their talents or dignity. Compared with them I seemed vain, not willing to enter any profession but the one for which I was trained. Not many couples would have resolved to try any longer in a situation which seemed hopeless. So reluctant was I to leave bookselling, and so convinced that returning to it would be impossible if I left, that we agreed to maintain the business another year, put every ounce of our energy into it, try every new and fresh approach we could think of, do more traveling, make more phone calls. Then, if we failed, we would have to accept the reality of the situation and build a different kind of life.

Success begets success and failure generally brings forth more failure. Part of this is psychological. This I experienced in Bucharest as a salesman. If successful you become more aggressive, bolder, more positive, and your attitude has an effect on customers.

My first major American sale, major in the light of the times, came later in that same year. Hanni was pregnant now, for real (without martinis), making our situation even more critical. Frantically I wrote letters to well-known American collectors, asking if I could call on them and bring along some of my books. Nothing would come of this mail campaign, I was pretty certain. These prominent collectors were already good customers of the leading rare book dealers. Why should they want to have anything to do with someone almost totally unknown in this country and barely able to speak its language?

One day the break came. Lessing J. Rosenwald, one of book-collecting's legendary figures, invited me to his Jenkintown, Pennsylvania, estate. To a beginner in the rare book trade this was comparable to a singer getting an audition for the Metropolitan Opera. I sold him books for $4,500 on my first visit, a fabulous amount for a poor immigrant like me. The story of that historical visit to Rosenwald is told later.

Now I had no doubts about the future.

Before depositing the check I showed it triumphantly to my father-in-law, who was duly impressed and could no longer say (as he had persisted in doing) that I would do better in the furniture business. That sale was my passport into the upper strata of rare book dealing. It reinforced my belief in myself and in the ability of books to find buyers even in trying times.

It also accomplished something else. It encouraged Mr. Zucker to lend me $10,000, to be used as working capital, which he would not otherwise have done. I spent it wisely, on books which in today's market are worth ten times as much or more.

In November 1940, my mother arrived in America. It was no longer possible at that late date to travel westward, as I had done, so she had to go east, through Russia, Siberia, Japan, and across the Pacific, a total of more than 20,000 miles. Since my start as an independent book dealer my mother had been my first employee and worked faithfully with me since then.

Mary Ann, our first child, was born in September 1941. Pearl Harbor was attacked in December. Being a father, I was exempt from the draft, though I realized that all exemptions, except for the unfit, would be revoked should the war intensify.

International trade, so vital to the book community and especially to someone like myself who specialized in European books, came to a standstill. When ordering from a foreign catalogue or buying at a foreign auction, there was no assurance the books would arrive. By wartime law the British booksellers could accept payments only in sterling, and this further complicated matters. One could not draw dollar checks but had to obtain sterling drafts. Yet we in America, despite all our difficulties, fared infinitely better than foreign booksellers, many of whom lost their stock through bombing and other acts of war.

Several unsurpassed opportunities to buy occurred during the war, most of them resulting from America's still-lagging economy. William Randolph Hearst's newspaper empire had been suffering losses for several years, prompting the aging multimillionaire to divest himself of some of his holdings. Rather than selling newspaper companies, he conducted a sweeping purge at San Simeon, his chief estate, as well as at his other homes and warehouses. Here were stored the fruits of a half century of world traveling and heavy spending: antiques of all varieties, paintings by old masters, tapestries, candelabra, bronzes, ivories, marbles, stained-glass windows. Most were supposedly purchased to furnish San Simeon, but Hearst continued to buy—by the carload, like an antiques wholesaler—long after it was filled to bursting. He bought antiques with as much gusto as Sir Thomas Phillipps bought vellum manuscripts. Into cellars and storerooms they went, where they remained for years. When Mr. Hearst decided he could live without a part of the collection, even he was surprised at some of the items in it.

Gimbel's in New York was designated to sell a portion of the treasures, where they made a rather spectacular display amid kitchenware, yard goods, vacuum cleaners, and the other merchandise Gimbel's normally stocked. Swarms of reporters and photographers attended the opening on the fifth floor, treating it as a social occasion, which it was in a way.

Spanish Antiphonals three feet tall and other manuscripts appeared at Gimbel's. Among the latter was a large Spanish Breviary of the Gothic era, beautifully illuminated and suggestive of the kind of book Archer M. Huntington had been buying for his beloved Hispanic Society of America. I knew little about Spanish illumination at that time—a difficult area of study calling for specialist knowledge—but felt that either Huntington or the Morgan Library might be a prospective buyer for such a volume. The possibility that they had already seen it at the store never occurred to me.

The price was high but I succumbed, then walked the few blocks to the Morgan Library (Gimbel's is on 32nd Street, the Pierpont Morgan Library on 36th) and placed it on Miss Greene's desk. Strong-willed, not easily charmed, Belle da Costa Greene, elder stateswoman of American rare book librarians, who had worked for the Library's founder (and had inherited much of his determination), was still at her post after nearly 40 years. She was fiercely devoted to the library, which her book knowledge and two generations of Morgan money had built. Nobody in the country had handled so many precious books or possessed such vast expertise. Her manner befitted her station: regal, aloof. I trembled.

"Young man," she said, after briefly examining the manuscript, "you have a splendid book here."

Elated, I tried to conceal my emotions; I expected her to summon the library's treasurer to write out a check. Then she fixed an icy stare on me. "Yes, a splendid example . . . of the work of the Spanish forger."

I left sheepishly, angry at myself for buying a costly book that I was ill-equipped to appraise, even angrier that my first meeting with Miss Greene should be so unfavorable.

I knew nothing of "the Spanish forger" but set to finding out. It seems he had been a talented artist of the 19th century who executed miniatures in mediaeval style. The next day an old friend came to call, Philip Hofer, renowned collector and author of books on graphic arts. He had visited my place in Vienna, one of few Americans to do so. I showed him the Breviary and explained the whole story. He expressed interest and asked the price.

"To pay for my foolishness," I said, "I will sell it at 10 percent under cost."

Even this I did not expect to get, since the book had been priced at Gimbel's as genuine and would be worth considerably less as a fake. I very frankly told him what I had paid; he thought the matter over, then bought it.

Thereafter my Spanish Breviary rose like a phoenix from the ashes. Harvard's experts reached the conclusion that it was perfectly genuine. When the Houghton Library published its exhibition catalogue of *Illuminated and Calligraphic Manuscripts* in 1955, it was described with this comment:

"This MS is so beautifully preserved that at one time the miniatures were suspected of being forgeries."

C'est la vie. Before it was in my hands, and after it left, it was accepted as authentic. Only while I owned it was it considered a forgery. But I had the good fortune in 1974, more than a quarter-century later, to buy it back from Mr. Hofer.

Had I not been intimidated by Belle Greene's reputation and manner—one had the feeling of being in a royal presence—I could have established by my own research that the miniatures were genuine. But I was a beginner and behaved like one. The miniatures are now identified as a major work by a 15th-century Dutch painter.

One of my most valuable purchases, not just in profit but in usefulness, was a portion of Wilberforce Eames' reference library. This singular individual, a biblio-eccentric if ever one lived, had been cast from the Dibdin mold. His more than 80 years were devoted largely to the study of books, not just rarities or books he chose to collect but the whole history of books from prehistoric times onward. He edited the last volumes of Sabin's *Bibliotheca Americana* for the Bibliographical Society of America, one of his master works.

All aspects of book production fascinated him and he became expert in their background and history: papermaking, calligraphy, typefounding, binding. His love of the science of bibliography encompassed catalogues of all types, especially those of booksellers and public sales. For many years Eames, who died in 1937, served the New York Public Library as its chief bibliographer, compiling many of its catalogues and other publications. Such was his addiction to books that he slept in a hammock with books piled underneath, so he could reach them without getting up. Few collectors ever put their books to so much hard daily and nightly use. Every volume was for Eames a "working copy" and, no matter how pristine when acquired (he carefully inscribed his name, with a calligraphic flourish, on the front flyleaf of all his books), the covers generally fell off in time.

At his death Eames bequeathed his collection, by far the largest of its kind in private hands in America, to the New York Public Library. After absorbing the titles it did not already possess, a process which took almost five years of card-catalogue checking, the library decided to dispose of the remainder. This, a grand melange of twelve to fifteen thousand volumes, comprised works on every aspect of bibliography as well as on the study of Oriental and ancient Near East languages and cuneiform texts (another of Eames' interests). For about $1,000 I was able to buy this entire lot. This gave me the start of the reference library I sorely needed and also established me as a dealer in "books about books," as I extracted items not needed for reference and made up catalogues of them. One was devoted to standard bibliography, the other to Orientalia. Both sold exceptionally well. Libraries ordered 30 or 40 titles at a time and the number of orders received for the same item (of which I had no duplicates in stock) showed that I could well have charged more and still made sales. I had learned that trade in such books was very lucrative in Europe; now I knew that this was true in America as well. Interest in the subject, among librarians and private collectors, was at an all-time high and many books that sold for $5 or $6 in 1943 are now scarce and command justifiably stiff prices. Fifteen hundred sale catalogues were sold to Yale for approximately $1,500.

With space becoming a serious problem, I rented the cellar of our building and the cellar of the adjoining building. Still we were hard pressed for room. Soon after the Eames purchase another opportunity was presented to acquire important bibliographies from the Pierce Butler collection. This scholar-collector, author of a book on the invention of printing and many important monographs, had amassed a large library of reference material. It was acquired by Chicago's Newberry Library, which then proceeded to sell duplicates. Many of these duplicated the Eames books, but could be profitably sold if not needed for my reference shelves. There was no alternative but to rent two more floors in the same building.

Business improved but the war, with its uncertainties, dragged on. Although we now had two children, Hanni had become sufficiently involved in the business so that she could run it without me should I be drafted. Assurance that it could continue in my absence provided some measure of comfort.

A new chapter—and a rather important one—began with my involvement in the Russian book trade. To be sure, I did not speak Russian, did not read Russian, and had very little knowledge of Russian literature or history. In 1942 there was an abundance of Russian books in New York, resulting from the disposal of works from the Czarist libraries at the Winter Palace, Tsarskoye Selo, and many private libraries seized during the revolution. Occasional dipping into the imperial treasure houses had gone on since the 1920s and brought about the much celebrated transfer of the *Codex Sinaiticus* from St. Petersburg to the British Museum. These collections, so little known or appreciated in the West, included fabulous material, more Eastern European rarities than had ever been seen in this hemisphere. The Czars and Czarinas had among their ranks a formidable number of book collectors. In addition to books they purchased, they received many presentation volumes, printed on special paper, luxuriously bound in silk or morocco with the imperial crest.

Having no time for a proper sale, the Russians merely shipped these books to their New York agency, Amtorg. From Amtorg they found their way into the hands of a pair of local secondhand booksellers, Israel Perlstein and Simeon Bolan. The prices must have been extremely low because Perlstein and Bolan sold the books by size, $2 a volume for octavos, $4 to $5 for quartos, $10 to $20 for folios. No effort was made at closer examination. It was ridiculous. Even people without book knowledge could see that many were worth considerably more, even if only as art works or library furniture. Memories of the 1933 Thun-Hohenstein sale in Prague came to my mind. But Perlstein and Bolan, not in the practice of issuing catalogues or catering to the sort of buyers who might appreciate such books, thought only of turnover as rapid as possible. By the time I arrived, several librarians had already picked through the treasure-lode and I knew that most of the choicer volumes must be gone.

Nevertheless, what remained was worth in aggregate far more than the sum total of Perlstein's and Bolan's prices. After long negotiations, at which these gentlemen displayed well-developed talents, we arrived at a favorable figure; I bought out their entire holdings.

My experience with Polish booksellers led me to demand that they seal up their storerooms upon conclusion of our transaction, fearing they might continue to sell while I arranged for removal. To humor me, and convince me of their good faith, they complied. Later I saw that such precautions were unwarranted. These men, one of whom (Bolan) later came to work for me, were absolutely honest. I continued to have successful dealings with them for many years. What I did not know at the time, but subsequently discovered, was that Perlstein and Bolan had an agreement to buy back the whole lot from me, if I found—as they were certain I would—that Russian books suited neither my taste nor the tastes of my customers. I admit that it did seem odd for a dealer who spoke no Russian to buy such books. I must be a wild speculator, they imagined, who in time would come to his senses.

Naturally I could not hope to catalogue the collection myself, but this presented no insurmountable obstacle. New York had many Russian intellectuals, refugees from the Communists who were glad to find this kind of work. I hired half a dozen on a temporary basis, to go over the lot, and transliterate all title pages, and provide English translations. Among them were a former official of the Czarist government, a lawyer or two, and a journalist. Colonel Nicolajewski, one of my translators, had been tutor to the Czar's children. These men did an excellent job. It was a pleasure to work with them. But still the question remained: would the books sell? That they were good books and *deserved* to sell, none of us had any doubt. As the work progressed many rarities turned up, copies of which had never appeared on the American market. Still it was a highly specialized subject. How many American collectors appreciated the significance of Russian books? How many could read them? Practically none, unfortunately. As for American libraries, which I counted on to buy, there was no way of being sure of their reaction. Russian studies had been expanded at many universities, but would this mean increased shifting of acquisitions funds to the purchase of Russian books and periodicals?

I had gambled but, as usual, I felt that books bought at well below their real value were a gamble worth taking.

Among the highlights was the first Russian Bible printed at Ostrog, which had cost me $20 but appeared at the much more sensible figure of $350 in my list. Albums of colored plates of Russian army uniforms went up from $10 to $150, sets of multivolume chronicles were priced at $600 to $800 instead of a few dollars per volume. And most important for the business, there were thousands of volumes of journals in many fields, publications of Russian academies, encyclopedias, and collected works of Russian authors.

Despite my multiplication of the Perlstein and Bolan prices, they sold remarkably well. These initial lists went to libraries, but later I issued a full-scale catalogue of Russian books from the lot, the first catalogue of its kind to appear in America. It had an introduction by the well-known Russian scholar Roman Jakobson. This too brought in a good stream of orders. I became within a short time the leading dealer in Russian books in America.

The success of my Russian book venture was quite visible. It was talked about in the library world and among dealers. This encouraged Bolan to join me in what became a very profitable and agreeable partnership. We bought from his old private clients the books he had sold them at very low prices. Since the prices of Russian books were now (thanks to me) much higher, we could resell them very profitably.

We knew that Chicago had two great libraries, the Newberry and the University of Chicago, both interested in Russian books. Boland and I packed up four large suitcases and went by train to Chicago. It was no pleasure to travel during wartime. Fortunately we had our suitcases upon which we could sit. We arrived in the evening, and had to wait an hour at the railroad station before getting a taxi. We had rooms reserved at the Palmer House, one of the city's best hotels. Upon arrival we found to our great dismay, after standing half an hour in line, that the rooms had not been held. Back in a taxi, we cruised by at least twenty hotels, all booked solid. It was nearly midnight and we still were in the taxi with our four heavy suitcases. The situation was rather desperate. Finally the taxi driver brought us to a hotel under the Loop. He warned us that the place rented rooms by the hour—not very respectable—but we were ready to accept the worst. It proved even worse than our fears. The furniture consisted of one bed, a chair and an iron washstand, the bed dirty and unmade. Bedbugs ran along the ceiling. Of course the bed was unusable. So we sat all night on our suitcases as we had on the train. We were tired and nearly asleep when a terrible screaming woke us. People were running up and down the hall. Police knocked at our door. "A girl was killed," they told us. Luckily we weren't witnesses. The next morning we moved to the Palmer House. The trip ended well, however: we sold all our books and returned with empty suitcases. It was a hard-earned success.

During the war I established close relationships with the three deans of the American rare book trade, Dr. Rosenbach, Gabriel Wells, and Lathrop Harper. Their large, diverse stocks, built up over a period of years and comprising books from many noteworthy libraries, provided me with some of my best sources of supply in those early times. None of them had a reputation for pricing his books below the market. Nevertheless one could find in their stocks many volumes that were good buys, especially if you dealt (as I did) in categories of books in which these master dealers chose not to specialize and for which they did not cultivate customers.

Though Dr. Rosenbach's clients included ardent bibliophiles who were experienced collectors, the bulk of his sales went to rich men who bought because they considered it the fashionable thing to do. The elder Morgan was partly responsible. When Morgan assembled his greatly talked-about library at the turn of the century, other men of wealth decided that they too must own good books, just as they must own paintings and fine furniture. Many knew nothing about book collecting. They depended entirely upon the dealer's advice about what to buy, and how much to spend. Because Rosenbach had a reputation for building great libraries for rich men, they placed confidence in him. They had large incomes and paid extremely low taxes compared to today's. In recent times the complexity of book dealing has changed considerably. The level of expertise and connoisseurship among American collectors, including the wealthy, is higher. Not many people collect books as status symbols any longer. Today's collectors often know as much about their books, if not more, than the dealer who sold them.

Once a week I called on Dr. Rosenbach at his New York office, not because his stock changed that frequently (it hardly changed at all), but many visits were needed to absorb it all. I was always graciously received and allowed to browse about at will on the fourth floor, which housed miscellanea. Here I found items to which, because of their highly specialized nature or comparatively small value, Dr. Rosenbach had not given much attention. I was able to sell them at fair profits to university libraries and occasionally to private parties.

At heart Rosenbach was a collector and, like myself, could not always bear to part with an item that specially appealed to him. He set aside, from time to time, "books too good to sell," and over the years they amounted to a substantial collection. Part is now in the foundation bearing his and his brother's names. The renowned Rosenbach Collection, that of early American children's books—of which he compiled an excellent bibliography—was given not to the Foundation but to the Free Library of Philadelphia. The catalogue, *Early American Children's Books*, was soon out of print and in 1966 we issued a reprint which sold well.

In personality, style, and habits we were miles apart. Rosenbach was a bachelor, a lavish party-giver, a hard drinker. I am rather an introvert, a family man, and only a social drinker.

My best purchase from Dr. Rosenbach was a large collection of Luther tracts, including many first editions. Some I sold to Harvard and there made the acquaintance of William A. Jackson, Librarian of the Houghton Library, bibliographer of Thomas Frognall Dibdin, and a bookman's bookman. Selling to him was a pleasure. He possessed the taste of a Renaissance Pope. No sales talk was ever needed. He recognized at once a book's rarity and significance. But he was also shrewd in the best sense of the word. On one of our first meetings I showed him the first edition of *De educatione puerorum* by Aeneas Sylvius (Cologne, 1470), the earliest book on education. I knew it was not in the Harvard collections.

"Yes, I suppose we should have it," he mused. "How much?"

I said $300.

"That's outrageous."

I had learned to counter such protests. "It is nevertheless a great book, and Harvard, the great educational institution, ought to own the first printed book on education."

This was too much for Jackson. "If you think so strongly that we must have it, why not give it to us?"

Though in no position to make a gift of that size I could not refuse the challenge. The book went to Houghton Library as my gift. It was hard to explain: A poor immigrant (I was still poor by the standards of other booksellers, who held large stocks and big bank accounts), making a gift to an institution whose endowment was over $100,000,000! "Hans," my wife scolded, "you behave like a millionaire."

It was my first grandiose act in America and accomplished its purpose. My friendship with Jackson was cemented, Harvard was in my camp as a client, and it drew attention. Sometimes, giving can be as profitable as selling.

Another very successful bookseller, and also colorful, was Gabriel Wells. His real name, Weiss, was changed to Wells after World War I. For the twenty years, from 1920 until I made his acquaintance, he had provided the chief competition for Rosenbach at auctions. Neither bought very extensively for stock but carried out commissions from clients. Each wished to best the other, not just for the 10 percent on each lot but for the prestige of buying the most important items at a big sale. They fought, too, for the patronage of valued customers, each trying to lure heavy spenders away from each other. The most lasting mark Wells made on the antiquarian book trade came in 1921, when he purchased an incomplete Gutenberg Bible in Europe. Instead of selling it as a book, he broke it up to sell the leaves individually. Each was bound in blue tooled morocco by Stikeman, a New York binder, and sold along with an essay entitled "A Noble Fragment" by Wells' good customer A. Edward Newton. Today, a copy of "A Noble Fragment" with the leaf sells for nearly as much as Wells paid for about 600 leaves.

Wells was a George D. Smith kind of bookseller. Smith, king of American dealers in the pre-Rosenbach era, knew practically nothing of the literary, historical, or physical aspects of rare books. Only the prices interested him, and in those he was expert. Today such a dealer, who did not know his merchandise, would be at a serious disadvantage. Wells had perhaps some limited knowledge of rare books but no personal taste for them and no desire to learn. For his lack of knowledge he made no apologies, nor did he consider it a handicap. It hardly could have been, in light of his success.

Once, when I was in his shop discussing a book, I asked to consult his reference library. He had none.

"We don't need a reference library," he replied. "We do good business without one." Then he added: "Believe me Kraus, you cannot sell a book easily when you know too much about it."

What he meant, I suppose, was that the emotions which prompt a collector to buy are instinctive and can only be encumbered by details. But if this held true 35 to 40 years ago, it does no longer. Buyers now demand full bibliographical records with their purchases. In fact it is said by some booksellers, not entirely facetiously, that university librarians buy the description, not the book.

Lathrop C. Harper was of a different sort, conservative in manner and dress, European in his scholarship and approach to bookselling. Americana and incunabula were Mr. Harper's (everyone always called him "Mr. Harper") chief specialties. In his long career he bought and sold more early printed books than any other American dealer. He treated them very unlike Rosenbach or Wells who—with ordinary or lesser-valued incunabula—aimed for sales in quantity rather than endure the task of identifying and describing volumes with a $35 or $50 price tag (which, striking as it may appear today, was the price range of many incunabula four decades ago). Never did Rosenbach or Wells issue a catalogue of incunabula showing the full range of titles they had in stock. Harper meticulously catalogued and described everything. He loved incunabula and put out catalogues of them reminiscent of Joseph Baer's, the Frankfurt dealer, and of Jacques Rosenthal's. Much more than sale lists, they served as bibliographies, in an age when English-language bibliography of incunabula was still a wasteland. One series of Harper's catalogues subsequently appeared as a bound volume entitled *A Selection of Incunabula*. It listed 1,000 15th-century books.

Harper was neat, orderly and soft-spoken, which most great American bookmen of his time were not. He wore high collars and, like John D. Rockefeller, continued doing so after they went out of fashion. A derby in winter, a straw boater in summer served as his standard headgear. He favored salt-and-pepper tweeds and in England was always taken for a native. I think he could have been very much at home there.

By the time I came to know Lathrop Harper he had been in the business for nearly 60 years, since the 1880s. When things got slow he would reminisce about the Good Old Days. His memories were as rich as his stock. Listening to his stories was like hearing an aging army general recount details of battles from long ago. He had known everybody who was anybody in the book world, and their fathers and grandfathers. Most were friends, many had been customers. Morgan and Huntington, the princes of American book buyers, were among his clients. He had a phenomenal memory for his customers and sales. When somebody offered him an incunabulum, he looked it up and would dismiss it with a wave of his hand: "Morgan has it, Huntington has it, everybody has it."

I bought few books from Mr. Harper but profited immeasurably from knowing him. I felt in his presence like an apprentice learning from the master. He could see I was eager to learn and perhaps spent more time with me than he would with other dealers.

As the war intensified, the armed services began calling up draftees previously exempt. Younger and older men were being taken, as well as those with families. Early in 1944, the regulations were changed to cover fathers of two, and I was summoned for a preinduction physical.

The duty to serve my adopted country in time of war was one which I recognized, but military service was for me far different from the ordinary draftee. The agreement I had signed on release from concentration camp provided for immediate arrest and confinement in Dachau, if I ever returned. There was little doubt that, if inducted, I would go to Europe rather than to the Pacific, as was usual for soldiers who spoke German.

I had a restless night, and at 6 A.M. of the appointed morning I reported to the examination station, the 34th Street Armory.

Upon arriving I discovered that I had forgotten my draft card and raced back to the apartment. Hanni would, I felt certain, be nervously pacing the floor: instead she was sound asleep and never knew of my return. I admired her calmness under the circumstances.

I was one of a group of 25 men being examined that morning. We went stoically down the assembly line, having ears, eyes, blood, reflexes, and other physical indications checked. I heard the current joke of the day, "If your skin is warm, you're drafted," and was beginning to believe it. The doctors seemed in a rush. I was passed by each until I reached the psychiatrist's desk. He listened attentively, with more concern than I had expected, to my concentration-camp experiences. I told him of the time, for example, when I had been assigned to an outside work unit at Dachau to clean up a road leading to the camp. We were guarded by storm troopers armed with automatic rifles, who were under orders to shoot us if we came within 30 feet of them. One prisoner in our group did not believe that a soldier would kill in cold blood a defenseless prisoner who walked up to him with a smile of peaceful intent. He put his confidence to the test; without warning, shots rang out and the foolish fellow fell dead. I trembled, dropped my shovel and was hit by a guard. Was the dead man really foolish? I asked myself as we resumed work. He had been liberated from the cruel life of the concentration camp and was at eternal rest.

I trembled again as I told this to the psychiatrist. My interview had taken half an hour, and those who were waiting outside became impatient. The doctor rose and shook my hand. I would, he assured me, be classified 4-F, unfit for duty on grounds of health.

Still, one could not be certain until formal notice arrived, and that took time. Each morning we waited anxiously for the mail. When it contained nothing from Selective Service, Hanni called out "All clear." Finally my revised draft card was delivered. It did indeed read 4-F.

We celebrated this good news with our first real vacation since our honeymoon. Off to the mountains of Virginia we went, for a taste of quiet and clean air that New York could not offer, and a chance to make plans for the future. Knowing we would not be parted by war, we could set our goals and priorities with some hope of achieving them. "Our first general meeting," we called these sessions, borrowing a phrase from the conferences of Roosevelt, Churchill, and Stalin. We agreed on more children, a home with a garden in the suburbs, and moving the book business into a building of its own. Hanni was then, as now, a realistic planner with both feet firmly on the ground, counterbalancing my tendency toward wild fantasy.

CHAPTER 11

16 East 46th Street

IN A MUCH SHORTER TIME than we had hoped, our goals came to be realized. We found a house in New Rochelle in Westchester County, about 30 minutes from midtown Manhattan.

Then an opportunity came to purchase just the kind of centrally located building suitable for our business. Although the war had eased economic problems, real estate remained low-priced by postwar standards. Nearly every block around Grand Central Terminal had houses whose mortgages were taken over by banks. One, located at 16 East 46th Street, midway between Fifth and Madison Avenues on the south side of the street, had served as the store of an "antiques" dealer. Its five floors were filled with old furniture of all descriptions, which one might only in a generous mood refer to as antiques. The building was owned by the Union Dime Savings Bank and offered for sale as a parcel along with the one next door. It was twice as much space as we needed, but price and location seemed right. With aid from my father-in-law and his brother Ernest we bought both buildings, making a small down payment and receiving a long-term mortgage. A few years later, when real estate began going up again, we sold the adjacent building for almost as much as we had paid for both.

With the "antiques" removed (except for 16 large tables, which we bought for $90), we faced the task of turning five bare floors into a hospitable, well-appointed place of business. It was much more than a matter of bringing in bookcases and transferring the stock.

While strolling along Fifth Avenue one day I passed the old Union

Club, across the street from St. Patrick's Cathedral. This landmark building was about to be demolished to make space for Best & Co. (now the site of Olympic Tower). I watched as workmen carted furnishings into waiting trucks. This, it appeared, might be a good source for the furniture we needed, but I was told that all the furniture had been sold.

However, no buyer was yet found for the oak paneling that adorned the club library. Handsomely carved in old-world manner, it carried devices of renowned printers (Caxton, Aldus, and others). I bought it on the spot for just $100, on condition that it was to be removed within one week at my expense. This time limit could not be extended because demolition crews had a schedule to meet; if not out in a week, my paneling would end up beneath a mound of rubble. Frankly I had no idea how to do this. First the paneling had to be eased away from the walls, without cracking or splintering, then carefully loaded on trucks for the trip to 46th Street. By some miracle (the whole story is too lengthy to tell here), we succeeded in meeting the deadline. Setting it up took somewhat longer but was well worth the effort. It was installed on the second floor, in a spacious room with high ceilings, and was to house my already extensive reference library as well as the offices of Dr. Hans Nachod, my assistant, and several cataloguers.

Shortly thereafter I succeeded in buying a number of showcases formerly used by the Morgan Library at the bargain price of $5 each. It was a good omen, we felt, placing our books in cases which once contained some of the world's most precious volumes. They furnished part of the first floor. The rear was set aside for my office, at first shared with Simeon Bolan. Not only had I bought his stock of Russian books, in his days as an independent dealer, but also a set of elegant mahogany bookcases from a Russian imperial library. Suitably stocked, they made a perfect addition to the office and are still there today. The furnishings taken as a whole blended harmoniously, and seemed made exactly for the uses to which we placed them. We could not have done this, we kidded each other, without the experience gained in mixing and matching old furniture from the Salvation Army.

As for the rest of the building, two of the three upper floors were set aside to contain the bulk of our stock, on library-style metal shelving. The remaining floor became the bookkeeping department. This still left ample room for expansion. Expand we did, at a pace well beyond our expectations.

We loved the new location and wanted to learn something of its history. Obviously it was quite old, since private houses such as No. 16 had not been built in that area for many years. The neighborhood had been residential for a long time and was then rapidly being taken over by business. Old houses disappeared, replaced by skyscrapers and office buildings. Finally, the building of Rockefeller Center in the 1930s completed the area's change of face.

With some investigation we succeeded in assembling the history of this site. Until 1866, the year after the Civil War ended, the whole block was a vacant lot. It was then bought for $315,000, the equivalent of millions in modern money and a huge sum for real estate in those days, by John D. Phillips and Samuel Cohen, a pair of speculators. In 1868 four houses went up on selected lots, including the present 16 East 46th. Three years later the building changed hands. Jesse Seligman, the banker, was the next purchaser, the seller one Reuben H. Cudlipp (of whom we were unable to learn anything). One needs only a bit of imagination to picture the site in 1871, the block still largely vacant, the street void of cars and noise. This was still "uptown" as the plan of the city went. Wealthy bankers and business executives who settled in this area did so to escape the downtown turmoil, which meant Wall Street and environs. Only a few miles to the north there were still farms. In 1877, Emanuel Lehman, senior partner of the cotton-brokerage firm of Lehman Brothers, is recorded as owner of No. 16. He died there on January 11, 1907. His son Philip Lehman, the banker, then owned it and is believed to have lived in the house until 1922. In the early years it was apparently a summer residence, with garden and adjoining stables.

In a few months the entire task of cleaning, refurbishing, and redecorating the building was completed. Books and personnel were moved in and we opened for business.

Without question we had one of the handsomest bookshops in New York, if not in the whole country. Soon it was to become the only rare-book business in the city to occupy an entire building, as Dr. Rosenbach gave up his townhouse and took an apartment on 57th Street (now used by his successor, John Fleming). Within seven years I had advanced from near penniless immigrant to the owner of a prestigious business.

My success depended not only on the traditionally recognized ingredients of hard work, skill, and luck. A number of other factors were involved, without which we could not have come so far so fast. The war's end revitalized the antiquarian book trade as never before. Dealers and collectors began buying again, owners of fine libraries who hesitated selling during the war placed their properties up for sale. In the two years following World War II, 1946 and 1947, more fine books appeared at auction than in the previous six. American postwar prosperity led many more individuals to take up collecting.

It had been my practice since Vienna to show pictures of my salesrooms in catalogues, and No. 38, the first issued from 46th Street, contained a photo-layout at the new address. Many people who saw the photos but had not visited the shop could not quite believe it. "But of course you don't own the whole building?" they asked incredulously. It gave, really, the appearance of far greater wealth than we possessed.

Since then the building has witnessed a number of changes, though still in many ways reminiscent of its appearance in 1946. The staff has increased, our catalogues have become more substantial and, in the 1950s, we began to deal in rare books of the first magnitude. It may safely be said that in the third quarter of this century 16 East 46th Street has served as home for more great book rarities than any other dealer's address in the world.

It has done so, if I may be allowed some boasting, in a style befitting their estate. We do not merely turn over merchandise. Every valuable book is subjected to the most rigorous examination. Page-by-page checking is done to determine if all leaves are original, in good condition, and if any are inserted from another copy. (An ultraviolet lamp is used to discover facsimiles and repairs.) We research every aspect of a book that can be researched: the binding, any heraldic devices that may appear on bindings or bookplates, ownership signatures, and other particulars. Never do we rely on the previous owner's description, even if he is a recognized dealer, because it is unlikely that he has facilities for research comparable to ours or that he has such an expert staff. Our reference library contains most of the important—and many of the less-than-important—bibliographies and reference works in every European language. In addition we have facilities for researching all fields of subjects in book collecting. This is the one thing in which I take greatest pride, that when a book has passed through our hands it gains an unquestionable pedigree.

With the purchase of the 46th Street building a new chapter had begun in our lives. So had a new type of business: Periodicals.

It was a typical sort of American success story. It had all the classic ingredients, especially that of stepping in to fill a void and finding the void larger than anticipated. In Vienna I had done a successful trade in early runs of scientific and learned serials, buying sets from defunct libraries or library duplicates and reselling them at handsome profits to other institutions. There was, in Europe, more money in this kind of operation than in rare books. Why, I wondered, could it not be done in America?

A thriving periodicals trade would supplement our rare book operations and bring a steady day-to-day flow of income. That is always a thorn in the rare book dealer's side. Only two or three letters may arrive in a day, to order or inquire about something in a catalogue. There are simply not enough customers for rare books to generate big bundles of mail every day. On the other hand a periodicals business may draw hundreds, as we do now.

I wanted to buy an automatic letter-opener, after we settled into 46th Street. Hanni chided me, because we received so little correspondence. "You'll never need that in our business," she observed. And of course we didn't. It was she who suggested starting trade in periodicals, to be supplemented by out-of-print scholarly books aimed at university libraries. This sort of venture cannot be started overnight. One must build a stock, have capable people to organize it, then issue catalogues. It requires a much larger warehousing and shipping operation.

In the spring of 1946 I hired, at the then very respectable salary of $60 per week, a former Viennese jewelry salesman, Frederick Altman. He knew nothing of the book business but was blessed with the memory of an elephant and a virtuosity in languages. He soon managed our department of periodicals and scholarly books and compiled our first catalogue of them. This was list No. 100, a fat mimeographed catalogue offering Orientalia, duplicates purchased from the Cleveland Public Library. It became an instant success. It was an amazing achievement to accomplish this feat single-handed.

As a newcomer to the book business, Altman was able to grasp the rudiments of the trade within a month, which others take at least a year to learn. He was a crackerjack salesman and by his amiable nature established good personal relations with librarians. I gave him considerable independence with the periodicals and later with the reprint business and this was a happy relationship until he retired as president of the company in 1976.

Storage facilities were inadequate at 46th Street and we preferred not to buy another building in the city because of the high cost. Renting the necessary space in a public warehouse would be even more expensive. So we tried to find something out of town and eventually rented part of an old rubber-goods factory in Mamaroneck, New York. It was not far from the city and near our home. Architectural appeal was hardly a consideration.

We then divided the business into two branches, H.P. Kraus Rare Books and Kraus Periodicals, Inc. Altman was installed as manager of the second.

Stocking a periodicals business is more difficult than building a working stock of rare books. A few auction purchases might provide the basis of the latter. Long runs of periodicals are rarely sold at auction. Within the space of just a few years we acquired a tremendous stock, by seizing every opportunity, and became one of the foremost specialists in the trade. Thus we were able to supply needed material to university libraries all over the world.

Our first large-scale purchase was the stock of Universum Co., a firm with 30,000 volumes of journals in the field of chemistry and physics. Desperately the owners had sought a buyer for liquidation but, despite the material's desirability and very low price, none could be found. All New York dealers had space problems and wanted to pick and choose; we were willing to take everything and got it for $3,000, 10 cents per volume. This was followed up with a much larger acquisition, the stock of an old dealer in scientific periodicals named B. Login & Son, Inc. He had been successful but died without leaving a successor, and his whole inventory was for sale. It amounted to 300,000–400,000 volumes. Included were rare sets and thousands of valuable out-of-print titles. The sets of *Chemical Abstracts* alone (always in demand) amounted to about 20,000 volumes.

After this purchase, the strain on our storage space proved even greater than that on our finances. With help from Hanni's family we purchased the entire building in Mamaroneck. Parts of the space not immediately needed for our own use we rented to others. But even this was soon to become inadequate, due to the pace at which we expanded, and we had to add a new building. Our next buy was the enormous stock of H. W. Wilson's periodicals department, over 1,000,000 issues. The Wilson Co., noted publishers of indexes and union lists of periodicals, had also done a thriving trade in back issues. It was now abandoning this to devote full time to publishing. The price was not low, as this was no distress sale: $50,000, our largest purchase of any kind up to then (not counting real estate). It was a large sum to invest, but we never hesitated or regretted this transaction. We were able, using odd volumes from the Universum, Login, and Wilson collections, to build many complete sets of periodicals, which were greatly in demand. After news of the Wilson purchase was reported, we became recognized as the leading dealer in back issues of scholarly periodicals. It was time to organize another new firm, or rather another branch of the old one: Back Issues Corp., Inc.

CHAPTER 12

Europe Revisited

I LOOKED FORWARD to visiting Europe again after the war. If European dealers had not already taken the initiative, the earliest arriving Americans should, we felt, have choice opportunities to buy books. This war had scattered books more than any previous war in history. It reduced many wealthy persons and descendants of nobility to near-poverty, obliging them to part with possessions that would not otherwise be sold.

In June, 1946, I was able to make arrangements for the first trip.

With Hanni pregnant and unable to travel, I went with my father-in-law, Mr. Zucker, and William H. Schab. Buying books was the chief aim but we had no firm contacts or leads in that direction. We would simply try to look up old acquaintances and had no idea what might be found.

We went by ship, a relic known as the SS *Brazil*. She had served as a troop transport during the war and was still laid out for military use. We had to sleep in bunks, 16 persons to a cabin, and wait in line each morning to wash and use the community toilet. There were no baths and no hot water for showers. This definitely was not a luxury liner. After ten uncomfortable days we reached Cherbourg. Evidence of war was noticeable before we left the ship. Most of the piers and buildings around the wharfs lay in ruins. We had to drop anchor outside the harbor and passengers were discharged in shallow-draft lighters. We ended up in a meadow, where all the baggage lay strewn. Everyone dug through the piles of bags and boxes to find his possessions, like a treasure hunt. A confused American woman turned to a French customs officer and asked deadpan, "Sir, can you give me the address of the Black Market in Paris?"

It was a comic scene.

Mr. Zucker's Paris representative met us with a rented car, the availability of which so soon after the war surprised us.

Cherbourg had lost much more than its harbor. Most of the city was gone. I unthinkingly suggested that we dine on our way to Paris and was told that hardly any restaurants remained between Cherbourg and Paris. It was hard to believe. In a pre-war *Guide Bleu* lying in the car I found a three-star restaurant near Caen, not far from the road we were on. I asked the chauffeur to find it. "Ah, monsieur . . ." he began, about to explain that the odds on this establishment's still being in business were much against us. But he only shrugged, drove on, and within a short time we were being served a meal. Not only had the restaurant escaped damage, it seemed to be thriving. And the food was excellent; we got three stars' worth and more.

We found Paris more or less as anticipated, recovering slowly, business dull, booksellers selling very little. For grocers, clothiers, and others who dealt in essential products, the postwar period was not so gloomy. But the trade in art, antiques, books, stamps, and coins was slow. Most book sales were made to libraries rebuilding their damaged collections, but this business hardly compensated for lack of buying by private collectors. Discounts were offered, as well as opportunities to buy in bulk which would never have existed otherwise.

An old Parisian book dealer, the owner of Maisonneuve, had died and his widow found herself unable to carry on the business. The whole stock was available at an attractive price but nobody in the city wanted it. I bought it en bloc: Orientalia, periodicals of all descriptions, scholarly remainders, and a small but select sprinkling of antiquarian books. It was my first European purchase as an American book dealer. The books were crated and shipped back to New York, where they would await my return.

From Paris we went to Geneva, Switzerland, and a few days later Schab and I decided to go to Lyons to visit Paul Lardanchet, proprietor of the well-known Librairie Lardanchet. Like many French dealers, Lardanchet was book-rich and cash-poor. He was anxious to move to Paris and in need of money. We were the first Americans to call on him after the war, and he was delighted to see us. At his home he showed us the cream of his collection, volume after volume of French incunabula. Strange as it sounds today, books of this nature were not easy to sell in the U.S. 30 years ago. They were considered highly esoteric material. Few collectors appreciated them, unless, of course, a book had beautiful woodcuts, in which event it might appeal to someone like Rosenwald. But the exquisite typography of French 15th-century presses and the rarity of many of their works were yet to make an impact in this country. Schab and I drooled over the books but wondered if our customers would buy, and how much they might pay. I can recall only one specific item, the first French translation of St. Augustine's *City of God*, printed at Abbéville by Pierre Gérard and Jean du Pré, 1486–7, with 23 large, handsome woodcuts, and bound in contemporary calf.

We asked for prices. If Lardanchet was as eager as he claimed to raise cash, they might be low enough to allow some margin of profit.

"Not on an empty stomach," was his reply. "We'll have lunch first, which I've arranged at the Mère Brazier, then return here and talk business."

We were treated to the biggest luncheon we had ever eaten; various apéritifs, eight or ten courses, red and white wines, champagne, and a genuinely old brandy. All this in 1946, one year after the war ended! After two hours of nonstop eating and drinking, I felt miserable and the bumpy ride back to our host's house only aggravated matters. I collapsed on a sofa, Schab on an easy chair, and we both fell into a deep sleep.

We had driven to Lyons from Geneva on a 12-hour entry permit to France and were facing a three-hour drive back. Lardanchet, aware of this, felt that time was running out on him. Desperately he shook Schab and tried to conclude a deal. When that failed, he began to work on me. I was in no mood to buy any books, old, rare, or otherwise.

Lardanchet named a price for the lot we had selected before lunch. As we had feared it was too high.

"Too much," Schab replied, sounding as uninterested as I felt.

"Let's go back," I said.

Lardanchet countered with an offer of a 10 percent discount, then 20 percent, then 30 percent. Still we said no.

At that point the taxi driver stepped in and announced it was time to leave, to be certain of getting back in time.

This was all the nervous Lardanchet had to hear.

"Fifty percent off," he cried, almost pleading.

"It's a deal," I said feebly. Schab nodded his approval.

The transaction was consummated on the spot. I opened my valise and handed over a wad of franc notes (I carried cash in those days), the books were piled hastily into the taxi, and we reached the border on time. Lardanchet had succeeded in financing his move but made no boast about the sale. He called it the most expensive luncheon he ever gave and made certain in future to conduct business when the customer's brain was clear. Never, he was convinced, would he have been obliged to offer such a discount, if we had been in full possession of our senses.

Our next stop was the home of the recently deceased Italian Senator Patetta, at the little village of Cairo near Genoa. Patetta had lived in ducal splendor in a 13th-century Hohenstaufen castle, furnished with antiques and numerous works of art. Aside from Italy's churches and museums, it was hard to imagine a more authentically mediaeval atmosphere. The widow, in need of money like everyone else in the country, wanted to sell not only the library but the whole estate. Quite a package it was, including hundreds of acres of lush countryside, several lakes, and surrounding villages. The price was about a third of what it might be in better times. I could probably have gotten back the cost just by selling the furnishings in America. But I declined, and to this day regret my decision. I turned down the kind of opportunity that comes to few of us, the chance to live like a mediaeval baron.

The library was my main concern, if Signora Patetta would consent to sell it by itself. She was only too anxious to. I had no idea what it contained but went to look with my usual high expectations. There is always the chance that a library in a centuries-old building contains valuable manuscripts and printed books. There is also the likelihood that if anything significant had been included, it had long since been disposed of. We found the Patetta collection rather disappointing, though it would not be considered so today. The bulk was law books, some of them old. A scattering of incunabula was included and even a few manuscripts but nothing that specially excited us. The Patetta incunabula were mostly of the class that could, in those days, be had from the shelves of Lathrop Harper for well under $100 apiece. Schab dismissed it as deadweight, feeling there was no logic in buying books here that we could get cheaply back home. I too concluded that the library as a whole represented a questionable investment, but since Signora Patetta had given me carte blanche I picked out some of the more interesting pieces.

Fully loaded with books, we went on to Milan and found an opportunity to add further to our baggage. Dr. Erardo Aeschlimann, head of Hoepli's antiquarian department (for years Olschki and Hoepli had ruled the Italian rare-book market), wanted to sell a warehouse full of books because they had to be moved. These were not, alas, the gems that adorned Hoepli's big opulent catalogues, but the firm's day-to-day stock of 16th- to 19th-century Italian books. Here again this same material, viewed from the standpoint of today's demand, would now be considered an attractive lot. Schab took one look at the yards and yards of theological treatises, late editions of Greek and Latin authors, philosophers, and the like, most of them from undistinguished presses and in ordinary bindings, and announced, "I am not a garbage collector."

I wasn't, either, but the collection seemed to bear some potential. It was low-priced and contained many books that probably could, in time, be sold at a good profit. There was also one outstanding treasure, much too good for the company it was keeping, a set of four monumental wall maps of the continents, dating from the late 16th century by the famous Venetian cartographer Giacomo Gastaldi. They had come from the Orsetti Library and were in their original frames. More than 20 years later I sold these maps to the University of Texas at Austin for about ten times my investment in the whole Hoepli collection.

All in all, the Hoepli books proved one of my best purchases on this trip. Because I was willing to gamble, and had patience to wait for buyers, I made almost a hundred-fold profit on them—and I am still selling them. They provided me with the best stock of Italian books in America. As interest grew in Renaissance studies, humanism, and Italian literature, many of them increased greatly in demand. Patience is the key to success in this business, patience and capital.

The following year I returned to Europe. This was the time to buy; prices were still low, with sacrifice sales continuing, and in those circumstances I had no objection to being overstocked. Accompanying me again was Schab. Hanni was able to join us later.

My major bulk purchase was the duplicate periodicals of an academy in Haarlem, Holland, the Teyler Endowment Library. The collection was so huge that I went half shares with the Dutch dealer Nijhoff, but afterward bought out his interest. The library had for generations been exchanging runs of periodicals with other learned societies all over the world and built a formidable collection. I doubt if we ever again owned so many sets of publications of European universities and academies. Many of them sold very quickly, before we could even publish a catalogue. The rest were featured in our Catalogue 50, our first large catalogue devoted to periodicals. Once again it was good business and good promotion.

From the Netherlands we went on to Lugano to call on the widow of Giuseppe Martini. He had only recently died and we wanted to get first choice of his books if possible. A world-renowned bookseller, he had dealt in precisely the sort of books which interested Schab and me: incunabula (mostly Italian), paleography, humanistic manuscripts, and early Italian literature. For years he had bought the choicest material in these fields. Martini was a sort of gentleman dealer, a collector by nature.

The stock was for sale individually. I picked and chose, Schab did likewise, and together we took some of the best volumes. Schab was unwilling to join me in buying the remainder (about one thousand volumes) as a whole, so I decided to try to buy it alone and opened negotiations with Signora Martini. An American by birth, she was nevertheless temperamental and emotional, like an Italian, especially when her late husband's books were concerned. It became evident at the outset that she either had no idea of their real value or was not serious about selling.

She began by naming an exorbitant price. For two weeks we bargained, exchanging offers and counteroffers. Her mind was changeable. Whenever we reached what seemed like an agreement, she thought things over and decided she should either not sell, or that the price ought to be higher. I could sympathize with her somewhat. She undoubtedly knew the prices paid for some of these books before the war and expected to get a profit; but times had radically changed. Feeling sure we had reached an accord one evening, I began to pack the books. She burst into tears, I unpacked them, and a fresh round of negotiations began.

Hoping that the sight of money might succeed where mere mention of it failed, I went to a bank and withdrew bundles of Swiss notes in denominations of 20 and 50 francs. A shipping firm was called and told to be waiting near the Martini house with a van and a full crew. Then I showed the banknotes to Signora Martini and tossed them on a table. I told her what they added up to, and that it was my final offer.

She would take it, she murmured, but I had heard that before. A yes from the Signora could not be regarded as anything more than tentative. I worked fast and had the books moved out by the waiting movers before she could change her mind. Hanni, who had just arrived from Zurich, acted as attention-diverter, placing the banknotes in piles, counting them, shuffling them, preventing Signora Martini from looking at or thinking about the movers going in and out laden with books. Finally, the money was counted, the bookcases were empty; she sighed and commented, "I'm glad it's over."

We were more than glad. The collection was one of the best of its kind we would ever have the opportunity to buy. Martini's connoisseurship showed in his books. They had been picked for special reasons, physical beauty in typography or binding, or the importance of the text.

I still have some of Martini's manuscripts and books. Far from slow movers, as this might indicate, they proved excellent investments whose value has increased greatly over the years. Many were listed in my catalogue 44.

Later Hanni and I made a pilgrimage to Lucca, Giuseppe Martini's hometown where he was born and is buried. Lucca is, like many Italian cities, a mediaeval town with many old buildings and narrow twisting lanes surrounded by perfectly preserved ramparts of the 13th century. The streets were designed for vehicles no larger than a donkey or at most an ox-cart. Yet here we were, driving through them in an American car. After a while the inevitable befell us. Going through a particularly picturesque but narrow street we got stuck, literally stuck. We were wedged in fast, between the buildings on each side of the street, with a steadily increasing band of small Italian cars behind us, drivers honking and shouting. A standard-size American car had its limitations in this part of the world. Finally the racket brought a policeman. Instead of berating us he hopped into the car and, with the aplomb of one who had been through just such situations before, squeezed it free.

Was this, I wondered, Signor Martini's vengeance for my purchase of his beloved library? Had he caught me in his snare to ponder if I were a worthy owner of his treasured books? I was determined to find the cemetery and promise at his grave that I would cherish his books and price them high enough so that they would not fall into undeserving hands. He must have smiled on us from above as we were extricated from our dilemma and probably concluded that I was a worthy possessor of his library. Later we noticed a warning about Lucca in the guidebook: "Do not take large cars inside the ramparts of the city."

On that same trip I bought in Paris the papers of Louis Polain (1866–1933). Known best for his catalogue of incunabula in Belgian libraries, the standard work in the field and among the most frequently cited incunabula reference books, Polain was a sort of French Wilberforce Eames, a tireless scholar, a passionate lover of old books and their mysteries. Like Eames he left behind a storehouse of papers: memoranda, lists, plans, letters, files. Every copy of every 15th-century book Polain had examined, and he had examined thousands, was carefully recorded in lengthy bibliographical detail. The files also contained numerous photocopies of incunabula pages, made to compare type designs and illustrations. It was, without exaggeration, the product of his lifetime—the work of 50 years as a bibliographer.

I bought the papers from Mlle. Eugénie Droz, a learned specialist in the French Renaissance and a very successful publisher. I was introduced to her, and to the Polain papers, by a fellow dealer, Lucien Scheler, a nonconformist poet and a great antiquarian. Mlle. Droz lived near Scheler in the historic Rue de Tournon in Paris. Her home could not have boasted a more fitting background, having been the house of Clément Marot four centuries earlier. It had changed little since then, still served by the same courtyard toilet that the great poet had called his own. Much as I was impressed by walking in Marot's footsteps, I felt no particular emotion over his toilet. It was designed for standing use only. Walking across the yard to it at night in the pitch darkness, flashlight in hand, took one back 400 years. Both arms being needed for support in this situation, I was too embarrassed to ask Mlle. Droz to hold the flashlight, so my friend Scheler assisted me in this crisis.

Lardanchet had needed money to come to Paris; Mlle. Droz needed it to leave. We completed the transaction without delay and both got what we wanted. Included was also the manuscript of the Pellechet-Polain catalogue of incunabula in French libraries, that ambitious project whose publication was halted after only three volumes.

Marie Pellechet (1840–1900) was the first woman bibliographer of any importance. She undertook the monumental task of cataloguing all the incunabula in French public collections. Unfortunately, she lived to see only the first volume of her work published. Two more volumes appeared, substantially her work, but with Polain's revision. Then the work stopped. Preparation of the catalogue had been sponsored by the government, costing the French Ministry of Education more than one million gold francs.

Mlle. Droz claimed to have hidden this archive from the Nazis during their occupation of France; the Germans wanted to incorporate it into their *Gesamtkatalog der Wiegendrucke*, designed as the ultimate catalogue of 15th-century printing. This I could not help but question. Mlle. Droz was said to have been sympathetic to the Germans. In any case she retained the manuscript after the war, rather than turning it over to the French government so that publication could resume. I felt it only fair to do this and presented it, along with the other Polain papers, to the Bibliothèque Nationale. In gratitude I was awarded the decoration of Chevalier of the Légion d'Honneur. I cherish my red ribbon and wear it in my lapel every day.

The hopes entertained for seeing the work in print were not soon fulfilled. Faced with the enormous cost of editing and publishing more than two dozen volumes, the French government delayed. When 20 years had passed with not a single additional volume published, we intervened. Our reprint company brought out a facsimile of the manuscript in 26 volumes in photo-offset, with a learned introduction by my dear friend Frederick R. Goff, former head of the Rare Book Division of the Library of Congress and a great incunabulist.

CHAPTER 13

H. P. K.'s Family

TO BE HAPPILY MARRIED for many years is an art in which few succeed. I am proud to say that nearly 40 years of married life proved that we could do it, with great happiness. The gods were merciful in letting me choose the right wife. Good teamwork overcame the early disadvantages of no money and an uncertain future. We built a family, four lovely girls, Mary Ann, Barbara, Eveline, and Susan, and a fine boy, Hans Peter, Jr. First came the girls. Obsessed with dynastic ideas, I hoped for a boy. When the fifth child was due, I waited, as usual, outside the delivery room, where Hanni, undisturbed by the events to follow, routinely read the proofs of a forthcoming catalogue. After a night of nervous suspense the doctor came.

"It's a boy," he announced. "Congratulations."

"Are you sure?" I blurted out, delighted and a little delirious.

The doctor was irritated. "I think after 35 years of practice I should know the difference."

Hanni and I were both in heaven!

One of the rare bones of contention between Hanni and me had always been the question of a name. If it was a boy I wanted to call him Hans. Hanni contended that she had enough with one Hans. My idea was that as long as we could not agree, we would not have a son. When number five was due, we both refrained from discussing names. But when I heard the good news I acted independently. I went to the office of the hospital and registered the name of the baby as Hans Peter Kraus,

Jr. It was too late for Hanni to object. Later we agreed to call the boy John.

I adored my children and invented a whole cycle of bedtime stories to entertain them, which they asked to hear again and again. After a brief retirement from story telling, I am now doing it again for my seven grandchildren.

I love sports of all kinds and imparted this love to my wife and children. We played tennis and golf together. In Vienna I had gone horseback riding when I could afford to, and continued to do so soon after I came to America. All my children rode and I felt pride in seeing all five on horseback, sometimes winning blue ribbons in shows. Before I became ill with colitis I was a passionate mountain climber. With the older girls and a guide I climbed quite a few peaks in the Italian Dolomites, all of us roped together.

I am very happy and lucky that my oldest daughter, Mary Ann (Mrs. Raymond W. Mitchell), has been working with us for the past 15 years and is now my able assistant and trusted partner.

In 1966 we bought a most beautiful home, the former residence of *Time-Life* publisher Henry R. Luce in Ridgefield, Connecticut. This house we filled with works of art of all kinds, periods, and cultures: from prehistoric bronzes to modern sculpture, Renaissance to Victorian paintings, oriental and mediaeval miniatures. The variety results not only from a catholicity of taste on my part but from a wish to expose my son, eight years old at the time we bought the house, to great art of all styles. I personally love everything beautiful of all periods, all the more when I can buy and possess it. So it is evident that I enjoy spending money. One cannot live in the 20th century like the Renaissance princes, but to surround oneself with art as they did is no less enjoyable and satisfying today than it was five centuries ago.

Until now I have chiefly written about myself and my wife and children. The picture that I gave would be incomplete without further mention of my mother, to whom I owe so much. In 1927 she became a widow. When in 1932 I opened my own business, mother worked with me as my first employee, and when my business grew she ran the office so that I could concentrate on buying, selling, and traveling.

She took care of me, spoiled me, made my life agreeable. In the Vienna days I had lunch at home and then I usually napped for half an hour. Mother always worried about me. She became much concerned about the fact that I, a young man of 21, did not have any sex life. One day she said to me: "Hans, my son, you are old enough to have a girl friend. You should not sit alone at home and read every evening."

"Where shall I go?" I answered. "To the park?"

My efficient mother was prepared for this. To open the way she rented a room for me. It was a part of a large apartment, too big for the tenant, an old widow; a bedroom and bath, with a separate entrance. Mother gave me the key with this advice: "I hope you will use it. It is expensive but don't worry, I have already paid three months rent in advance."

I took the key but was a little uneasy about using it.

As a matter of fact I could not find a proper subject to use it with. At this time I was a romantic, sentimental young man full of ideals of pure love and instead of taking advantage of this bedroom I poured out poetry. After a few weeks mother reprimanded me: "Hans, you have never used the room."

"How do you know?"

"The landlady told me that the bed is never slept in. I paid for the laundry, so that the bed linen could be changed. What a waste."

I blushed and promised to do my best, so that the money should not be wasted. From then on I made a pilgrimage each week to the lonely bedroom, all alone, and mussed up the bed linen. After a while I felt by the proud look of my mother that she was happy with the love life of her son. Soon, though, I had very sweet girl friends but I did not get married because of the comfortable home my mother made for me.

When the Gestapo took me away in 1938, mother showed her courage and stamina. By sending me money regularly to the concentration camp, she helped keep me alive. She hired lawyers and stood for hours every week at the Gestapo office to work for my release. These stubborn efforts finally succeeded.

In order to join me in America she went, in 1940, on an odyssey, a two-month trip via Siberia and Japan. Soon after arriving in New York she resumed working for me and continued to do so up to the age of 86. Everyone who knew her loved her; members of the family, all our employees, friends, even the postman. I never knew anyone with such charisma, always friendly, never complaining. She was the most wonderful mother. In 1972 she died at the age of 89.

PART II

CHAPTER 14

Success at Jenkintown

I HAVE ALREADY SAID that my first major sale in the U.S. was to Lessing Rosenwald, who through the years remained a most valued customer. Born in 1891, he is the son of the Chicago industrialist and financier Julius Rosenwald. As an executive of Sears Roebuck, he moved from Illinois to Pennsylvania to supervise its Philadelphia branch and settled in Jenkintown. There, and on his periodic trips to New York, he was introduced to prominent rare book dealers and became one of the most important collectors of our time. So devoted was he to his books and prints that he retired at an early age to make his hobby a full-time occupation.

Lessing Rosenwald is a dedicated, serious collector who not only loves fine books but realistically appreciates them as works of art and historical objects. At first he collected printed books and prints from various periods—whatever was rare or beautiful—but without special focus. Later his attention settled on great illustrated volumes and for many years he reigned as the foremost American buyer in that field. In Jenkintown he built a beautiful home, called Alverthorpe, a wing of which houses his books and prints. In 1952 the collection was presented to the nation, to be kept at Alverthorpe during his lifetime and at his death to be turned over to the Library of Congress. His superb collection of prints is to go to the National Gallery in Washington.

Rosenwald is a farsighted collector. When incunabula were relatively unpopular in America, he was buying 15th-century works, selecting volumes with illustrations, mostly woodcuts.

He bought Caxtons during the depression years, when prices were extremely low, and assembled one of the largest private collections of works by this famous printer. He bought when many other wealthy bibliophiles had stopped. Moreover, Rosenwald has the temperament to enjoy what he buys. Book collecting is a merry adventure for him, a vehicle for making friends, traveling, having good times, sharing common interests with other collectors. He has an ebullient personality and is a man of good cheer. Yet he is at the same time a practicing scholar, not a mere book accumulator; he owns not only a great collection of books but a fine refergence library of thousands of volumes.

Another of his qualities, luckily for me, is approachability. Some collectors are difficult to reach, even if one is offering books they would like to own. They confine their buying to a select group of dealers and want nothing to do with the rest of the trade, least of all with newcomers.

Early in 1941, having been in this country less than two years and struggling to support myself and my wife, I had made little headway in the book business and was desperate for money. I wrote to Rosenwald, whom I knew by reputation only, asking if I could come to Jenkintown and show him some books. Much to my surprise he extended an invitation. I had few rare books in my possession at that time but was able to get enough on consignment from other dealers to assemble a fairly impressive lot. Once again, as on our honeymoon, I borrowed my father-in-law's car and Hanni and I, with several suitcases of books, headed south to Pennsylvania.

A more miserable trip can hardly be imagined. For three hours fears and apprehensions went through my mind. I didn't know the way, was sure to get lost and not arrive on time. Would Rosenwald already have most of the books, perhaps in better condition? Would he consider the prices too high, or the volumes not good enough for his library? Would he deem it a waste of time trying to understand my poor English? Was he expecting me to be somebody I was not?

To calm my nerves I flipped on the car radio, but what we heard proved anything but calming. Hitler had invaded Greece; France had capitulated. Europe was now almost wholly in the Nazi grasp, Russia would probably fall in time, and Hitler's attention would then turn to America. No vivid imagination was needed to picture storm troopers parading along Broadway. "It can't happen here," Americans asserted. But that was what was said in every country before it was invaded by the Nazis.

I expected to find Rosenwald (who must have heard the news) morose, not wanting to buy or even look at books.

Instead he gushed charm and was in the best of humor. If the world was not at peace, Jenkintown surely was. Rosenwald mentioned nothing about the news reports.

"Aren't you upset by Hitler's conquests in Europe?" I could not refrain from asking.

"No," he said emphatically. "Why should we be upset in this great, strong country? Losing one battle doesn't mean losing the war."

"But aren't you afraid the Germans will come here?"

This sort of question he was not expecting. A German invasion was the farthest thing from his mind. "No, my friend. We are not afraid," the "we" meaning America as a people.

He was then 50 years of age and I was 33, but much more than 17 years separated us. Rosenwald was the kind of individual I had not encountered in Europe, an American aristocrat. He behaved like anything but a lord of the manor. There was nothing formal or overbearing about him.

I put my books on his library table, surrounded by the treasures he had gathered, while he looked on with rapt attention. Loosely inserted in each volume was a typewritten description. He picked up every book, examined it quickly, read the description. I noticed he was making two piles and assumed, or hoped, that one consisted of items he wished to buy. All the while his expression never changed; a smile remained on his lips, masking his emotions. He asked no questions, made no remarks. He had the finesse of a professional with long experience.

When one pile began to outgrow the other I could no longer stifle my curiosity.

"Which is the one you are considering?" I asked.

He made no reply but went through the piles again, re-examining some of the books, shifting several from one to the other. Finally he pointed to the larger pile. "Figure out your price for those. And sharpen your pencil!"

With that he left the room.

By "sharpen your pencil" he meant "Give me the best price you possibly can." But the phrase was new to me and I was puzzled by it. After a few minutes of calculating I was approached by a secretary and asked for the figure.

"Mr. Rosenwald wants to know for how much to make out the check."

It amounted to $4,500, by far my largest American sale up to then. A moment or two later Rosenwald strode in and handed me his check. I had sold four and a half thousand dollars worth of books without uttering a single word about them. I could hardly believe the coolness and smoothness with which he carried out the transaction and I don't think my amazement was very effectively concealed.

"Come again," he said, showing me to the door.

"Mr. Rosenwald," I could not help but ask, "what did you mean by saying that I should sharpen my pencil? It was already quite sharp."

He laughed heartily. "You made more money by not knowing what I meant."

I made no further inquiries.

Outside, I broke the good news to Hanni, waiting in the car. It was my policy in those days not to introduce her to clients, for fear of making the visit seem like a social call and taking attention away from the books. Her annoyance at being kept waiting like a chauffeur soon vanished.

Rosenwald was to remain a good customer and valued friend. Quite a few of his chief acquisitions, especially during the 1950s and 1960s, after the death of Dr. Rosenbach (from whom he did most of his early buying), came from my shelves. In the 1940s, after more than 20 years as a collector, he had already formed a marvelous library, its riches too numerous to be described here, but had yet to take the firm direction toward illustrated books and graphic arts for which this collection is now famous.

"Is it still possible," he asked at the time, "to build a great private collection of illustrated books today, when so many are already in institutions?"

"Of course it is," I replied. "If you are prepared to pay enough for them, the books will come running to you from all parts of the world."

And they did. For the next quarter-century important woodcut volumes, illustrated books of the 15th through 20th centuries, engravings, Blakes, and anything else significant in the history of book illustration gravitated to Jenkintown. My warning about prices seems hardly valid in light of the present market; most of what Rosenwald bought would now be fabulous bargains at the prices he paid. Not a haggler, he did expect, and I was willing to extend, a 10 percent discount on all his purchases. Time and circumstance were on his side. The disappearance of books into institutions, which Rosenwald feared would hinder the formation of such a collection, was more than counterbalanced by a slump in the market and the general lack of appreciation for these important volumes. Many woodcut books of the 15th century were considered just interesting curiosities. For example I sold Rosenwald a copy of Ingold's *Das Goldene Spiel*,(Augsburg),1472, the first illustrated book on sports. My price of $600 was normal for that time. Fifteen years later, after illustrated incunabula mushroomed in interest and price, I quoted him another copy, having forgotten that he already owned one. Now it was $10,000. He beamed and showed me the old bill for $600. Many of his purchases reflected similar advances, in a relatively short span of time. To some degree he was responsible for the boom in illustrated books; one great special collection tends to promote emulators. The catalogue published by the Library of Congress in 1954 focused attention on the subject and showed that building such a collection was still possible in the 20th century.

Of course when one collects 15th-century woodcuts, some of the most desirable come not in books but as single prints or even as playing cards. To early binders they were nothing more than waste paper to be used for stiffening the leather of book covers. How many early woodcuts are imbedded in old bindings at this very moment one cannot begin to imagine; it must be a huge number, but the chance for any but a tiny fraction of them being discovered is virtually nil, as such discoveries are made only in rebinding or through some accident.

In 1941, not long after paying my first call on Rosenwald, I ordered a manuscript from the catalogue of a small Parisian bookseller. When it arrived I found it failed to match the description. Instead of the interesting contents promised, it was nothing but a legal text. I was angry and asked my secretary to fetch the catalogue and our copy of the order. When neither could be found I became still angrier.

"Shouldn't you at least look through the book?" my secretary pleaded, trying to calm me. But I was not to be pacified and flung the book into a wastebasket, whereupon the rather fragile old binding broke.

She fished it out and looked at it forlornly. "Now we can't even return it."

Later, when my anger subsided, I examined the binding to see if it might be repairable. It was limp blindstamped leather of about 1500, probably French. In handling the detached covers I noticed some small specks of red and blue peeking out of the torn edges. Having made two major discoveries of rare items in the covers of old books (the unique Fust and Schoeffer Indulgence and a fragment of the Parsifal poem in Middle High German), I peeled it away slightly and saw what appeared to be the edges of a colored woodcut. My impulse to remove the whole pastedown had to be checked; the contents might be damaged unless expertly removed. I consigned the job to Rudolf Wien, a restoration specialist. He brought forth from the covers several copies of a brilliant and hitherto unrecorded 15th-century woodcut, in color, in folio size. In three sections, it depicted the Resurrection in the upper portion, monograms of Christ and Mary in the center, and, in the lower portion, a monk (probably St. Bonaventura) preaching and a procession through a mediaeval town. To one side was a shield blazoned with a crosscut saw and the letters J CRO. Campbell Dodgson of the British Museum, to whom I sent a photo, called it a sensational discovery of a wholly unknown woodcut. Dodgson, the great authority on 15th-century woodcuts and engravings, wanted to publish it but died before he could do so. The cut is now believed to be the first printed in five colors by stencil.

Rosenwald found my discovery as irresistible as I suspected he would. I brought two copies to Jenkintown and even before discussing the price he called for his wife to "see what I've just bought." It was worth while, in this case, to own two copies: each had lost a bit of margin to careless scissors, but each in a different place; what one lacked the other supplied. The catalogue of Rosenwald's print collection, presented to Washington's National Gallery, refers to them as being among the most interesting in the collection (*Fifteenth Century Woodcuts and Metalcuts from the National Gallery of Art*, Washington, 1965, nos. 208 and 209).

Though not an enthusiast of manuscripts, Mr. Rosenwald bought choice ones from time to time. Among the purchases were two manuscripts of Valturius, *De re militari*, with drawings relating to the woodcuts of the 1472 edition from the Voynich estate (see Chapter 31). I got them on consignment and sold them to Rosenwald for $20,000. They became items five and six in the catalogue of his gift to the Library of Congress.

In the early postwar years Rosenwald bought many of the fine books and prints that Schab and I located on our European trips. In Paris Schab had the good fortune to buy with me a nearly complete collection of the prints of Jean Duvet, "Master of the Unicorn Engravings" and one of the more important figures in French 16th-century graphic art. Nothing could be more tailor-made to Rosenwald's taste. With this purchase he owned the finest Duvet collection in the country.

For a collector like Rosenwald, who did things in a big way, no acquisition could have been more appropriate than the so-called Giant Bible of Mainz, a 15th-century manuscript in elephant folio size. It came from the library of the Duke of Gotha. In the partitioning of Germany after World War II, Gotha became part of the eastern or Soviet zone. The library of the Dukes was claimed as national property. Nevertheless a certain number of volumes had been smuggled out on the Duke's behalf and in 1951 began to appear on the western European market. Included was the finest known copy of Ptolemy's *Cosmographia*, Ulm, 1482, printed on vellum with maps contemporarily hand-colored, now in the collection of Harrison Horblit, and an *Ars Memorandi* blockbook, which I later owned.

I was able to establish contact with a representative of the Duke, Landrat Voigts. I met him at one of the Duke's estates, Coburg Castle, near the border but in the western zone. When I asked if he could sell me anything from the library, I was offered—much to my surprise, as it seemed the kind of item least suitable for smuggling—a huge manuscript Bible in two volumes, "beautifully written" according to the description. When the massive crates arrived in New York I could scarcely believe they contained just two books. These volumes are nearly as large as the Audubon *Birds of America* and considerably thicker, being on vellum rather than paper. With a real sense of awe and wonder I studied them, never having seen a manuscript Bible of such proportions; manuscript Bibles were hardly ever written on so large a scale. As promised, the calligraphy was masterful and in addition the borders bore historiation and floriation from the hand of an accomplished, though regrettably anonymous, artist. (See Fig. 3).

Even without further recommendation, this was a mighty piece of workmanship, deserving attention on physical grounds alone. But the more I examined it, the more I became convinced I had seen its marginal decorations elsewhere, while the calligraphy bore striking resemblance to the 42-line or Gutenberg Bible type. Further investigation led to the discovery of several dates. The scribe had conveniently recorded, at the end of each section, the year of its completion. So enormous was the task that it carried over from one year to the next. The dates were 1452 and 1453, exactly contemporary with the 42-line Bible.

That evening, after having spent most of the day with my new acquisition, I was as usual reading reference books. Suddenly something hit my eye. In Max Geissberg's book *Das älteste gestochene deutsche Kartenspiel* (1905) I came upon almost precise duplications of the marginal drawings, which were designs of early engraved German cards, the work of an anonymous artist called "The Master of the Playing Cards." Intertwined miniatures of stags, bears, lions, and hunters within tendrils seemed copied from or inspired by those in my Bible, or vice versa. If a connection could be established among Gutenberg, the Master of the Playing Cards, and my Bible, it would rank as a sort of bibliographical "missing link."

Next morning, after a night of little sleep and much excitement, I rushed to the office and summoned my two experts, Drs. Hans Nachod and Hellmut Lehmann-Haupt. Together we examined the marginal decor, compared it with the illustrations in Geissberg's book, and agreed that they could not have been independently created. Theory and counter-theory then presented themselves. The possibilities were numerous. Was the playing-card designer related to Gutenberg? Did Gutenberg

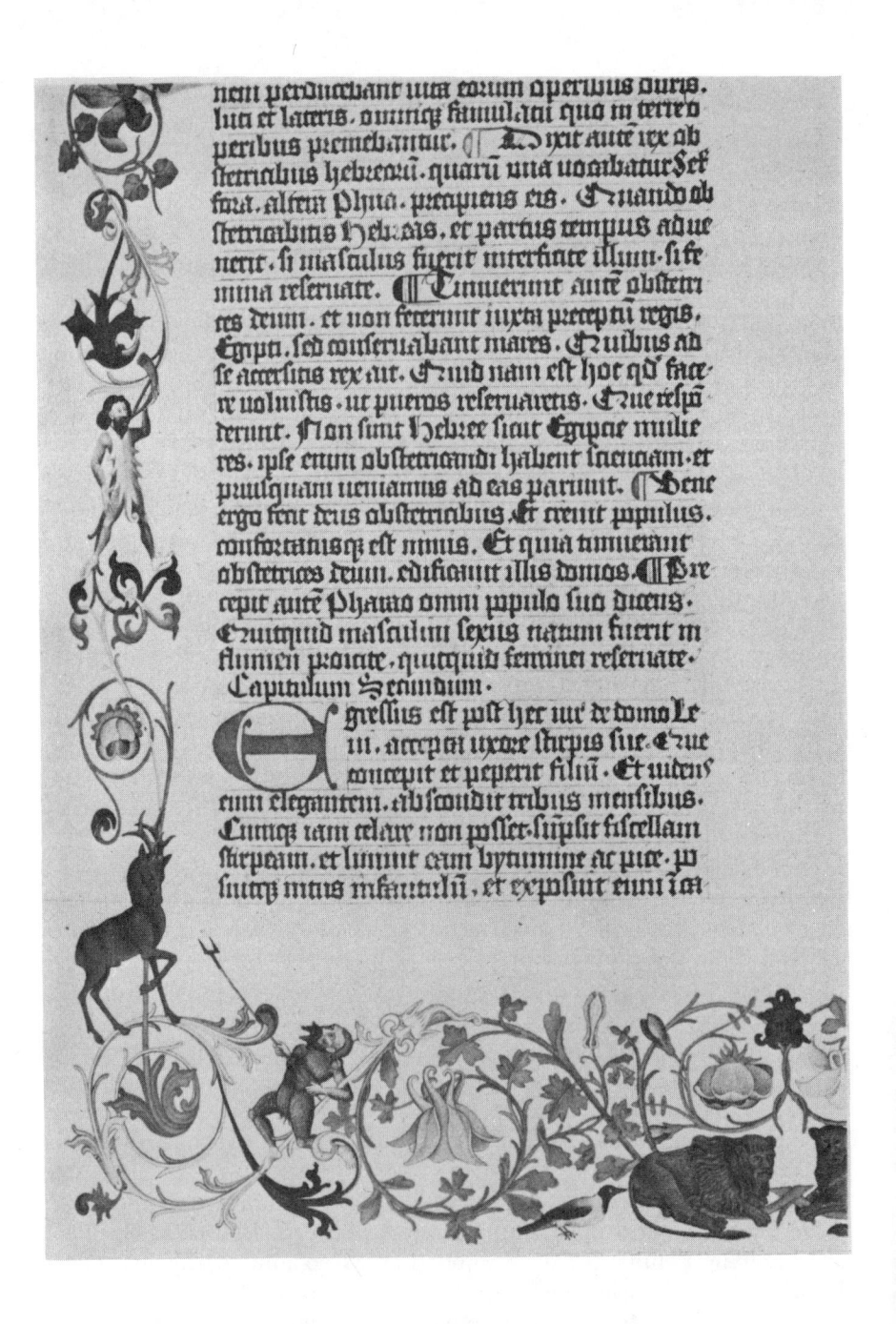

Fig. 3. Giant Bible of Mainz. Portion of a leaf (much reduced).
(Library of Congress, Washington–Rosenwald Collection.)

himself design and print the first playing cards? Was the Giant Bible in Gutenberg's possession, and did he model the 42-line Bible after it? Going a step further, had Gutenberg dreamed of printing decorations in the margins of books to make them approximate even more closely the appearance of manuscripts? Careful, unhurried investigation was called for. In 1966 Lehmann-Haupt published his authoritative book, *Gutenberg and the Master of the Playing Cards* (Yale University Press), exploring the matter from every possible angle. But this was 15 years later; in 1951 my concern was not merely with solving bibliographical puzzles but with selling this expensive item.

Rosenwald struck me as the logical prospective buyer of such a work, not because he had any special interest in Bibles or manuscripts but because it bore squarely on subjects dear to him, the origin of copper engraving and the development of book illustration. If he bought the manuscript it would be his costliest purchase from me, and I wondered if he could be persuaded to go that high for a manuscript.

I decided this was a perfect opportunity to put on a show.

Rosenwald paid occasional visits to 46th Street, when he was in town. To prepare for his next, I set up a pair of lecterns on a second-floor table, each displaying an open volume of the Bible—opened to pages with the most lavish and handsome illumination. The lights were turned down and overhead spotlights focused on the lecterns. It was a breathtaking sight that no collector could witness without emotion. Rosenwald was given no warning. I simply told him there was something upstairs he ought to see and escorted him there. The room was totally dark. At my signal the spotlights were turned on, and a very surprised Rosenwald reacted just as I hoped he would.

"Congratulations, Kraus," he beamed. "That was worthy of Joe Duveen."

I was not at all displeased at being compared to the century's foremost art dealer.

I had barely begun telling about the manuscript when Rosenwald asked that it be brought to Jenkintown so that he might inspect it along with his librarian-curator, Elisabeth Mongan. I had brought many books to Jenkintown but none of this bulk. A pair of oversized suitcases was found, into which they just fitted, and Hanni and I drove down with them. As usual, she waited outside while Rosenwald sent two of his household staff to bring the suitcases in. Nobody would believe that each suitcase contained a single book, but these men, being in Rosenwald's employ, knew that anything was possible.

For an hour we huddled together in the library, Rosenwald, Miss Mongan, and I, with the volumes opened before us. Slowly, lovingly, each leaf was turned, every border examined. Rosenwald wanted to buy but had doubts. So monstrously large were the volumes that they would not stand upright in any of Alverthorpe's bookcases; they would have to be laid flat or a special case built for them. Even at that, their weight would require Rosenwald to call for help every time he wished to move one.

"Don't keep them here," I advised. "They deserve to be on permanent display at the Library of Congress."

"Let's sit down and talk about it," he replied.

Here I felt was an ideal opportunity to discuss in detail the manuscript's background and the important findings we had made concerning it. I had just begun to mention Gutenberg and the Master of the Playing Cards when I was silenced with a wave of the hand.

"Don't tell us any more," he cried, "or I won't be able to afford it." Then, after a brief pause, "By the way, how much do you want for it? And don't forget to sharpen your pencil."

The price was $35,000. Even then it was a modest figure; today I would gladly pay ten times as much for it. But this item will not pass through my hands again. Rosenwald gave it, as I suggested, to the Library of Congress, where it is kept on exhibition in a bulletproof case and draws its share of gasps from tourists. Even those who know or care nothing about investigations into the origin of printing and engraving are duly impressed; never have they seen such a book.

CHAPTER 15

Five Significant Failures

THOUGH I CAN TAKE NO CREDIT for the discovery of the Dead Sea Scrolls, I can take no small measure of blame for failing to buy them. This opportunity, this once-in-a-lifetime chance, was placed before me in 1949, not long after they were found. It could have been one of the supreme acquisitions of my career, but it seemed at the time an unpromising gamble.

Eleazar Lipa Sukenik, Professor of Archaeology at Jerusalem's Hebrew University, came to my office—entirely without warning or appointment—and laid two or three scrolls on a table. Dr. Sukenik was also, I learned later, the father of Yigael Yadin, Chief of Staff of the Israeli Army in 1948 and now Professor of Archaeology. Dr. Sukenik had been carrying the scrolls through the streets, despite their fragility, thrust under his arm like loaves of French bread.

I must admit that they aroused little enthusiasm on my part by their physical appearance. They looked ancient enough to be sure, but so blackened and battered that any attempt to read them seemed hopeless.

Dr. Sukenik gave me the full story of their discovery, which by now has been retold in dozens of books and encyclopedias. They were Hebrew script on leather, dating approximately from the time of Christ, he explained, and, as best as he could judge from reading the first few words of the stiff, ossified scrolls, were Biblical texts. He had bought them from some local Arabs for his own account and he wished to sell. They had been found by Bedouins, he said, in a cave near the Dead Sea where they lay hidden in a Genizah, or place of concealment for worn-out and disused sacred texts, to prevent their profanation.

The asking price was $100,000. Knowing what I know now, but could not possibly have known then, I would have written out a check then and there. But I was not willing to invest such an amount in a surprise package at that time. There was a question whether an expert could successfully unroll the scrolls, and whether they truly contained anything of significance. The whole text might prove to be illegible or unimportant. Perhaps those first few words were preserved and nothing else; or maybe the scrolls contained nothing more than business records (interesting historically, to be sure, but not worth $100,000). I would have to pay another large sum for restoration and deciphering, and this would require a great deal of time. Meanwhile my investment would be tied up. Even if all went well—if they could be unrolled intact and did carry significant Biblical texts—I might still find it hard to resell them. I had never handled material of this nature and had no real idea of its price potential.

Dr. Sukenik assured me that experts could open the scrolls with a minimum of loss and wanted immediate cash, before I could consult with anyone. It was vital that he raise money right away, he said, because there were other similar scrolls in the hands of peasants which he wanted to buy. "I must buy them at once before they are damaged," he explained.

I said no, to my eternal regret, and had no second chance. They never did come on the market but went into the Jerusalem Museum, to become part of the "Shrine of the Book" exhibit. The scrolls proved to be everything he so steadfastly hoped, and which I just as steadfastly doubted. But nobody wins them all.

Few private libraries from the Middle Ages and Renaissance survive intact. Unless the owner was a king or other important person, whose books would pass to his successors, a library was likely to be scattered. Even a great collection like Grolier's was eventually broken up. Only in the most fortunate circumstances would such a library be preserved, and the chance to buy one is practically unheard-of.

Nicolaus Cardinal Cusanus (1401–64), pre-Reformation priest, was one of the great minds of his era. Born Krebs, he took the name Cusanus from his birthplace, Kues or Cusa on the Mosel River in Germany. His record as an intellectual and freethinker was rivaled by few. He was a member of the Council of Basel, at which he assailed the genuineness of the 8th-century forgery, "the Donation of Constantine," which purported to be a grant from the Emperor Constantine to the Pope, Sylvester I, of temporal dominion over Rome, Italy, and the provinces, places, and *civitates* of the western regions. Based on this claim America was divided between Spain and Portugal.

Later Cusanus staged various crusades: on the importance of mathematics, against the mediaeval devotion to Aristotle, reform of the calendar (later undertaken by Gregory XIII, along lines similar to Cusanus' proposal). He dabbled in science too, designing scientific instruments with graduated scales, and he advanced the theory, then revolutionary, that the earth moved in orbit and was not the center of the universe. He possibly knew Gutenberg; in any event he took great interest in the new craft of printing. Another of his claims to fame was designing the first printed map of Germany, a copy of which was in Catalogue 69, my first big catalogue of incunabula (*The Cradle of Printing*). It was the Prince Oettingen-Wallerstein copy and was sold to Otto Schäfer.

While doing research on maps I learned that the Cusanus library, assembled five centuries earlier, was still in existence. I had no idea what it contained, but I felt I must find it. In 1949 we went to Kues in quest of it. Before long I discovered the library in the Hospital of St. Nikolaus, nestled away like a jewel in an antique setting. How it got there was not difficult to determine. In 1464 the hospital was established by the Cardinal's will, which provided additionally for its long-range support. Since the 15th century the hospital had sold wine from its famous vineyards, which were included in the Cusanus bequest.

The library and what little remained of Cusanus' personal effects could be viewed on the second floor of an ancient building in the hospital complex, an ideal setting in terms of atmosphere but one where they seemed totally lost to scholars. Father Eismann, a delightful old priest, had charge of the books. He received me and we chatted amiably. It was apparent that he had few visitors. I explained how greatly I admired Cusanus. He showed me a number of items, including some astronomical instruments of the Cardinal's design and holograph manuscripts of his works.

I could not look at any of these treasures without wanting to buy them. They seemed almost to be going to waste. Yet suggesting a sale was a delicate matter, because the Cardinal had such a personal connection with the institution, and even more so because money was not badly needed.

I decided to use the wine as my opening gambit.

"Is it possible," I asked, "to buy any of the fine wine that your vineyards produce?"

He smiled. "Which kind? We make quite a few different wines."

Descending to the wine cellars, we tasted a number of varieties. He tasted, I tasted, we supplemented our tasting with a few nibbles of cheese and bread, and had a fine time. I arranged to buy a case of one of the most expensive wines. Then, the foreplay being over, I got down to business.

"Would it be possible," I asked, "to buy one of the great Cardinal's manuscripts? To own one of them would fulfill a life's dream."

Father Eismann was not shocked at the proposal. "Come again next year, my son," he said. "Then perhaps I can do something for you."

I returned the next year, and the one after that. I kept returning to Kues during my annual European visits, paying a call on Father Eismann, tasting more wine, talking more about Cardinal Cusanus and his books. The next time, I was always promised, there might be a manuscript to buy. It never came to pass. On my fifth visit I was informed by the new librarian that Father Eismann had died. There would be no more wine-tasting, no more visits to Kues, no more hope of buying any of Cusanus' books. The collection remains intact today. The old priest was a good friend and I believe he held out the hope of "next year" to lure me back, so we could talk books and drink wine.

While staying in St. Moritz in the summer of 1947, I received the following handwritten letter on stationery bearing the name of a prominent music publisher:

Milan, 3rd July, 1947

Dear Mr. Kraus,

I am a customer of Mr. ――― and have been informed by him that you are at present in St. Moritz for a short period, and that later on you will probably spend a day or two in Geneva.

My brothers and I have inherited from our late father, who was a keen book-collectioner [sic], a very rare Italian piece, which, as we now wish to divide our property, we should like to put for sale in the States. The book is of extreme importance.

I believe the matter might interest you. I should therefore be obliged if you will kindly write to me, or wire, in which days you will be in Geneva, and at which hotel, as I should come to meet you and show you the book, which we are keeping in safe-custody in Geneva.

With best regards, sincerely yours,
―――

I replied at once by telegram, though I had no idea what the book was, informing my correspondent that I was about to leave St. Moritz and had an uncertain schedule thereafter. I received a quick answer:

Milan, 7th July, 1947

Dear Mr. Kraus,

    I have received your cable and I thank you.
    I regret to hear you are leaving St. Moritz on July 12th, as I am unable to leave Milan until that date.
    Anyway! The book I have written you about is Dante's first edition (Foligno 1472), a perfect specimen, with wide margins. The price we wish to obtain is one hundred & eighty thousand Swiss francs. Please let me know if you would be interested in trying to sell the book in the States, as we should be quite willing to leave it with you on deposit for 3 or 4 months.
    In case you might have fixed by now your program after leaving St. Moritz, and we might therefore meet in Switzerland before you leave, please let me know by cable, keeping in mind that I should first have to go to Geneva where I keep the book in safe-custody, and therefore should not be able to withdraw it on a Sunday.

Best regards, sincerely yours,

    I shall be grateful if you will keep all the above absolutely confidential.

The meeting was arranged at the Hotel Neues Schloss in Zurich. The Dante seemed an excellent specimen, crisp clean leaves, wide margins, a few insignificant wormholes, and a good solid contemporary binding. I was prepared to buy. In fact we had the check written. It amounted, after some negotiation, to the equivalent of about $30,000. I collated the copy. This was an easy task. The copy was perfect.

"Could there be some leaves in facsimile?" Hanni whispered. "It seems to be too perfect."

This possibility had not occurred to me. But then I, too, had second thoughts.

At this time the deal was as good as completed. I could not ask for more time for examination. Therefore I said, "I hope you won't object if I take a few moments to enjoy the music of the old paper? You, a publisher of music, will understand." The owner had no objection.

I was seated at a window and had the book on a table before me, bathed in sunlight. Gently I flipped the pages one after the other, sounding each with a sharp push of my finger; it gave the authentic old-rag-paper crackle. The tune of the paper should always be the same. I was not merely delighting in the "music," however. I was looking for watermarks. When I found one, it carried the number 1911. Could this be a date?

"What does this mean?" I asked the owner, who fortunately was still the owner (we had not yet handed over the check).

"I have no idea," he replied, and I believe he meant it. I had with me a copy of the *Census of Incunabula in American Libraries* and there, in small print, was mentioned that in 1911 a full facsimile of the Foligno Dante had been published for an exhibition in Turin, one of those exact reproductions in which even wormholes are reproduced. The 1911 binding would have given it away, but at some time it had been removed and a neat job of "remboîtage" performed, as the French call it. The book was fitted perfectly into a genuine 15th-century Italian binding and, to complete the masquerade, wormholes in the covers corresponded to those in the leaves. The owner, thinking he owned a valuable book, turned ashen. I believe he was absolutely honest. His grandfather had bought it 30 years earlier, he explained to us. Very likely he paid a great deal of money for it and was duped.

Of the great finds that I made over the years but was unable to buy, none caused quite such bitter disappointment as the Sarezzano Purple Bible. This was a manuscript of indescribable importance, equaled in age, beauty, and historical interest by perhaps only a dozen manuscripts in the entire world. I fought to overcome each obstacle standing in the way of this purchase and came within hours of owning it.

Miss Meta Harrsen, colleague of Miss Greene at the Morgan Library and author of many books and monographs on illuminated manuscripts, alerted me in 1953 that this volume was for sale. It had a romantic background, having been found in the wall of a chapel at Sarezzano, near Tortona, in Piedmont, Italy, during renovation. At some time in the far past, a monk fearful of pillagers had hidden away his prized book in a niche and covered it with plaster. There it reposed soundly, safe not only from the barbarian tribes or whatever enemy he had in mind but from the hands of collectors as well. The volume was incomplete but even in that state commanded respect.

A Biblical text in Latin, it dated from the 5th century, prior to St. Jerome's revision of the Gospels, and was transcribed on purple-dyed vellum, suggesting imperial use. (The practice of dyeing vellum prevailed in various parts of Europe until the later Middle Ages; purple was the usual color.) With the only two known 4th-century Bible codices in national libraries, the British Museum and the Vatican, it was unquestionably as early as any that could reach the market.

One must negotiate in person, I was advised. The citizens of Sarezzano mistrusted letters as much as they mistrusted checks. Should I be successful, the Morgan Library would presumably be interested. I wrote to Padre Domenico Botto, Arciprete di Sarezzano. I got, in due course, a friendly reply inviting me to come. This was encouraging.

Here the situation was quite unlike going into a library, browsing, and finding books to buy. The good people knew exactly what they had and meant to sell it—for which nobody could blame them—for the best price. It was not so much a problem of bidding against other prospective buyers, which I was willing to do, but getting there in time and having the chance to bid at all. For all I knew, half a dozen people might have already made offers. Perhaps the manuscript was already sold.

In Milan I enlisted the aid of Professor Mario Armani of Hoepli's Antiquarian Department, a connoisseur of the first rank, who had enough love of manuscripts to accept my invitation to join me. He would act as a second pair of eyes and much-needed interpreter. My Italian, though good enough for a restaurant, was not to be trusted with delicate negotiations.

We rented a car and drove to Sarezzano. The place had obviously seen better days. It was one of many old Italian villages which thrived in the 15th and 16th centuries but now suffered from a shortage of industry and noble patrons. It was very picturesque. Several local dignitaries received us, including the priest and the mayor, who was also a butcher. We were led to the only two-story house of the village, into a room where the Purple Bible lay seductively on a table. One glance told me I must have it. The script was in faint silver and gold uncials on vellum of the deepest, richest purple. "The color of emperors," I said to myself. Could it have been prepared for a 5th-century ruler? Rome still had emperors in the west until A.D. 476; they undoubtedly owned libraries; and if they possessed Bibles, which is not unlikely, none finer could be imagined.

After two hours of the liveliest haggling of my entire career (which the dignitaries seemed to enjoy a great deal more than I), we worked out a price: five million lire. This was much more than it is today, but still was reasonable considering the book's quality. All the while, as bargaining went on, a crowd of villagers milled in the street outside, aware of what we were doing. They awaited news of the outcome with as much anticipation as the election of a pope. When the priest addressed them from the balcony and announced, " *La Biblia è venduta*" (The Bible is sold), bedlam broke loose, a band played, there was applause, dancing, and hats hurled into the air.

"Why the celebration?" I asked the priest. "Why all this excitement?"

"I can explain," he replied. "The people have always been poor; the village also. It has never possessed a noble church. For six centuries one was promised, by various popes, dukes, and emperors, but, while neighboring towns received churches to be proud of, Sarezzano's dream remained unfulfilled. By selling the Bible we no longer need to rely on a patron's beneficence; we can finance our own church. Plans are already drawn up. Every able-bodied townsman has vowed to take part in the construction, working one day a week without pay."

Everyone was well satisfied with the outcome. I would have the book, the priest had his sale, the village would get a church. In the square a fiesta was held, to which we were taken as guests of honor. After being plied with a choice assortment of the region's food and drink, we returned elated to Milan.

For the next several days I was kept busy with the financial details of the transaction. Buying in these circumstances is not so simple as writing a check. One must produce cash, and raising that much cash in a foreign country is no small challenge. It took me three days to assemble it, in sheaves of notes held together with rubber bands.

As I prepared to leave again for Sarezzano and complete the deal, I glanced at the headline of the *Corriere della Sera*: AMERICAN BUYS PURPLE BIBLE OF SAREZZANO FOR FABULOUS AMOUNT.

As much as I like publicity, it was unwelcome this time. I wanted things kept quiet until the book was in my possession. Once the news circulated throughout Italy, the government or maybe the Vatican would step in and prevent the sale on grounds of protecting a national treasure. Of course I could sympathize with such actions, but as a bookseller intent on making a purchase I had to place my own interests first.

Racing to Sarezzano, my suitcase bulging with lire notes, I went immediately to the big house. Upon entering I knew there was trouble. A wake seemed in progress. The jubilation of several days earlier had turned to gloom. Just yesterday, I was informed by a downcast priest, a papal courier had come and whisked the Bible away. There was nothing to be done about it. Under church law, any property of an Italian church belongs to the Vatican and can be removed at any time. I did not get my purple Bible and the town would not get its church.

Anyone who collects English literature, reference works, British history, or, in fact, rare books in almost any category, has at one time or other come into possession of volumes bearing the handsome heraldic ex-libris of the Bibliotheca Lindesiana, showing a pair of unicorns. This library, remarkable in size and content, belonged to the Scottish noble family of Lindsay, Earls of Crawford and Balcarres.

The immensity of the Bibliotheca Lindesiana, as it existed in the late 1800s and early 1900s, is not easily put into words. Mere numbers fail to suffice. The printed catalogue, a very, very costly labor of love, comprised no less than 8 volumes in large quarto, four of them (dealing with printed books) thicker and bulkier than the volumes of the British Museum's general catalogue. In aggregate value the library was certainly matched or surpassed by those of other British collectors—Christie-Miller and Spencer, possibly Huth—but in diversity, in its broad spectrum of subjects and variety of its choice rarities, none came close. Unlike libraries assembled by collectors with specialized tastes, the Bibliotheca Lindesiana was conceived as a great general collection reflecting the history, literature, and art of all peoples. Haigh Hall, one of the Crawford homes, which housed the library, contained books on tobacco, glassmaking, numismatics, Quakers, stamp collecting, and many other topics, with rarities in almost every one.

The ancient beginnings of the family might lead one to presume that its library grew gradually from century to century, with Shakespeare folios bought when published and perhaps Caxtons purchased from Caxton himself. Such was not the case. In the mid-19th century, after 800 years of Crawfords, Haigh Hall possessed no formidable library. Most of the collection was acquired from 1860 to 1880, the result of whirlwind buying by the 25th Earl. His appetite for books knew few parallels in the history of collecting. About 100,000 volumes must have been acquired in that period. While other Scottish noblemen fished or hunted, the Earl of Crawford surrounded himself with miles of books. However, in order to raise some £26,000, the 26th Earl sold, in two Sotheby sales (1887 and 1889), his Gutenberg Bible, many of his finest incunabula, and his beautiful chivalry romances. Later, in 1924 and 1925, his son sold the collection of French historical documents in three more sales at Sotheby's and then sold the bulk of the library (about 80,000 volumes) to Quaritch, retaining only the sections on fine arts and bibliography, the remainder of the incunabula collection, and some other rare books. Years before this gigantic sale most of the illuminated and Oriental manuscripts had gone to the John Rylands Library, shortly after the founding of that institution. The reasons for these huge sales were various—one was to provide extra capital for one of the family businesses, another to pay out a family settlement under the will of a previous Earl, and there were others.

Among my fondest memories is a dinner in 1951 enjoyed in one of the Crawford houses, at Balcarres. Built in 1595, in the reign of Elizabeth I, this mansion had been extensively renovated in the 19th century but retained the palatial dining hall, the grand staircase, and the thick-walled bedchamber known as Oliver Cromwell's room. With little imagination, one could hear many a ghostly footstep.

When visiting a collector, one hopes that he will either buy or sell. I knew that the house contained many desirable books, even if just a fraction of what the family once possessed. It was presided over by David, 28th Earl of Crawford, now deceased. Though perhaps not so voracious a book buyer as his great-grandfather, he had a strong interest in the family library and was a member of nearly every major bibliographical society in the English-speaking world. He was a handsome gentleman, scholar, and gracious host.

Before dinner was served I committed a faux-pas. Lord Crawford asked what I would have to drink. Being in Scotland I asked for whisky. Gently I was reminded that the custom dictated sherry. Scotch appeared later and had its medicinal benefits. The spacious hall, thanks to its thick walls, retained December's chills until mid-May. This was April and my teeth chattered, despite a roaring fire. I admired my host's ruggedness, as he seemed unaffected and comfortable. At length I could not refrain from asking his secret.

"Woolen underwear," he answered, undoing a button of his dress shirt to display it.

Next morning I was granted my wish of being allowed to browse in the library. It lived fully up to my expectations, being still a very choice, impressive collection. Knowing that the manuscripts had been sold long before, I had no hope of finding any, but nevertheless several fine specimens were present, including a superb *Roman de la Rose*. I was also quite taken by a rare broadside of Martin Luther's theses. Lord Crawford expressed no objection to selling, so I selected a group of the best items and made an offer for them. It was, I believed, a very liberal one, more than I might have paid under other circumstances. I wanted to show my willingness and eagerness to buy, hoping he might always sell to me rather than anyone else.

His Lordship knew market prices—his penciled notes of prices fetched by other copies were found in many of his books—and he was expecting to get the full retail value. There was no margin for profit, but the Crawford books so thrilled me that I found myself unable to resist.

After having reached an agreement I discovered that matters did not end there. Lord Crawford poured another round of drinks and exclaimed, with typical nonchalance, "Of course, I shall be expecting you to take care of the extraneous expenses as well." (This happened more than 25 years ago and I can unfortunately not recall what he meant by this.)

I gulped. "Surely that cannot be a large amount?" I asked, thinking of something like a sales tax.

"Oh yes, quite," he replied. "Sixty to eighty percent." (I believe I heard him mention inheritance taxes.)

That ended our negotiations. I would be paying almost double the price I had offered. Even for books of such quality it was unthinkable. I returned from Scotland without books. This was one of the libraries from which I could not extract a single item. Later, when I had another opportunity to purchase a treasure from the Crawford collection, luck and fate again went against me. This time the problem was of a different sort.

When visiting London in 1961 Clifford Maggs showed me one of the most extraordinary English documents I had ever seen, a land grant of 1067 to 1075, signed by William the Conqueror. Owing to the king's illiteracy (shared in good measure with a number of his early successors), the signature appears in the form of a cross against which the king's name was transcribed by a clerk. The rarity of anything signed by England's first Norman king is of course legendary. To find such a document on the market astounded me. It had belonged to the Earl of Crawford, who had sold it to Maggs. I thought to myself, "This belongs in a museum." Later these sentiments returned to me only too bitterly.

A well-preserved folio sheet of vellum, it contained 18 lines of Latin text written in a good early Anglo-Saxon hand. It concerned a grant by Walerand, count of Meulon, of the church and endowed lands of St. Mary, Bury St. Edmunds, to St. Stephen's Church in Caen, Normandy, "for the good of William, King of the English and Duke of the Normans, and for the good and salvation of the soul of Walerand, and for the souls of Walerand's father, mother, wife and children, the Abbot of Caen to the place fit for God's service, and for a settlement of monks, to confirm which at Walerand's prayers, his lord the king has signed it with his own hand. . . ." The gift also included a yearly stipend of 200 pigs and cattle. St. Stephen's was built by William as a penance for his irregular marriage with Matilda; the Pope had granted the King and Queen dispensation on condition that a portion of the royal wealth be used for "worthy works." Incidentally it was at St. Stephen's that the curfew was first instituted in England: beginning in 1061 a bell was sounded, on order of the king, at a certain hour each night to clear the streets.

The price of the document was not high (£800). The collector in me, not to mention the dealer, succumbed instantly.

"May I take it with me?" I asked Maggs.

"Unfortunately, no. We must secure an export license from the British Museum."

Those words, "export license," have caused me some of my most uneasy moments. How could such a license be granted for a document of this kind? What could be more of a "national treasure"?

"Don't worry," he assured me. "It's been in two of our catalogues. The Earl of Crawford bought it, then sold it back to us. If the museum wanted it, I imagine they'd have sent for it by now."

A decision would be forthcoming in a few days. Until then the document had to remain with Maggs Brothers.

At lunch I told my children, in London on holiday with me, all about it. Having just studied about the Battle of Hastings, Mary Ann was fascinated. She could hardly wait to see it. "Well," I suggested, "why don't we pay a call on the British Museum? We'll look at their specimen and see how it compares with mine."

"Do they have William the Conqueror's signature, Daddy?"

"Well, it's the national library, the greatest collection of British historical documents in the world."

We strolled through the museum's exhibition halls and found the royal documents. It was a stunning spectacle: case after case of letters, charters and other manuscripts, reflecting the whole panorama of British history. Elizabeth I, the Henrys, Richards, Edwards seemed amply represented; the Charleses and Jameses, Anne and Marys, we found in abundance. But look as we might, there was no trace of William the Conqueror.

"They can't have everything on public display," I said, trying to reassure myself. "It's probably stored somewhere for safekeeping."

An attendant whom we questioned seemed puzzled. "We must have it," he remarked. After thoroughly checking the displays he shook his head. "I will ask the Keeper of Manuscripts," he said, and departed.

A few moments later the Keeper of Manuscripts was introduced to us. "I was positive we had a signature of William the Conqueror," he explained. "Otherwise we'd have bought the one from Maggs Brothers. They had a fine example in their last catalogue. I must find out if it's still available. . . ."

The awful truth was that the British Museum, which everybody thinks has everything, did not own a signature of William the Conqueror. This soon was corrected by purchasing the Maggs specimen. Never again, I was sure, would the chance come to buy a signature of this king. But it did, just four years later. It came from the Phillipps collection and was sold at Sotheby's. As it now had one, the British Museum made no objection to granting an export license for this document. It is now part of another renowned collection, the Bibliotheca Bodmeriana near Geneva.

CHAPTER 16

Unsold for Twenty Years

I N MY YEARS as an antiquarian bookseller I've made discoveries of rare items in monasteries, churches, cellars, and in the possession of people who had not the slightest notion that they owned valuable books. Some of my best buys have also been found on fellow dealers' shelves.

When Gabriel Wells died in 1946 his business was not carried on by successors, like Rosenbach's and Harper's. The executors put the books up for sale. At first they were offered for sale, *sans* fanfare, then nearly a decade later the still unsold items went up for sale at Parke-Bernet.

Wells was not a connoisseur of illuminated manuscripts. In fact he really had no interest in that kind of book at all; nevertheless at his death he still owned two manuscripts of what can be called "museum quality," the *Anhalt Gospels* (see Plate 14), and a splendid 15th-century French Missal.

The more important artistically was the *Anhalt Gospels,* dating from the 10th century, in neat Carolingian bookhand on choice vellum. It came from the library of the Dukes of Anhalt-Dessau. This was a magnificent manuscript illuminated with full page miniatures, one of those rare treasures of great antiquity which can hardly be found anymore in private hands. I wondered for a while how it could have remained unsold for 20 years; Wells had bought it in 1927. Then I wondered no longer. Wells had paid, in a paroxysm of stock-buying frenzy, £9,000. With the pound then at $5, this equaled $45,000. Two years later the crash came, prices plummeted, and few investments could be sold for more than pennies on the dollar. Wells held determinedly to his price, hoping at least to get back his cost. Stupendous though the volume was, nobody had that kind of cash in the depression.

I bought the manuscript from his estate at $36,000, a stiff price at that time though well under the 1927 figure. It was the most expensive book or manuscript I had owned up to then.

The French Missal, though belonging to a more plentiful class of manuscripts, was one of the finest examples of its kind. Beautifully illuminated, it captured all the glories of French Gothic art and bore testimony to the virtuosity of its artists. No less than 107 large miniatures, far in excess of the customary total, and 428 smaller ones adorned its pages. The hand of Jean Fouquet's disciple Jean Colombe was seen in the paintings; subsequent study resulted in an attribution to followers of Fouquet and determined the date as about 1475. Charles VI's coat of arms, emblazoned on a beautifully colored page, appeared to be a later addition. But even if this volume was not created for royalty, even if it had not been touched by the brush of France's greatest miniature painter, it was nevertheless a manuscript whose artistic peer was not likely to appear on the market for a long time. As long ago as 1879 it brought 76,000 gold francs in Firmin Didot's sale in Paris, the highest price in this star-studded auction.

I had to have this manuscript, too, but my bank account balked at the prospect of two such gargantuan purchases. So I called upon my friend William S. Kundig of Geneva, the well-known dealer; he agreed to join me and we worked out an arrangement whereby Kundig took a half interest in the *Anhalt Gospels* in exchange for helping to finance the Missal purchase. The plan was that I should try to sell the *Anhalt Gospels* in New York, while he sought a buyer for the Missal among his European clients.

My first call was on Miss Greene of the Pierpont Morgan Library. I announced that I could offer her the *Anhalt Gospels* for $46,000. She was already familiar with the manuscript. Wells had obviously tried to sell it to the library.

"If I want to buy it," she said in her best ice-coated tones, "I don't need you. I can deal directly with the Wells estate."

"Miss Greene, I *own* the *Anhalt Gospels*," I replied. She obviously thought I was acting simply as an agent, trying to skim off 10 percent.

"Nonsense," she snapped. Interview over.

I looked at the manuscript back at 46th Street and noticed the receipt from Wells' executors still tucked between the front cover and first leaf.

Here was positive proof of my ownership. Should I return to the library and place it before Miss Greene? Or would this be looked upon as a defiant act?

In the midst of this dilemma the phone rang. It was Miss Greene. Apparently she had spoken to Wells' executors. "Send me the Gospels," she instructed, in a rather different tone of voice.

Instead of sending the book I brought it personally and the following week received a check in full payment. I could not help wondering what effect this little episode might have on my future relationship with her. I never found out, because she retired shortly thereafter and died in 1950. She was indeed a unique individual.

Meanwhile, over in Geneva, Kundig's exultation over the Missal had little trouble inspiring a customer to share in it. Within sixty days the manuscript was sold to a private collector, for a sizable price. As I could well understand, Kundig had no wish to share this client with another dealer and kept his identity secret. Twenty years later, I think it was in 1968, I finally learned that the buyer was a Frenchman named Paul-Louis Weiller, a man of great wealth. Still very much alive, he lived in a former residence of Mme. de Pompadour, Marshal Göring, and Dwight D. Eisenhower (in that order), in Versailles. Eisenhower had used the house briefly after the liberation of Paris and it still retained the memory: it was surrounded by battlements with gunnery stations.

There, I felt, was a fitting home for a book of such value!

I was invited to lunch. My hopes of buying back the manuscript were not high. Weiller did not seem to be anxious to raise money. But it would be a treat in any case to see his library, of which I knew nothing, and to make a new client.

After a sumptuous lunch replete with wine from his own vineyard and Sèvres china, I was ushered into his curio-filled library. Instead of the manuscripts that I expected, there was very little except books from Mme. de Pompadour's library.

"Monsieur Weiller," I said, "your library is really lovely, but that Missal hardly suits its character." I went on like that for a while, and then got down to business. "Would you like to sell it?"

"How much will you offer?"

I named a considerable sum. He named one 25 percent higher. This is the standard tactic of people unaccustomed to selling. They get a price from the buyer, then try to raise it.

But I was not in a mood to argue. "Very well, I accept," I said. We shook hands. The deal was closed, or so I presumed.

Within a few minutes his countenance changed. He was thinking it over, telling himself he was a fool to conclude such a big deal without more bargaining. If I agreed to 25 percent over my offer, he must have been figuring, I probably was prepared to go much higher.

"The deal's off," he cried.

"No, it's not." I stood firm. "We shook on it. I'm holding you to it."

And I did.

We both knew he was getting a good profit.

A month later I showed the manuscript to Herman W. (Fritz) Liebert, the first librarian of the Beinecke Rare Book and Manuscript Library of Yale University. As with most pairings of great books and people equipped to appreciate them, it was love at first sight. He in turn showed it to Edwin J. Beinecke, then putting together a collection of illuminated manuscripts for Yale. For a quarter million dollars it became one of the treasures of the Beinecke Library, now catalogued as Yale MS 425.

Having crossed the Atlantic from Wells' storerooms in New York to Geneva, to Versailles, then back again, its journey was now ended. There would be no third chance to buy it.

CHAPTER 17

The Buenos Aires Ghost

A FASCINATING ASPECT of rare books is the chance for discovery, for turning up a near-priceless volume when least expected. And *where* least expected. A copy of Edgar Allan Poe's *Tamerlane*, the most valuable American book of poetry, was once discovered by a sharp-eyed browser in a 10¢ tray outside an antiquarian bookshop. Its value, now over $100,000, was sizable even then. Just recently (1975) came news of part of an unrecorded Gutenberg Bible found in the choir loft of a church in Immenhausen, Germany, where it had nestled far from bibliographical eyes for nearly 500 years. (True enough, this was just half the precious work, but not a bad "sleeper" for any bookman to unearth.)

Having no substantial investment in them, many early owners treated their books with as much reverence as we pay a paperback. They were left behind when the owners moved. They were sold and resold, and eventually—if things got bad enough—sold to a bookbinder, who ripped out the leaves and used them to line the leather covers of his bindings. Then there were wars, floods, fires, forced evacuations by plague and religious persecution, immigration, and carelessness, all serving to scatter books far and wide. The result is that nobody knows exactly how many copies of a rare book exist. You have a certain number of "recorded" specimens: the British Museum copy, the Morgan copy, and so forth. In addition there may be unrecorded copies, hiding who-knows-where, in the possession of people who are ignorant about rare books, or of knowledgeable individuals who prefer to maintain a low profile and keep their collections secret.

Then there are what I might call semi-recorded copies; books that were sold at auction decades ago but whose present location can't be learned. In this business, you never assume that six copies exist because six are recorded. There could be another one. There could be, though not likely, another six. Also, you never assume that a rare book can't turn up in this place or that. This sense of excitement, this possibility that the next man who walks through the door carrying a bundle, or the next letter you open, will introduce you to a "lost" specimen of a fabulously rare book, is one of the professional dealer's great thrills. Every day you face that chance.

All dealers receive offers of books for sale, from other dealers, from collectors, from the general public. The more renowned the dealer, the more offers.

Mostly the general public wants to sell books found in the attic, bought decades ago by great-uncle Silas, which it hopes will be valuable on grounds of age alone. A collector may have switched from books on aviation to those on food and cooking. Now he has the former to dispose of. There are any number of reasons why people sell. Only on occasion do these "quotes," as the trade terms them, amount to anything. The books offered may be worthless; they may be good books in damaged condition; or the owner may have an over-inflated notion of the value, making a purchase impossible. Nevertheless, the rule to keep religiously is: read every letter, whether postmarked Topeka or Taiwan. Study every list, neatly prepared with full bibliographical references or scrawled on pages from a grade-school tablet.

Without much doubt, the most exciting list I ever received arrived in April 1954. It came from Buenos Aires and the envelope bore some handsome stamps, but I held out little hope for its contents.

It seemed that a private collector, one Jorge Beristayn, was interested in disposing of a part of his library. The list he had prepared consisted of 120 titles, mostly early printed European books of high caliber. This was obviously a collection to be reckoned with, but two of the books seemed too good to be true. Among the lot was a Durandus *Rationale Divinorum Officiorum*, printed by Fust and Schoeffer in 1459 and another work that, for reasons soon apparent, I dubbed "The Ghost Book."

Mr. Beristayn minced no words in describing it, tossing it off with a colossal lack of enthusiasm:

```
      /45N°51-(HORAS) HEURES A L'USAGE DE ROME. Paris; Ph.Pigouchet para Simon
              Vostre. 9 June 1487. Red morocco binding. A beautiful copy.
        N°52-S.HIERONYMUS. Vitae Santorum. Ulm; Johannes Zainer; circa 1478.
              Hain 8594. Contemporary stamped calf on oak. Very broad. Fine copy.
           N°53-HISTORIA DE JOSE DANIEL ESTHER.Pfister 1462. Hain 8749. 49 woodcuts
              Missing five woodcuts. Leather binding. Good state.
       105 N°54-HYGINUS, C.JULIUS. Poeticon astronomicon opus. Venice; Erhard
              Ratdholt. 22 January 1485. 210 x 148 mm. Hain 9063. Brown levant
              morocco binding. Beautiful copy.
```

Fig. 4. Inconspicuous listing of the Pfister "Ghost" Book.

"HISTORIA DE JOSE DANIEL ESTHER. Pfister 1462. Hain 8749. 49 woodcuts. Missing five woodcuts. Leather binding. Good state."

Albrecht Pfister of Bamberg, a pioneer printer from the art's earliest days, was the inheritor of some of Gutenberg's printing types. His books, real masterpieces, are excessively rare. This particular volume, issued in 1462, is among his most significant: the second dated and illustrated book in a language other than Latin (German), recorded in only two other copies, at the John Rylands Library in Manchester, England, and the Bibliothèque Nationale in Paris. No American library owned it; it had eluded even incunabula collectors like Huntington and Morgan.

But rarity alone fails to convey the significance of a book like this. Neither does price. Here is a woodcut picture-book containing 49 large illustrations printed from wooden blocks, from an age when no other printers were doing anything comparable. Yes, there were blockbooks, with text and cuts carved from wood. But Pfister, almost as much a pioneer as Gutenberg or the first Chinese to print from wood blocks, combined the new art of movable-type printing with the older one of woodcut illustration. He was the first to do this, and his name will forever be graven on the hearts of bibliophiles.

Finding an unrecorded *Historia* by Pfister would be the bibliographical event of the year, if not of many years. Could there really be an unknown copy in Argentina, over 4,000 miles from Bamberg, Germany, its place of birth?

Many times, people have offered me a book, thinking (or hoping) it was a certain edition or came from a certain press, and on examination it proved to be a facsimile or something else disappointing. I've learned to prepare for letdowns.

The list was a paradox: Without any doubt, Beristayn had knowledge of books. He was quoting Hain numbers (from Hain's bibliography of incunabula), and you have to know something about books to know Hain numbers. Otherwise I might have had no confidence at all in the list. At the same time his offhand manner in describing a book of such stature led me to wonder. Was this a collector who, to sell his books, wanted it believed that there was extra icing on the cake?

Then another question came to my mind. If this Beristayn truly had a Pfister, did he know its value and importance? Maybe he inherited the library and was just copying out the descriptions from an old catalogue made by the former owner. His book was worth at least $300,000.

This called for action—and discretion. My initial impulse was to take the next flight to Buenos Aires and settle the thing without delay. But book buying demands diplomacy, as great and sometimes as intricate as in negotiating an arms treaty. With the utmost coolness I sent a letter—not an attention-getting cable—to my correspondent.

What, I asked casually, is the binding's condition? By the way, those woodcuts, are they plain or colored? I asked about the cuts in several other books, too, pretending to be equally interested in them. After an almost endless wait, the reply came.

"The Pfister cuts are colored."

Now I felt sure the book wasn't a figment of somebody's imagination. Wanting desperately to make the trip myself, I doubted my ability to retain composure. So off went one of my colleagues, Nachod, in my place.

Nachod and I had a code system for cables, not trusting anything to chance. On seeing the Pfister he was to cable confirmation of its existence. We would then take matters from there, once we knew we weren't just goose-chasing.

I am not the most patient person on earth, and biding time until that cable arrived was agony. After a full week had gone by, I became convinced that my trusted associate had fallen into the hands of headhunters somewhere along the way.

Then came, instead of a cable, Nachod himself.

He did not wear the look of a conquering hero.

Yes, he had seen Beristayn. No, he had not seen the Pfister.

"He claims the book is in Uruguay. His daughter has it."

A black cloud settled over 46th Street.

It is usually a bad sign when a prospective seller claims that the books are not available for inspection. But this time, after following the quarry so far, I was not about to give up so easily.

I dashed off a series of letters to Beristayn. Polite answers were received to each, but we were getting nowhere. What I wanted was an invitation to visit him. After five months of hint-dropping, it was time to take a new approach. Hanni and I decided to leave for Buenos Aires, figuring we'd get to see him somehow.

Beristayn received us cordially, as if we were expected. He was Basque, tall, swarthy, regal, a Velazquez canvas come to life. Right away we developed respect for him. About 70, he introduced us to his beautiful, blonde wife, Ingrid, a German girl of 20.

His home, as Nachod had told us, was straight out of Renaissance Spain. Across the street were stately homes, residences of retired cattle ranchers, of the city's wealthy business executives, and of descendants of old noble families from various parts of Europe.

More treats for the eye awaited us inside: walls hung with pictures, furniture of carved oak in Moorish style, glittering chandeliers, silver, cut crystalware, all manner of objets d'art. Beristayn was living like a lord of the manor and behaved every inch a nobleman. One had the feeling that, with a snap of his fingers, a string quartette would appear in the parlor. However, as we discovered, Beristayn had spent too regally for his income and now had to raise cash. Parting with books hurt less than parting with works of art.

His library was not large, but selected with the care of a connoisseur. It stood in a series of Spanish-Gothic cases. Just glancing at the spines made my heart palpitate. Here were about 120 incunabula, mostly in contemporary bindings. Many were illustrated. Eyes darting from shelf to shelf, I sought out the Durandus of 1459 (the Pfister I did not expect to be included, and it wasn't): It proved all a bookman could ask.

The *Rationale* of Durandus is not the sort of book anyone would stay awake nights to read. A religious treatise compiled by a famous mediaeval theologian, it is not light reading. But typographically, few grander monuments to the printer's art could be named. Every collector of great books covets the Durandus. Most have to settle for a leaf or two. Here was a whole one, and on vellum. Being in the original binding it had not suffered the fate common to many of its brethren, of being trimmed down by successive generations of binders. It was tall, magnificently tall. And with a book like this, when condition is everything, half an inch of additional margin can mean thousands of dollars.

It was printed by Gutenberg's associates, at a time when no other printers were active anywhere in Europe. Indeed, it was only the fourth book printed from movable type. An extra attraction in this copy was that it came from the library of the Duke of Gotha. Beristayn owned other books from this library, including a brilliant copy of the not-nearly-so-rare but just as delectable *Hypnerotomachia Poliphili* by Columna, printed by Aldus in 1499. This was in a contemporary German binding, unusual for an Aldus. Most of his books were "trade bound" in limp vellum and sent all over the continent.

What do you do in a situation like that?

The experienced bookman returns such books to their shelves, keeps a deadpan expression, and starts talking about the weather.

For Beristayn, I was too good an actor. My feigned disinterest offended him. (Later he wrote: "Really your visit to Buenos Aires was an exciting experience for me. At the beginning when you began to look at the Poliphilus with a certain unsympathy I nearly burst. I have to confess to you now that in that very moment I was going to sit at the piano and play a Scherzo and not to talk any more about books, as you did on Tuesday. But you are clever and attractive. The storm faded and now I am your friend and I took a great liking to your person, tact and knowledge.")

After a long pause I popped the question. Would you consider selling me a few books?

To this kind of query, not having mentioned any particular books, I was pretty confident of a positive reply. After all, he had approached me with the idea of selling.

Instead I got a shake of his noble head and a disheartening "no."

When you're trying to buy books, "no" can mean a lot of things. It can mean, "I'll sell if the price is high enough." Or, "I don't feel like talking business today." Seldom does it mean "no" flatly and unequivocally.

Here I was pretty sure it was just a case of getting to Beristayn. I was not playing the game the way he liked it. A change of tactics might succeed. I quit talking about books. By good fortune, Hanni and I were invited to dinner at his home the next evening. This was going to be crucial. Without doubt, it would be our last meeting with him. If this opportunity slipped by, we'd be returning empty-handed. In my dreams that night I saw the Durandus, the Aldus, and other prizes from his library equipped with wings, flying out the window.

The situation called for strategy, but my mind was blank. I could think of no way to broach the subject again, without drawing another unfavorable response.

It was a sumptuous dinner, with the fair Ingrid lavishly bejeweled. ("A lucky girl to have such jewels," I complimented her, but she nearly burst into tears. "As soon as you leave," she wailed, "I have to return them to him.") But neither mind nor palate could enjoy the delights at hand. Suddenly I had a thought. The fastest way to many a man's heart is through his profession.

Beristayn was a renowned portrait-painter. Not internationally known, in Argentina his reputation roughly paralleled Bonnard's. He had made a career of painting the country's aristocrats and their ladies, and his pictures hung in every museum and gallery in his country.

I asked if he'd paint my portrait (and I laid it on thick). "I have seen so many of your beautiful portraits and I would be deeply honored if you would paint one of me." No bookman is beneath bootlicking when the situation demands. Suddenly the barriers between us came down. Yes, he would paint me. With a little encouragement he'd have painted all my family and ancestors. It was a way of raising cash without selling me any books.

He named a substantial fee. Being in no position to bargain, I agreed. Next day, and for a week thereafter, I sat for him. "You must look into my eyes," he commanded, "so our minds will communicate." This didn't exactly thrill me but I figured, well, when in Rome. . . .

At week's end I owned not only a picture but the Durandus, the Aldus, and a 1501 Aesop. Cost of the books: $50,000. Expensive but worth it. Today these volumes would cost $200,000 at a conservative estimate. But my friend's defenses remained up on the Pfister. Even after having his palm crossed with so much silver, he persistently parried my every thrust concerning it.

Was it in Uruguay, as he led Dr. Nachod to believe? Well, yes, today it was. Uruguay, definitely. Tomorrow, well, it might be right here in the house but mislaid. Why am I always mislaying books, Beristayn asked himself with a wry smile?

The big fish got away. What went wrong? What was the real story? I was never able to find out, despite repeated inquiries.

One little detail remained, before we could write finis to our assault on the pampas. Getting back home with a painting and $50,000 worth of books shouldn't be much of a problem, we said to ourselves. Books go duty-free and everybody—including customs officers—could see that the painting was no old master. But Beristayn sensed the fate that awaited us. He followed us to the airport to witness the fun.

First the painting was examined. Gravely the customs chief shook his head. Being the work of a renowned native artist, it could not be taken out of the country without special permit! He referred to it as a "national monument," as if we were laden with pre-Columbian pottery. The fact that the picture was of me made no difference. It was too much. We threw in our hand and decided to leave the painting in Buenos Aires. Beristayn beamed, taking in all this from a distance. We guessed he had observed such scenes before.

Then came the moment of truth: the opening of Hanni's suitcases, containing the three books. Losing the painting was one thing. For the books we were prepared to fight.

I couldn't bear to watch.

"What are these?" the inspector asked and seemed ready to doubt us, no matter what we said.

"Don't you see?" Hanni explained, with the slight annoyance that always helps in such circumstances. "These are some old books."

No truer words could be spoken. The declaration was accepted, the books repacked, and we were off—but not before I had planted a kiss on Hanni's cheek, as a reward for a virtuoso performance.

Still another hurdle remained; the U.S. point of entry at Miami.

Something about old books, especially valuable ones, rankles customs people. They get vaguely (or openly) suspicious, of you, the books, and your motive in buying them. Pictures and antiques worth hefty sums they understand; books they don't.

As usual, our three precious volumes drew an icy stare. Then our customs form was checked. There, for all to see, was the damning evidence: $50,000 worth of books. I had written down the full price.

"Why on earth did you declare such a high price?" one irate inspector cried, as if I'd inflated the value. "You know what this means? We've got to contact Washington, ask them how much duty to charge."

"There's never any duty on old books," I protested. But I might as well have been whistling in a silo.

"Not for ordinary old books," came the reply. "But these aren't ordinary. I can't find it in our tariff schedule, but I tell you this. It's going to cost plenty to get them into the country."

Now we faced not only an uncertain delay, but the always conceivable possibility that somebody in Washington might look in the wrong book or misunderstand. Instead of no duty we'd end up ransoming our books from the customs dock.

After several fidget-filled hours, during which time every customs-regulation manual in the entire capital must have been consulted, the answer came. We were safe. No duty. Apologizing profusely, the inspector released our books to us. Our plane to New York had long since departed, but it didn't seem to matter any more. "I sometimes wish," I said to Hanni, "our clients knew what we go through to get books for them."

William H. Scheide bought the Durandus, adding it to his many-splendored collection. Otto Schäfer took the *Hypnerotomachia Poliphili*, incidentally my first sale to him.

But the Pfister? Beristayn died several years ago. I cannot help but think his ghost strolls about with that volume clutched under its arm, casting furtive glances over its shoulder.

CHAPTER 18

An Old Noble Family Sells

To MOST AMERICANS Liechtenstein is known only as a place which produces very handsome postage stamps. They confuse it with Luxembourg, are unsure where it is, or how to spell it, or, indeed, if it still exists. I frankly had no particular knowledge of this tiny central European country either, until it entered my life in a big way.

Liechtenstein occupies some 62 square miles, one fifth the size of New York City but considerably more picturesque. It is situated on the east bank of the Rhine, in the northern Alps between Austria and Switzerland. Its population of 22,000 speaks German. Liechtenstein's history is long and colorful. Originally there were the county of Vaduz and the lordship of Schellenberg which passed through many hands, until both were sold to the Princes of Liechtenstein. This noble Austrian family, embracing several branches, was of venerable antiquity. It reached as far back as the 12th century and in its early history included the minnesinger Ulrich von Liechtenstein who died in 1275. The Princes of Liechtenstein owned two castles, one in Styria, another near Vienna, and numerous other estates when, in 1699, they became also the Lords of Schellenberg and, in 1713, owners of the county of Vaduz (today the capital of Liechtenstein). In 1719 these new acquisitions were united as the Principality of Liechtenstein. Residents lived on the princes' own personal property and lived well—it was traditionally one of the continent's more idyllic spots. After World War I Liechtenstein entered into a customs union with Switzerland and adopted Swiss currency but continued to issue, in fact made a major industry of, its very distinctive postage stamps. These have brought the country a handsome revenue. Within the past few decades it has become headquarters for foreign companies because of attractive tax benefits.

During the centuries the Princes of Liechtenstein, like most prominent members of the nobility, adorned their estates with art and antiquities. Their collection of old-master paintings is internationally known. Many of the princes were also ardent bibliophiles and, with their taste and wealth, each generation adding to the inherited riches, the library became particularly noteworthy.

The first book collector of the family who can be identified is Hartmann II von Liechtenstein und Nikolsburg, whose fine vellum tomes bear his initials and the dates 1577 or 1578. In the 18th century, all books owned by various members of the family were combined into one large family library, to which other collections were added. Most spectacular was the purchase of the library of Franz von Hauslab in 1883. This by itself would have assured the eminence of the Liechtenstein library, even if nothing else had been collected. Hauslab, a Tyrolean by birth and a tutor to Emperor Franz Joseph I, spent the better part of his life collecting incunabula, volumes with woodcut illustrations, prints, maps, and globes. A cartographer himself, he introduced crosshatching on maps to indicate altitude.

I was introduced to the Liechtenstein library in the late 1940s. No major additions had been made for a number of years and the present owner, Prince Franz Josef II, was considering selling. E. V. D. Wight, Jr., an American banker stationed in Europe before World War II and instrumental in arranging loans to Austria and Hungary, put me in touch with the Prince and the Prince's brother-in-law, Arthur, Count Strachwitz, then Liechtenstein's Ambassador to Switzerland. Later Mr. Wight came to work for me, helping to establish and manage our periodicals and reprint businesses in Vaduz.

In the summer of 1948, while Hanni and I spent our vacation at the Palace Hotel in Gstaad, Switzerland, one of the loveliest spots in the Alps, Wight set up a meeting for us with Count Strachwitz to see the illuminated manuscripts of the Liechtenstein collection. The excitement of this occasion was intensified by the fact that no catalogue had ever been published, making it a real surprise party. The magnificent works I was shown included a *Concordantia Caritatis,* a picture book of Biblical instruction. Only four manuscripts of the *Concordantia* were known, this being the finest artistically if not the earliest in date, painted by a Bohemian master around 1400. Some miniatures were not completed, drawn only in outline, but still of great beauty. The price asked for this manuscript was reasonable and I bought it at once, together with Schab.

Most of that night was spent, back at the hotel, looking through the *Concordantia*—not collating, not checking, simply admiring. I studied one miniature then, certain it was the finest in the volume, flipped to another and immediately revised my opinion. Each was superb. The hours flew by. "I should be a manuscript," scolded Hanni, already in bed, "so that you'd pay more attention to me." Then she added, on reflection, "Maybe it's just as well you have this passion for manuscripts; it's better than fooling around with other women."

Today the *Concordantia* is in the library of one of book collecting's grandes dames, Clara Peck of New York. Chiefly a devotee of sporting books, Miss Peck, with her love of the beauty in book design, succumbed to this princely volume.

A few months later I was shown more manuscripts: the *Theatrum Sanitatis* of the early 15th century, containing 130 full-page miniatures, depicting various trades; a very imposing manuscript of Duke William the Affable of Austria; and Thomas Aquinas' *Historia de Corpore Christi* (now M 853 at the Morgan Library), with a large miniature by Nikolaus of Bruenn, the head of the principal atelier which created fine books for the court of Vienna in the early 15th century. These and several other manuscripts I purchased as appetizers with hopes of more to come.

The following year I launched an all-out effort to buy the bulk of the library. Convincing the prince to sell was unnecessary. He had already arrived at that decision and sent a number of consignments to Sotheby's. The library's incunabula, a quite considerable collection though not including any single item of momentous stature, were already gone. However a great deal of other material remained: thousands of 16th-century and later books, plus an untold quantity of maps and engravings. Unfortunately it was divided up between two locations, part in Liechtenstein and the majority at the Prince's Vienna palace. The Russians still occupied parts of Vienna but could not, under international law, prevent the Prince, a sovereign ruler, from removing his property. This he did, shipping about 20,000 books informally and very hastily packed, by truck to Liechtenstein. Instead of Vaduz, they went to the tiny village of Schaan for storage in a schoolhouse. It was August and the school reopened in September, making the Prince doubly anxious to find a buyer.

When we saw the books, it was obvious that no thorough examination could be made. We could do little but survey bindings and read titles from spines. Even on the strength of that sort of cursory inspection we were impressed. Many highly salable volumes were in the lot, plus others that would undoubtedly grow in value if I could not immediately sell them. When negotiations began, the Prince's agent asked an unrealistic price. We met and talked, met and talked, until September. We both budged somewhat—he came down, I offered to go up—but an agreement seemed distant. I felt sure of losing the books to an auction house. Finally I was given a "rock bottom" price, conditional on immediate payment and removal within three days, after which pupils would start pouring into the schoolhouse.

How we would manage the removal of 20,000 volumes in only three days I had not the slightest idea, but Wight, who knew the terrain better than I, gave his solemn assurance that it could be accomplished. So I paid the "rock bottom" price, and immediately thereafter one of the not-to-be-forgotten spectacles in bookselling history unfolded.

For three days utter chaos reigned in and around Schaan. Wight hired some 20 farmers and their wives, and three open trucks which stood waiting on the road below the hilltop schoolhouse. A human chain passed the books hand-to-hand into the trucks. These were people who had never handled books, not to speak of rare ones, and it showed. Morocco bindings got jostled like bales of hay. I stood by to aid in directing operations but could hardly bear to watch. It proved, however, to be only a prelude to a much more nervewracking experience. As the open, overloaded trucks trundled along unpaved roads they bounced and rocked and—despite Hanni, Wight, and his secretary seated atop the book piles, trying to keep them intact—each bump in the road dislodged a few more books. I followed in a car to pick up the fallen volumes, working frantically to keep pace. Meanwhile, villagers stood along the road and observed this strange scene in disbelief.

Despite our difficulties we succeeded in making the three-day deadline. The books were taken to a shipping agent at Buchs, a small Swiss town across the Rhine from Schaan, and from there forwarded by freight to New York. About five tons of material were involved. The cataloguing, an immense task, cost nearly as much as the books. After nearly 30 years, a number of volumes bearing the Prince Liechtenstein bookplate are still on the shelves at 46th Street. All, I am pleased to state, have increased greatly in value since acquisition.

The best of the Prince Liechtenstein books, not counting the illuminated manuscripts, was an unpretentious volume that might easily be overlooked: a collection of 16th-century French chapbooks and poetical works including the first edition of *Les grandes et inestimables cronicques du grant & enorme geant Gargantua* (Lyon), 1532. (See Fig. 5.) Only one other copy was known—not surprisingly in the Bibliothèque Nationale. Rather than trust it to a shipper I personally mailed the small book to New York. A large part of catalogue 56 and the entire catalogue 66 (527 numbers) consist of Liechtenstein treasures.

A year later I purchased the map collection, discussed in Chapter 46.

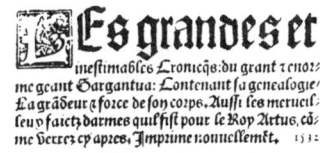

> **Es grandes et**
> inestimables Croniqs:du grant tenor:
> me geant Gargantua: Contenant sa genealogie
> La grãdeur a force de son corps. Aussi ses merueil-
> leuy faictz darmes quil fist pour le Roy Artus, cõ-
> me verres cy apres. Imprime nouuellemẽt. 1532

Fig. 5. The Rabelais source book (one of two known copies).

The huge collection of books and prints of military costumes is now owned by Mrs. John Nicholas Brown of Providence.

One event worth relating unfolded when we discovered among the Liechtenstein books a group of volumes, both printed and manuscript, bearing the bookplate of the Kress von Kressenstein family. At first they struck us as curious, containing a variety of pictures of the Kress family in festive costumes. We soon realized that these came from the archives of the Nuremberg patrician family, complete with meticulously preserved portraits of generations of Kresses, watercolors of their participation in festivals, pageantries, and parades, so-called Schembart Books, and chronicles with references to the family as early as 1193. On historical grounds alone this material would be valuable and salable; many libraries and even private collectors might be interested.

This, the name Kress, made me remember an old friend from Vienna, Professor William Suida, an art historian and specialist in Italian Renaissance painting. Author of many important books, he was working as advisor to the Kress Foundation in its art purchases, most of which went to Washington's National Gallery and to various smaller American museums. Samuel and Rush Kress were the founders of the famous dime-store chain. They became multimillionaires and devoted a substantial portion of their wealth to the cultural enrichment of this country.

Since it was concerned mainly with paintings, I never seriously considered the Kress Foundation as a potential customer for rare books.

It seemed that I should at least offer the Kress Foundation first refusal on items bearing directly on the family, so I wrote to Professor Suida and announced my discovery. He replied that I should bring a few of the manuscripts to the foundation's headquarters at West 57th Street. An appointment was made and I arrived on schedule. For some reason I expected to find a quiet office.

What I did not know, and Suida did not tell me, was that Rush Kress personally inspected everything offered for sale to the foundation. Because of his age and infirmity he came to the office infrequently and on each occasion interviewed numerous dealers for potential purchases. The scene was that of a waiting room populated by hopeful individuals (in this case mostly art dealers) bearing parcels of assorted shapes and sizes. This was discouraging; I perhaps would have to wait hours and it was already afternoon. Soon after I took my seat, Dr. Suida appeared and motioned me to come in. Everyone was astonished as I strolled past them. I was taken directly to Mr. Kress' office and introduced to him; very possibly I was the first bookseller he had ever received there. He showed great interest in the manuscripts. Stopping at a portrait of a 17th-century Kress von Kressenstein he remarked, "I don't read German, and I'm not sure if these are my ancestors, but please translate this page for me."

I did, and he asked for another page to be translated. After half an hour those waiting in the anteroom became impatient. One gentleman, I suppose an art dealer, was so bold as to come into the office. Tapping me on the shoulder, he said in a sarcastic tone, "Do you intend to stay here overnight? We also want to do some business." Suida, standing by all the while, smiled, and Mr. Kress asked for more translations. When I finally left, Kress left with me. The others were informed that he would see no further visitors that day. "I saved quite a bit of money staying with you," he commented. He purchased most of the Kress manuscripts from the Liechtenstein collection, and I was grateful to Suida for his role as an intermediary.

Later (in 1959) Dr. Suida published two of my important Italian illuminated manuscripts in the *Arte Lombarda*: the *Borromeo Hours* with miniatures by Giovanni Ambrogio de Predis, a gifted pupil and collaborator of Leonardo da Vinci, and a Graduale illuminated by Ludovico de Gazis from Cremona. Both are described in my catalogue 88.

CHAPTER 19

Clandestine Literature

CLANDESTINE LITERATURE—"underground" books—has always had its appeal for collectors. Since ancient times there have been such works, banned by church or state (or both), smuggled, bought under the counter, mailed in plain brown wrappers. Clandestine literature falls into various classes: pirated books, pornography, blasphemy, treason. With the Inquisition in progress and the Reformation spreading across Europe, emotions ran high and no printer could risk openly offending the authorities. Even in our own century, many works destined to become classics—*Ulysses* and *Lady Chatterley's Lover,* to mention two of many—could not be imported into America until long after publication.

Attitudes toward pornographic or libertine literature have varied through the centuries. In England the social and legal position has swung from one extreme to the other: from the forthright bawdiness of Shakespeare's time to Victorian gentility. But even on the continent, which usually took a more liberal view of spicy books, one had to be careful. Indelicate works by Aretino, Cellini, Crébillon, Voltaire, and de Sade were published under a smokescreen to escape censorship. The Vatican published its first index of prohibited or proscribed books, the *Index Librorum Prohibitorum,* in 1559 and added to it assiduously thereafter, employing a staff of censors to read new books as published. Today, authors would fight to get their books on this list; in the 16th, 17th, and even 18th centuries it was deemed wiser not to invite the apostolic wrath.

All sorts of ruses were used to throw authorities off the track. So long as those responsible for an offending piece of literature could not be identified, there was no risk (except to the booksellers, who might have their stocks confiscated and burnt). London printers put "Antwerp" on their title pages, when issuing something especially titillating. Rome printers went farther and gave Peking as the place of publication. Other locales appearing on the titles of clandestine European literature are Canton, Astracan, Paphos, Cythere, Libidinos, Gazneh, and Luxuriopolios, the last three totally imaginary. One Parisian printer used the imprint "Aux Enfers," the name now applied by the Bibliothèque Nationale to its sequestered collection of erotica. Others, like Mirabeau, assigned their provocative work to the Vatican Printing Office, not only to confuse but to shame the enemy.

Most best-selling authors had their books pirated by one or more publishers, who issued and sold them without paying any compensation. The Elzevirs of Holland had their attractive little books pirated unmercifully, to the point where imitators even imprinted them with the Elzevir name and mark. Even as early as the turn of the 15th century, Albrecht Dürer complained to the town magistrate at Nuremberg about a peddler who was selling fakes of his engravings in the market square.

Political clandestineness is of long precedent. An edition of *Le Prince* by Jean-Louis Guez, Sieur de Balzac (not to be confused with the 19th-century novelist), was printed at London in 1632, not—as stated on the title page—at Paris. It slung mud at the late and much-revered Queen Elizabeth and received the traditional treatment: public burning. Richard Whitaker, the publisher, was found out, but instead of losing his head lost only about £66 in fines. That dangerous enemy of orthodoxy, Voltaire, had to publish clandestinely; the earliest editions of *Candide* (1759) give no place of publication but were in fact printed at Geneva and Paris.

Without doubt, Russia leads in its output of clandestine, underground, seditious reading matter, issued mostly but not entirely before the revolution. Only the major works of Marx, Engels, Lenin, Trotsky, and other revolutionaries are known to the public. These are valuable, in first editions; but in addition there exists a great and equally valuable body of what might be called revolutionary ephemera, mimeographed or even handwritten sheets, on perishable paper (sometimes cigarette paper for compactness). They were not meant to be classics of philosophy but to circulate among the revolutionary workers and to spread the word. Of some only a few copies could originally have been made. If one or two survive, that may be all. The delicate paper did not lend itself to preservation.

There is no question about the historical importance of this material. It may be the work of fanatics, it may represent ideas or philosophies disagreeable to some, but its effect on the 20th century and the whole course of human existence is overwhelming.

For years I have actively collected this type of literature, buying choice items when the opportunity arose. Though always scarce, it used to be rather inexpensive, since westerners took no special interest in it. Today, the prices are very high, even for tiny scraps, with so many prominent libraries eagerly buying. Such items cannot be taken out of the Soviet Union. This represents a complete reversal of the original situation, when the revolutionaries had their books printed at Geneva, Dresden, and Paris and stealthily smuggled them *into* Russia, where the Czar forbade them. Trotsky's writings are especially rare, and those by Lenin issued before the revolution command increasingly high prices.

Russian state archivists, who look upon anything touched by Lenin as sacred, try to buy whatever comes on the market, or to obtain it by other means. They consider nothing a crime toward that end, feeling it must be rescued from the hands of infidels. So much do they treasure this material that they refuse its loan for exhibition anywhere, even to their own Communist satellite nations. When visiting the Deutsche Staatsbibliothek in East Berlin during the Grolier Club trip in 1970, we were shown an elaborate display of revolutionary books and manuscripts, including some by Lenin. The library's director, Dr. Horst Kunze, obliged my request for a closer examination and opened some of the cases, whereupon I discovered that every item was a facsimile.

"Yes," he admitted, "these are facsimiles. The originals are preserved in the great library at Leningrad or at the Marx-Engels Institute at Moscow."

I said I owned original first editions of many of the printed works, but he seemed not to believe me.

In my early days as a bookseller in Vienna I bought a number of sets of Communist or radical periodicals, to which nobody attached special importance in those days. Russia's revolution had taken place 20 years earlier; reading about the plans for it seemed an anticlimax. Today they fetch healthy prices. Among them are sets of Lenin's first journals, *Iskra (The Spark)*, which began in Munich late in 1900 with the battlecry "From spark to flame" as its motto; a complete run of *Vpered* (January 1904–May 1905), the outlawed Bolshevik weekly, founded and edited by Lenin; Alexander Hertzen's famous journal *Kolokol (The Bell)*, issued at London and later at Geneva, from 1857 to 1867, and related items.

One of my major purchases in the field of clandestine literature was the collection of Frederick B. Adams, Jr., former director of the Morgan Library. It is now at the Karl-Marx-Haus in Trier, Germany, a research center. The Adams collection was one of the largest in radical, Communist, and anarchistic literature ever assembled in America, totally impossible to duplicate today. It was big even by Russian standards. Only an Adams, in his association with so many booksellers and librarians around the world, could have assembled it. Included were many presentation copies from the authors, and the famous *Communist Manifesto (Manifest der Kommunistischen Partei)* was represented by the first 1848 edition and by over a hundred later editions in various translations. (See Fig. 6). One of the most translated books of the 19th century, nearly every first edition of each different translation is valuable. Also included were a number of American radical publications in first editions.

I took the whole Adams collection home, where I could study it at length. I read many books on Marx and Lenin and the history of Anarchism and Communism. Before offering it for sale I supplemented it with material I already owned and filled in gaps with new purchases.

Included were a number of sub-collections, large and important themselves. One of them consisting of more than a hundred items pertained to the Haymarket riots, possibly the largest file on this subject anywhere. (See Fig. 7). This was the first large-scale labor disturbance in America. On May 1, 1886, a group of Chicago strikers fought with police, leaving one of the former dead and several wounded. A group of anarchists supporting the strikers staged a protest rally four days later. It proceeded without incident until police arrived and ordered the demonstrators to disperse. (According to one account, it had started to rain and the police wanted to go home.) The protesters became unruly and suddenly a bomb was thrown at the police, killing one and wounding nearly 70, of whom six later died. A wholesale roundup of anarchists was made; eight went to trial and were convicted. Four were executed, one committed suicide in his cell by setting off a blasting cap in his mouth, the other three eventually received pardons. Most of the memorabilia in Adams' collection comprised the personal file of Julius S. Grinnell, the Illinois state attorney who tried the case for the prosecution. A catalogue of the Haymarket collection material, unused by any historians of the affair, was prepared by John (Jack) S. Kebabian and published as Volume IV in my "Rare Books Monographs Series." To allow Kebabian easy access, I moved the collection back to 46th Street. One morning he came rushing into my office, considerably agitated, holding what looked like a copper cigar butt.

"It's part of a bomb," he announced, setting it down gingerly on the table. "And it may still be alive."

Many a heart-throbbing object has been placed on that table in 30 years, but never one which brought quite so swift a reaction. We wasted

Fig. 6. Marx and Engels. *The Communist Manifesto*. First Edition.

Attention Workingmen!

GREAT MASS-MEETING

TO-NIGHT, at 7.30 o'clock,

AT THE

HAYMARKET, Randolph St., Bet. Desplaines and Halsted.

Good Speakers will be present to denounce the latest atrocious act of the police, the shooting of our fellow-workmen yesterday afternoon.

Workingmen Arm Yourselves and Appear in Full Force!

THE EXECUTIVE COMMITTEE.

Achtung, Arbeiter!

Große Massen-Versammlung

Heute Abend, ½8 Uhr, auf dem

Heumarkt, Randolph-Straße, zwischen Desplaines- u. Halsted-Str.

☞ Gute Redner werden den neuesten Schurkenstreich der Polizei, indem sie gestern Nachmittag unsere Brüder erschoß, geißeln.

☞ Arbeiter, bewaffnet Euch und erscheint massenhaft!

Das Executiv-Comite.

Fig. 7. The Haymarket Meeting. Circular. First issue calling for armed uprising.

no time calling for the police. Within minutes a big wire-covered bomb-disposal truck pulled into the block, while lunchtime strollers scattered and traffic came to a halt. It was no false alarm. The item proved to be a detonator or blasting cap, used to set off an explosive charge but deadly enough itself at close range. An identical cap was used by the jailed anarchist to commit suicide; when placed in his mouth it blew away the whole lower part of his face. I shuddered to contemplate the damage it might have caused to our building, and to us. It still, after nearly 100 years, contained fulminate of mercury and could have been discharged by any spark or even a sharp blow. The bomb squad, very understanding about the whole thing, took it away, cleaned it, and returned the empty cylinder. It had been one of the state's exhibits during the trial and had been labeled and preserved by Grinnell, who never bothered to have the fulminate of mercury removed. Whether Adams was aware of its danger, I do not know. If so, he had far more faith in Providence than I. The mere thought that I had had this in my basement at home for six months made my skin crawl. We had moved the collection around with no more caution than that normally accorded rare books.

Letters of Lenin, Trotsky, even Stalin (I say "even" because the public expects Stalin's autographs to be plentiful or at least obtainable, since he lived into the second half of the 20th century; but such is not the case), can usually only be had, if they can be had at all, from the persons to whom they were originally addressed or their families, rarely from collectors. But there are exceptions. In 1950, long before buying the Adams collection, I purchased a pair of genuine holograph letters of Lenin, among the few ever sold, from Dr. Hans Strahm. Dr. Strahm was historian of the Canton of Bern, Switzerland, and director of the state and university libraries there. Both letters were written in September, 1915, to a delegate to the first conference of European Socialists opposing World War I, held at Zimmerwald near Bern. It was at this epochal gathering that the party's more radical wing, led by Lenin, broke away from the moderate Mensheviks and formed the nucleus of the Communist International. At the time of the purchase, Dr. Strahm provided no background on his ownership of these letters. But we met again, 20 years later, and then I got the full story. They had been discovered by a restaurant busboy in Zimmerwald, apparently in a wastebasket. With great presence of mind he turned them over to a conference member, who did what he considered the noble social thing—to sell them to Dr. Strahm, then a young collector. The busboy had become a farmer and was still living in the area. "Of course I remember that Lenin," he recalled, with something less than awe, when asked by Strahm. "A busybody who talked all the time and never tipped. Thank goodness nobody ever heard of him again!"

I also sat on Lenin's bed and almost bought the library that was in the same room. It belonged to an old-time Bolshevik, a man who had been active in the cause long before the revolution, Nicolai Alexandrovich Rubakin. I visited him after World War II at his home in Lausanne, Switzerland. At 84, after giving 60 years or more to the party, he was active as ever and just as enthusiastic. Rubakin had been a fellow student of Lenin's older brother, who was executed for plotting the Czar's assassination, and a friend of Lenin and his wife Krupskaia. His lifelong struggle was on paper rather than on the battlefield, to educate the proletariat—not only in Communist philosophy but all aspects of learning. From 1887 to 1920 he wrote 280 books and pamphlets explaining every branch of science in popular terms. More than twenty million copies of his writings had circulated by 1920, one for every five or six adults in Russia, and they remained in print thereafter. For most of his early life Rubakin lived in St. Petersburg, where he brought together a large library for his own use and that of the people. After the suppression of the 1905 revolt, when wholesale arrests of Communists began, he moved to Finland and from there to Switzerland, where he settled. His beloved library stayed behind, left to the Pan-Russian League for Popular Education. In Switzerland he resumed work, and book collecting. From scratch he built another library, which reached proportions nearly as formidable as the first. It consisted of over 20,000 pieces, mostly rare early socialist pamphlets. Several important libraries of Communist literature were incorporated into his own: that of the socialist Gustav Brocher, and of the daughter of Alexander Hertzen. Rubakin accepted books as his due, preferring them to money as reward for his labors. "To whom should they go," he asked, "if not to me?"

Among his major accomplishments was the publication of a series called *Sredi knig*, "Among Books." It appeared from 1911 to 1915 and comprised a reading list with lengthy introductions of more than 24,000 titles in all fields of science and literature, all of which I was told he had personally read. In his biography written by his son he is said to have read and studied nearly 200,000 volumes.

He had rosy cheeks and a white beard and looked like Santa Claus, hardly one of his heroes. I was received hospitably in his small study, lined with shelf after shelf of the kind of books that only a fellow Communist or a collector could appreciate. His working library, the books and pamphlets he referred to each day, comprised rarities in the original editions, a treasure-trove of radical "incunabula."

Of course I wanted to buy it. But this was no mere collection, assembled as a hobby or investment. It represented the life work of its owner. I had to be diplomatic.

I explained that American students could learn about the history of Communism through such a collection, if it were in their country. I struck the right chord; his eyes lit up. He saw the gospel of Communism spreading across the U.S.

But he would not part with his beloved books.

"You may have them," he said, "after my death, which must be soon. Bide your time. My housekeeper, who will inherit them, will let you know and you can buy them from her."

It was more than I could have hoped. I was overjoyed, though I kept my emotions in check.

During our meeting I had been seated on an iron cot, the only furniture in the room besides his desk and chair. "Sitting on that bed is a great privilege," remarked my host. "Lenin slept on it once, after a night of talk, when it was too late for him to return to Geneva."

We embraced and parted.

A few months later I received word from his housekeeper that he had died, and that I should come to buy his library. With the keenest anticipation I made the trip to Lausanne. The acquisition of this collection would give me the preeminent stock of rare socialist books.

On arrival I found crews of workmen taking books from the house, loading them on a truck.

The housekeeper met me in tears.

For years the Soviet government, she explained, had been paying the old man a pension and felt itself entitled to his library. Rubakin's son was of the opinion that his father had formally bequeathed the collection to the Lenin Library at Moscow. I found this hard to believe, unless his memory had faded and he had forgotten the terms of his will. In any case the books went to the Lenin Library, where they are kept separately as the Rubakin Collection. My disappointment at not being able to buy this collection was understandable; but I appreciated that its usefulness intact would be far greater than if sold and scattered. With this kind of very personal and very specialized library, the ideal would have been to sell it intact to an institution. Perhaps I could have done that. The availability of such a collection in this country would not, I am quite sure, have advanced the cause of Communism, as I led Rubakin to think, but certainly could tell scholars more than they are likely to discover about its background in any other way.

CHAPTER 20

Three Gourmets

LOVE OF RARE BOOKS and manuscripts seems to prolong life. There are, of course, tragic exceptions such as Harry Elkins Widener, one of the victims of the *Titanic* disaster. But a host of bookish people have lived into their eighties or nineties, among them William Beckford, Sir Thomas Phillipps, Bernard Quaritch, and Horace Walpole. Nearer our own time were William Loring Andrews, George Arents, Edwin J. Beinecke, Sir Sydney Cockerell, Wilberforce Eames, Lathrop Harper, Thomas W. Streeter, Chauncey B. Tinker, and Lawrence Wroth. Happily, Frank Altschul, Sir Geoffrey Keynes, Wilmarth Lewis, and Lessing Rosenwald are still going strong at this writing.

The accumulated knowledge of books of such men is nearly as valuable as a large reference library—more valuable in some ways, for they have memories of collectors, sales, and bibliographical details that cannot be found in print. For the sake of this, I have cultivated my acquaintance with the older members of the book fraternity, and always found their conversation entertaining and instructive.

One such person was Dr. François Ritter, the well-known bibliographer of Alsace. He knew my catalogues and received me kindly, when I visited him in the mid-1950s. He was then probably over 80, and, like most bookmen, a very likable man.

In his office, I met another octogenarian, the librarian emeritus of Strassbourg University. We exchanged some lively book-talk, much of it concerning the *Constance Missal* (see Chapter 33), which I had recently purchased. I was then convinced on the best authority that this missal was a Gutenberg production preceding his famous 42-line Bible. We had endless discussions on all the exciting possibilities and Dr. Ritter brought out for me all the often contradictory literature concerning its probable date and place of printing. We concluded our discussion on an optimistic note and he suggested that this happy meeting should be celebrated.

How does one celebrate in Strassbourg? With a special *déjeuner*. We repaired to a small restaurant with only five or six tables, sawdust on the floor, a waiter in shirt-sleeves. Its modest appearance belied its cuisine: we had a superb lunch; fresh escargots, Strassbourg goose liver, a perfect rack of venison, crêpes suzette, cheese, all accompanied by regional wines of the kind never exported, as well as champagne and cognac. All during the meal the old boys told me stories about the book world from times that were only legend to me.

I cannot say how many bottles we emptied, but I began to feel very happy and drunk. My aged companions were also considerably elevated, though they were more used to drinking than I. We were the only diners left in the restaurant, and about 4 P.M. we were told it was closing.

We all found it hard to rise, but by helping each other we managed to get up, and, still holding on, to reach the street. There, across the way, was the ancient cathedral of Strassbourg, beckoning to us in its cool, quiet splendor. The church was empty; we settled down in the nearest pews, and were asleep in a moment. Not even the quarter-hour bells of the famous astronomical clock disturbed us.

But suddenly the boom of the great organ shook us awake. The vesper service had begun, there was a considerable congregation, and those nearby were staring at us with disapproval. A friendly verger led us out a side door.

I loaded my friends into a taxi and took them to my hotel, Der Rote Hahn. In my room we stretched out on the bed and continued our interrupted naps.

I had to catch an evening train for Paris, so about 8 o'clock I managed to slip out of the room without waking my friends. At the desk, I instructed the hall porter to let the two gentlemen sleep, paid my bill, and left for my train.

A few days later, I received from Dr. Ritter an affectionate letter of thanks. The two old boys had slept through the entire night.

CHAPTER 21

Walking Up the Main Staircase

THE ENGLISH CHANNEL was a dangerous place in 1568, infested by pirates. Some were Dutch rebels against Spain's rule of the Netherlands but most were Englishmen, piloting their own ships, whose activities could always be disavowed by Queen Elizabeth but who could, in the event of war, become part of the Royal Navy by the stroke of a pen.

Two hundred miles east, Don Fernando Álvarez de Toledo, Duke of Alba, governor-general of the Netherlands, and Spain's great military leader, was seeking to suppress religious and economic freedom among the Dutch with the aim of creating a seat of Spanish government there and, ultimately, of dominating all Europe. He had the men and political influence, but lacked one important ingredient to the execution of his designs, money. Genoese bankers were prevailed upon to lend him £85,000 and in December of that year a fleet of four Spanish ships carrying the money arrived in English waters. The danger of this fortune being taken by pirates was of course great; the Genoese agent in London, fearing it would fall into English hands, announced that it belonged to the bankers until the Duke received it, but added—in a coolly calculated gesture—that Elizabeth's credit stood better than Philip of Spain's. The Queen, taking the cue, declared that she was borrowing the gold, and the chests promptly found their way to the Tower of London.

To negotiate the matter, Philip II appointed the Duke as his special envoy to Elizabeth, in a document dated July 20, 1569, and signed "Phillippe" rather than the usual "Yo el Rey" because she was, after all, the sister of his late wife (Mary I of England).

Having acquired this document, I offered it in 1947 to the current Duke of Alba, feeling certain he would want to own such an important piece of family history. I was not quite prepared for the news contained in his reply:

> I thank you for your letter etc. As is natural, I possess in my archives exactly the same document as the one you offer me. As you know, it was the custom in the 16th-century to duplicate and even triplicate such documents.
> Yours truly,
> Alba.

That ought to have taught me a lesson. But a few years later, when the chance again came to purchase early Spanish archival material, I had all but forgotten the Duke of Alba document.

In 1950 I received a letter from an antiquarian bookseller in Madrid, informing me that it might be possible to buy some of the papers of the Conde de Revilla-Gigedo (1740–1799). An enlightened statesman and administrator who served with distinction as viceroy of Mexico from 1789 to 1794, he patronized the arts, established the Botanical Gardens, set up an orderly national archive, built and lighted streets in the capital, pacified and founded schools for the Indians of Mexico, and sponsored the exploration of the Pacific Northwest. The dealer could not afford to buy the papers himself, but would get a commission from me if I bought them.

Without delay I flew to Madrid.

The dealer and I walked to the Palacio Revilla, the stately family mansion, on one of Madrid's main streets. When I rang the front doorbell, my companion went pale. "No, no," he admonished. "We are tradesmen and must use the servants' entrance. You have spoiled the deal."

But the door was opened for us by a liveried butler. We were admitted and I handed him my card. After a few minutes the Conde appeared at the head of the great staircase and beckoned for us to come up. For my companion, more familiar than I with the traditions of Old Spain, it was too much for him, a common tradesman, to use the main stairway. I had to take him by the arm and pull him up.

The transaction proved to be an agreeable one. We discussed the collection at some length, the Conde showed me special items from it and explained their background. He named a price for it, I accepted, and in less than an hour after we had entered I owned the papers.

Later, while we celebrated at the dealer's home, he told his wife and children in breathless tones that we had actually walked up the front stairs. It was this, rather than the purchase and his commission, which we celebrated as the highlight of the day.

The acquisition of the papers of Count Revilla-Gigedo was certainly reason enough to celebrate. New Spain included parts of Mexico, Louisiana, Texas, California, Florida, and claims to the lands northwards to Alaska. Revilla-Gigedo's interest in and devotion to exploring enterprises in the Pacific from Alaska to the southern tip of the California peninsula won him fame. Some islands still bear his name today. The papers purchased are contained in 37 folio volumes comprising some 18,500 pages. Of these, 12 are monographs by explorers and scientists in copies made for the viceroy, many presented to him by their authors, and 25 contain his hitherto unpublished copies of the day-to-day correspondence with the Spanish ministers. The crown jewel is the unpublished diary of the leader of the Nootka expedition of 1792, Francisco de la Bodega y Quadra. Nootka is on Vancouver island where Captain John Meares established a settlement which nearly led to a war between Spain and England. A companion volume contains watercolor drawings of Nootka Indians, views of settlements, flowers, birds, and many detailed maps. The great importance of the collection is clear.

Later it was found that exact duplicates of the Revilla-Gigedo papers exist, some volumes in the archives of Mexico City, some in Madrid. I need not comment on the decreased salability of manuscripts which are not unique. Again I learned my Duke of Alba lesson.

I sold the papers in 1956 to a collector in California but in 1973 I bought them back and I am as happy to own them now as I was in Madrid, when I bought them the first time.

CHAPTER 22

Joint Ventures

IT IS QUITE COMMON among rare book dealers to join forces in handling large transactions. To have complete trust and confidence in one's partner is a *sine qua non*. Never is a contract signed. Your word is your bond. In this fashion I have made transactions of hundreds of thousands of dollars and created long-lasting friendships.

Usually we—my partners in these ventures and I—each offered our joint property to his customers, in the same manner as other stock. If it had not been sold after a mutually agreed upon time, say one or two years, it would be auctioned off privately between the partners. Excitement and poker tactics enlivened these private auctions. Both played at being bored, pretending not to want the item at half the cost. After such silly preliminaries the real sale began, low bids advancing slowly to high amounts. The partner who was the successful bidder had to pay half his bid to the loser. Such was the game.

During the last years in Europe and the first ten in America, William H. Schab was my trusted friend. Many profitable transactions, including purchases from Sydney Cockerell, Martini, and Lardanchet (as reported in other chapters) were joint ventures. Later Schab decided to concentrate mainly on graphic arts and I remained with printed books and manuscripts, putting an end to our partnerships.

Soon, business in Americana, mainly books relating to America's discovery, increased and I often joined forces with Roland Tree of New York and Maurice Chamonal of Paris. We became close personal friends. Tree (nicknamed Roly) was the typical well-bred English gentleman, full of good humor and charm, and with profound knowledge of Americana. From 1949 on he occupied an office in our 46th Street building and I saw him daily. Our many trips in this country and Europe were very profitable. Our roles were generally divided: I bought and he sold. The prominent Americana collectors were his clients, through his connection with the venerable English firm of Henry Stevens, Son & Stiles. His wife was the granddaughter of the famous rare book dealer Henry Stevens of Vermont, the Green Mountain boy who settled in London in the mid-19th century. His clients had included James Lenox, a founder of the New York Public Library, John Carter Brown of Providence, William L. Clements of Ann Arbor, Michigan, and others of special note. Roland Tree carried on the business in the third generation, very uncommon in this trade.

My first contact with Tree was in 1941, when he sold for Schab and me our precious atlas, the *Atlantic Neptune* (see Chapter 46) which I owned jointly with Schab.

In 1950 a sale of rather important Americana took place in Paris, the private library of a dealer, the late C. H. Chadenat, who specialized in French- and Latin-American books. Like most prominent French dealers, he had built up over the years a large collection of his own. At this sale Tree, Chamonal, and I worked together.

Chamonal was the most knowledgeable dealer in all Paris. Although lacking in formal education, he possessed an unerring instinct for rare books and a reliable memory. Nobody challenged his knowledge of Americana. Like Tree, who knew English Americana, he knew early French and continental Americana and owned a very impressive collection which he kept at his home rather than at his store.

In 1952 I went with Chamonal to Tours to visit the archivist and historian of the Rochambeau family, J. E. Weelen. Here I saw for the first time the headquarters papers of the French expeditionary force that landed at Newport, Rhode Island, under the command of General Rochambeau, with 6,000 men on July 10, 1780. Louis XVI had sent them as a kind of token support for America's rebels against the British.

There were two Rochambeaus, father and son. The father, Jean-Baptiste-Donatien, Comte de Vimeur Rochambeau, Marshal of France (1725–1807), was the general, famous in American history. His son, Donatien-Marie-Joseph, Vicomte de Vimeur Rochambeau (1750–1813), was a French general and Governor of Santo Domingo. Later, as commander of the Antilles, he succeeded General Victor-Emmanuel Leclerc (died 1802), husband of beautiful Pauline Bonaparte (sister of Napoleon). Pauline later married Prince Camillo Borghese. Rochambeau the younger fell at the battle of Leipzig.

H.P.K. age three

H.P.K. age ten

H.P.K. age four with mother

Dr. Ignatius Kraus, grandfather

Dr. Emil Kraus, father, in 1915

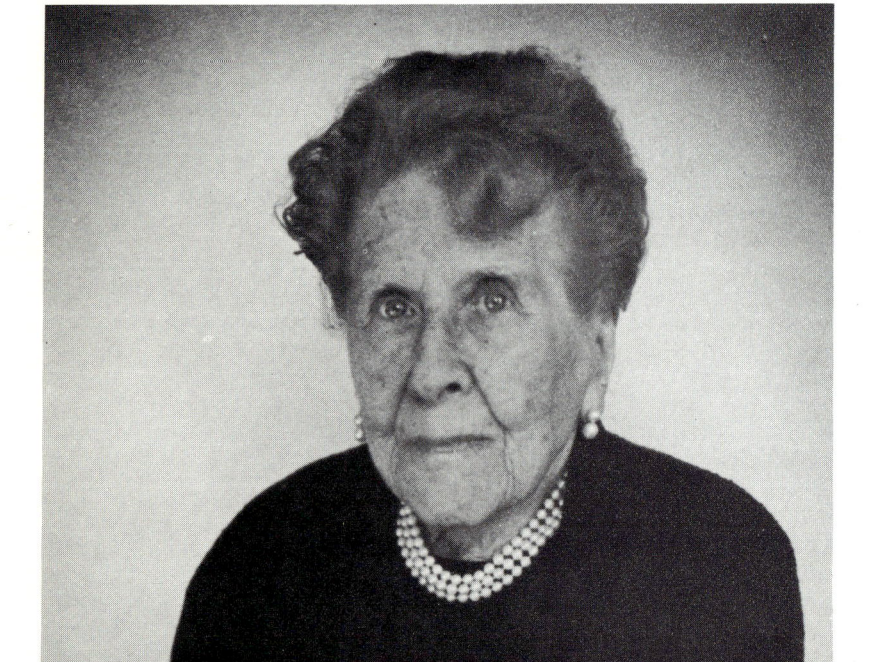

Hilda Kraus, mother at eighty-eight

H.P.K. with parents, grandmother and family members

H.P.K. with Hanni, her mother, five children, their husbands and seven grandchildren

H.P.K. with Mary Ann, 1942

H.P.K. with H.P.K., Jr., 1962

The riding family, 1966

H.P.K. and family, 1962

Hanni Kraus

H.P.K. and Hanni at work

Vienna quarters, partial view

Quarters at 64 East 55th Street

16 East 46th Street: first-floor showroom

The third floor at 46th Street

Vault at 46th Street

The three chief assistants: Dr. H. Nachod; Dr. H. Lehmann-Haupt; J. Kebabian

Exhibition room at 46th Street

Reference Library at 46th Street

French Consul confers the Légion d'Honneur on H.P.K.

A cocktail party at H.P.K.'s

H.P.K. with partner, Lord Thomson of Fleet (Chapter 51)

Office and warehouses of Kraus Thomson Organisation, Ltd. in Liechtenstein and Millwood, New York (Chapter 51)

Egyptian Cross, ca. 400 (Chapter 29)

The Chelles Sacramentary (Chapter 29)

The Anhalt Gospels (Chapter 16)

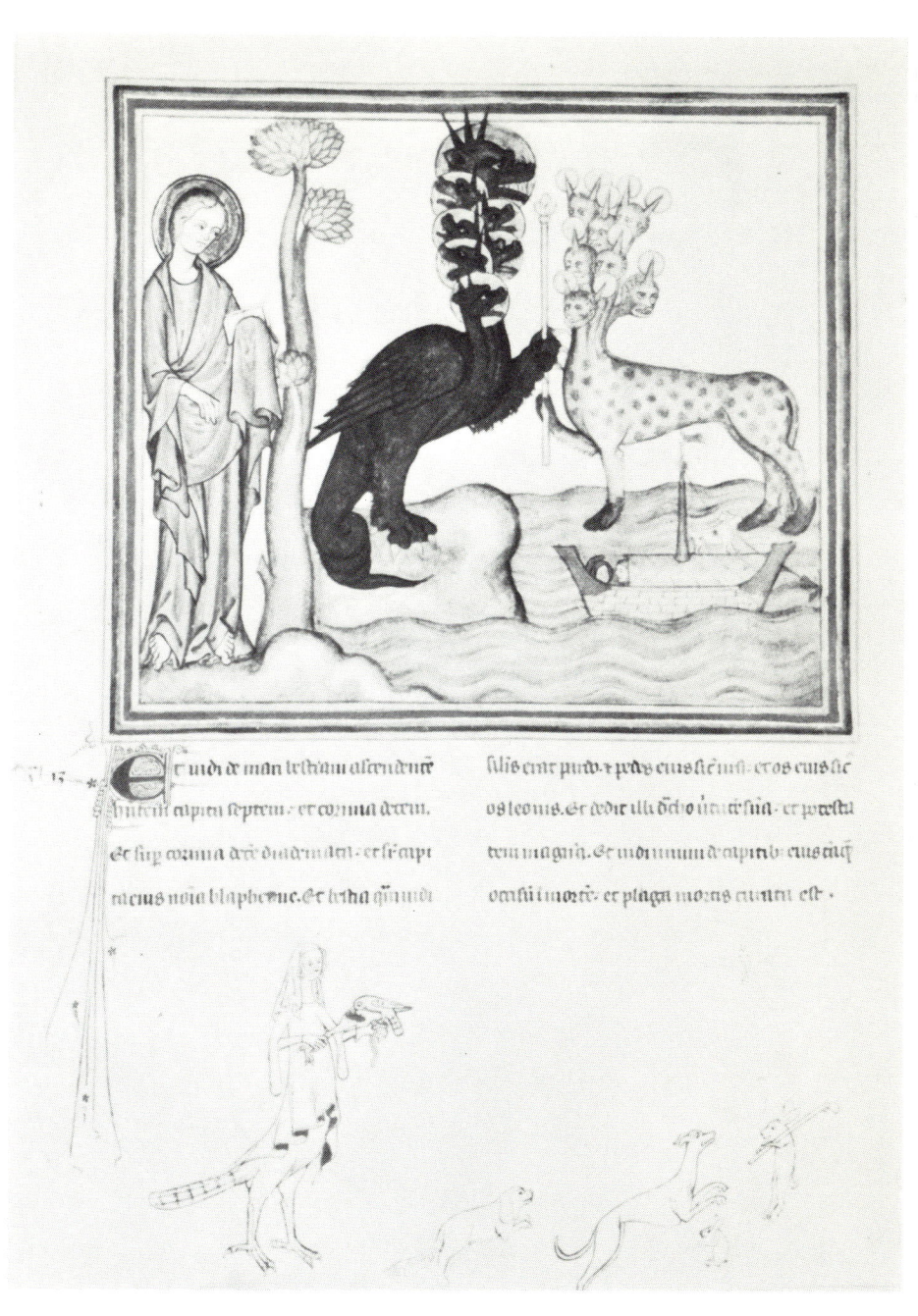

The Rothschild Apocalypse (Chapter 38)

Golden Fleece postal stamps
(Chapter 23)

A

The great Coronelli Globe, 1686
(Chapter 35)

B

16

In a somber, poorly furnished room, heaps of papers lay piled on a table, papers that had witnessed the great events of American and world history. Though dirty, primitively bundled, and very unimpressive, the first package to be opened contained letters sparkling like diamonds: one after the other, letters signed by Washington, Rochambeau, and Lafayette. Visions of the historical events came to my mind: the celebrated march of the combined French-American forces to Yorktown, the surrender of General Cornwallis, the redcoats beaten, final victory.

There was little hesitation on our part. We bought. This was a day to rejoice—and rejoice we did, celebrating that evening at the famous Paris restaurant, "Tour d'Argent." Our papers—how proud I was to say "our papers"—dealt with the greatest, most glorious chapter in U.S. history.

The story of the sale of these papers is a perfect example of how unpredictable the market is and how apathetic and insensitive American clients, librarians, and private collectors can be, neglecting the opportunity to acquire the most important historical documents. It sounds unbelievable that it took six years to sell the collection. The market was quite obviously America, and we asked Tree to join us. And still it took us, though being among the ablest dealers of America, that long. We all complained about the lack of spirit of our clients. If someone had offered this collection to me in the middle of a rainy night on the condition that I walk twenty miles, I would have done so without hesitation. The "don't care" attitude of the book-collecting public is most exasperating.

To make matters worse, shortly after we bought the Rochambeau collection the abortive sale to Clendening Ryan occurred (see Chapter 24).

It was not until November 21, 1958, that a rare coincidence happened: The Ryan library was sold at Parke-Bernet, and Paul Mellon decided to buy the General Washington-Rochambeau papers. It was like a miracle. As a kind of celebration I bought at the Ryan sale the most expensive book, the first edition of Rudolph E. Raspe's *Baron Münchausen's Narrative of His Travels*, Oxford 1786, sewn, uncut, one of three copies known. It also was purchased later by Mellon for $6,500 (Cat. 90, No. 25).

Paul Mellon of Upperville, Virginia, is a great collector of paintings and drawings; one of his chief interests is English art, especially of the 18th and early 19th centuries, of which he has brought together very large holdings, with emphasis, natural to a horse-breeder and rider, on English sporting scenes. He has also assembled fifteen books printed by Caxton, a remarkable achievement in our time, and he has bought other English incunabula and later books, many of them special copies in fine condition.

This marvelous collection he gave to Yale University, and to house it properly he built in New Haven a splendid museum, the Yale Center for British Art. Many of the Caxtons and early books came from me, and when I discovered his interest in the history of Virginia, I offered him the General Washington-Rochambeau collection.

Among the papers we bought at Tours, we discovered significant portions of the Leclerc-Rochambeau papers of the West Indies. They comprised parts of the government archives during the reigns of the generals. This collection consisted of about 3,400 letters and documents and 21 manuscript maps, some in very large size, of Martinique, Guadeloupe, Haiti, etc.

We handled the Leclerc papers separately, their interest being largely Napoleonic. The supreme Napoleon collector at that time was a Cuban, Julio Lobo, a sugar magnate. He was sent a detailed listing of the collection but did not respond. Another attempt at correspondence met the same fate. Finally we realized that Lobo did most of his buying through Sotheby's, so we put the collection up for sale there. This represented a very considerable gamble; if for some reason Mr. Lobo was ill or just not interested, the sale would hardly be a success. There were few other collectors of Napoleonica. Luckily he chose to take part, not in person but through his agent. Another bidder, whom we did not expect, appeared as an agent for the Haitian government. Chamonal and I attended the sale and, when possible, made bids. We acted discreetly and never got stuck. The whole sale realized £23,000, quite profitable, since more than the investment had been recovered earlier with the Washington-Rochambeau material.

The General Washington-Rochambeau deal was probably the largest joint venture in my life. After that came many other less impressive ones. We bought low and sold high; that was always the scenario. A few deals, however, were significant enough to warrant a report here.

The first is the Conway story, involving the well-known collector Thomas Gilcrease of Tulsa. The late 1920s saw the arrival of early Latin-American documents, letters, and other archival material on the rare-book market. Most of them came clandestinely. Prince Pignatelli, a descendant of Hernando Cortez, was expelled from Mexico for having smuggled out the Cortez papers. A hardly less enterprising collector named G.R.G. Conway had built up a substantial collection of Latin Americana in the usual manner, buying from dealers. But, finding not enough available on the market to suit his appetite, he began to investigate the possibilities of buying "at the source," in Mexico and elsewhere.

This led him to purchase from private individuals, and he soon found out that most of what he was offered had been stolen from official archives or institutional libraries. At first the prospect of owning such material repelled him; he returned a valuable document to the archive to which it rightfully belonged and took the cash loss. Soon thereafter, the same document was offered to him again. Conway realized that the Latin American government collections were being plundered on a large scale, that the items could never be all reunited, and that, since other collectors showed no compunctions about taking advantage of the situation, he should not either. In addition to acquiring items for his own collection in this fashion, he also sold extensively to dealers, especially Rosenbach, serving as a kind of liaison between them and the black market in manuscripts. The Mexican government was furious; in the U.S. the general feeling was that such documents could only be properly appreciated and studied in this country, that Mexican officials did not take adequate care of their manuscripts, and that the means by which they arrived need not be too critically examined.

In 1949 Hanni and I took our first trip to Mexico. We left in a snowstorm and arrived in the midst of a Mexican heatwave. The furor of two decades earlier over disappearing manuscripts had by then become just a memory, but the individual most responsible for it remained very much alive and active. Conway, no longer the daring young collector but now an aging business executive (president of Mexican Light & Power), still owned large portions of his collection. They included parts of the Cortez Papers, documents relating to the Inquisition, and a number of pre-1600 Mexican books. Canadian by birth, Conway kept his library in Canada. I was anxious to buy it, if possible, and talked over the matter with him at his club.

The price of $160,000 was reasonable but I could not raise that much cash by myself. They were not Schab's kind of books, so I turned to Roland Tree. His principal client, Thomas Gilcrease, was just the sort of collector who might buy the Conway library. An oil millionaire and one of the most singular and colorful of bibliophiles, Gilcrease had assembled a very valuable collection on American Indians. He himself was partly of Indian blood, I believe an Osage. While still a youth, he discovered oil on the family's land and became a millionaire by the age of 20. He retired young and devoted his life to improving his education, traveling extensively in Europe. His collections are housed now in a museum bearing his name. Here were gathered bronzes of the Old West, pre-Columbian artifacts, and American Indian relics of all kinds, in addition to books and manuscripts relating to Indians. It was acknowledged to be the finest collection of its kind owned by a private individual, and it grew rapidly. Gilcrease was known to be an almost certain buyer of any important item in his field. At the time I was negotiating with Conway, Gilcrease was buying lavishly from the Robinsons of London, who, thanks to their acquisition of the Phillipps manuscripts, then owned some of the finest American documents in any bookseller's hands. He also was a customer of Rosenbach's.

Tree and I showed him the Conway catalogue. He was interested and willing to buy, but not without special arrangements. Even millionaires can overextend themselves. Gilcrease's buying had run somewhat ahead of the returns on his oil wells; he owed huge sums to a number of art dealers, booksellers, and, undoubtedly, other creditors. He would require some time to straighten things out, and could agree to purchase the Conway collection only if we extended special terms. The collection was to be deposited in a bank near his home. Gilcrease would pay the full price within one year, the collection to be delivered then. Tree and I acted, in effect, as agents for Conway. We had no money of our own invested in the books; we would receive a commission only when Gilcrease paid.

But Gilcrease did not pay.

With most of his capital in oil, and oil quotas reduced by the state, Gilcrease was—on paper at any rate—broke. Liquid cash went toward the completion of his museum, while creditors waited. After the museum opened, its public displays were well overshadowed by material stored in the cellar; this was where Gilcrease kept yet-to-be-paid-for items. Then Conway died.

After two years of waiting, Conway's daughter and heir asked us to start proceedings against Gilcrease. Tree and I went to Tulsa trying to collect, with no more success than others. He died a few years later without having paid. All creditors were paid by the State of Oklahoma, which took over the Gilcrease Museum and floated a bond issue to clear the debts. Miss Conway, Tree, and I received full payment, and the Conway books and manuscripts are now among the prime attractions of that institution.

While in Tulsa, I called upon another of that city's important collectors, mining engineer Everett DeGolyer. His library of works on the history of science was already on deposit at the University of Oklahoma, but he continued adding to it. I was able to supply Mr. DeGolyer with an occasional rarity that he might not find elsewhere. I brought to his office a manuscript from the Liechtenstein collection, the Mining Book of Schwaz—a Tyrolean village. This richly illustrated, unpublished mining handbook dates from the 16th century. It contains more than 100 strikingly beautiful watercolors, pen drawings, and a pictorial dictionary of mining terms. (A good description with reproductions is in my catalogue 80, item 123.) No volume could more perfectly suit this collector's tastes, and the price, about $4,500, was quite reasonable. I was sure he would buy.

After examining each page with rapt attention he asked the price. "Too rich for my blood," was his reply. I have heard this exasperating phrase again and again from the lips of wealthy collectors, who spent twice as much on trifles. Just then the phone rang and he disappeared for a long while. I waited half an hour. I think he felt sorry for me—he knew of my Gilcrease problems, knew I was disappointed not to sell the mining book.

"Look here," he said. "I just got news that one of our affiliated companies, Amerada Petroleum, found a big oil deposit in the Williston Basin. I'm not a stock tipster, but you cannot lose."

This news probably meant millions for him, yet he would still not buy the book. After leaving him I called my New York broker and placed an order for shares of Amerada Petroleum. They brought greater profits than many *Mining Books of Schwaz* could produce. Later this manuscript was sold to the Bergbau-Museum in Essen, Germany.

James C. McCoy (1862–1934) was well known in the book world as the foremost collector of the Jesuit Relations of Canada, a field in which he had specialized since 1920. These relations were published yearly from 1632 to 1673, and served as records of the experience of Jesuit missionaries in French America during that period. The catalogue of McCoy's collection, compiled by Arthur Rau and published after McCoy's death in 1937, has not been surpassed as the standard book on the subject. Rau had supplied many of McCoy's chief acquisitions over the years.

I met Rau, the grand old man of the French book trade, before World War II when he managed the Paris office of Maggs Brothers. Until his death in 1973 we did much business together. Upon retiring from the trade in the late 1960s he trusted me to sell our common stock. As in all our joint ventures, trust was mutual.

In 1951 Rau, Tree, and I were seated together at the Café de la Paix in Paris, talking business. Rau asked, "Do you think the McCoy books would sell well?"

I, not familiar with the name, said, "Who is McCoy?"

Tree knew. "Jesuit Relations," he remarked. "Hundreds of them."

Rau: "Many in various issues. The largest collection in the world."

I: "Who needs so many? Couldn't we break it up and sell separately?"
Tree: "I'm sure it can be sold as a collection."
Rau: "McCoy's widow asked me to sell. The amount is big; let's do it together."

We agreed quickly and a three-party joint venture began on a beautiful spring afternoon at the Café de la Paix. When the library arrived at 46th Street, it proved to contain not only the Jesuit Relations but many other valuable Americana. My staff compiled descriptions and Tree took charge of selling. Everything sold within a few months. I never experienced such a fast success. All the Jesuit Relations went to James F. Bell of Minneapolis, the other books to Henry Taylor, Thomas Streeter, Robert Dechert, and a few others.

Americana rode high as one of the great collecting fields in the 1950s. I say this in the past tense, because most of the great collectors of Americana have died during the last ten years and no big ones have come to take their place. The list of the departed reads like an honor roll of famous bibliophiles.

J. K. Lilly of Indianapolis, Chairman of Eli Lilly & Co., one of the largest pharmaceutical manufacturers, started with English literature and first editions. His collecting covered many other fields, including stamps and tin soldiers. I met him rather late in his life, after he had gotten interested in the history of science and medicine. He also bought, in a rather smaller way, Americana from Tree. In 1956, when the Americana collection of Baron Hardt in Lugano was offered to me, Tree wrote to Lilly describing it in a general way. After some time he visited 46th Street. It was late afternoon, Tree had gone home, so I did the explaining and selling. We went through the catalogue and I pointed out the highlights, their importance and value. The first item, I remember, was the Columbus Letter in the first Roman edition, ca. 1493 (G.W. 7173; Goff, C 757). After half an hour's talk the question of price for the collection came up. It was $100,000.

"All right," he said, "send it to my home in Indianapolis."

I was astonished.

"You have not seen the books," I exclaimed. "They are still in Europe."

"I have full confidence in you and Mr. Tree. I always do buying rather quickly."

His check came a few days later and within six weeks the Baron Hardt books arrived at Indianapolis. It was a splendid lot and all parties concerned were satisfied. Unfortunately one can seldom do business in such a smooth and speedy way.

Indiana University at Bloomington today owns the entire Lilly Collection. At this same library are also the Poole books, thanks to the generosity of Mr. Lily. (See Chapter 24.)

Another benefactor of Indiana University was my friend, Dr. Bernardo Mendel. He bought from me in the old prewar days in Vienna and was my oldest client in America, visiting New York several times a year from his home in Bogotá, Colombia. He was an amazing person, a successful businessman, well educated and cultured, a music enthusiast, and a genuine expert in his chosen field of Americana. His knowledge of Americana being greater than mine at first, he sometimes profited from my ignorance. Later I caught up to him. His greatest coup was purchasing the Conway Mexican incunabula (books printed in Mexico before 1600), twenty volumes for $20,000. This was in 1950. Later, in 1954, when he moved from Bogotá to New York, he outbid me for Lathrop Harper's business, which was for sale after Mr. Harper's death. So he finally became a rare-book dealer. He was then my able competitor and the boss of my friend Otto Ranschburg. Indiana University benefited enormously from his vast knowledge of Latin American books and manuscripts. As advisor to the Library, he helped it acquire quite a few important collections and archives.

CHAPTER 23

Discoveries Celebrated by Postage Stamps

STAMP COLLECTING was not an unknown hobby to me. I have told of my father's collection and how I helped him; but this never attracted me. Nevertheless, I believe I am the only dealer whose books have been honored twice on commemorative stamps of foreign governments.

First there was one depicting the title page of the earliest book printed in the Philippines. I like to refer to this story as the Galanti Caper. Blasio Galanti, the most mysterious bookseller in Paris, was an Italian. He was born at Imola and died in 1969. Rumor had it that Galanti possessed one of the finest stocks of choice books and manuscripts in Paris, but he preferred not to display them to browsers. His bedroom served as headquarters for his chief treasures. I was never allowed to enter.

Out front in the office, stacks of miscellaneous books ringed the floor, leaving room for only a chair. To look at a book near the bottom of a pile, everything on top of it had to be removed. This task was complicated by the fact that the topmost volumes were usually thick folios, apt to topple without warning.

Every visit to Paris included a pilgrimage to Galanti at 13 rue René Bazin. Luckily he lived on the ground floor or the weight of so many books might have brought the building down. Around 1949 Schab and I paid our usual call. Atop one book-mountain we discovered a blockbook printed in strange eastern and Latin characters. The title-page imprint read Manila, 1593. By chance I was familiar with Manila printing, having read José Toribio Medina's bibliography. The first work listed by

Medina was a "ghost book," a *Doctrina Christiana* printed in xylographic or block-book form in Spanish and Tagalog, the native language of the Philippine Islanders. No actual specimen had been seen, hence the name ghost book. Its existence was based on reports in old local chronicles.

I knew I had a treasure in my hands.

Needless to say, we bought it, paying a very modest price. Galanti was no beginner but apparently his knowledge did not extend to early Philippine volumes. Schab and I headed straight to the Bibliothèque Nationale to confirm my hopes. It was just as I suspected, and a sensational discovery. A few months later Lessing Rosenwald bought the book at a substantial sum. He got his money's worth. The Library of Congress published a facsimile edition and the Republic of the Philippine Islands issued a stamp to celebrate the book's discovery. Mr. Rosenwald sent me a whole sheet of the stamps. (See Fig. 8.)

Religious texts accounted for most of the early books printed in Latin America and Asia, mostly editions of the *Doctrina Christiana*. I own the original manuscript of the first book printed in South America, which came from the press of Ricardo at Lima. This is a *Doctrina Christiana* in the autograph of José Acosta and signed by the bishops of Latin America at their council at Lima, 1584. (A pair of broadsides had preceded it, but these cannot be considered books.)

Fig. 8. Doctrina Christiana, Manila, 1593. Stamps commemorating the discovery of the unique copy of the first Philippine book. (Library of Congress, Washington–Rosenwald Collection.)

The supply of unrecorded book treasures in Paris seems never to run dry. On another occasion a gentleman invited me to see his manuscripts. His apartment was not far from Galanti's and I could combine both visits.

He owned a few illuminated manuscripts, but his conversation impressed me even more than his books. It seems that one of his relatives had a great castle in southern France filled with mediaeval and Renaissance manuscripts. To gain his confidence and friendship I bought a manuscript, *Armorial of the Golden Fleece*, with portraits of the early grand masters Philip the Good, Charles the Bold, and Maximilian, the later emperor. The likeness of Maximilian was especially accurate; this, with my Austrian background, I could see at first glance.

The book proved to be another "find" of major proportions: It was an authentic work of Simon Bening and the most beautiful manuscript of the many existing ones of this text.

This was a splendidly illuminated record of the Order, historically one of the great knightly orders of Europe. The Order is significant in European social history as the last great attempt to realize the mediaeval ideal of the "chevalier," the noble man whose nobility depends not only on his birth, but on his high qualities of "chevalieresque" character.

I was lucky to find in the literature (*Le Beffroi* II 309) the warrant for payment of the manuscript ordered by the Chancellor of the Order in 1537. The payment warrant for Simon Bening was also reprinted in an article by T. Frimmel and Klemme in the *Jahrbuch der Kunsthistorischen Sammlungen des Allerhöchsten Kaiserhauses*, V (1887).

Such documentation is the wish fulfillment of every antiquarian. Artists' names are rarely confirmed by documents.

The Royal Library of Brussels bought it, notwithstanding its rather stiff price. But the Belgian government recovered its investment and must have made a good profit by issuing a set of commemorative stamps with surcharge, featuring portraits of the knights. (See Plate No. 16a.)

I paid the Parisian collector many visits in subsequent years, but he was never again able to offer anything even approaching this manuscript's importance. At least my first visit had paid off.

CHAPTER 24

Some Bibliomaniacs

THE ECCENTRICITIES AND ODDITIES of book collectors, immortalized as long ago as 1809 in Thomas Frognall Dibdin's *Bibliomania, or Book-Madness,* know no bounds. Great books and manuscripts apparently contain some catalyst which promotes odd behavior in otherwise rational individuals. For a confirmed collector the desire to own a certain book may become an obsession, and the obsession can continue long after it was acquired. Henry C. Folger, oilman, partner of John D. Rockefeller, founder of the Folger Shakespeare Library, did not stop at his first copy of Shakespeare's First Folio. He bought, and bought, and continued buying until he had amassed 78 copies of the same book. Most of his books—which totaled tens of thousands, as he purchased every edition and translation of Shakespeare and every work related to the Bard—he never saw. Too numerous for storage at his home, they went into a warehouse, well protected but out of sight.

In my career I have not been victimized by any swindlers or cheaters. But of the lesser orders of biblio-nuts, the overspenders, the bankrupts, the ultra-eccentrics, the hermits, I have been acquainted with my share.

Self-denial for the sake of books was carried to the extreme by one of my old Vienna customers, Count Koziebrodzki. To this individual, the spiritual nourishment of books was preferable to bodily nourishment. To say that the venerable Count worshiped his books would probably not be stretching things too far. When contemplating a fine binding or a particularly well-printed volume, he seemed lost in a vision. As his collection grew larger, the Count grew thinner and paler, spending all his waking hours in admiration of it and neglecting the necessities of life. At the time he was buying from me, I knew nothing of his bizarre lifestyle, nor did I care. He was a good customer, paid cash, and never gave me any trouble; I wished I had more like him. But I did notice one peculiarity in his behavior. Whenever the Count bought a book, anyone else (including myself) was prohibited from touching it. He insisted on packing all his purchases himself and taking them away with him. I'm not sure if he, like the Moslems, regarded anything handled by others to be defiled, or whether he feared we might injure the books. In any case he would pack them gingerly into valises or cartons, handling them like high explosives.

He was Polish but beyond that I knew nothing about him. I had no idea whether he was a real nobleman or a pretender. Polonica and 16th-century printing comprised his chief interests; passions would be a better word. I had quite a fair stock of such material in Vienna and he came to browse through it twice a year. He resembled Rasputin as closely as anyone I could imagine. He had eyes like a deer and a long bushy beard. A kinder, more polite individual could not be found. He thanked me for every book I sold him, as if I had presented it as a gift.

After a few years I was informed of his death and invited to come and appraise his library. I went to Poland, expecting to find a castle of the 16th or 17th century, filled with books and art. But the Count's conduct should have warned me to prepare for the unexpected.

He lived in a small village about four hours' drive from Lemberg (Lwów), a city with which I was familiar from my days as Wasmuth's representative. I made inquiries for Koziebrodzki's castle but found nobody who could direct me. Finally I was sent to a ramshackle old barn. The Count's housekeeper, an old woman, admitted me. Inside was nothing but an iron bed, a primitive washstand, and a few rustic, bare tables and chairs. There was not a single bookcase. Piled on the floor in heaps were hundreds of books. This was the fate of the volumes he wished no one but himself to handle.

The housekeeper told me the story. The Count had indeed lived in a castle 30 years earlier, but used all his income to buy books and had to sell it to finance more purchases. He moved to the barn, taking along only the bare minimum of furniture, and lived like an Indian holy man for the rest of his life. He ate little, never saw friends, went abroad only to buy books. His entire occupation from sunrise to evening consisted of arranging and rearranging the piles, admiring the bindings, leafing through volumes here and there, and recalling the good purchases he had made. Book collecting was more than a way of life for him; it *was* his life. I bought the library, not out of sympathy but because it was a good library.

My first major catalogue was published in 1954. The 69th in the series, it bore the title *The Cradle of Printing* and contained nothing but books of the 15th century—mostly incunabula but with a few manuscripts relating to printing. In its descriptions, this catalogue was a model of excellence, each having been prepared by my two chief assistants, Nachod and Lehmann-Haupt. Though this was less than a quarter-century ago, the prices at which these books were offered seem unbelievable today. Many of the items are unobtainable now at any price. Those which can be had today cost many times more than we asked. Among the highlights was a vellum leaf from the Fust and Schoeffer Psalter of 1457, one of the great rarities of early printing and the first book recording the printer's name, and the date and place of publication; a leaf printed by Albrecht Pfister of Bamberg about 1463, the only specimen in America of his press; the first Caxton edition (circa 1478) of Chaucer's *Canterbury Tales,* probably the most famous of all Caxtons and most coveted by collectors (single leaves now fetch over a thousand dollars); Dame Juliana Berners' *Book of Hawking and Hunting,* 1486, from a press scarcer than Caxton's, that of the anonymous "Schoolmaster of St. Albans," and without question the most celebrated of its productions; the first engraved map of Germany, by Cardinal Nicolaus Cusanus; and a unique proof sheet of the Gutenberg Bible. Such an all-star cast had not been assembled in an American bookseller's catalogue for many years. But it drew a less than enthusiastic response.

The Library of Congress, owner of the Vollbehr Gutenberg Bible, asked to have my proof sheet on approval. I sent it along with a discount of $400, making the price $1,800 instead of $2,200 as it appeared in the catalogue—a price which seems utterly ridiculous now, when ordinary Gutenberg Bible leaves bring three times that much. Yet the Library of Congress turned it down. Lessing Rosenwald ordered the Caxton Chaucer and the Book of St. Albans on approval, and likewise returned them. It was not a problem of price with Rosenwald. Both books were incomplete and, despite very dim prospects of any other copies being available in the near future, he objected to this condition. It was hard to believe. I never thought it possible that books of such stature could fail to find eager purchasers, especially at the very reasonable prices we asked. Does one ever get "stuck" with a Caxton, I asked myself, or a specimen from the Fust and Schoeffer press?

The only bright spot in this gloom was provided by Otto Schäfer of Germany, who ordered (and kept) the Cusanus map. It marked the beginning of a long and mutually agreeable relationship (see Chapter 41).

But the sale of only one important item, from a catalogue offering dozens, did little to lift our spirits. We had put an enormous amount of time and effort into preparing the catalogue, not to mention the capital for acquiring the books. I began to wonder whether, after all, American buyers really did appreciate the monuments of European printing.

Then an unforgettable character entered our lives, in the person of George A. Poole III of Chicago. When he came to 46th Street on his first visit he was a total stranger. We had never heard of him. It was Catalogue 69, seen at the Newberry Library, that prompted his visit. He had read it with interest and wanted to make a purchase. He bought not just a selection of items but nearly every important book in the catalogue. This is not the sort of thing that happens very often.

"Bill" Poole was amiable enough but a nervous, insecure person who seemed torn by doubts whenever making a purchase. He had a fear of making the wrong move. He wanted a guarantee from me to take back any books within a year for a full refund. The catalogue had done poorly and I could not turn away an order of such size, but I would be placing myself in a vulnerable position. Within a year's time, other orders would be received. If we informed these clients that the books were sold, we would lose sales, and then might have to take the books back. So I told Poole that I could not accept his terms. After lengthy haggling (he was a customer to whom the act of buying was just as enjoyable as acquiring a book), he reduced the period of guarantee to three months. He returned nothing and, I believe, never had the slightest intention of doing so. The clause was merely for his peace of mind, in case he started up out of a nightmare asking how he could have spent so much money.

He became a steady customer, one of our most profitable ones during the 1950s. I almost said "good customer," but Poole gave us a run for his money. The more he bought, the more he haggled, and the more he complained (even after buying) that the prices were too high. A client who buys and complains is much to be preferred to one who complains without buying. Nevertheless, I was becoming annoyed at his behavior and decided to teach him a lesson.

I had sold him the first three editions of the *Canterbury Tales* (including the Caxton returned by Rosenwald). Such an opportunity, to own the first three printings of this classic of mediaeval English literature, might never occur again. Yet Poole chose to accuse me of overcharging. I was curious to see whether he was really so concerned about a few dollars. "Bill," I told him, "I've received many orders for those books since selling them to you. If you think I've charged you too much, why not return them. I am prepared not only to refund your money but to give you a profit."

He accepted my offer, returned the books, and I brought the three volumes to the Fifth Avenue office of Arthur A. Houghton, Jr., the great collector. He had inquired about them, and a Houghton inquiry was not to be taken lightly; he was one of the nation's foremost book collectors. I mentioned nothing about the books having already been sold to someone else and being no longer my property.

At his office, there was no vacant table so Houghton and I knelt on the floor to examine the books. I could tell he wanted very much to buy them. We settled on a figure and he requested 24 hours to think it over.

Early next morning I received a call at home from Poole. He asked if I had sold his books.

"I will know today," I told him frankly.

"I withdraw," he replied. "Please return them."

I explained that a client had them and they could not be returned.

"Call them back," he demanded.

"But my client . . ."

"Call them back," he repeated and hung up angrily.

Both Poole and Houghton were valuable customers. I had no wish to lose either. Yet it seemed I had to offend one or the other. Houghton, on the verge of buying, had to be informed of the situation. On my way to him I felt as I had in Vienna, many years before, when two periodicals dealers ordered the same sets and threatened to sue me if I failed to deliver. A face-to-face explanation is the best measure in such circumstances. Houghton said that he understood perfectly, though he could hardly be blamed for being disappointed. "This Poole doesn't seem to like me," he commented, handing over the books. A very relieved Poole got his Chaucers back.

What had happened in those 24 hours I never discovered. Was it possible that Poole, a Yale man, learned that a Harvard man was going to buy his books? Or (which I consider more likely) did the prospect of losing the books affect Poole more deeply than the prospect of a profit? If so, it would not be unprecedented. There have been cases of collectors bidding at the auctions of their own books, to retain ownership of favorite volumes.

I was sure this had cured Poole of complaining about my prices. It had cured *me* of attempting to sell books on consignment from clients, rather than purchasing them outright. Later, however, he found another way to incur my displeasure.

During my illness in November, 1958, at the time of the first Perrins sale, Poole called from Chicago and asked if I would be interested in buying his library. I said that I would and asked how much.

"Three hundred and fifty thousand."

"Please send me a list."

The list arrived soon thereafter and contained all the books I had sold him in the past four years plus a number of other good items acquired elsewhere. At $350,000 it was not exactly a bargain but, as the prices of rare books had risen steadily and Poole had computed his price on the basis of his cost, I considered it a worthwhile investment. I called to arrange for a meeting and was told, curtly, that the collection was already sold.

I was furious.

He had offered the collection to me and had not even given me the chance to buy it. But I had company, as I found out later. Poole played dealer and sent his lists all around the market. Another dealer bought the collection over the phone, then was informed it had already been sold to someone else. The lucky buyer, if anyone who dealt with Poole could be called lucky, was a Chicago bookseller. The collection is now in the Lilly Library of the University of Indiana.

Another unpredictable gentleman with whom we dealt was Clendenin J. Ryan. A grandson of Thomas Fortune Ryan (associate of Pierpont Morgan and co-founder of the Guaranty Trust Company), Clendenin Ryan had the kind of background and credentials that would inspire anyone to extend credit. As a bibliophile he was less than well known, but the rich can plunge and build large libraries overnight. He had to be treated as a serious customer.

Shortly after Roland Tree and I had acquired the General Washington-Rochambeau papers (see Chapter 22), Ryan paid us a call. I do not remember the purpose of his visit, whether he came to browse or had specific business. He asked to see Tree rather than me. As they spoke, Ryan's glance fell on the sheaf of Rochambeau letters and documents lying on Tree's desk. Immediately infatuated with them, he voiced no objection to the price of $180,000 and within a few minutes agreed to their purchase. Even millionaires can have obligations, so we bowed to his request for 30 days' credit. He gave us a $20,000 down payment and would, he assured us, pay the balance of $160,000 within four weeks. At that time he would take possession of the collection.

Ryan was a highly persuasive person: dynamic, energetic, a crusader against crime and corruption, just the sort of individual with whom one ran no risk (or so we believed) in business dealings. But the ways of a man with a book, or in this case with $180,000 worth of historical documents, can be strange. Some collectors continue buying even when faced with other obligations; the overextended bookman (A. Edward Newton coined the term "busted bibliophile") is not exactly a rare species. So strong is the drive to buy that they continue spending even when nothing remains to be spent. Little did we suspect that in Ryan we had that kind of customer.

I made inquiries about his financial reliability at the Guaranty Trust Co. and received firm assurances. His $20,000 check was good, we had no reason to anticipate problems, and we still had the manuscripts.

The 30-day period passed without further payment. Two months, six months, a year went by. We heard nothing from Ryan and failed in our efforts to reach him. Because we still had his down payment we continued holding the material for him, but could not reserve it indefinitely. Then one morning I picked up the *New York Times* and read on the front page the news of his suicide.

Our bill for the balance of $160,000 was rejected by Ryan's executors, who not only refused to pay but demanded return of the $20,000 deposit. This, we protested, was legally ours as liquidated damages, to pay for holding this valuable property and turning away other potential buyers. The matter was settled in our favor, after months of negotiations. We kept both the down payment and the General Washington-Rochambeau papers, which were afterwards sold to Paul Mellon.

All in all, however, collectors comprise one of the most honest segments of all mankind. With millions of dollars yearly changing hands in this business, the instances of fraud—bounced checks, nonpayment, and other foolery—amount to a tiny fraction of all transactions.

One wealthy customer who challenged our patience was Howard Samuels of London. Samuels collected mostly with an eye to profit. He read *Book Auction Records* like balance sheets and bought books that seemed to offer the greatest growth potential. I have no objection to selling to investors, though their cold approach, their lack of appreciation of a book's historical or artistic merit, can be disheartening. To make matters worse, Samuels was an inveterate haggler. Catalogue prices meant nothing to him. He treated them merely as a starting point for bargaining. Knowing he enjoyed gambling, I invited him to toss a coin for his discount. By the law of averages, I assumed, we would each win an equal number of times, giving him half the discount he wanted. I soon learned the dangers of trying to beat one's opponent at his own game. Samuel's skill at coin-tossing proved equal to his abilities in the world of real estate, from which most of his fortune came. The result was that he usually got the full bargain, and I made very little profit on books sold to him.

Another way in which he failed to endear himself to us was to telephone at odd hours whenever we visited London. A night owl, he would call his friends between two and four in the morning. They, perhaps, shared his habits and welcomed calls at that hour. We did not. After a number of disturbed nights, Hanni answered the phone and told him, in no uncertain terms, what he could do with his telephone henceforth. Never again did we hear from him during the night.

When Samuels' books had sufficiently "matured" (he kept close watch on the book market), he sold many back to me at handsome profits. Once again we tossed coins. A year later he drowned while swimming in the Mediterranean. From his estate I bought one of his most valuable possessions, a set of the Four Folios of Shakespeare.

This was the Trowbridge set, the first rare books which James F. Bell, from Minneapolis, bought, about 1925. During an ocean voyage Bell met Rosenbach in the smoking room. He said he had some extra funds to invest and wanted to start a collection. Rosenbach had, at that time, a complete set of the Four Folios which Bell bought right there. This started him as a collector. Later he switched to early travel books and sold the Shakespeares.

CHAPTER 25

Finding the Hours of Catherine of Cleves

THE FACT THAT the Duke of Arenberg was selling from his library provided ample cause for excitement in the book world. Here was one of western Europe's oldest, most coveted private collections, a collection not generally believed likely to be sold. Descendant of a noble and wealthy Belgian family, Eric-Engelbert, Prince and Duke of Arenberg, had left Belgium after the war, taking his art works and books to Villa Encar at Cap Ferrat in the south of France. There he encountered space problems and wanted to sell.

In 1954 a small selection of illuminated manuscripts from the Arenberg library was offered for sale in New York. Germain Seligman, the art dealer, had them on consignment. They were exceptional and I could hardly restrain myself from buying, yet restraint seemed necessary in light of the prices. When Seligman was unable to sell most of the lot after several years, my point of view seemed to be confirmed.

Then in 1955 Schab offered me a collection of 100 incunabula from the same source. The lot consisted almost entirely of Dutch and Belgian imprints and at the asking price of $100,000 would look irresistible today. Even then it was a worthwhile investment and I should have bought them. Some important works, salable at big prices, were included, and even if many titles remained in stock for years they were not the kind of books anyone would object to having on hand. To my everlasting regret I declined, but did have the presence of mind to take the best volume. For $35,000, or more than one third of the whole collection's price, I got Boccaccio's *De la Ruine des Nobles Hommes et Femmes* printed in Bruges in

1476 by Colard Mansion. In this copy the nine engravings, to be pasted in the blank spaces, were not present, and a pair of miniatures filled the first two spaces. The possibility of ever securing a copy with the engravings seemed at the time very small. (See Chapter 41.)

In the Spring of 1957 I succeeded in gaining an introduction to the Duke. Hanni and I settled into Cap Ferrat's Grand Hotel, next to his villa. No effort was made by the Duke to conceal his desire to sell. All the great books on his shelves were up for sale, individually or in lots, depending on one's preference. Many more illuminated manuscripts were involved than I had expected, some of them in the family for generations. They had not, with few exceptions, been exposed to the critical gaze of art historians and hence no identification had been made of their artists, schools, places of origin, or other background.

So far as prices were concerned, I was not in the sometimes delicate position of making offers. The Duke had, like few princes with books to sell, done his own pricing.

Early during my visit, the Duke showed me three of his finest manuscripts: the *Hours of Philippe of Cleves*, the *Hours of Catherine of Cleves*, and the *Grandes Heures d'Arenberg*, the last named having been executed for a Renaissance ancestor. All three carried dazzling miniatures, were in the freshest of condition, and could easily be ranked with the most luxurious Horae. The *Grandes Heures* were signed by the artist, Willem Vrelant, an eminent 15th-century Bruges painter. Sander Bening, father of Simon Bening of Ghent, was the painter of the *Hours of Philippe of Cleves*. The *Hours of Catherine of Cleves* was the work of the yet-to-be-identified "Cleves Master" of about 1430; artistically it stood as unarguably the finest of the trio. Their high prices failed to discourage me; I bought the three without hesitation.

I was in my office in New York, talking to a collector who had never made a purchase from me, when the *Hours of Catherine of Cleves* arrived. It came by registered airmail in a small, unassuming parcel, packed in corrugated paper. While we continued chatting, I unwrapped it, to put at rest the anxiety one always feels about having a valuable book mutilated in the mails. My visitor asked to see the new arrival and became intrigued by it. After glancing at some of its miniatures he asked the price.

"Eighty thousand," I replied, without really taking time to think. This was the price I had tentatively decided to charge, but I had not intended offering the manuscript for sale before thorough study.

"Well, I think I'll buy it," he announced, to my utter shock.

In this unlikely fashion did I make my first sale to Alastair Bradley Martin, a man of wealth and a scholar-collector, more noted as a buyer of objets d'art than manuscripts. Items from his big, sprawling collec-

FINDING THE HOURS OF CATHERINE OF CLEVES 193

tion, ranging from Egyptian to mediaeval, are on loan at the Metropolitan and Brooklyn museums.

Eighty thousand seemed a decent enough price; it brought an instant profit. But when a customer buys that quickly, it cannot fail to arouse nagging suspicion that the price was too low. Here I had underpriced drastically. I had a manuscript worth, after proper research and disclosure of its background, well over $150,000. I was then unaware of the manuscript's significance, beyond its visible beauty. In 1963 the Morgan Library bought another *Book of Hours of Catherine of Cleves*, formerly belonging to a Rothschild, and discovered that it and my (then Martin's) volume were two parts of the same book. Around 1850 it came into the possession of the Paris dealer J. J. Techener. Unable to sell this costly book, which was above the purse of his customers, he split it into two halves, had them bound separately and sold them to two different purchasers. (While this kind of vandalism is rarely practiced in the antiquarian book trade any longer, other varieties flourish: the breaking up of costume and other color-plate books to sell the plates separately, and especially the breaking up of atlases.) For over 100 years the two halves not only remained apart but each owner believed he owned a complete book, blissfully unaware of the other's existence.

I had tried, almost since the day I sold Martin my half of the manuscript, to buy it back. For a long while thereafter, every time we met, he complained of being overcharged—other Books of Hours were bringing considerably less on the market. I offered him a profit if he would return it. This he refused to do, though he continued complaining. When both manuscripts received publicity, ten years later, through the publication of the facsimile edition, Martin became convinced that he had not paid too much.

While in Munich in May 1970 I received a letter from him, offering to sell the manuscript, but at an enormous price. By coincidence it was the same day I received news of the purchase of the Michelino da Besozzo manuscript by the Morgan Library (see Chapter 37). After returning to New York we sat down to negotiate. An hour of spirited haggling resulted in a price which pleased neither, but on which we could agree.

"Of course I'm expecting cash," Mr. Martin announced.

This was out of the question, since I had just a month earlier bought the Houghton Gutenberg Bible and, also in the recent past, spent heavily on manuscripts from the Rothschild collection. To pay cash now would dangerously drain our capital and cause sleepless nights. When I reminded Martin that he had been extended credit of one year to pay for the manuscript originally (four quarterly installments of $20,000 each), he generously reciprocated and allowed me the same terms. Long before the final payment was due the volume had been sold to the Morgan Library. This time they paid cash instead of swapping duplicates. Both parts of the manuscript are now reunited, a happy ending to a bibliophilic thriller.

A few years after purchasing these three manuscripts from the Duke, I returned to Villa Encar. My daughter Mary Ann was with me, to serve as a needed foil: she was to involve the Duchess in conversation, giving me and the Duke a chance to talk business. Since my previous visit he had suffered crippling losses through investments in the Congo, then on the brink of independence and civil war, and his desire to sell had increased proportionately; but instead of books he hoped to interest me in other items. We went to the garage. It was cluttered with packing boxes, in the midst of which stood the Duke's stately new Rolls-Royce. Every possible luxury was built in, he explained: air conditioning, phone, bar, etc. He was selling it only because of an accident on one of its early trips, which forever jinxed it for him. Would I be interested? Yes, but the price stopped me. For that kind of money I'd rather have an illuminated manuscript.

"By the way," I asked, "what do these boxes contain?"

"Old papers, probably of no value," he replied. "They're in my way, and if you want them"—which he said in a tone of disbelief that anyone wanted such a quantity of old papers—"you can gladly have them just by paying the transportation."

We returned to the house and the Duke showed me three paintings of very large size that he also wished to sell: Views of Amsterdam, Antwerp, and Brussels, painted by Jean Baptiste Bonnecroy for an ancestor of the Duke in 1657. For years they had hung in the Arenberg castle, Heverle, outside Brussels, then were removed after the war to Cap Ferrat, where they were somewhat out of scale. Not only that, but the Duke and Duchess contemplated another move, and the prospect of finding accommodations for such huge works was not bright. "They are in my way," he moaned. So I bought them, confident that they would not be in *my* way. The views of Brussels and Antwerp are now in our home in Ridgefield. Amsterdam, largest and most beautiful of the three, seemed ideal for a second-floor wall on 46th Street. But baroque artists failed to anticipate the dimensions of 19th-century townhouses; Amsterdam refused to fit either elevator or stairway. Hoisting from outside, our last resort, also proved futile: the picture would not even fit through the second-story window. Finally we had to trim away several inches of sky—no great loss, since the top had been damaged in shipment. Recently we moved this painting to Ridgefield.

FINDING THE HOURS OF CATHERINE OF CLEVES

Before returning to New York I reached an agreement to buy the remainder of the Arenberg books. These included the incunabula not already taken by Schab, some manuscripts, and quantities of books from the 16th to 19th centuries. It proved a good purchase. The Arenberg volumes expanded my stock in a number of important areas and provided salable material for many catalogues. I still have a few on hand, without the slightest regret. But the most profitable acquisition was that garage-load of boxes, which the Duke had dismissed as "worthless old paper." They contained the archives of Nordkirchen, a castle in Germany belonging to the Arenberg family, and were documents and text manuscripts of the 15th to 17th century with a wealth of material on Westphalian history. I easily sold the entire collection to the University Library of Münster. Mary Ann also made a profitable transaction on this trip. The Duchess presented her with a fine tortoiseshell purse, which my daughter had admired, in exchange for a quite ordinary one from Bloomingdale's.

CHAPTER 26

A Lucky Purchase

DESPITE HAVING BEEN BORN in the 20th century, at least a hundred years too late, one might think, for making major finds, I have sometimes succeeded. Several which seemed relatively minor at the time would now be newsworthy, while others, such as the *Constance Missal* and the *Sigenulfus Codex* of Monte Cassino, rank with the most celebrated of all time.

I take pride in my finds because most have involved early manuscripts. One must be a connoisseur and lover of books to make headway in the search for important manuscripts. To find a Mark Twain first edition may involve luck but there is little problem in identification once the work is found. With manuscripts, especially mediaeval ones, an entirely different situation prevails. The value of a manuscript may hinge upon its decoration, as well as its paleography or history, the identification of which is an expert's task.

Not that I have always been right. The story of my experiences with a Czech Bible believed to be Polish has been told earlier.

Age may play a vital role in determining the value of a manuscript. Here one must depend upon his knowledge, since a manuscript rarely carries a date or any reference by which it can be approximately dated, such as the name of a ruler in whose reign it was written; I must admit being envious of collectors of Roman coins in that regard. Handwriting, text arrangement, page layout, and other evidence must be weighed in judging age. Then, too, an acquaintance with Latin, Greek, and vernacular European literature is required, as one may encounter texts of

Aristotle, Pliny, and Gower in the same library. Woe to him who is unaware that any manuscript copy of Chaucer's *Canterbury Tales* dating before the first printed version is immensely valuable, even if the calligraphy is sloppy. Fifteenth-century manuscripts of a Greek or Latin text may be fairly plentiful, while the same work in a manuscript of the 11th or 10th century can be positively rare.

In the spring of 1962 I received a letter from a book scout in Switzerland. He was offering what he termed an Aesop manuscript, described as beautifully illuminated and approximately 1,000 years old. As for the dating (which would place it in the 10th century, and Romanesque Aesops are not exactly plentiful), he had this on trust from a priest of his village who had examined the volume. One learns to take evaluations of nonexperts cautiously; but even with some margin for error in the age, any manuscript of Aesop with good miniatures merited investigation.

I did not know the writer of the letter. He knew of me, I suppose, because of my recent purchases at the Perrins sales, which had been reported around the world. I admit to having not been overly impressed with the letter. It seemed to have been written by an uneducated person, and his statement that the book turned up "in an attic" was familiar and not altogether convincing. Still I was interested. He asked $60,000, too much to gamble but a reasonable price if the volume lived up to its description.

It happened that we were leaving soon for Italy to join the Grolier Club trip of that year, a pilgrimage to Italian libraries chronicled in the Club's *Iter Italicum*. Hanni and our daughter Mary Ann planned to join me, and we intended it strictly as a vacation, but this was too good an opportunity to miss. We went to Zurich and inspected the volume. Under such circumstances one is prepared for anything; for the book not being there, or for it being very different from the description, but also (with great luck) for it living up to the claims. In this case the description was substantially incorrect, but the manuscript proved anything but disappointing.

It was not an Aesop at all. In his simple way, the man had identified it as such because several of the initials showed animals and Aesop was the only text which he associated with animals. Actually it was a Breviary, extremely beautiful and extremely old. The village priest had not missed by much in his estimate. There was a manuscript ex-libris of Monte Cassino, and a special prayer in the text for the scribe Sigenulfus. The monastery chronicle added at the end of the manuscript reached to the year 1153, thus dating the codex exactly. In the codex were many large initials embellished with animal figures in elaborate interlaced vine patterns of Celtic style, reminiscent of Irish art, though considerably later.

Yes, $60,000 was a fair price. Today it would seem very low. I was prepared to buy but began to get suspicious that the book had been stolen from the Monte Cassino monstery during the war, in which event the monks would still have a legal claim to it. The partly erased ownership inscription on the first leaf added to my doubts. As much as I wanted the manuscript, I had to be careful. I casually mentioned this suspicion to the seller, not aggressively, but to see if he might have any information. He felt offended and left quickly. I breathed a sigh of relief at having resisted the bait.

But I could not forget the book.

When we arrived at Naples with the Grolier Club, we heard mournful stories of the fate of rare books during the war. Librarians from all parts of Italy told us of the destruction of their collections and sacking (mostly by American or German forces) of their choicer possessions.

Monte Cassino, we learned, was turned into a shambles during the long battle in 1944. Returning from Naples to Rome, we paid a call at the Monte Cassino monastery. It had been, and was again in its rebuilt state, a major religious shrine, the chief monastery of the Benedictines and for many years the home of the order's founder, Benedict of Nursia. Even before entering I grieved for the loss of its books.

But they were not lost at all, we discovered. The librarian, who must have told this story to more tourists than he cared to remember, explained how the monastery had shipped its valuable books off to the Vatican prior to the hostilities and lost nothing of consequence. All its manuscripts escaped injury; the collection remained intact.

I became more curious about the Breviary. If the library had not been decimated, could the Breviary have been stolen in some other fashion? Or was it not stolen at all? One does not ask directly about such things. Instead I requested to use the catalogue of manuscripts.

"We have one," the good father replied, without much encouragement in his voice. "It's handwritten, it was made in the late 18th century, and it gives very little information, but you're welcome to use it if you can read it. The printed catalogue came out later, but is not as accurate."

It consisted of a set of bulky volumes, the typical catalogue found in monasteries. One of the first entries was the Breviary. I asked if I might examine it, hoping he would not wonder why.

"With the greatest regrets, no," he said, pointing a finger at the bottom of the page. There, beneath the lengthy description, was a note indicating the codex had vanished at the time of preparing the catalogue, about 1799. "A pity," I said, but the tears welling up in my eyes were for joy. Had it been missing that long, it was no longer the monastery's property under law and nothing stood in the way of its sale. I could buy it without fear.

Then it occurred to me: I had lost the seller's name and address and had no way of contacting him. Very likely he had sold the volume elsewhere by now.

The hotel in Zurich where he had been living could give no forwarding address. I asked around but nobody knew him. But then, at the depth of my dejection and expecting any day to read news of the manuscript having come on the market, a letter arrived at 46th Street. It was from my scout. He was still in Zurich; he had left the hotel but hadn't gone far. The Breviary was still his and for sale.

He had been thinking over the matter (but not for as long as the letter, sent surface mail, took in transit) and concluded that, to be perfectly fair, he would lower the book's price to half the quoted amount, $30,000 instead of $60,000. Within 48 hours I was back in Zurich and completed the transaction. By waiting, agonizing though it was, I saved $30,000. This is not advisable for anyone with weak nerves or intestinal disorders. Incidentally, the scout persisted in referring to the manuscript as an Aesop, even after I had explained what it really was. He believed, undoubtedly, that I was trying to cheapen it by denying it was an Aesop.

I said of the *Sigenulfus Codex* in my catalogue *Monumenta Codicum Manu Scriptorum* (1974) that it is "one of those masterpieces which it is not at all necessary to praise. Like all great works of art, it speaks for itself in its decoration, its gem-like script, and, not least, in the historical value of its texts. As a work which originated at the height of Italian Romanesque art and at the very heart of European monastic culture, this manuscript constitutes a new landmark among masterpieces of mediaeval illumination."

Soon after the purchase I sold it to Dr. Peter Ludwig of Aachen. Its provenance, which we succeeded in putting together roughly, runs as follows. Upon completion by the scribe in 1153 it went into the monastery library and remained there for somewhat more than 150 years. Early in the 14th century it was removed to San Vincenzo al Volturno, a house allied with the monastery, and was there until 1505. At that time it was returned to Monte Cassino and stayed until 1799.

The Monte Cassino catalogue says that the codex was lost "in Gallorum direptione" (in the pillage by the French). This must refer to the events of 1799, when a French army occupied the monastery; such pillages took place all over Europe during the French Revolution and under Napoleon.

Though Monte Cassino contained many priceless manuscripts, this one was described as early as the 1700s as the "most outstanding." "Praestantissimus" it was called by the monk Fredericus, in the 18th century.

Where it was during those more than 150 years, from 1799 until 1962, we could never learn. It dropped completely out of sight and was presumed destroyed. References to it during that period were based on the monastery catalogue, not on examination of the book itself. As for my scout, I could not discover how it came into his possession, other than "found in an attic." He would say no more, I suppose, to conceal the fact that he had acquired it for practically nothing and was making a large profit.

CHAPTER 27

From the Victorian Past

SIR SYDNEY COCKERELL (1867–1962) was a remarkable individual, a scholar, an authority on and connoisseur of illuminated manuscripts, a collector whose activities spanned more than 70 years, and a friend of three generations of collectors and dealers. Though not wealthy, Sir Sydney had, thanks to good connections (he had been the Fitzwilliam Museum's Director for many years), some means; and this combined with meticulous taste built a collection modest in size but large in every other way.

Sir Sydney was one of the elder statesmen among English book collectors, like Sir Alfred Chester Beatty, who lived past 90. Sir Sydney had, by the time I knew him, long outlived his era but was rich in memories. He belonged to the age of William Morris—had been Morris' bookkeeper for the Kelmscott Press, implausible as that seems for someone who lived into the 1960s (Morris died in 1896). Frail and crippled in body, he was rich in booklore and memories. Bernard Quaritch? Yes, he knew Quaritch. He knew Toovey, Leighton, and all the Victorian booksellers. Sir Frederic Madden of the British Museum was a personal friend. Cockerell's life even overlapped with that of Sir Thomas Phillipps, the famous manuscript collector, who was born in George Washington's presidency!

Few people ever handled as many precious manuscripts as did Sir Sydney, in his official capacities, as collector, and—a role he also filled—advisor, consultant, and agent for collectors and dealers. He became in later years a Bernard Berenson of manuscripts, to whom everyone within reach turned for an opinion. Did the miniatures in an illuminated manuscript contain overpainting? Sir Sydney would know. Does this Psalter or Bible date from the 13th or the 14th century? Is something missing here? His word on such matters was the equivalent of law. No lover of modern scientific instruments, he relied usually on his eyes, his instinct, and his decades of accumulated knowledge. Late in life his eyesight weakened but it seemed always to remain keen for details of illumination.

Sir Sydney lived in a setting ideally befitting his tastes, background, and elder-statesmanship, the villa at Hammersmith where Morris had lived and in which the Kelmscott Press was born. I visited him there in 1956 accompanied by Schab. The furnishings had not changed much in 70-odd years, nor the atmosphere. Morris' presence was still to be felt in the low doorways, beamed ceilings, the bare furniture of massive oak that bespoke the neo-mediaeval craftsmanship in which Morris so delighted. Morris, openly expressing contempt for the classic and its various revivals, turned Hammersmith into a sort of glorified 15th-century dwelling. Mediaeval manuscripts in contemporary bindings fitted the mood. But Morris could at best be called a perfunctory collector. He was unwilling, perhaps because of his socialist philosophy, to spend the kind of sums necessary to acquire great books (which, in his time, meant two or three hundred pounds for an outstanding mediaeval manuscript). Cockerell was not so grandiose a personality as Morris, made no crusade to revive mediaeval art, but clearly enjoyed living out the Morris legacy. He was looked upon as the last link to Morris, a patriarch in the eyes of Morris-worshippers.

No secret was made of Cockerell's desire to part with certain books. Over the years he had sold quite a good deal. Now, feeling he could not live too much longer, he stepped up the pace. I went to Hammersmith with high expectations, though a little regretful that my knowledge of manuscripts could not, at that time, approach his. Schab, who had more experience with them, was not an aggressive buyer. Together, we hoped, each could compensate for the other's shortcomings.

A routine had been established to deal with buyers. Sir Sydney's secretary escorted you to the second-floor library, where you could browse at will. After having made your selections, you were ushered into the bedroom, where Sir Sydney, supine and deathly pale, nearly paralyzed, negotiated the price. The flesh was weak, but Sir Sydney's spirit bubbled. Talking about books seemed to resuscitate him. At haggling he was without peer and knew to the shilling the present market values of every book he owned. He countered each offer, parried every thrust. Even in his state of health (we imagined him at death's door, though he survived a number of years thereafter) he could rise to the occasion, and extract just the sort of profit he felt was his due. Finally, after a long session, we succeeded in purchasing the *Fountains Abbey Bestiary* (see Chapter 45), a Shah Abbas leaf, a Florentine pictorial chronicle with miniatures from the school of Fra Angelico or Jean Fouquet, and a 15th-century manuscript: Joachim of Floris' *Vaticinia* containing the prophecies of the Abbot of Floris beginning with Pope Nicholas III (1277–1280).

The "Shah Abbas" leaf, the most important of our purchases, had a romantic history. It was once part of a volume of miniatures illustrating the Old Testament, painted in Paris in the 13th century; a volume which is one of the finest surving art objects of that era. In 1604 it belonged to the Polish Cardinal Bernard Maciejowski, who sent it as a present to the King of Persia, Shah Abbas the Great, for whom Persian translations of the captions were added in the margins; subsequently Hebrew translations were also added. Later it passed into the Phillipps collection, and it was sold by the Phillipps heirs to the younger J. P. Morgan for £10,000, in 1916. At some time in the past, three leaves had become detached from this great manuscript; two are in the Bibliothèque Nationale, and the one we bought from the Cockerell collection is now in the collection of Dr. Peter Ludwig.

The Florentine chronicle, artistically the finest of the group, cost us £1,500. Even at $2.80 to the pound this was a good buy for $4,200, or so we imagined. Schab and I set a selling price of $14,000 on it, which seemed fair in the light of prices then being fetched by comparable manuscripts. We offered it to U.S. clients, like Philip Hofer at Harvard and the Metropolitan Museum. Until December of the following year nothing happened. The Morgan Library politely declined after six weeks of examination. I had quoted $12,600 but it felt the price was too high. At this point Schab, despairing of a sale, sold out his half-interest to me, along with his share in the other Cockerell purchases.

Normally I am firmly opposed to breaking up books. I cringe at framed prints from Audubon's *Birds of America*, despite their beauty. I shudder at the thought. But there comes a time when one must abandon scruples and take a realistic view. Anthony Hobson of Sotheby's, who knew the manuscript from Sir Sydney's library and admired it just as much as I, advised breaking it up and selling the leaves individually. It consisted of just eight leaves, each very beautiful. With some reluctance I did this, placed them with Sotheby's for sale, and was more than pleased at the result: they realized £9,400, or about $25,000. The Morgan Library's refusal turned out to be a blessing; I made twice as much. But I was not induced, as a result of this episode, to practice the breaking up of manuscripts. As a general rule a manuscript is more valuable intact, and of far more artistic significance.

While visiting Sir Sydney, I glanced into every corner of each room, never knowing where some choice volume might be found. Behind his bed lay a ledger in a drab binding. Anywhere else it would merit no notice, but this was Hammersmith, and nothing could be taken for granted. It proved to be the original book of accounts kept by Cockerell for the Kelmscott Press. To a collector of private-press books its value would approximate that of a Kelmscott Chaucer. It carried detailed records of sums paid for every phase of the press: to Burne-Jones for his Chaucer woodcuts, for ink, paper, all sorts of equipment.

Assuming he would not wish to sell an item of personal attachment, I chose a different approach.

"You should," I said, "present this to me as a souvenir of our transaction."

"Why do you want it?" he asked. It was obvious he knew why I wanted it.

"For my collection of bibliography and the history of printing. It would fit in perfectly." I was thinking fast, but nobody thought faster than Sir Sydney.

A smile cracked his timeworn features. "Well, I will give it to you. But to prevent your being tempted to sell it, I will inscribe it to you." This he did, in his minute, characteristic hand—the famous Cockerellian script.

With the ledger safely in my possession, and without having to pay for it, I ought to have rejoiced. But private-press books and everything pertaining to them did not excite me greatly in those days. (I have since warmed considerably to them, having owned two copies of the Kelmscott Chaucer on vellum, the most valuable private-press book.) Unable to sell a book inscribed to me, I got the best of foxy Sir Sydney by presenting it to the Morgan Library. What better final resting place for a memento of the man who had once, 60 years earlier, worked as London agent for the first J. P. Morgan?

CHAPTER 28

My Greatest Disappointment

For the lover of illuminated manuscripts, Ireland will always be more than just another place to visit. No greater or more historic manuscripts exist than those created in mediaeval Ireland: the *Book of Kells*, the *Book of Durrow*, the *Lindisfarne Gospels*, and many others. Had Ireland never produced a poet, a playwright, or a novelist, its cultural achievement would be secure with these masterpieces of illumination, the work of a school of book painting that sparkled brilliantly while the rest of Europe was engulfed in the Dark Ages.

Barely two centuries after the fall of Rome, Ireland's monks began to exhibit their skills in book decoration. The *Book of Kells* (Trinity College, Dublin) dates from approximately 650 years before the invention of printing. Ireland's great manuscripts were already old by the time Ghent and Bruges emerged as important centers of illumination.

The chance of finding an unrecorded Celtic manuscript is of course very slight; even a single page would be a noteworthy discovery. But every book collector who goes to Ireland has that hope, no matter how unrealistic.

Unfortunately my romantic expectations of Ireland failed to materialize. I returned without any books and without any more illusions. With less luck and presence of mind, I might not even have gotten out of the country alive.

In 1959 Sir Alfred Chester Beatty (1875–1968), the legendary collector, whom I had visited repeatedly, invited me to Dublin to make him an offer for his Western manuscripts. Well over 80, he had been a noted bibliophile since almost the turn of the century. Born poor in Brooklyn, he made a fortune in copper and spent much of his life in England, Ireland, and France. His chief collecting interest was illuminated manuscripts, both Oriental and Occidental. In his early years he assembled a collection comparable to the best of that time, on a par with the one of Perrins, but had to sacrifice most of it at Sotheby's in order to raise money during the depression. Those sales in 1932, documented in quarto-size, color-plate catalogues, were the talk of the book world. They occurred at the wrong psychological and financial moment, when the purses of many collectors were thin, but they realized £43,000. At $5 to the pound, this was better than $200,000. But the world had not seen the last of Chester Beatty as a manuscript collector. His finances improved and he began buying again, not perhaps on quite so lavish a scale as before because of rising prices, but often enough to place him in the first rank of postwar bibliophiles. He was a low-key buyer, taking advantage of good opportunities as they came, rarely making headlines. Most of his acquisitions came from Sotheby's and English dealers. He seldom bought anything in America. After Dyson Perrins, it was clear that Sir Chester owned the finest private manuscript collection in the British Isles.

I was tense and nervous on the flight from London. What might prove to be one of the biggest transactions of my career lay ahead. It was also my first visit to Ireland, and I had a tourist's natural curiosity. Having the luck, or so I believed, to be seated next to an Irishman, I put various questions to him. After brief and less than enthusiastic replies he said, "My dear sir, if you want to be entertained, I will do my best, but I prefer my own thoughts." That ended our conversation. It was an omen of worse embarrassment ahead.

I checked into the Shelburne Hotel late in the evening. It was after dinner but I had not eaten and hoped to get at least a snack before retiring. Sitting in the lobby, wondering if I should try to find a waiter, I saw a man in rather shopworn formal attire. Here, I felt sure, was a waiter. I got his attention and called out, "A ham sandwich and a whisky soda, please."

He whirled around.

"Could you repeat that?"

"Ham sandwich and whisky soda."

"Please follow me."

I did so, expecting to be led to a dining area. Instead we landed in the courtyard.

"I did not want to create a scene in the lobby," he blurted out in highly agitated tones. "You have deeply offended me and I want to have satisfaction. I am attending a Charity Ball, and you had the insolence to ask me for a ham sandwich and drink as if I were a waiter."

He was boiling. "I would hit you if you were not a gentleman." As an alternative he suggested a duel on the morning of the second day; 24 hours were needed to permit his friends to make the necessary arrangements.

This was not exactly the way travel folders portrayed the country.

Unwilling to risk my life over the incident, I tried to pacify my adversary. While he steamed and fumed I delivered the following speech: "As you with your most acute eyes must recognize, I am a stranger, absolutely unfamiliar with the customs of your great Irish Republic. I was completely exhausted after a long, strenuous journey. My eyes were clouded by fatigue. Therefore I made the inexcusable error of mistaking you for a waiter. I offer my most humble and heartfelt apologies and hope you will do me the great honor to drink a whisky with me."

If he doubted my sincerity, he must at least have admired my acting. He accepted my apologies and the offer of a drink. True, I was unfamiliar with the customs of Ireland, but I knew that raising a glass settled most disputes in any part of the world. One drink led to another. Soon all was forgotten. We shook hands and parted friends. It was a close call.

Going through Beatty's collection was the kind of delight a bookman gets only on rare occasions and hardly ever with a private collection. The manuscripts were of a quality of which any great monastery could have been proud. That the collection could have been assembled by only one person and largely within the space of 20 years (some manuscripts that he bought early in life were withheld from the 1932 sale, but not many) seemed remarkable; it was a tribute to his dedication. Here were Psalters, Breviaries, Books of Hours, mediaeval Bibles, and early copies of literary works, with the handsomest illuminations, and a number of them in contemporary bindings. I could imagine the reaction of some of my customers to these treasures. I would have no trouble selling them, if Sir Chester accepted fair prices. I had no way of knowing what value he placed on the collection; undoubtedly he hoped for a good profit and deserved it, since prices of manuscripts had increased considerably. The first Perrins sale had just taken place, reaching record-setting prices. Having seen the collection, I went to Cannes where Sir Chester lived at that time. I had carefully calculated the value of the collection and wanted to submit my offer.

The Beatty collection comprised 76 European manuscripts, of which two stood quite dramatically above the rest, a Statius and the famous Psalter of Philip II; the remainder were valuable but not quite in that category. I was unsure whether he might be enticed to part with these two gems and, if so, whether his prices might make a deal impossible. Since I would still be willing to buy the balance of the collection, I submitted two offers: £230,000 for the 74 manuscripts, £300,000 with the two included. The pound was then $2.80, so I offered more than $800,000. It seems low today.

"I have to calculate, give me half an hour," he replied, and withdrew to his study. I prepared for possible bargaining. In precisely half an hour he returned, smiling. "You give me great pleasure with these figures, Kraus," he announced (I was never Mr. Kraus to Sir Chester, more than 30 years my senior). "You have offered me three times my cost. This is wonderful. I always thought I paid too much. Thank you, yes, thank you indeed," he beamed.

I was elated to have the deal closed so quickly.

"When may I pick up the books?"

Suddenly his expression changed. "Oh, I'm not selling."

"What?"

"I'm not selling. I never mentioned anything about selling."

"But you said . . ."

"Oh, it's a very fair offer, yes. But what should I do with the money? I am an old man. I have oatmeal in the morning, eggs or some meat at noon and evening, not even wine. Thanks ever so much. You have made me very happy."

He had not made me happy in the least. I had gone out of my way, wasted time and expense, for what amounted to a free appraisal. For the next few years I had no further association with Sir Chester. Then, shortly before his death, in 1967, I received the following letter:

Palais Ermanno
27 Boulevard Albert 1er
Monaco
Principauté de Monaco
Tel. 30-35-53

29th June, 1967

My dear Kraus,

I was going through some old files and came across your letter of December 15th, 1964, in which you said, "I am still dreaming of the day when you might decide to sell me some of your choice Western manuscripts."

After much thought, I have now decided to sell some of the manuscripts, and I want to give you the chance of handling the sale for me, as we are such old friends, and I know you will get them good homes in the universities and museums in America, where the public will have the full benefit of seeing them. I have had so much pleasure from them myself, and I want future generations to enjoy them too.

Sometime when you are in Europe (there is no great hurry) I suggest you go to Dublin and look over the whole collection of Western manuscripts and give me your ideas. None of them is tied up in any way, except that I have promised to make a gift to the Irish nation, and I imagine I will leave them the bulk of those on exhibition . . .

This matter, I think, should remain very, very confidential, because the newspapers can make such a terrible lot of trouble.

With kindest regards,

I am,

Very sincerely yours,
A. Chester Beatty

This letter, after the earlier disappointment, made me understandably very happy. Arrangements were made with Dr. R. J. Hayes, the new director of the Chester Beatty Library in Dublin, to show me the Western manuscripts again. The world famous and fabulous Oriental section of the collection was not for sale and was bequeathed to the Irish nation. It was agreed that in one or two months I should go to Dublin and make a new offer. Before I could do so, Sir Chester died. Still I went, examined the manuscripts once more, and submitted an offer larger than the first. Dr. Hayes thought I had offered too much. But the luck of the Irish was, once again, not with me. The manuscripts went to Sotheby's, where they realized even more than I had offered.

During my visit in 1957, Sir Chester spoke at length of his friend Wilfred Merton, a scholar who published the monumental catalogue of his collection. He was the owner of the publishing firm Emery Walker. A student of paleography and a collector in his own right, Merton lay seriously ill in a Monte Carlo hotel. He died a few months later and I wrote immediately to Sir Chester, to put me in touch with his executors. I hoped to buy the collection or, if it were not available as a whole, at least portions of it. It was too late, he informed me; Bernard Breslauer, the London dealer, had already bought Merton's books.

One cannot be everywhere at once. Breslauer in London was nearer to the Merton Collection and had an advantage over American buyers. Nevertheless, I was unwilling to give up. It was possible that Breslauer would hold the collection intact for a time and might be persuaded to sell en bloc.

On my next visit to London, in 1958, I asked Breslauer to dinner at the Ritz.

He was in good spirits, reveling in the Merton books. "The catalogue is nearly finished," he proudly proclaimed.

"I should very much like to see the collection."

"And so you shall. But I warn you, nothing is for sale."

This admonition, coming from a bookseller, especially one with whom I had done considerable business through the years, took me by surprise.

"I thank you for your company, but I'd prefer going to bed," I told him. "If I want to see beautiful books that I cannot buy, I can go to the British Museum."

But on his insistence I went to his office, late in the evening, examined the books, and discovered his resolve not to sell was not so strong as it had appeared. I found that in fact he had already been selling; both Maggs and Robinson were allowed to buy Anglo-Saxon manuscript fragments (which I bought from them the next day). The bargaining was long and tedious. Breslauer had the upper hand (and knew it) with first-quality material which could be sold without difficulty in England. There was no question of any discount. Without many years of experience I could not have succeeded that night. I played my part well. The chief rule in buying is not to show emotion, no matter how beautiful the books, no matter how badly you want them. Be unimpressed, even if all of western civilization's treasures should be spread before you.

I went back to the Ritz with some of the best Merton items: two uncial leaves, a manuscript of the Coronation of King Charles IV of France, the *Sacre de Reine Claude,* wife of François I, and others. Not at all bad acquisitions from a lot of which nothing was for sale.

CHAPTER 29

A Book-Collecting Banker

I DID NOT HAVE the pleasure of knowing William S. Glazier very long. We met in the mid-1950s, and by 1962 he was dead, unexpectedly and prematurely, at the age of 55. I do not say "pleasure" out of etiquette. Knowing him was truly a pleasure; born and educated in America, he became a scholar-collector in the best old-world tradition. His field was illuminated manuscripts and his knowledge of them primarily self-taught. In 1936 he bought his first manuscript at the age of 29, "for reasons not much more profound," he commented, "than that it appealed to me, and that it seemed to complement two printed Books of Hours already in my possession." Beginner's luck was with him: it proved to be one half of a Book of Hours—Paris, about 1470—of which the other half appeared at a Sotheby sale in 1954 and was recognized and bought by him.

Gradually Mr. Glazier bought manuscripts, not spending large sums, not over a thousand pounds, I believe, until later in life. An investment banker by profession, a partner in Lehman Brothers, he became a trustee of the Morgan Library and made provisions that his collection be deposited there after his death. For the last four or five years of his life he was without doubt the most respected American collector of manuscripts. He had gathered not just a formidable array of picture books but representative manuscripts encompassing 11 centuries and practically the whole length and breadth of European miniature painting. He had done it all at a time when everyone claimed it was no longer possible to collect illuminated manuscripts. He was meticulous, in his contacts with dealers, in his study of catalogues, in his bidding at auction.

I first heard of William Glazier at the Hachette sale in Paris on December 16, 1953. Arthur Rau bought the day's best manuscript, with me and Maurice Chamonal as underbidders. A French text of Colonna's History of the Trojan War (*Histoire de la Destruction de Troye*), it dated from 1474 (signed and dated by the scribe) and contained one large miniature and 48 charming watercolor drawings. Rau, I felt certain, though as much an enthusiast of French manuscripts as anybody, was not buying for stock. I learned he was the agent for a mysterious New York collector.

Soon thereafter I made the acquaintance of this collector. We got on very well. He was impressed with my stock of manuscripts, not so large as it became in the post-Perrins years but still the finest selection in America. I in turn was impressed with his enthusiasm. Never did he haggle over a price. Never did he protest, "That's too much," as some great collectors do.

He listened attentively. He wanted to learn all about every manuscript, not just the price.

He was my kind of customer except in one regard. He never was moved to spend beyond his limit. Elsewhere (in Chapter 36 on the Dyson Perrins Library) I tell about his interest in the *St. Albans Apocalypse*. It would have been his greatest manuscript but he would not, could not, allow himself to go high enough to acquire it.

Among the books he bought from me was the *Chelles Sacramentary*, an illuminated manuscript of about 860. (See Plate 13.) In 1958, the year of the first Dyson Perrins sale, a European dealer showed me a large manuscript obviously of prime importance. Its script was without any doubt Carolingian. This placed it very early in the Middle Ages but did not identify the place of origin, as Carolingian script flourished throughout Western Europe. The calligraphy was beautiful, the illumination no less so. It struck me as a jewel.

"Well, what is the price?" I asked the dealer.

"The price is not fixed yet," he explained. "The book does not belong to me. It was given to me for appraisal."

Having no real notion of the value himself, he asked my opinion.

"Many thousands of dollars," I said, or words to that effect, then added—in tones betraying my anxiety—"Look, we have to buy this and buy it quickly. Any delay and the owner will get other ideas. I have had experience in these matters. Whatever you do, don't let it get back in his hands; you'll never see it again. Pay any reasonable price."

At our next meeting he had the book, and at a price that could be called low. I offered him a profit of $10,000, and he instantly accepted.

Most dealers like an immediate profit. Of course he might, for all I know, have given the owner $1,000 for it, but I do not trouble myself about the other person's profit so long as the price to me is right.

I went back to New York with the manuscript, full of excitement. What would American art experts have to say about it? They would be astounded, I was pretty sure. It isn't often that an unrecorded Carolingian manuscript comes to light, and the decoration of this one was of very high quality.

Professor Harry Bober, astute authority on early manuscript illumination, examined it carefully and lovingly, matching it against the literature on Carolingian manuscripts. The result was a more detailed provenance than I could have hoped for. Bober identified it as the Sacramentary of Hermentrude, Queen of France and Abbess of the Convent of Chelles (855–869), wife of Charles the Bald (Charles II). It was executed by the monks of St. Amand, about 860, then presented to the Royal Abbey of Notre Dame de Chelles, probably by the Queen-Abbess herself. As an example of Franco-Saxon art it had few surviving peers. Bober could say with assurance that in all the world's museums and libraries there were only a few similar manuscripts to equal it.

But a spectacular book does not guarantee a spectacular sale. Such are the vagaries of the great collectors. Some are not such connoisseurs as to appreciate such an item sufficiently. It is frustrating. Dr. Ludwig, one of my best customers for manuscripts, turned it down on the grounds that it had "initials only" and no separate paintings. Though the initials were brilliant full-page paintings of elaborate ornamental design, they were not historiated, nor did they have portraits of the Evangelists or of royal personalities, like other great manuscripts of that period.

This set me back a few paces. Ludwig judged it on the basis of a 15th-century Book of Hours. The lack of separate miniatures would lessen the appeal of a Gothic prayerbook; but the *Chelles Sacramentary* was 600 years earlier, from an era earlier than that of large paintings. Carolingian artists did their best work in initials and borders.

In February 1960, Mr. Glazier paid me a call and took an immediate liking to the book. With studious attention he went over Bober's notes, examined the manuscript page by page, then abruptly announced, "I'll take it." The price, to which he as usual raised no objection, was $175,000. This amount included a few uncial leaves of the 7th century, from the Phillipps collection. It was one of my biggest single sales up to then; I was basking in Perrins glory at the time, having garnered headlines on my purchases, but most of my acquisitions from that sale had not yet been catalogued. I knew that with Glazier the *Chelles Sacramentary* had a good home.

Another, probably his most important purchase, was a complete codex on vellum of the *Acts of the Apostles* in Coptic from the 4th century. This is an unbelievably early date for a manuscript. (See Plate 12.) The script is similar to that of the famous *Codex Sinaiticus*. The original binding is preserved—wooden boards, morocco back with blind stamped decorations—and the last page is decorated with a full-page miniature of an ankh, or Egyptian cross, between two peacocks. This is, according to scholars, the earliest miniature in a Christian Codex (for details see the two chapters in my Festschrift, *Homage to a Bookman*, 1967). Glazier came, saw, and bought. This was about a year before he died. I never saw him so thrilled. He exclaimed proudly: "This is my first Irish miniature." He was right. The style showed unmistakably the influence of Egyptian-Coptic art on Irish paintings. Rightfully I could boast that within a short time I had been able to supply Glazier with two fabulous treasures, the dream of collectors: newly discovered, unknown, and great art of the earliest periods.

Glazier's death occurred suddenly. We were together the previous day and he even made a purchase from me—a most uncharacteristic one, a wooden tally stock of the Elizabethan era. The tally stock was a very primitive and curious method used by the English Exchequer for keeping its accounts. When cash was paid in to the Exchequer, a tally stock was prepared. It was a wooden stick (usually hazel wood) with various notches cut across it, the number and size of the notches indicating the amount paid in. The stock was then split lengthwise, one half being given to the payer as his receipt, the other half being kept by the Exchequer for its records. The same information was also written in ink on the stock, with, in addition, the name of the payer.

In the evening we met at the Grolier Club and he spoke about plans for future collecting. He was in the full prime of a collector's life. Next morning, when I called to ask where the tally stock should be delivered, to his home or his office, his secretary informed me that he had passed away during the night. She said it without emotion; the news had probably been given already to many other callers.

I had lost a good friend.

"Collecting illuminated manuscripts may not be easy," Glazier once told a Morgan Library gathering, "and I doubt that it will prove to be a popular pastime—but it can be done." No better proof could exist of that statement's truth than the collection he built.

CHAPTER 30

There Was No Silver Lining

LOUIS H. SILVER BELONGED to an illustrious circle of Chicago bibliophiles which included George A. Poole III, Everett D. Graff, Frank C. Deering, and John H. Wrenn. Imposing in appearance and manner, he was a man who made his presence felt: tall, lean, with ample grey mane, fiery eyes, and flamboyant temperament. I could not help but think of him as an Old Testament prophet. During the 1940s and 1950s he was without doubt one of the major buyers of rare books in America, and his acquisitive pace came near matching that of the great collectors of yesteryear.

He owned six Caxtons, including the Bruges and Westminster editions of the chessbook of Cessolis; a fine Shakespeare First Folio and a few Quartos; but his pride was a French *Speculum Humanae Salvationis* from the Holford Collection, a manuscript with 168 fine miniatures. This was his most expensive item, and the jewel of his library.

Silver did most of his business with Rosenbach, until the latter's death in 1952. It was not until 1956 (if I recall correctly) that he sought to introduce himself to me, with rather unhappy results on the first attempt. While staying in New York, he paid an unannounced visit to 46th Street to see a book that had been listed in one of my catalogues. Unfortunately he arrived just at closing time. I had already departed and Dr. Nachod was preparing to leave. Not realizing that this stranger was an important collector, Nachod told him politely to come tomorrow. Silver, accustomed to booksellers going out of their way for him, became furious.

"I am Louis Silver," he shouted.

To this Nachod answered calmly, "I am Hans Nachod."

That was too much for Silver. He stormed out and did not return the next day. When the incident was reported to me, I regretted it of course, but I could not easily soothe Silver's ruffled feelings. For two years he boycotted me. It was bad for both of us; he missed many choice books and I missed many good sales. Finally we met in London, established good relations, and he accepted an invitation to visit me. This time I was prepared. Nachod was made invisible and I sold Silver a major item, the original manuscript of the proclamation of the Louisiana Purchase. This important document, which I acquired from that collector of all-encompassing tastes, Dr. Otto Fischer of Detroit, was the copy by which Thomas Jefferson made public the purchase of Louisiana from France. It began with a copy of the treaty ceding Louisiana (dated at Paris, April 30, 1803), followed by the convention regarding the price paid (60 million francs, $11,250,000) and the manner of payment, and another convention dealing with payment by the U.S. of various claims of American citizens against France. It was signed by Jefferson and bore the Great Seal of the United States. No other copy of this manuscript is recorded; it was possibly intended to be sent to the French government or the French prefect at New Orleans. Evidently written in haste, it bore erasures and corrections in many places. The Louisiana territory includes Missouri, Arkansas, Iowa, Minnesota, North and South Dakota, Nebraska, and Oklahoma in their entirety and most of Kansas, Colorado, Wyoming, and Montana. This document, one of the largest real-estate transactions in history—about 1,000,000 square miles, five times the area of continental France—gave Silver, a real-estate magnate, a special thrill. From then on he became a steady client and good friend. His wife Amy, a sweet lady of even temper, was just the opposite of her husband in personality but took equal interest in his hobbies. The Silver catalogue was entirely her work.

In 1962 he fell terminally ill and, in need of money, told us that his library was for sale. Kebabian and I went immediately to Chicago to see his books. I was in poor health myself, suffering from colitis. After going through the library we selected a small, choice group of volumes and offered $600,000 for them. This we knew represented a good profit for Silver, most of them having been purchased 10 to 20 years earlier from Rosenbach at low prices. Nevertheless it was painful to do business with someone whom we knew was near death. Whether or not he was aware of his situation I do not know, but he gave no evidence of it; quite the opposite, he seemed to enjoy the role of playing dealer. He would let me know his decision. It was negative; he had decided to keep the library intact. There was no Silver lining in the clouds for me. Six months later he died and his books went to the Newberry Library of Chicago, after having been rumored to have been bought by the University of Texas, for about $2,500,000. Some of the books, mostly duplicates, came up at Sotheby's in the winter of 1965. The auction was a great success and many of the prices were staggering. The total amounted to more than $800,000. I succeeded in buying the most expensive item of the sale, the *Ars Memorandi*, a block book printed in Germany about 1470, a perfect and beautiful copy from the library of the Duke of Gotha. Although this is one of the rarest of all block books, I paid only the modest price of £29,000 ($81,000). It is now in the library of Otto Schäfer in Schweinfurt.

Among my other important purchases at this sale was an item about which I had been dreaming from the time I saw it first in Silver's home. This was an autograph letter by William Harvey (1587–1657), the famous discoverer of the circulation of the blood; the only letter ever to appear on the market, and the only one in America. It is now at the Morgan Library.

CHAPTER 31

The Most Mysterious Manuscript

WILFRED MICHAEL VOYNICH was a towering figure in the rare-book trade at the turn of the century. I never met him (he died in 1930) but two manuscripts brought us together. The first was a Valturius manuscript about which I spoke in Chapter 14, the second, the "Cipher Manuscript" of international fame. This manuscript has created a sensation among scholars and resulted in a flood of literature, even up to the present time. Since 1912 it has tested the skills of many learned cryptographers, none of whom could break the cipher.

Around 1912 Voynich was introduced to the Jesuits of the Collegium Romanum at the Villa Mondragone in Frascati near Rome. The library of the Collegium was sold to the Vatican but with the help of one Father J. Strickland, S.J., Voynich was able to buy a group of the most extraordinary manuscripts, now dispersed among American libraries.

The only one of them which he retained was the so-called "Roger Bacon Cipher Manuscript." Convinced that it represented an enormous historical and cultural treasure, he reportedly asked the equivalent of $160,000 for it before World War I—much more than any manuscript or book of any kind had previously realized. Voynich had made a fortune through the sale of the other Mondragone manuscripts and therefore was in no hurry to sell; he hoped that one day the cipher could be broken.

Voynich was a colorful man. Born in 1865 of Polish parents, he attended universities in Warsaw and Moscow, and joined the Russian revolutionary movement. He was arrested and sent to solitary confinement in the Warsaw fortress, from which he escaped after one year. Arrested again after a few months, he was sent to the Siberian salt mines. He escaped again and made his way to England, arriving in 1890. There he met and married Ethel Boole, novelist, author of one of the world's bestselling novels, *The Gadfly*. Translated into eighteen languages (there were over 100 editions in Russian alone), *The Gadfly* served as the basis of a play, two films, and three operas.

This is not the place to write the biography of Voynich. All I can say is that he rose like a meteor in the antiquarian sky and his catalogues testify to his abilities. It was my good fortune that his longtime secretary, Ann Nill, later worked for me for at least ten years. She was a tiny woman, with a perfect memory and a very even temperament. That was her most important quality. She was so soothing that when I got furious and started yelling about some insignificant matter, she would look at me with her large, dark doe eyes and I would calm down.

Ann Nill was the longtime companion of Mrs. Voynich and inherited the Cipher Manuscript on the latter's death in 1960. I bought it from her on July 12, 1961, for $24,500. Such a manuscript is not easily described in a few words but I will try. It is small in size, about 230 by 160 mm, and consists of 102 vellum leaves with many colored drawings of fantastic-looking plants. On other pages are found astrological diagrams of concentric circles followed by magnificent and powerfully conceived drawings which suggest graphic representations of the universe. There are small-scale drawings of female nudes immersed in and emerging from fluids flowing from interconnecting tubes, giving the impression that the artist was struggling with the very mystery of the creation of life itself. (See Fig. 8a).

Many of the best cryptologists have tried to break the code since 1912 when Voynich acquired the manuscript. In 1921, Professor William R. Newbold announced that he had solved the cipher and in 1928, after his death, Professor Roland G. Kent published Newbold's findings. Unfortunately, later publications disproved Newbold's theory. The great cryptologist W. F. Friedman, who succeeded in breaking the Japanese code in which the attack on Pearl Harbor was revealed, tried for some twenty years to read the manuscript, without success.

Space does not permit the mention of all the scholars who have tried to solve the riddle. The latest attempt is being made by Professor Robert S. Brumbaugh of Yale University.

The manuscript's provenance is fascinating. It enters recorded history on August 19, 1666, when Joannes Marcus Marci sent the codex from

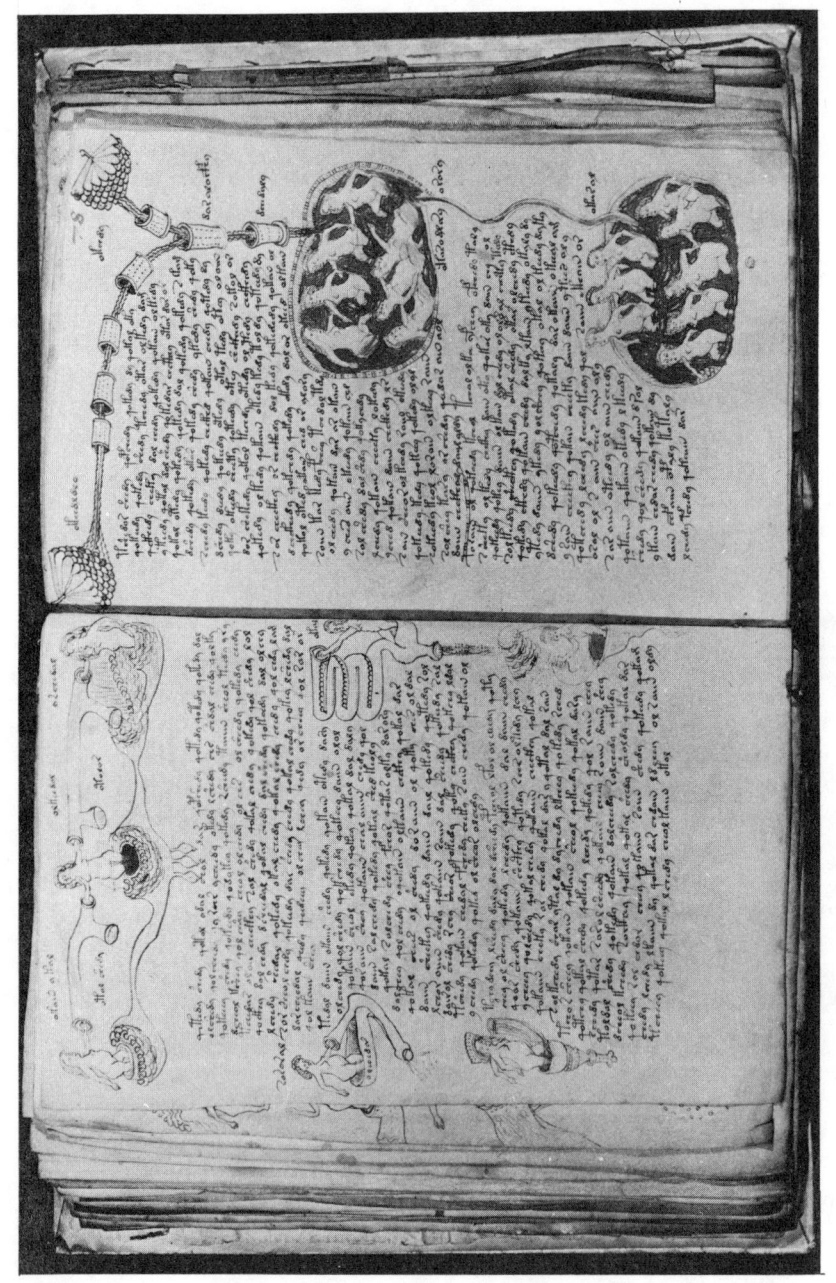

Fig. 8a. 2 leaves from the "Roger Bacon Cypher Manuscript" (Yale Beineke Library.)

Prague to Athanasius Kircher, S.J., in Rome, with a signed autograph letter which is loosely laid into the manuscript. It reads as follows (translated from the Latin):

> Reverend and Distinguished Sir, Father in Christ: This book, bequeathed to me by an intimate friend, I destined for you, my very dear Athanasius, as soon as it came into my possession, for I was convinced that it could be read by no one except yourself.
>
> The former owner of this book asked your opinion by letter, copying and sending you a portion of the book from which he believed you would be able to read the remainder, but he at that time refused to send the book itself. To its deciphering he devoted unflagging toil, as is apparent from attempts of his which I send you herewith, and he relinquished hope only with his life. But his toil was in vain, for such Sphinxes as these obey no one but their master, Kircher. Accept now this token, such as it is and long overdue though it be, of my affection for you, and burst through its bars, if there are any, with your wonted success.
>
> Dr. Raphael, a tutor in the Bohemian language to Ferdinand III, then King of Bohemia, told me the said book belonged to the Emperor Rudolph and that he paid to the bearer who brought him the book 600 ducats. He believed the author was Roger Bacon, the Englishman. On this point I suspend judgment; it is your place to define for us what view we should take thereon, to whose favor and kindness I unreservedly commit myself and remain,
>
> At the command of your Reverence
Joannes Marcus Marci
Of Cronland
>
> Prague, 19th August, 1666.

Here is an original witness to the history of the manuscript in the 17th century. Emperor Rudolph II (1562–1612), a scholar rather than a ruler of the empire, devoted most of his time to the study of alchemy and astrology. He lived in Prague, was patron of Tycho Brahe, Kepler, John Dee, and assembled a large collection of books and art objects. The manuscript passed from Rudolph to a succession of other owners before Athanasius Kircher (1601–1680), the foremost Jesuit scholar of his time, who was keenly interested in problems of cryptography. His work on codes and ciphers, *Poligraphia*, was published in 1663.

From the letter we learn that the manuscript was believed to be the work of Roger Bacon (1214–1294), the famous English scientist and philosopher, and that Rudolph bought it for 600 ducats. Though it would be difficult to equate 600 ducats with a modern sum of money, it was a substantial price.

It is quite possible that Rudolph bought the manuscript from John

Dee while in Bohemia from 1585 to 1588. Sir Thomas Browne quotes Arthur Dee (1579–1651), the son of John Dee, "that he saw in his father's hand a book . . . containing nothing but hieroglyphics." (C. F. Smith, *John Dee*, 1909, p. 311)

The "Roger Bacon Cipher Codex" is indeed a sphinx, as Joannes Marcus termed it; its lair strewn with the bones of those who failed to solve the riddle, still awaiting the Oedipus who will give the right answer. The Cipher Manuscript is described in my Catalogue 100, item 20, with many plates and illustrations. The literature about it is vast.

In this catalogue it was offered for $160,000, the same price Voynich had asked 50 years earlier. Miss Nill was to get one half of the amount above the price I had paid her. Many clients, mostly scholars, expressed great interest, but nobody bought. I felt like Voynich, who had held the manuscript for such a long time. Dozens of scholars wanted to see it, other asked for photos. Institutions asked to have it on loan. I had to decline all such requests, to preserve its commercial value. There were no buyers. After seven years of happy ownership we felt that the right thing to do was to turn it over to an institution where it could be freely studied. We chose the Beinecke Library at Yale as the recipient. Along with it, Yale received boxes of correspondence, pamphlets, notes, and miscellaneous literature concerning the manuscript. To this we added Mrs. Voynich's *Gadfly* collection consisting of over one hundred editions of the book in various languages, as well as a film produced in Russia after World War II.

In 1963 we were in Rome and I visited Monsignor José Ruysschaert at the Vatican Library. I knew that he had published the catalogue of the Mondragone Library and I hoped to get information about the Cipher Manuscript. To my great surprise he thought that the manuscript was still in the library. I asked him: "Can you show it to me?"

"Yes," he replied, and headed for the stacks.

Soon he returned without it. I had to tell him that I owned the codex, and how it came to me.

CHAPTER 32

The Obsessed

I N 1944, IT BECAME KNOWN that the remaining portion of Sir Thomas Phillipps' library was for sale in its entirety.

Sir Thomas Phillipps (1792–1872) ranks without question among the world's greatest book collectors. Beginning when he was a teenager, he amassed about 100,000 volumes of manuscripts and printed books, many of great beauty and rarity, and a far greater number of autographs and documents. He was a bizarre personality, who sacrificed all his ample resources, as well as the happiness of his family, to his obsession of acquiring more and more. (Sometimes, I have to confess, I feel like Sir Thomas when I see a beautifully illuminated manuscript and am driven after sleepless nights to pay a silly price. Oh, bibliomania!)

The dispersal of this collection, begun not long after Phillipps' death, continues to the present day. From 1886 to 1913 there were 16 Sotheby sales of nearly 19,000 lots, realizing £71,277 but making no very noticeable dent in the vast material. My connection with Sir Thomas' library started in 1944. Charles Stonehill, the dealer of London and New Haven, suggested that we should jointly acquire the "remains" of the Phillipps Library. He had no money to invest and expected me to finance the deal. He claimed to be a friend and, if I remember correctly, a classmate of Alan George Fenwick, nephew of Thomas Fitzroy Fenwick (d. 1938) who was the son of John Fenwick, husband of Phillipps' third daughter. Fenwick had charge of liquidating the still-enormous remainder of the library. The sum required for the purchase was between

223

£100,000 and £150,000, a considerable figure in those days and especially for me.

In December 1944 the Robinson brothers, Lionel and Philip, offered Alan Fenwick £100,000 for the library and the collection of old-master drawings. This offer was refused. In February of the following year they made a fresh bid, £100,000 for the library alone without the drawings. The brothers approached William A. Jackson, Harvard's esteemed rare book librarian. In a cable they announced that they might be in a position to offer the residue of the Phillipps collection for £110,000. I remember very well Jackson's face when he broke the sensational news of this huge deal. We all were spellbound. He told me and some other friends that it would take only a few weeks to get the approval of Harvard's trustees. We congratulated him on this fabulous coup. However, after drawn-out negotiations the trustees balked and Harvard lost the opportunity to acquire this wonderful collection.

In the meantime Stonehill, supported by my financial backing, was still in the running. Hanni's uncle Ernest trusted my judgment and promised to advance the necessary cash. But there was a problem. All the books had been removed during the war from Thirlestaine House, which had been requisitioned by the Ministry of Aircraft Production. They were hastily crated, stored in the cellars for the duration, and inaccessible to a prospective buyer. Here, in the absence of any listings of what was left after all those sales, was a gamble—a real shot in the dark. This might well be the reason why the Harvard trustees had declined to buy.

Still I was ready to risk the amount asked. I had studied the Phillipps literature and was convinced of the great value of the remaining treasures. When I wanted to submit my offer, Stonehill could not be reached. I was told that he was abroad. So I lost the chance to make the biggest purchase of my life. The collection went to the Robinson brothers, who signed the purchase contract on September 3, 1945 (confirmed by Court of Chancery on December 13, 1945). The merchant bankers S. M. Warburg of London financed the deal. About 20 years later the same firm arranged the sale of half of our reprint business to Lord Thomson.

My Phillipps interest was not limited to my efforts to buy the remainder of his collection in 1945, but also included collecting his publications printed at his private Middle Hill Press.

Since Sir Thomas did not always encourage scholars to visit his residence at Middle Hill, he devised another way of making his historical source materials available; he had them printed by his own press. As my collection of about 400 titles attests, during the course of his long life he did indeed publish a huge number of documents, literary and historical

A CATALOGUE

OF

𝔅𝔬𝔬𝔨𝔰

AT

MIDDLE - HILL,

WORCESTERSHIRE,

1819.

SALISBURY:

PRINTED BY J. A. GILMOUR,

Fig. 9. First catalogue of the Phillipps Manuscripts.

works, indices, tax rolls, and other such research materials in political, social, and economic history. My collection of Phillipps publications, one of the largest in private hands, contains a great number of proofs with manuscript corrections in Sir Thomas' hand. Until 1844, he generally printed only 25 copies (and sometimes less). After that date editions consisted of between 50 and 100 copies, but again there were exceptions. All titles are of great rarity.

As A. N. L. Munby, the biographer of Sir Thomas, says, "By printing in exceedingly small editions (partly through parsimony and partly through impatience) and distributing these small editions in an unsystematic and arbitrary manner, he defeated his own ends. Many works he printed are almost as inaccessible today as if they remained in manuscript."

I was lucky enough to buy the stock of the remaining publications from the Robinson brothers, many in duplicate or multiple copies. My readers will understand that I look upon this collection of Middle Hill publications with great pride. (See Fig. 9.)

My collection is surpassed by that of Harrison D. Horblit, friend and neighbor, who owns over 450 titles and many memorabilia and photographs, certainly the largest collection in existence. Horblit is also a well-known collector of early books in the field of navigation and the history of science. The Grolier Club's publication, his *One Hundred Books Famous in Science*, is a standard work important to collectors and scholars.

As I read the galley-proofs of this book in November 1977, I can add, with pride, that we have just returned from London, where I succeeded in acquiring from the trust created by Lionel and Philip Robinson all the remaining Phillipps manuscripts. It is hard to believe that, after the many auctions, about 2,000 volumes of manuscripts and over 130,000 letters and documents remain. It will take time to catalogue this huge mass of material, much of it unknown to scholars, and I am confident that many discoveries will reward my venture.

CHAPTER 33

The Cradle of Printing

I HAVE ALWAYS REGARDED printed books as a secondary specialty of mine, after manuscripts. Nevertheless I have established myself as a dealer in great printed books, from the Gutenberg Bible to Shakespeare Folios to color-plate natural history volumes of the 18th and 19th centuries. Incunabula have interested me the most among printed books, first because they come from an age, the 15th century, contemporary with manuscript illumination and representing the outgrowth of this art; second because the field of incunabula offers so many mysteries and challenges. Over the years it has bewitched bibliographers, from Panzer and Hain in the early 1800s to Louis Polain, Margaret Stillwell, Curt F. Bühler, and Frederick R. Goff of the present day. Incunabula include, of course, many of book-collecting's fabled volumes: the Gutenberg Bible, the Psalters of Fust and Schoeffer, books printed by Sweynheym and Pannartz, the Foligno Dante, the Valdarfer Boccaccio, Caxtons, Jensons, and Aldines. The opportunities to buy and sell such volumes today do not compare with those of fifty or a hundred years ago. With most important incunabula, it is simply a matter of "not available at any price." Yet I have owned most of the major incunabula. I am the only bookseller in history, so far as I know, to have owned a Gutenberg Bible and the Psalters of 1457 and 1459 simultaneously—and "own" is here the correct word, as they were bought not for a client's account but for stock. Though I have handled copies of less than one tenth of the works printed by Caxton, that is still a remarkable total.

The stories of my adventures with important printed books would fill a separate volume. Here I shall recount my experiences with only a few of the most heralded incunabula.

Otto Hupp (1859–1949) looked like an El Greco painting of a Renaissance cardinal. A tiny man with bright luminous eyes and snow-white goatee, he was a fixture around Germany's antiquarian bookshops during most of his life. Hupp focused his researches on incunabula, particularly those of German origin. Not being a rich man, he was unable to build the kind of collection owned by some of his contemporaries. Still, the low prices of those days—he started buying a hundred years ago—enabled him to accumulate very many incunabula. With great precision, Hupp compared type designs, measured type faces, studied paper and binding, in an effort to add knowledge to published findings. He made small discoveries occasionally and always seemed on the verge of something big, historically—not monetarily, for few book collectors cared less about money than Otto Hupp. He was not only a collector, but an artist specializing in heraldic design and the graphic arts.

About 1880 Hupp discovered a Missal for the diocese of Constance in the stock of an antiquarian bookseller. Its type design seemed out of the ordinary. Though only 21 years old and no expert yet in such matters, Hupp knew enough about incunabula to judge that this was not just another volume. Exactly what it was he could not say. But he bought it, on the spot, a decision never to be regretted.

The more he studied the book, the more his interest rose. A small folio, it bore no indication of printer, place of publication, or date. Its type face was of extremely large size. That fascinated Hupp. After lengthy comparisons, he found that the type nearly matched that in the Fust and Schoeffer Psalter of 1457. This led to all sorts of speculation. As this type appeared more primitive than that of the 1457 Psalter, it could well be older. If older, it came from Gutenberg's press. If it came from Gutenberg's press, it almost certainly predated the 42-line Bible, believed then (and by some still) to be the first book printed from movable type.

All published literature on incunabula was checked by Hupp without finding any reference to his mystery book. Copies appeared in no dealer's catalogue, nor in any auction sale. No library seemed to own it.

After several years of intense research, Hupp published his findings in 1898 in a volume entitled *Ein Missale Speciale Vorläufer des Psalteriums*, followed by two other publications: *Gutenbergs erste Drucke* (1902) and *Zum Streit um das Missale Speciale Constantiense* (1917). Indeed, Hupp spent the better part of his life researching and writing about his celebrated acquisition. The conclusion he reached, not taken too seriously at first but gradually accepted, was that this Missal should be recognized as the first full-size book printed from movable type, the work of Gutenberg, and probably dating from 1445–50, a blank period for which there is no record of Gutenberg's activities. Hupp lacked most of the laboratory techniques available today for the study of paper and ink; but even using them, scholars have failed to convince everyone.

A few years later the early date of the *Constance Missal* was challenged, when a book of 1472 was discovered which was printed on identical paper. Speaking for myself, I believe that the *Constance Missal* is earlier than the Gutenberg Bible. A printer in 1472 could indeed have acquired a stock of paper that had been manufactured twenty or thirty years earlier.

In any event, the book was believed to be unique and gained unparalleled notoriety in Hupp's time. Content to live vicariously on his notes and monographs, Hupp consigned it to Ludwig Rosenthal who offered it for sale in his Catalogue 100 (1900) at 200,000 marks. No takers came forward. Later Domizlaff, the Munich bookseller, bought a half-interest in it from Hupp. After Hupp's death in 1949, his widow authorized its sale to the Bayerische Staatsbibliothek for 20,000 marks, with credit extended over several years.

In 1953 Hanni, Hans Mehltretter, my agent, and I visited Munich. As usual we paid a call on Helmuth Domizlaff. He had survived the war and was able to resume business in the same city. We got to talking about old times and the subject of the Missal came up. With Hupp gone, Domizlaff was probably the foremost living authority on it. He had certainly handled it more than anyone else. Mehltretter listened attentively to Domizlaff's stories. When we left, he whispered to us on the staircase:

"This *Constance Missal*—another copy has turned up in Switzerland. The old Capuchin monastery at Romont has one. Its prior is my neighbor in Lucerne. What do you say? Would you care to buy it?"

It sounded like a joke. A second copy?

"I'm sure I would!" I replied, still not convinced he was serious or had identified the book properly. "And for much more than the 20,000 marks poor Mrs. Hupp received." (That then equaled about $5,000.) We three stood for at least ten minutes on the stairs excitedly discussing the prospect of such a purchase. I believe that historical meeting should be commemorated by a bronze plaque on the spot.

Father Andreas, the prior, was willing to sell, but only at a price for which one could build a small hospital. After a few days of hard bargaining we finally agreed on a price acceptable to both of us. To this a 10 percent commission for Mehltretter had to be added. I was sure that when I paid I could take the book with me. How mistaken I was. Father Andreas explained that he had to get permission to sell from the

Vicar General of the Capuchin order in Rome, a matter which could take many months. Life in a monastic world is timeless. I asked: "Why not telephone?" He said no. It required a formal letter in the channels of monastic bureaucracy, which might sit on desks for weeks or months before a reply. Not able to wait in Lucerne, I returned to New York. Mehltretter stayed behind to handle things. Meanwhile I alerted the Director of the Morgan Library, Fred Adams. In confidence I reported what was going on and gave the Morgan Library first refusal in the event of a successful purchase.

After a few months of waiting I received good news. The Vicar General in Rome had agreed. I immediately flew back to Lucerne. Permission to sell was granted on the condition that the Missal was older than the order of the monks, which was the case.

I had hoped for a quick transaction, now that all obstacles were cleared away. Once again, reality failed to match expectation. The monks allowed me only to collate the Missal; removing it from the premises was impossible until *official* approval came. Official approval consisted of a signed, sealed document delivered to the monastery from Rome by special courier. Still clinging to the old mediaeval distrust of the mails, Rome conducted its affairs by courier only, and as usual he was late. When he might arrive nobody had the slightest idea. I shuddered to think he might be traveling on foot.

The Missal was not in the Romont monastery's library but in a Capuchin house in Lucerne on a shelf in the refectory cupboard, wrapped in none-too-clean newspaper. It was indeed a genuine *Constance Missal*, exactly like Hupp's. The more I examined it, the more my impatience grew. I felt sure the monks must be negotiating with another buyer. I could see the book slipping from my grasp.

"Can't they phone?" I demanded of the beleaguered Mehltretter, who must have felt sorry that he ever brought up the subject.

When this possibility was put to the monks they recoiled. No cash in the budget for long-distance calls. Even if I paid, the appearance of a toll call on the monastic phone bill would cause talk.

So we brought Father Andreas to Mehltretter's house to use his phone.

While I was on a side trip to Marburg, selling for Kraus Periodicals to the Westdeutsche Bibliothek, news came of official approval. Guests with whom I was dining had no idea why I suddenly became ecstatic but, not the ones to bypass a celebration, they joined in. Many bottles of champagne were opened that night. Marburg had not, I am pretty sure, witnessed such merry-making since Charles V's days. I was delirious. Only one small detail remained: coming up with the cash.

THE CRADLE OF PRINTING 231

Unable to finance such a purchase single-handed in those days, I had enlisted the help of two partners, Hanni's father and William Schab. That, however, solved only part of the problem. The monks demanded cash. My pockets bulged with Swiss banknotes; I felt like a padded scarecrow. In addition to the price of the book there was Mehltretter's commission. I'm sure this was his biggest payday.

My reception by the monks this time could not have been more enthusiastic had I been the Savior incarnate. The money, I well realized, meant a lot to them—but the book meant even more to me. Suddenly a sobering thought crossed my mind, as Schab and I completed our rounds of handshaking and well-wishing and left with it. It wasn't insured. Losing the book would be just the same as losing the money; even worse, as it could not be replaced.

We agreed that it must not leave our sight, even for an instant. In the car it would ride on the seat between us. On foot, one or the other would clutch it to his bosom.

Like victorious Roman soldiers returning from the field, we regaled ourselves with food and drink. We stopped at the Grill of the Baur au Lac in Zurich and feasted on caviar and crêpes suzette, interspersed with no small number of toasts. By dinner's end we had clearly over-toasted ourselves. When we left the waiter ran after us with a newspaper-covered package. He called, "Mister, mister, does this belong to you?" We had forgotten the book. (See Fig. 10).

That night I slept with the book under my pillow.

Next morning it was shipped by air to New York for Hanni to collect. Of course, at customs the parcel had to be opened and inspected.

"Is this a book more than 50 years old?" the inspector asked. "Otherwise it's subject to duty."

The book was safely in my vault at 46th Street and I was breathing more easily. Nobody in the book world knew of its arrival except for Adams and Dr. Curt Bühler, the great incunabulist from the same institution, both committed to secrecy. It was now up to them to persuade the trustees to approve the purchase for a considerable amount. It was, I was told, not too difficult to convince them not to miss this star piece, which was not likely to come on the market again. And regardless of what may be decided about the Missal by future generations of bibliographers, there is no doubt that it occupies an important place in the history of the invention and development of the art of printing. The problem was that the Morgan Library did not have the cash available to buy the Missal outright. My two co-owners had already been paid. I succeeded in closing the deal by taking part cash and part duplicates. I was paid $58,000 in cash and received the following books: The first edition of

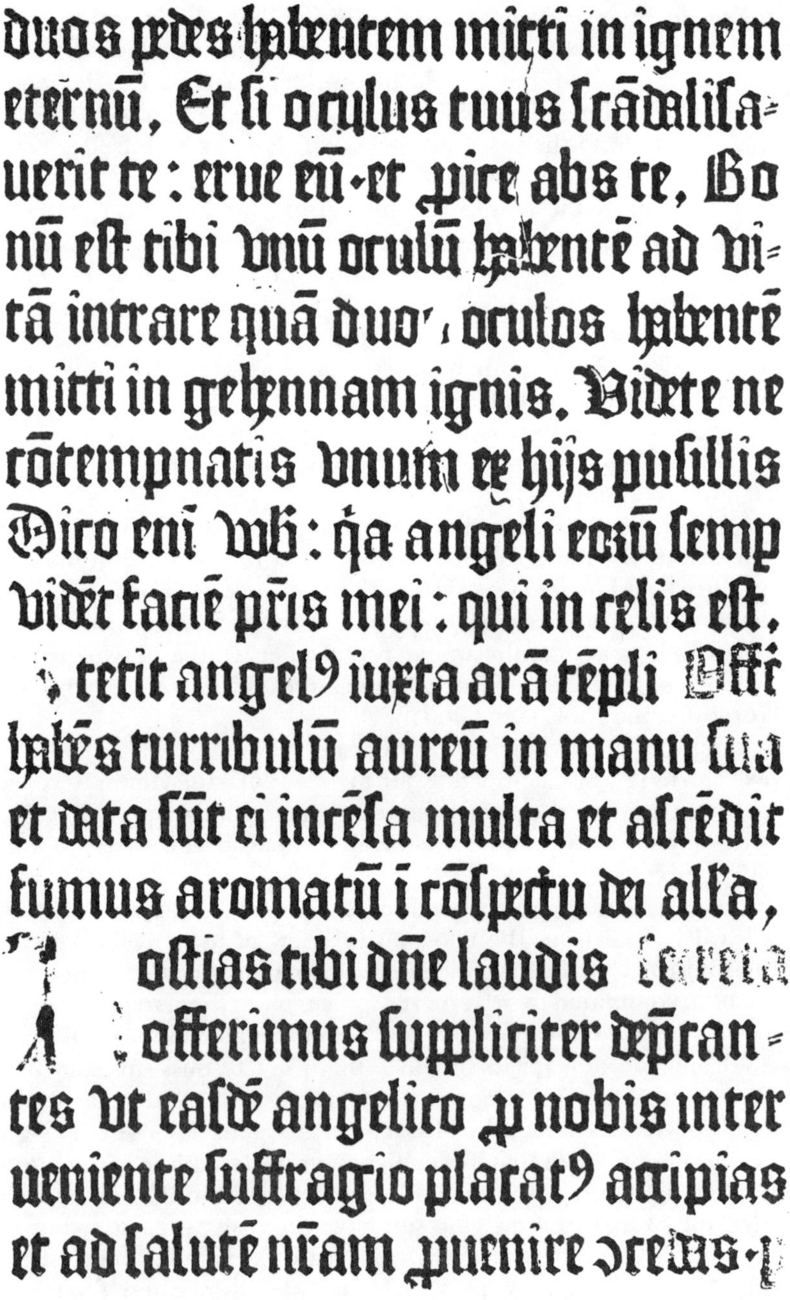

duos pedes habentem mitti in ignem
eternū. Et si oculus tuus scādalisa-
uerit te: erue eū et pice abs te. Bo
nū est tibi vnū oculū habentē ad vi-
tā intrare quā duos oculos habentē
mitti in gehennam ignis. Videte ne
cōtempnatis vnum ex hijs pusillis
Dico eni vob: ɋa angeli eozū semp
vident faciē pris mei: qui in celis est.

⁂ tetit angelꝰ iuxta arā tēpli Offi-
habēs turribulū aureū in manu sua
et data sūt ei incēsa multa et ascēdit
fumus aromatū i cōspectu dei alta,

ostias tibi dñe laudis   secreta
offerimus suppliciter depcan-
tes vt easdē angelico ꝓ nobis inter-
ueniente suffragio placatꝰ accipias
et ad salutē nram puenire cōcedas.

Fig. 10. One page of the Constance Missal. (Morgan Library.)

Chaucer's *Canterbury Tales* printed by Caxton (lacking 7 leaves), the *Myrror of the World*, the first English illustrated book, also printed by Caxton, complete; the *Booke of St. Albans*, the first English sporting book, printed by the Schoolmaster Printer in Oxford, complete.

This was a transaction of major proportions. It also was an event which had to be appropriately celebrated. That was arranged by the Morgan Library in a grand way. The opening day was February 25, 1954. The exhibition was to include a "very important book, recently acquired and never seen in America." There was an exclusive story in *Life* magazine which was to come out the day of the celebration. But nobody remembered or was told that the magazine would be on the newsstands a few days before the cover date. So the cat was out of the bag and everybody knew what the great secret was. Part of the celebration was a dinner given in the great library room of the Morgan Library, to which many notables of the book and financial world were invited. Junius S. Morgan, the head of Trustees, bravely ignored the incident of the unexpected early publicity and gave his talk as though nobody knew what was coming. At the reception afterwards, Adams patted me and Lehmann-Haupt on the shoulders and said: "Well, you guys certainly can keep a secret," as indeed we had. But there is the story that David Randall, at that time head of the Rare Book Department at Scribner's, called up Adams before the celebration and asked what the mysterious book was. Adams, of course, would not tell him about the *Constance Missal*, and after more banter, Adams was about to hang up when Randall called out to him: "Well, constantly yours."

The publicity was fabulous. My name was for the first time on the front page of the *New York Times*. The *New Yorker* published a piece calling me the "Missal Merchant," alluding also to the publication of our first reprint, *Jet Propulsion*, when the news about the successful launching of the Sputnik by the Russians electrified the world. The story was on the ticker and was printed in newspapers all over the world. However, the publicity had adverse reaction in Switzerland where severely critical articles appeared in the press. There were demands for legislation, similar to Italian and French laws, prohibiting the export of nationally important art treasures. Two years later, when I wanted to visit the library at the monastery in Disentis, the door was slammed in my face when I mentioned my name. The great publicity alerted the librarians of many institutions to scrutinize their catalogues. The Missal was published without date, place, or printer, and therefore it was possible that other copies might have been misdescribed and escaped the attention of learned bibliographers. And, in fact, another complete copy was discovered on the shelves of the Zentralbibliothek in Zurich. There was no jubilation in

Switzerland, but national pride was restored. The "new" copy was transferred from the shelves where it had lain for hundreds of years to a bank vault. It is hard to believe that still another copy, the fourth, was found a few years later in the Stadt-Bibliothek in Augsburg.

What was the pinnacle of my bookselling career? What better encore, after buying and selling a *Constance Missal*, than buying a Gutenberg Bible, the king of all book rarities?

Gutenberg Bibles are a vanishing race, so far as the market goes. The great libraries of the world have them, in some instances even duplicate copies, but as a book for the private collector or dealer to acquire, the Gutenberg Bible has seen its day. Some 48 copies exist, as against four of the *Constance Missal,* two of Pfister's *Historia,* and less than ten of many Caxtons. But of this total, nearly all are owned institutionally and thus are "out of circulation." A hundred and fifty years ago, the situation was quite different. Fewer than 40 copies were known, about equally divided between private and public ownership. Gutenberg Bibles came up for auction regularly then; buying one was mostly a matter of having the money and the courage to plunge. Collectors would in fact debate the relative merits of their copies, one having handsomer rubrication, another being in a contemporary binding, yet another taller. Bernard Quaritch (1819–99), the German-English dealer, bought and sold about ten copies of this celebrated book—not different ones, of course, some being the same copies resold. Even in the 20th century, Rosenbach handled at various times four or five specimens. But circumstances then bear no relation to those of today. The highest cash price paid in America for a Gutenberg Bible before I bought mine was $106,000. I am sure that was a staggering sum at the time (1926) but it is about one-twentieth of the present value. The 1926 figure would buy only about 20 leaves today.

To buy a copy for stock, without immediate prospect of sale, was risky, considering monetary uncertainties and the threat of recession. No bookseller could tie up that much capital. Or so it was believed. The doubts persisted on that day in 1970, unforgettable for me, when the world learned of my acquisition of the Houghton copy.

Questions kept being put to me. For whom did you buy it? Nobody but myself. What dealer was your partner in the purchase? None. Who was your sponsor? What sort of backers do you have? None. None at all. I bought the book in exactly the same fashion as I buy others. I wrote out a check. This they found hard to believe. I confess the whole affair was hard for me to believe too. Nobody gambles like that with his own money. But I do not consider it a gamble. While the book is mine, I enjoy it. If and when I sell it, the price will be profitable. Meanwhile I've gained more publicity and stature by owning the book than any amount of cash could buy.

Naturally I always *wanted* to own a Gutenberg Bible, from the earliest days of my involvement with rare books. What bookman doesn't? In prestige, fame, beauty, and its role in typographical development, no book comes near it. For two centuries or more, historians of printing bestowed the ultimate honor on this work, calling it the first volume printed with movable type.

While this Bible was preceded by some printed ephemera (such as Indulgences) and perhaps even by some volumes (of which only fragments survive, except for the possibly earlier *Constance Missal*), it still may be called the first surviving printed book. It unquestionably was among the handsomest works ever produced, the editio princeps of the greatest book in the world, the Bible.

Gutenberg is almost positively established as the inventor of printing with movable types and the Bible is his tour de force. It is an amazing book, far more masterful than most works of other incunabula printers. Lines are even, pages well balanced, types a near-perfect imitation of 15th-century German bookhand, but with significant and very clever modifications from that used in the *Constance Missal*, in an effort to bring type closer together and render it more compact. The story is often told that Gutenberg, afraid of dislike for machine-made books, tried at first to sell his Bibles as manuscripts. To aid in the deception he left blank spaces for initial letters at chapter heads, to be filled in by rubricators. (Some copies bear elaborate floral décor in the margins in addition to handsome painted initials. My copy is fully and contemporarily rubricated.)

The "42-line Bible" is another name bestowed on this masterpiece as most pages contain that number of lines. Yet another is the "Mazarin Bible." It was in the library of the venerable French cardinal that a much-publicized copy came to light, 300 years ago. To this day, French scholars persist in calling it the Mazarin Bible.

As late as 1750, a London bookseller named Richardson proudly placed a copy in his catalogue at one pound sterling, which seems today as good a bargain—or maybe better—than Peter Minuit's purchase of Manhattan Island from the Algonquins for $24 worth of trinkets. By then, however, the book had achieved some notoriety. Every collector intent on building a fine library was trying to get one, especially in England. It may seem surprising, but it was the English who popularized the Gutenberg Bible and drove up its price in the salesrooms. They remained its champions all during the 19th century and into the 20th, when Americans came into the picture. It is significant to note that no auction sale of a Gutenberg Bible has occurred in continental Europe since 1858, nor has any continental European bookseller owned a copy in the 20th century except the Paris branch of Maggs Brothers, which bought the Czar's copy from Russia after the revolution and sold it to Martin Bodmer. The great incunabula specialists of the Bible's homeland, Germany, never had a complete one, and theirs is an illustrious list of names: the Rosenthals, Baer, Hiersemann.

After the Duke of Roxburghe sale in 1812, when incunabula suddenly came into vogue, the Gutenberg Bible was in heavy demand. The price rose to £500 in two decades. By the century's end it had risen tenfold to £5,000, the price listed in a catalogue by Quaritch. The first copy in America arrived in 1846, thanks to James Lenox who bought it for £500 in a London sale against Sir Thomas Phillipps.

After Lenox, a whole roster of Americans owned Gutenberg Bibles, in some cases more than one. A copy even ended up in the library of an Americana specialist who normally eschewed incunabula, George Brinley of Hartford, Connecticut. Pierpont Morgan owned two and a half, Robert Hoe had two (one of them on vellum), and various other collectors one each, including Carl H. Pforzeheimer, John H. Scheide, and Henry Huntington.

On Monday, February 2, 1970, out of the blue, Arthur A. Houghton called me at my office. He asked me to come for cocktails to his Sutton Place house. I had invited a few friends for dinner at the Opera Club that evening and I had to be on time because the opera started at 8 o'clock. I did not want to accept the invitation, but his Gutenberg Bible came to my mind. I knew Houghton and he wasn't the sort to invite anyone for smalltalk. I had a hunch he might be ready to sell, or at least to explore the possibility, so I accepted his invitation.

Arthur Houghton, president of Steuben Glass, had started young as a book collector. I met him first in 1940, when he was curator of rare books at the Library of Congress. He is one of America's great collectors and his library consists of rare and beautiful books and manuscripts that struck his fancy: composers' manuscripts and English literature, French 18th-century drawings and also the most famous Persian manuscript, the Book of Kings with 258 marvelous paintings, seven of which brought £785,000 at Christie's in November 1976. Houghton very generously presented 75 of these paintings to the Metropolitan Museum.

After hanging up the phone, I decided to do some homework on Houghton's Gutenberg Bible, just in case. It was the Shuckburgh copy, described at length in Don Cleveland Norman's *Pictorial Census of the Gu-*

tenberg Bible, Chicago, 1961. Up to 1950 the Shuckburgh copy was unknown to bibliographers (except for T. F. Dibdin's *Library Companion*, Vol. II, p. 13, note) and its discovery and subsequent sale by Quaritch and John Carter of Scribner's was the subject of an essay full of drama: "Operation Shuckburgh" by John Carter published in his *Books and Book Collectors*. The copy had been acquired in the 18th century by Sir George Shuckburgh.

If Houghton wanted to sell, what would be his price? Would he allow me to buy just the Bible, or tie it in with the sale of other books?

Houghton came right to the point. After exchanging amenities, during which he probably sensed that I knew what was coming, he announced:

"I want to sell the Bible."

He said it as matter-of-factly as if the item had been an old lawnmower. Those words danced in my ears. "I want to sell the Bible." It was sweet music. Though hard negotiations might follow, I knew the book was mine.

The decision, he explained, had not been reached overnight. Houghton had owned a Gutenberg Bible, first the very incomplete duplicate of the Stadtbibliothek Trier bought at Sotheby's in 1937 and then this one, for more than 30 years. His fascination with the book had not diminished in all that time, but his insurance company insisted he keep it in the bank and he did not want a book he could not keep at home. The urge to sell comes to many collectors, especially in a bull market. In 1970 the bulls definitely had the best of the antiquarian book trade.

I was not Houghton's first choice as a buyer. He had tried at first to sell to the University of Texas. It was a logical target. The University of Texas at Austin spent heavily on rare books, but did not have a Gutenberg Bible. Houghton offered his at $2,000,000, not an impossible price for the University's oil-rich benefactors. But the trustees paused to consider, took an option, and eventually let the option expire. Houghton was now free to deal elsewhere, and instead of trying to play dealer again he was turning to me.

I immediately made a substantial offer.

This took him by surprise. He expected me to go over the book with a magnifying glass for several hours before talking price. But I already knew as much about its condition as I could learn from examination.

"How will you pay?" he asked.

"Cash."

This, too, proved a surprise. Not every bookseller is in a position to write out a seven-figure check.

After minor bargaining we reached a firm price. This was later reported in the press as "between one and two million dollars." I agreed with Houghton not to reveal the exact sum.

In about five minutes the whole thing was over, with so quiet a conversation that nobody could have guessed what was going on.

In a hurry to reach the Metropolitan Opera Club in time for a 6:30 dinner, I rose to leave. Then I said as a parting shot, "That is the highest price ever paid for a book and the biggest profit ever made on one." Houghton had, we both knew, made a much better profit on the Bible than I could ever hope to make.

At the Opera Club we had as guests my daughter Mary Ann and her husband, as well as William H. Scheide (see Chapter 42) and his librarian, Mina Bryan. I was not yet free to disclose the news, or even to mention the book by name until full payment had been made. This was arranged for April, but I knew I would burst long before then if not permitted at least to drop some hints. In the midst of the dinner I seized a quiet moment and announced: "I have just bought the greatest book in the world."

Scheide, who also owns a Gutenberg Bible, knew instantly what I was talking about. "That must be a Gutenberg Bible," he exclaimed. "From whom? I still have mine. Was it Bodmer's or Pforzheimer's?"

I maintained a stony expression. "No further information. That was agreed with the seller."

Scheide did his own guessing and settled on Pforzheimer. It just seemed, to him, the least illogical of the two possibilities.

The dinner was, from that moment on, electrically charged. Hanni and Mary Ann, who knew from whom the purchase had been made, knew only that; I had not had a chance to mention the price even to them.

In a euphoric state we carried on business for two months. Then, on a notable day in April, we met in the vaults of the Manufacturers Hanover Trust Co. on Fifth Avenue and 57th Street, where the Bible was kept. In addition to me, the party consisted of Kebabian, Mary Ann, Houghton, and his secretary Sally Walker. I presented Houghton with a certified check and the Bible was mine. The date on the calendar did not disturb me at all; it was April Fool's Day. (See Fig. 11).

Back at the shop I phoned Sanka Knox of the *New York Times*. She came to get an interview and pictures, and next day I was on the front page of the country's most prestigious newspaper. The wire services picked up the story and it appeared in the international press. The following day I was horseback riding with William Randolph Hearst, Jr. "That was the best piece of merchandising I ever saw," he commented.

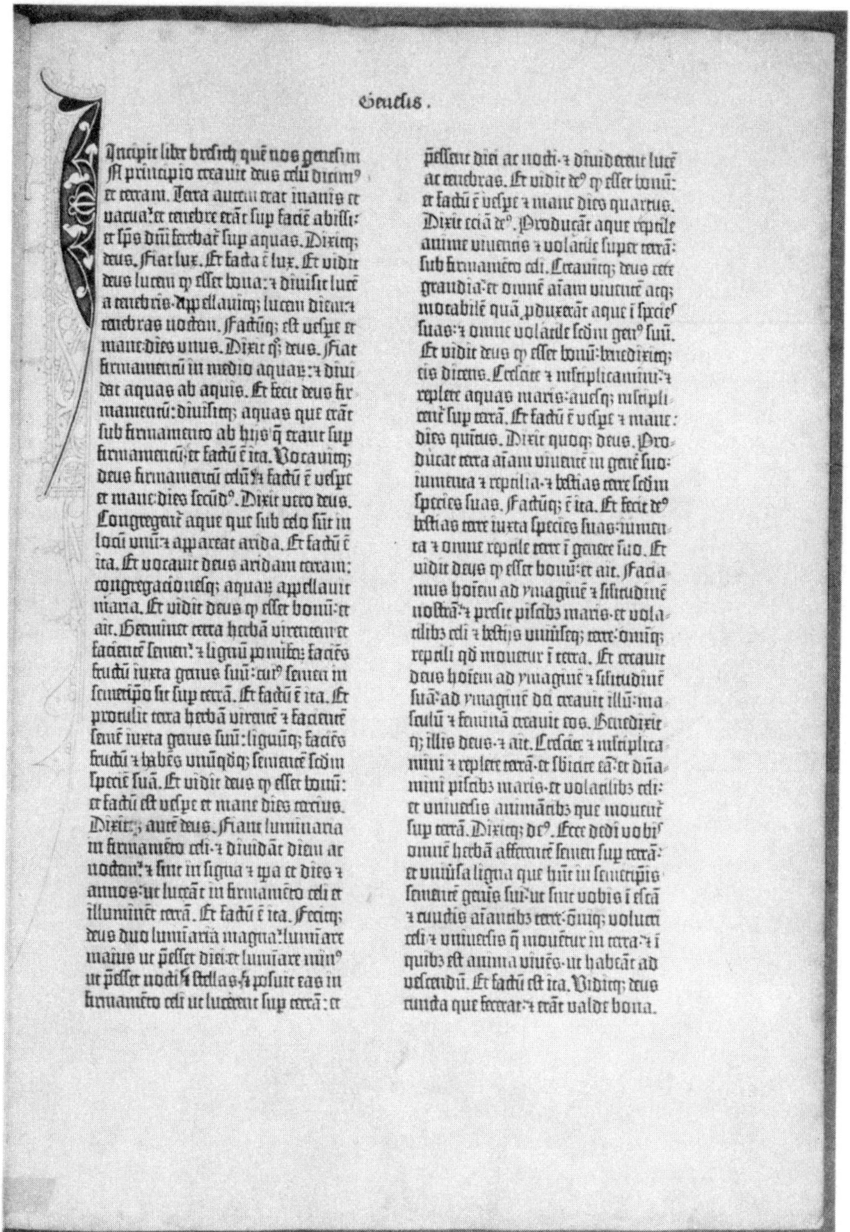

Genesis.

Incipit liber bresith quē nos genesim
In principio creauit deus celū dicimꝰ
et terram. Terra autem erat inanis et
vacua: et tenebre erāt sup faciē abissi:
et sp̄s dn̄i ferebat̃ sup aquas. Dixitq;
deus. Fiat lux. Et facta ē lux. Et vidit
deus lucem q̄ esset bona: ⁊ diuisit lucē
a tenebris. appellauitq; lucem diem: ⁊
tenebras noctem. Factūq; est vespe et
mane dies vnus. Dixit q̄q; deus. Fiat
firmamentū in medio aquaꝝ: ⁊ diui
dat aquas ab aquis. Et fecit deus fir
mamentū: diuisitq; aquas que erāt
sub firmamento ab hiis q̄ erant sup
firmamentū: et factū ē ita. Vocauitq;
deus firmamentū celū: ⁊ factū ē vespe
et mane dies secūdꝰ. Dixit vero deus.
Congregent̃ aque que sub celo sūt in
locū vnū: ⁊ appareat arida. Et factū ē
ita. Et vocauit deus aridam terram:
congregacionesq; aquaꝝ appellauit
maria. Et vidit deus q̄ esset bonū: et
ait. Germinet terra herbā virentem et
facientē semen: ⁊ lignū pomiferū faciēs
fructū iuxta genus suū: cuiꝰ semen in
semetipo sit sup terrā. Et factū ē ita. Et
protulit terra herbā virentē ⁊ facientē
semē iuxta genus suū: lignūq; faciēs
fructū ⁊ habēs vnūqdq; sementē scd̄m
speciē suā. Et vidit deus q̄ esset bonū:
et factū est vespe et mane dies tercius.
Dixitq; autē deus. Fiant luminaria
in firmamēto celi: ⁊ diuidāt diem ac
noctem: ⁊ sint in signa ⁊ tp̄a et dies ⁊
annos: ut luceāt in firmamēto celi et
illuminēt terrā. Et factū ē ita. Fecitq;
deus duo lumīaria magna: lumīare
maius ut p̄esset diei: et lumīare minꝰ
ut p̄esset nocti: ⁊ stellas. ⁊ posuit eas in
firmamēto celi ut lucerent sup terrā: et
p̄essent diei ac nocti: ⁊ diuiderent lucē
ac tenebras. Et vidit deꝰ q̄ esset bonū:
et factū ē vespe ⁊ mane dies quartus.
Dixit etiā deꝰ. Producāt aque reptile
anime viuentis ⁊ volatile super terrā:
sub firmamēto celi. Creauitq; deus cete
grandia: et omnē aīam viuentē atq;
motabilē quā p̄duxerāt aque ī species
suas: ⁊ omne volatile scd̄m genꝰ suū.
Et vidit deus q̄ esset bonū: benedixitq;
eis dicens. Crescite ⁊ multiplicamini: ⁊
replete aquas maris: avesq; multipli
centur sup terrā. Et factū ē vespe ⁊ mane:
dies quintus. Dixit quoq; deus. Pro
ducat terra aīam viuentē in genē suo:
iumenta ⁊ reptilia: ⁊ bestias terre scd̄m
species suas. Factūq; ē ita. Et fecit deꝰ
bestias terre iuxta species suas: iumen
ta ⁊ omne reptile terre ī genere suo. Et
vidit deus q̄ esset bonū: et ait. Facia
mus hoīem ad ymaginē ⁊ silitudinē
nostrā: ⁊ presit piscibꝫ maris: et vola
tilibꝫ celi ⁊ bestiis vniuersq; terre: omniq;
reptili qd̄ mouetur ī terra. Et creauit
deus hoīem ad ymaginē ⁊ silitudinē
suā: ad ymaginē dei creauit illū: ma
sculū ⁊ feminā creauit eos. Benedixit
q; illis deus: ⁊ ait. Crescite ⁊ multiplica
mini ⁊ replete terrā: et subicite eā: et dn̄a
mini piscibꝫ maris: et volatilibꝫ celi:
et vniuersis animātibꝫ que mouent̃
sup terrā. Dixitq; deꝰ. Ecce dedi vobis
omnē herbā afferentē semen sup terrā:
et vniūsa ligna que hūt in semetipis
sementē generis sui: ut sint vobis ī escā
⁊ cunctis aīantibꝫ terre: omniq; volucri
celi ⁊ vniuersis q̄ mouentur in terra: ⁊ ī
quibꝫ est anima viuēs: ut habeāt ad
vescendū. Et factū est ita. Viditq; deus
cuncta que fecerat: ⁊ erāt valde bona.

Fig. 11. A page of the Gutenberg Bible.

"That amount of publicity is worth more than the cost of the book." However, I am sure that without the mention of a huge sum of money, the transaction would not have generated such public interest. It was the money, and not the fact that a Gutenberg Bible had changed hands, which fascinated people. I told Sanka Knox that I would sell the book for two and a half million. All the other papers picked this up and made a grandstand play of it. It was not just talk. After we had catalogued the Bible, I did indeed place a price of $2,500,000 on it. (Usually, the stellar items in my catalogues are listed with the note "Price upon request," but, to avoid a steady stream of calls from people curious to know what a Gutenberg Bible sells for, I authorized Kebabian to print the price.)

After the initial excitement died down, reality began to settle in, and I must admit it was rather scary. It was not just a matter of this book; it and other purchases had cost some five million dollars in the space of a year, with very little sold and no immediate prospects of sales.

Then, in the midst of gloom, a savior (or one we took to be such) appeared. Lew David Feldman, a New York antiquarian bookseller (whose firm "House of El Dieff" is a play on his initials), came and bought the Bible. He gave me a 10 per cent deposit, the balance to be paid within one year. Until then the Bible was to stay with me. After a year he failed to make any further payments and forfeited his deposit.

I bought the Houghton copy in April 1970 and in December a bomb exploded nearly shattering my hope that no other copy would be discovered. I learned from Dr. Bühler of the Morgan Library that venerable Eton College in England had published an exhibition catalogue which recorded a "newly discovered Gutenberg Bible at Blandings Castle." I wrote to Patrick Strong, Keeper of the College Library, asking for a description of the Bible and the location of Blandings Castle. I could not find it on any map and even the British Information Service could not help. On January 8, 1971, I received from Patrick Strong the following answer:

> I'm afraid the Blandings Castle Gutenberg is a ghost: it was brought into *Something Fresh*, one of the early novels of P.G. Wodehouse. Sir Robert Birley could not resist putting it into *One Hundred Books* (in the Eton College Library). The T.L.S. alluded to it in the *Commentary* after we reopened in the fall of 1969; whereupon Mr. Goff of the Library of Congress asked similarly for details . . .
>
> So the canon of known copies hasn't had an addition that would startle us all . . .

So that was the end of the Blandings Castle ghost. I had one less worry— one less possible competitor. At that time I had no idea that in

1978, two more copies of the Bible were going to be offered for sale in New York.

In March 1978, when my memoirs were already in page proofs, I had to ask for the indulgence of my publisher in order to add the happy ending to "Operation Shuckburgh."

In January 1978, when it became public knowledge (*New York Times*, January 15, 1978) that in addition to our copy, two more Bibles were being offered for sale in New York, the interest in the Gutenberg Bible suddenly sparked. I was asked by the German Television Network for an interview and to comment, primarily on our own copy. After this appearance I received a telephone call from Dr. Hans Halbey, the Director of the Gutenberg Museum in Mainz, and in mid-February two gentlemen, Dr. Anton Keim, Mayor for Cultural and Educational Affairs, and Dr. Halbey came to New York on short notice (while Hanni and I were enjoying a vacation in Nassau) to look at the three copies of the Bible. Upon our return to New York I was told of the forthcoming auction at Christie's of the copy belonging to the General Theological Seminary. The next day, Dr. Keim informed me by telephone from Germany that they had decided to buy our copy. Official release of this news was to take place simultaneously with the payment, no later than March 10.

It is especially gratifying to us that our copy goes home, not only to the country but also to the city of its birth.

In April 1962, I attended the sale of a portion of the famous Shuckburgh Library at Christie's in London. Following soon after the Perrins sales, it provided a richness of printed books almost comparable to the Perrins richness of manuscripts, and some exquisite manuscripts as well. My purchases included Caxton's *Christine de Pisan* of 1489, Wynkyn de Worde's *St. Albans Chronicle* of 1497 (not the first edition from the "Schoolmaster Press," but a valuable item nonetheless), the 1460 Balbus *Catholicon* believed to have been printed by Gutenberg, Cicero's *De Officiis* of 1465–66, also a Mainz imprint, and fine illuminated Renaissance manuscripts of Vergil and Caesar.

After the sale I went to Chelsea to call on my friend John Hayward in his Cheney Walk apartment. I admired this great bookman. Hayward, then editor of *The Book Collector*, as well as of Donne and Swift, had a well-deserved reputation for always knowing the latest news and gossip of the book world and loved to talk about books at any hour. His catalogue of English poetry is a landmark. Despite a severe handicap—he was partly paralyzed and confined to a wheelchair—his activity and accomplishments were most remarkable. For many years he was sustained by the devoted companionship of T. S. Eliot, with whom he shared quarters in London.

The then current issue of *The Book Collector*—Spring, 1962—mentioned a long-forgotten copy of the very rare 36-line Bible (rarer than the 42-line) which was still part of the Shuckburgh Library. Only about a dozen complete or nearly complete copies are known, none of them in America. A rare book indeed, considering the 48 copies of the 42-line Bible. The printing was until recently ascribed to Gutenberg, but later research points to Albrecht Pfister of Bamberg as the printer. Since it was not included in the auction, I wondered if there might be a chance of buying it by private sale.

Hayward gave me the lead I needed: he told me that Major Nigel Martin, present owner of the Shuckburgh Library, was currently in London, and he told me how he could be reached. A meeting was arranged for the following day at the Scottish National Bank, Trafalgar Square. I was to be there at two o'clock sharp, as Martin had a crowded schedule and had to catch a four o'clock train. No mention was made of my interest in buying the book. As a student of early printing, I merely expressed a wish to examine it.

I had called for a cab at the Ritz at 1:45, when a sudden cloudburst snarled traffic. At least twenty others, huddled at the hotel's entrance for shelter, also wanted cabs. After half an hour I became frantic; to keep the Major waiting, after explicit instructions to be on time, was unforgivable. To walk the distance would make me much later. Determined not to miss the appointment, I climbed into the back of a chauffeur-driven Rolls-Royce. The car was empty but for the driver, and I tried to look as if I had been expecting its arrival.

The liveried chauffeur, a man of great dignity, obviously accustomed to transporting noble personages, reacted with shock.

"Sir," he shouted, "would you remove yourself? This is a private car." I was ready for this. "Please forgive me," I said, slipping a five-pound note into his hand. "This is an emergency. Please be so kind as to take me quickly to Trafalgar Square."

The chauffeur recovered his composure, reacted like a gentleman, and within a few minutes we arrived at the Bank.

Major Martin accepted my apologies graciously. Fortunately there was still time to examine and collate the precious book. No matter how many valuable books one handles, to touch such a volume is always an emotional experience: one of the earliest of printed books, a superb example of typography, and an integral link in the story of Gutenberg. Although it was quite incomplete, I very much wanted to own it; the possibility of any other copy reaching the market seemed unlikely. Major Martin expressed no wish to sell, or even a hint in that direction, so I held my tongue. Before I left, he invited me to visit his home at Dorchester next fall and see his other books.

Would he then talk of selling?

There was always hope.

That year proved to be a good one. With substantial sales to Dr. Ludwig and—the day before our departure for England—the sale to Bodmer of a magnificent and expensive French 15th-century manuscript, the *Histoire de Thèbes,* with miniatures by the Wavrin master, I had the cash necessary for a large transaction. Since I was still suffering from colitis, Mary Ann accompanied me. In the plane we amused ourselves by totaling up the sums of recent sales and converting them into various currencies. In Italian lire, where they amounted to multimillions, they made us feel rich indeed.

I knew nothing of Dorchester except that Thomas Hardy had lived there. Rather than a guide book, I read Hardy's *The Mayor of Casterbridge* on the train from London. It had not changed much in the half century since his time; it was a peaceful little town of dairy farmers and Roman ruins, with all the appearance of an old aquatint come to life. The Martins gave us a pleasant dinner party with a number of their neighbors. I mentioned Hardy, thinking he was remembered among the residents, but nobody seemed to know whom I was talking about. Such is fame. Later, when we toured the town, we asked several people for directions to Hardy's home, but nobody had the least notion where it could be found.

My regrets at finding that Hardy's memory had not been perpetuated were more than surpassed by the discovery that Major Martin entertained not even the slightest thought of selling his 36-line Bible. It was not for sale, and that was final. Final for the time, that is. Circumstances and minds can change. Each year I send a Christmas card to Major Martin, hoping to remind him casually of my interest.

CHAPTER 34

The First Printer of England

CAXTONS ARE NO LESS ARISTOCRATS of the book world than products of the early Mainz press; they hold a venerated position among rare books because they are in English and mostly on secular subjects. Within recent years the number of them in circulation has steadily declined, to the point where it is now an event of some rarity for one to be sold, regardless of the work or its physical condition, and even this generally happens only when an institutional library chooses to release a duplicate. Nevertheless my stock of Caxtons has been increasing.

Caxtons in possession of private collectors are few, comparatively speaking, in contrast to 100, 50, or even 25 years ago. At the turn of this century and up into the twenties, most good English libraries put up at auction could be depended upon to contain at least one Caxton, often more. They had been assembled from the middle years of the 19th century onward, when Quaritch and other English dealers listed page after page of English incunabula in their catalogues. The Earl of Spencer, part of whose library is now in the John Rylands Library of Manchester, owned more than 60 Caxtons. In the early 1800s this was believed to be a more or less complete collection. We now know that Caxton printed some 100 works, but a third of them exist in only one or two copies, or fragments, or are known only by references to them.

Caxtons were never plentiful—not even in Caxton's own time, since he issued what amounted to limited editions for a small readership—but a collector like Morgan or Huntington could, 50 or 100 years ago, gather a shelf of them. But as years passed, the collections of these men were given to institutions or became institutions themselves, rather than returning to the marketplace.

Caxton's books would merit attention simply as productions of the first English printing press. But they have, in addition to typographical interest, a very legitimate literary and social interest as well. Caxton changed the whole culture of the English nation; he introduced the reading public to his own translations of Latin classics and French romances. Soon other printers issued translations, and then not only the university student versed in Latin, but the English public—anyone able to read and buy books—could enjoy Cato, Livy, Martial, and the rest. Caxton brought Aesop to the English people, and was the first publisher of Chaucer and Gower.

Much of what Caxton printed was popular literature, books to be read for entertainment or enlightenment, or to be enjoyed for their pictures. About a quarter of Caxton's books were illustrated by woodcuts. The dull lawbooks of other publishers, the endless religious and philosophical treatises, the cheap imitations of foreign books—these came infrequently from Caxton's press.

A surge of interest in Caxtons during the 18th century undoubtedly resulted in the preservation of many copies that would otherwise not exist today. At the same time it subjected them to the bibliophilic caprices of the day. One rarely sees a Caxton in original or contemporary binding, because 18th-century collectors disliked their appearance. Many were trimmed down, and some were even "shaved" (trimmed into the print).

Most Caxtons, like all English incunabula, are in bad condition. They lack text leaves, sometimes just a few, often as many as several dozen, sometimes even half the book. Of a number of Caxtons no complete copy exists. In a Caxton of 300 leaves or more, the lack of only three or four is looked upon as remarkably good condition. Why English incunabula fared a worse fate than other early books is not entirely clear. One theory is that a paper shortage in late 15th- and early 16th-century Britain led to the use of book leaves for wrapping paper and similar purposes. Another theory has the Englishman of late mediaeval time reading his books to pieces. Wherever the blame is placed, it ought not to be with the bindings. These were sturdily bound books. Caxton maintained his own bindery and the surviving examples of work from it are in no way inferior to continental bindings.

Efforts have been made to assemble Caxtons from leaves of defective copies. A leaf from a shorter copy is easily noticed; an added leaf from a taller copy may go undetected unless the book is carefully examined.

Though I never made a specialty of English books, I have bought and sold more Caxtons than any other living bookseller. I broke price records for Caxtons, paying six-figure sums for books that sold for a tenth as much when I first started in business. But Caxtons, of all the world's book rarities, still seem underpriced. The big Caxtons—the Chaucers, the Le Fèvre, *Recuyell of the Historyes of Troye* (both French and English editions), and *The Historye of Reynart the Foxe* deserve to compare in value with the Gutenberg Bible, and I think eventually they will. They are no less rare, and certainly no less appealing to collectors.

I have owned three different copies of the first edition of Chaucer's *Canterbury Tales* (Caxton, 1478). It is a feat not likely to be matched again. Of all Caxtons, this is the public favorite. Others are rarer, some handsomer, but the first edition of the *Canterbury Tales*, a book so many have read, does not require a collector to appreciate it. Here is the old orthography of Chaucer, with which we all grappled in college and most of us cursed, printed when the language was almost current; Caxton was born only 22 years after Chaucer's death. (See Fig. 12.)

My first Caxton *Canterbury Tales* was acquired in trade with the Morgan Library. (See Chapters 24 and 33.)

My second copy of the first edition came as a consequence of selling the first. When Indiana University acquired the Poole collection, a number of its choicer rarities duplicated items in the Lilly collection, presented to it a few years earlier (the kind of double blessing received by few institutional libraries). Not wishing to be accused of bibliophilic greed, the University chose to sell some of the duplicates. This noteworthy sale, at Parke-Bernet, drew world attention and very strong bidding. Among the items was Lilly's first Caxton edition of the *Canterbury Tales*, which I acquired. Mellon, the great collector of Caxtons, bought it from me, and gave me in exchange (as partial payment) his less complete copy of the same book, formerly the Rabinowitz copy. Thus I acquired my third, which I sold to St. Vincent College of Latrobe, Pennsylvania. I played round-robin with Caxton, but a better playmate could never be found.

In 1960 I purchased a unique copy of Caxton's *Vocabulary* (from the Ripon Cathedral Library) at Sotheby's for £23,000 (more than $60,000 at the then rate of exchange, but far less than the present value). An export license would be hard to get. I had a potential customer in the Cambridge University Library, but like most institutional libraries everywhere, it wanted more books than it could afford. Its librarian, my friend Richard Creswick, bemoaned the lack of funds. But if Cambridge was cash-poor it was certainly not book-poor; its shelves abounded in the kind of duplicates any bookseller longs for. So we worked out a trade. Creswick exchanged the library's duplicate for another Caxton, Le Fèvre's *Historyes of Troye*, printed in Bruges, the book that began Cax-

❡ The Frankeleyns tale

Thou art a squyer and he is a knyght
But god forbede for hys blysful myght
But a clerk coude do as gentyl a dede
As wel as ony of you it is no drede
Syre I releße the thy thousand pound
As now thou were cropen out of the ground
Ne neuer or now ne haddist knowen me
For sire I wol not take a peny of the
For al my craft ne for al my trauaylle
Thou hast wel payd for my vytaylle
It is ynow farwel and haue good day
And tok hys hors & forth he goth hys way
Lordynges thys question than axe I yow
Whyche was the most fre as thynkyth yow
Now telyth me er that ye further wende
I can n more my tale is at an ende

❡ Here endyth the frankeleyns tale
And folowyth the prologe of the wif of Bathe

Fig. 12. Chaucer, The Canterbury Tales (Caxton, c. 1484). First illustrated edition – (Schäfer Collection, Schweinfurt.)

ton's career as a printer, for the *Vocabulary*. We were both satisfied, and Cambridge got a dividend: I financed the facsimile edition of the *Vocabulary*.

A number of other Caxtons have passed through my hands, several of which also came as the result of trading. Two more were acquired as Morgan Library duplicates in 1969. Once the Morgan Library decided to dispose of duplicates, it sometimes used them instead of cash when making large purchases. This was most agreeable to me. When I sold the Michelino da Besozzo manuscript to the Morgan Library (see Chapter 37), I received in exchange three English incunabula, the English and the French editions of Caxton's *Historyes of Troye*, and the Pynson *Canterbury Tales*. To get three such volumes in a single transaction was extraordinary, especially ones which had not been sold in 60 or 70 years. The *Historyes of Troye* (see Fig. 13) was the work translated by Caxton for Margaret, Duchess of Burgundy, when he was in her employ at the Flemish court. He was then past 50 and had no intention of becoming a printer; he had made money in the fabrics trade and was now living comfortably ("with no grete charge of busyness," as he put it). He went to Cologne to learn printing, to render the translation more enduring, and this adventure changed not only his life but also the course of learning in Britain. The Morgan duplicates were of the first printing of the English version, undated, about 1473-74, and the French version, 1476, both issued at Bruges. Incidentally the latter was the first original work in French to appear in print.

Only 16 copies are known of the English edition, of which just three are complete. Like most Caxtons this copy carries a distinguished provenance. Before coming to Morgan, it belonged to the great English collector Richard Bennett, whose library Morgan bought en bloc. Bennett had gotten it from the Earl of Ashburnham, and it had earlier belonged to George Hibbert, an important collector of the late 18th and early 19th centuries. But my French edition boasts an even more impressive record of ownership. It too went from Ashburnham to Bennett to Morgan, but earlier was passed from the Duke of Roxburghe to the Earl Spencer. As no bibliophile needs to be told, Spencer amassed the most renowned library of his day, if not of all times. This book is considerably scarcer, with only seven copies known.

I had the pleasure of owning, briefly, a Caxton in the original binding from his own bindery. The book was Gower's *Confessio amantis*, a very influential work in its day. I bought it from James F. Bell of Minneapolis and sold it to Mr. James G. Hanes of Winston-Salem, North Carolina. It became the millionth volume in the University of North Carolina library at Chapel Hill, owners of one of the largest collections of incunabula

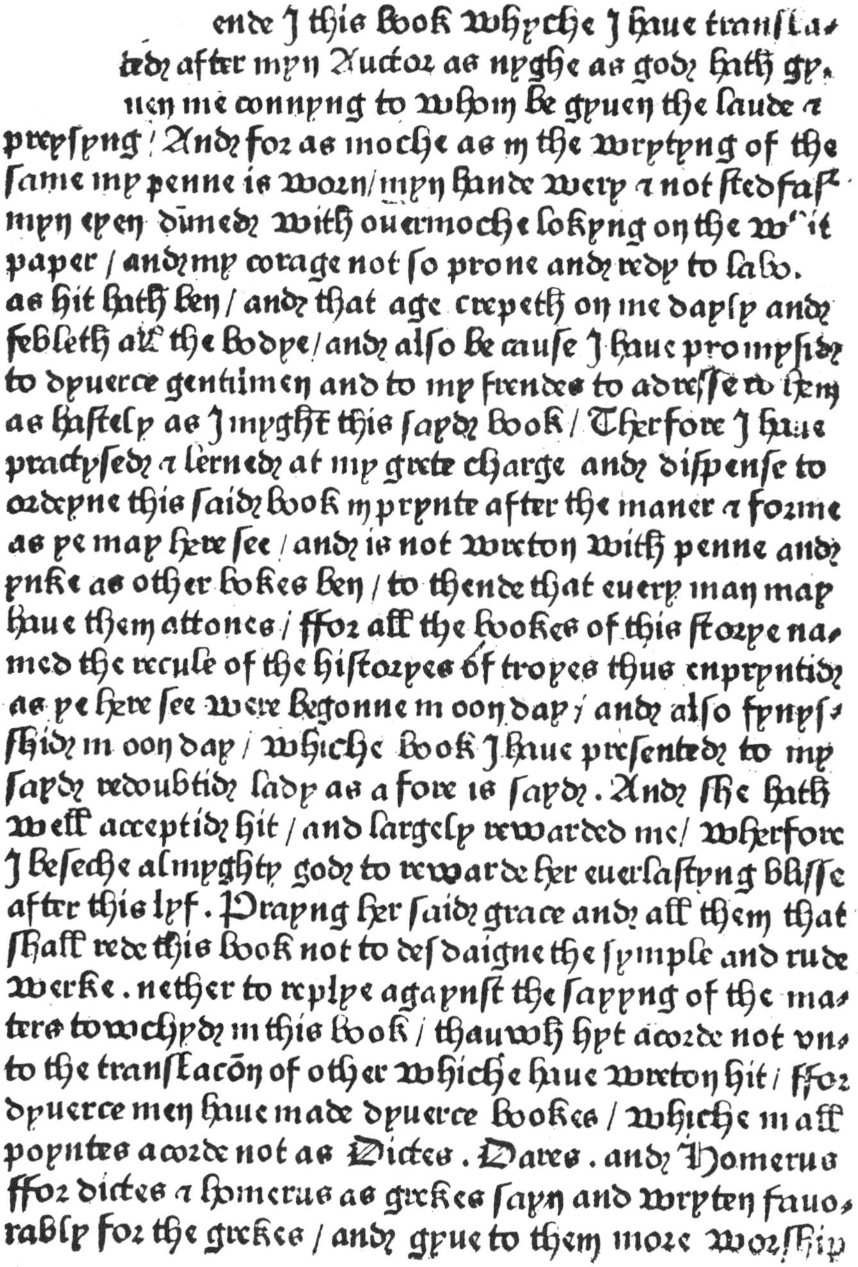

ende I this book whyche I haue translated after myn Auctor as nyghe as god hath gyuen me connyng to whom be gyuen the laude and
preysyng. And for as moche as in the wrytyng of the
same my penne is worn / myn hande wery and not stedfast
myn eyen dimed with ouermoche lokyng on the whit
paper / and my corage not so prone and redy to labo-
as hit hath ben / and that age crepeth on me daily and
febleth all the bodye / and also be cause I haue promysed
to dyuerce gentilmen and to my frendes to adresse to them
as hastely as I myght this sayd book / Therfore I haue
practysed and lerned at my grete charge and dispense to
ordeyne this saide book in prynte after the maner and forme
as ye may here see / and is not wreton with penne and
ynke as other bokes ben / to thende that euery man may
haue them attones / ffor all the bookes of this storye named the recule of the historyes of troyes thus enprynted
as ye here see were begonne in oon day / and also fyny-
shid in oon day / whiche book I haue presented to my
sayd redoubtid lady as afore is sayd. And she hath
well acceptid hit / and largely rewarded me / wherfore
I beseche almyghty god to rewarde her euerlastyng blysse
after this lyf. Prayng her saide grace and all them that
shall rede this book not to desdaigne the symple and rude
werke. nether to replye agaynst the sayyng of the ma-
ters towchyd in this book / thauwgh hyt acorde not vn-
to the translacōn of other whiche haue wreton hit / ffor
dyuerce men haue made dyuerce bookes / whiche in all
poyntes acorde not as Dictes. Dares. and Homerus
ffor dictes and homerus as grekes sayn and wryten fauo-
rably for the grekes / and gyue to them more worship

Fig. 13. Caxton's *Historyes of Troye*, Bruges, c. 1473-1474.
Caxton explains the beginnings of printing in the English language.

among American colleges (about 800 titles). There is no Caxton in England in its original Caxton binding in such superior condition.

Another Caxton we handled was a copy of the second edition of the *Canterbury Tales*, bought at Sotheby's for £30,000. This is one book nobody minds having in the second edition. It was the first Chaucer with woodcuts, since Caxton did not illustrate the first edition. These cuts, so charmingly crude, with cockeyed knaves and misshapen horses, served as models for the next three generations of Chaucer illustrators and still live today, through reproductions on playing cards, ceramic tiles, greeting cards, bookmarks, and wallpaper. Without question this is the principal work among illustrated English incunabula. I sold it to my best customer for this kind of material, Otto Schäfer.

On my shelves at the time this is written is a complete copy of one of Caxton's popular favorites, *The Historye of Reynart the Foxe*. Issued on June 6, 1481, it was the first English edition of this folk classic. Another complete Caxton in my possession is the 1489 *Book of Fayttes of Armes* of Christine de Pisane, translated by Caxton from the French. This copy is a particularly interesting one. A manuscript note by Francis Darwin, who owned it late in the 19th century, states that the book was "found at the bottom of an old hamper [at] Elston." What could tantalize a bookman more than the prospect of a Caxton lurking in the bottom of a basket? His family was a branch of the family of Charles Darwin, though the great naturalist never owned the book or even knew of its existence.

If anybody doubts that Caxtons are leaving the marketplace, the year 1976 is proof. In the year of Caxton's 500th anniversary, with the world so attentive to Caxton, with his portrait on postage stamps, no significant showing of Caxtons could be mustered for sale. I had by far the largest number on my shelves, and issued a special catalogue, though it "only" contained 6 items.

Fig. 14. Printer's device of Caxton.

CHAPTER 35

Window-Shopping in Florence

FLORENCE, THAT CITY OF DELIGHTS since the Middle Ages, was the scene of some of our more unusual purchases. In October 1966, Hanni and I spent an autumn vacation there, not to buy anything but simply to enjoy ourselves. We strolled the streets, which looked better in the clear autumn air than in summer's heat, ate, gazed up at the cathedral bell tower, and behaved generally like the tourists we were. Of course we chose the streets inhabited by most of the antique dealers and booksellers; their shops provide a ceaseless fascination for anybody in love with history and art. I will always be convinced that antiques, books, furniture, or anything old have greater appeal in a shop which is also old and on an ancient street.

My interest in early globes was strong at this time, because I had recently sold two collections of them to Shozen Nakayama, Shimbashira of Tenrikyo University in Japan. In England one often encounters English globes of the late 18th and 19th centuries, the Cary models and various library globes of domestic make. French antique shops generally can supply French globes usually not of any great age. But globes of the Italian Renaissance and Baroque eras, in good condition, are not so easily located, even in their country of origin. So it was with great interest that I noticed an early 17th-century specimen in a shop window in the Via dei Fossi.

Inspecting it, I discovered to my great surprise that its gores were hand-drawn and painted rather than printed. A relatively small globe about 25 cm high in its stand, it bore no name or date. At a reasonable price it would surely be a good buy.

"Sorry," the shopkeeper told me. "This is not for sale."

I was disappointed and at the same time angry, expecting that this might be some kind of game to test my degree of interest. "Why then do you display it," I fumed, "if you don't want to sell it?"

"Very simple. It attracts customers. Once they get in the shop, they usually buy something else."

It was useless to try to change his mind; if we appeared too anxious it would only have led to a fantastically high price.

"We're not apt to find another globe of comparable quality in Florence," I remarked to Hanni as we resumed our stroll. But within a few minutes we passed a chandelier shop that displayed a huge terrestrial globe, apparently just as early. This time we held our emotions in check. It's probably not for sale either, we agreed, or else it's a modern replica, the kind of work in which Italian craftsmen excel. Rather than make fools of ourselves we continued walking. A hundred yards further on, we looked at each other, decided we had nothing to lose by making a closer inspection and talking with the shop's owner, and returned.

After being assured that this globe was indeed for sale, I made a close examination of it. It was the largest early printed globe ever made, created by Coronelli, the great cartographer of baroque Venice, and it bore the date 1688. Not only was its condition better than could be expected, but it still retained, or so it seemed, the original mahogany stand on which Coronelli had placed it nearly 300 years earlier. I could not be sure of its authenticity, but had a certain feeling it might be an original and not just a replica.

"How is it," I asked the owner, "that a globe is for sale in a chandelier shop?"

It was evident that such items were not his usual stock in trade. He had acquired it from a client, he explained, who could not pay his bill and gave him the globe in settlement.

"It would be immensely valuable," he added, "if it were not a modern reproduction."

But it is *not* a reproduction, I almost said, then caught myself. This was the moment to talk about the price.

Fifteen hundred dollars was the sum he quoted, a ridiculously small amount. About ten years earlier I had bought a pair of Coronelli globes, terrestrial and celestial, from Hoepli of Milan for about $20,000, but the export license was not granted, and this one was every bit their equal, if not superior. But experience forbids one to accept the first price asked; the seller may think he has asked too little, and may find some excuse to raise the price or to declare that the item cannot be sold just now.

"Well, that's rather a stiff price for a replica," I replied, "and the cost of shipping it to the States will be enormous. Can you give me a discount?"

After some mild protests he accepted a price of $1,000 and I wrote a check. In the bill of lading he described the globe as a reproduction, which got it through customs without an export license. It was one of the most satisfying transactions I ever made. The most thorough examination, conducted after the globe's arrival in New York, confirmed my hopes that it was genuine and original in all respects and worth a substantial amount of money. Undoubtedly it was one of the finest surviving ones of this particular globe, perhaps even the bet. (See Plate 16b.)

We also visited a statuary shop on the Lungarno, where Hanni had spotted and fallen in love with a four-foot-tall bronze donkey. She thought it would fit well in our garden in Ridgefield; I had to agree, and to admit it was eye-catching. The artist had signed it on the base. It meant nothing to us at the time, but we made inquiries and discovered that the artist, Sirio Tofanari, born 1886, was not only still alive but residing nearby. The octogenarian sculptor received us cordially, showed us some of his works, and we gladly bought them. He claimed these to be the only ones left after a lifetime of sculpting animals. Next day I arranged for the shipping; the sculptures and the globe filled four large crates, on which we were promised speedy delivery.

Our stay in Florence ended on another high note, this time a bookish one. Prince Paul of Yugoslavia and Princess Olga, his wife, invited us to spend a day at the Villa Demidoff in nearby Pratolino, to see their grand estate and its library. Centuries of history and the handiwork of master artisans were in evidence. Even the gardens dated from the Renaissance and retained much of their old appearance, highlighted by Giambologna's 30-foot sculpture *Apennine*, cut into a natural rock formation by a pond. This work was completed in 1581 for the Grand Duke Francesco II de' Medici. It was the same Medici for whom the adjoining villa had been designed and constructed, as a gift for his second wife, Bianca Cappello. His first wife had been Archduchess Joan of Austria. Having had an opportunity to examine a portrait of Bianca at the villa, I realized that there was no mystery why she had inspired such extravagance: she was stunning, or at any rate the artist made her appear so. I recalled that I once owned a book bearing the arms of both the duke and his first wife, the Ghisolfi manuscript portolan atlas on vellum, in a superb mosaic binding, undoubtedly presented to them at their wedding in 1565 (Catalogue 88, no. 49). One of the fruits of this union was Marie de' Medici, future wife of Henry IV and Queen of France.

Our host was the brother of King Alexander of Yugoslavia, who had been assassinated in Marseilles in 1934 together with the French statesman and great bibliophile Louis Barthou. At lunch he told us the story of his villa:

The Medici home, which had stood for more than 300 years, fell victim to wanton destruction by cannon fire in the 19th century. It seems that an Austrian archduke, one of the last Medici successors, delighted in using it for target practice. The estate then came into the hands of Anatole Demidoff (1812–70), who reconstructed the house. One of the richest men in the world, Demidoff had vast landholdings, investments in gold, silver, and platinum mines in Russia, and was in the silk trade as well. Prince Paul, his direct descendant, inherited the estate and its contents. These comprised antique furnishings, works of art, and the library.

Had the latter been the original Medici collection, it might have contained untold treasures. But it consisted mostly of modern Russian literature, of very little interest to me and practically no monetary value. I almost despaired, looking over shelf after shelf of this material, of finding anything worthwhile. After a few moments of glancing about, my eyes fell upon a set of volumes in much handsomer bindings than the majority of its neighbors. Here was the only important book in the library: Prince Anatole Demidoff's famous description of his voyage to and scientific exploration of Southern Russia and the Crimea, the dedication copy to Czar Nicolas I of Russia, printed on vellum, with 79 watercolors of animals and geological maps. In addition it contained the hand-colored lithographs by Denis Raffet. How it came to be here, rather than at St. Petersburg, one could only speculate. Prince Demidoff had become persona non grata to the Czar and may have decided to keep the book for himself; or the Czar, if presented with it, may have refused the gift. Be that as it may, the work stayed in Pratolino and I was only too happy to purchase it. Paul Mellon bought it from me later. This was the only book I acquired from Prince Paul's library.

Not all the shelves at Pratolino contained books. Displayed on some were fragments of classical statuary, Roman and Renaissance. I assumed they had been part of the old Medici hoard. "Yes, in a way," the Prince explained. "But they've been here only briefly. You see, my grandchildren dive in the pond near Giambologna's statue and occasionally they find such relics." Apparently they had been thrown there when the Medici villa was destroyed. Shades of the attics of rural Austria!

Our Florentine adventures did not end without tension and suspense. While awaiting the arrival of our shipment (the globe and the crates of bronzes), news came of the devastating floods; the Arno had ruptured its floodgates and inundated most of Florence. Many persons were killed or injured, property loss ran high, and the city's activity came to a halt. If our crates had not already been shipped, they might well have fallen victim to the catastrophe. Cables to the chandelier shop, the sculptor, and our shipper brought no response. I sent my Paris agent to Florence to make personal inquiries at the various addresses; he reported that all were hard-hit and still under water. Now I was resigned to the loss and made preparations to file a claim for the insurance. Then, in mid-December, all our crates arrived safely. This was to become our most marvelous Christmas present.

£65,000 paid for book

Sotheby's sale to American dealer

Star Reporter

ANOTHER world record was broken at Sotheby's saleroom today. Hans Kraus, America's top dealer in rare books, paid £65,000 for an illuminated manuscript of the Apocalypse believed to have been written at St Albans in 1250.

The previous record price was the £39,000 paid by Mr Kraus at Sotheby's last December for a 12th century manuscript of the Gospels.

Both books were from the collection of the late G. W. Dyson Perrins, whose fortune came from Worcester sauce.

The first half of the collection fetched £326,620. The second half was sold today for a total of £293,030.

Altogether Mr Kraus spent £93,000 today on three lots. He considers the prices were very reasonable.

A Vienna-born victim of Hitlerism, he went to the United States in 1939. Now he is the boss of the world's biggest scientific periodical publishing company, a business which subsidises his antiquarian book buying.

DAILY EXPRESS WEDNESDAY

Nine nods from Mr. Kraus —£101,400

By JOHN RYDON

A LITTLE man in a clerical grey suit raised a well-manicured finger nine times at Sotheby's yesterday—and bought nine books and manuscripts for £101,400.

He was 49-year-old New York book-dealer Hans Kraus and he helped break some saleroom records at the first sale of illuminated manuscripts from the Dyson Perrins collection.

In one hour 50 lots fetched £326,620—three times as much as for any previous one-day book or manuscript sale.

The world record price for a manuscript —£33,800— was beaten three times and equalled once.

TO THE U.S.

Mr. Kraus paid the highest price —£39,000—for a Twelfth-Century book of Latin gospels.

Then he made arrangements for his new purchases to be posted back to the U.S. (insurance £200,000) and drove back to his suite at the Ritz Hotel.

He said last night: "I was astonished I paid such a low price.

"Today has been quite my best buy of the year, although I have paid more than this in the past.

"I think it was a reasonable price for such wonderful merchandise. I hope to make a sizeable profit."

Mr. Kraus, father of five and owner of a five-storey shop on New York's East Forty-Sixth street, began his business career at 17 as apprentice in a Viennese bookshop.

Daily Telegraph and Morning Post, Wednesday, December 10, 1958

RECORD £326,620 REALISED IN BOOK AND MSS. SALE

£39,000 FOR 12th CENTURY ITEM

By TERENCE MULLALY

A German mid-12th century manuscript of the Gospels in Latin was sold for £39,000 to Mr. H. P. Kraus, the New York dealer, at Sotheby's yesterday. This is a world record price for one lot in an auction of literary property.

Yet it was only one of many sensational bids. However remarkable individual prices may have seemed, the primary lesson of this and other sales, is that really first class objects, whether 12th-century manuscripts or Impressionist pictures, will fetch amounts that to the layman seem extravagant.

Yesterday, Sotheby's were selling illuminated manuscripts, a block book and four printed books, the property of the late Mr. C. W. Dyson Perrins. Fifty lots realised £326,620.

Huge Price For Book

LONDON. — The famed New York book dealer Mr. H. P. Kraus yesterday paid a record £23,000 for a book printed in 1480 by William Caxton, the first English printer.

The book, a "Vocabulary sale yesterday at Sotheby's and Conversation Book in auction rooms French and English," tells of English life in the 15th century, and was offered for sale. Sotheby's said that 2 lots were offered, and the Dean and Chapter of Ripon Cathedral, brought a total of £85,000 Yorkshire.

Of these nine lots which It is one of four known brought £40,000, came from copies, and the only one not Ripon Cathedral, which in a public library. is trying to raise money.

The book was offered for new choir school — t

NEW YORK HERALD TRIBUNE, THURSDAY, DE

$182,000 Book Arrives Here From London

A thirteenth-century illuminated manuscript copy of the Apocalypse, the Revelation of St. John, was received yesterday by H. P. Kraus, rare book dealer, at 16 E. 46th St. The book, bought in London by Mr. Kraus Dec. 1 at the record price of £65,000 ($182,000) in an auction at Sotheby & Co., was sent by air mail. The illustration above, one of eighty-two done on vellum in the Latin manuscript, shows an incident described in Revelations, Chapter 17, where an angel tells St. John of the judgment of Babylon, represented by a woman riding a scarlet beast with seven heads and ten horns. The woman is dressed in purple and scarlet and bedecked with gold and jewels and pearls. The manuscript was executed at the Benedictine Abbey of St. Albans, England, around 1250.

Fig. 15. Some newspaper clippings.

CHAPTER 36

The Battles of Three Auctions

IF IT IS TRUE that booksellers owe their reputations to the great auction sales of their time—Quaritch to the Ashburnham, Dr. Rosenbach to the Britwell—my chief debt would be the auctions of illuminated manuscripts from the library of C. W. Dyson Perrins, from 1958 to 1960. They brought high prices, international notice, and focused great attention not only on the manuscripts but also on their purchasers.

The Perrins collection, sold at Sotheby's in London, was the most valuable group of manuscripts to reach the market after World War II and indeed was equaled by only a very few collections in the whole history of manuscript auctions. At that time my love for illuminated manuscripts had developed at such a rate that it surpassed, to a certain degree, my interest in other book rarities. Each manuscript is unique, and presents the possibility of new and exciting discoveries. I envied the bookmen of old who could, in a single auction session, purchase half a dozen or more fine-quality manuscripts. Now here, with the Perrins library, was just such an opportunity in my own time.

Museums of art unfortunately have had a strong prejudice against illuminated manuscripts. Their paintings are small and, unless the manuscript is broken up into separate leaves, only one painting can be shown at a time. But this attitude is beginning to change, since mediaeval painting cannot be studied without manuscripts. The vast majority of panel paintings and even mural frescos of the Gothic period and earlier have been badly damaged through the years. From the Carolingian and earlier times virtually nothing exists. Those that look fresh have almost always been heavily restored and repainted. On the other hand, miniature paintings preserved in a book normally retain all the vividness of their coloring, and in most cases have not been touched by restorers.

A major innovation of recent years has been the exhibit of miniature paintings from color transparencies. With the original work displayed in the same room, and with expert photography and judicious lighting, transparencies allow one to appreciate the brilliant color of the mediaeval artist's palette.

C. W. Dyson Perrins (1864–1958), another long-lived English bibliophile, had been a contemporary of William Morris (who complained of the prices of manuscripts, in the days when a good Book of Hours realized ten or fifteen pounds), of Henry Yates Thompson, almost of Henry Huth. Having done most of his buying early in life, he lived to see his treasures rise manyfold in value. Unlike Yates Thompson, another memorable collector of manuscripts, Perrins rarely sold anything. In 1920 Sir George Warner of the British Museum compiled and Perrins financed a sumptuous catalogue of the collection. Though small, it was of the highest quality piece by piece, rich in English liturgies, Psalters, French and Flemish Books of Hours, Antiphonaries and miscellaneous picture books. To assemble it in the span of a comparatively few years, from Queen Victoria's death until World War I, ranked as an achievement.

Perrins had the look of a bibliophile; or, it might better be said, fitted the public image of one: emaciated, sallow-skinned, a wearer of wire-rimmed spectacles, a man very obviously at home with books. He was the Perrins of Lea & Perrins, Worcestershire sauce manufacturers, and easily one of Britain's richest non-landed gentry.

Each great collector carries his reputation before him. Some—Heber and Phillipps, to name two of many—are known for an insatiable bibliophilic appetite that resulted in mountainous accumulations. Others buy books like stocks and bonds. Perrins' reputation was for careful connoisseurship. An amateur scholar, he had the good sense early in life to cultivate the friendship of professional scholars; among his close friends and advisors were Montague Rhodes James, author of numerous works on manuscript illumination, as well as superb ghost stories, the aforementioned Sir George Warner, and Sir Sydney Cockerell. (See Chapter 27.) They served as an advisory triumvirate for Perrins, placing their accumulated knowledge at his command.

Though not given to bulk purchasing in the fashion of Morgan or Huntington, Perrins made one highly significant acquisition en bloc. In

1906 he bought a group of manuscripts from a fellow countryman, Charles Fairfax Murray, who also sold heavily to Morgan. From that moment on he was recognized as a prominent collector.

Perrins decided during his lifetime to sell his printed books, a less valuable collection than his manuscripts but still noteworthy. They went up for sale at Sotheby's just after World War II, an unfortunate time for important books to be auctioned. Though they were in fine condition, the prices for these Italian woodcut books, German incunabula, and miscellaneous fine printing were very low. They averaged fractions of the present values. Even the Perrins Gutenberg Bible (just one volume) fetched only £22,000.

But Perrins' manuscripts disappointed nobody. For three years they took the book world's spotlight, as Sotheby's strategically spread out the sales and gave buyers a chance to digest and recuperate. Not since the Yates Thompson sales of the early 1920s had such a group been auctioned. Those who could afford to buy were few, but they seized the chance and made no complaint about prices 50 percent or more above the estimates. Those unable to buy came to admire, while a few manuscript disdainers, annoyed that so much of Sotheby's sale calendar was given over to manuscripts instead of first editions, brushed aside the Perrins auctions as "picture sales."

Perrins died in 1958 and in December of the same year the sales began. They marked a turning point in my career, my emergence as a dominant buyer of illuminated manuscripts in the international auction market. Our financial position had improved very much, as Hanni's uncle, Ernest Zucker, died in May of that year, leaving a sizable inheritance. At auction one must be prepared to pay more than anyone else, to forget the past and be aware that the new high prices will be tomorrow's value standards. The only problem was that I, who created the new prices, had to follow through in future sales of similar material. It was my task to support the new price levels and demonstrate that the sums brought in that first sale were not artificially high, as was charged (with some validity) when the *Valdarfer Boccaccio* fetched over £2,000 at the famous Roxburghe sale in 1812. My strategy succeeded. Libraries, dealers, and collectors bid strongly against me, so it was not difficult to keep prices up. Of course I could not buy everything, but that was never my intent. I got the prime pieces and a number of the lesser ones as well, and was satisfied to see that the manuscripts I did *not* buy sold, proportionately, for just as much as those I purchased.

I was fully aware of the risks involved. In the winter of 1958 the onset of colitis made my life miserable, a state of affairs which continued until 1964 and became more and more severe. During this difficult period I behaved like a drunken sailor, paying ever-increasing prices, but my gambles paid off: miraculously I succeeded in selling most of these manuscripts at still higher prices. Here we have a perfect lesson in the psychological influence which one individual can exert on the market. Of course the Perrins manuscripts *deserved* high prices. They seemed extraordinary only because mediaeval manuscripts had long been underpriced, and sold for amounts that did not reflect their importance as works of art. I always insisted that a great book should command a great price, and so it was at these auctions.

My purchases at the three auctions amounted to £360,000, more than those of any other bidder. This was all the more significant inasmuch as nearly all buying was not on commission but for stock.

The first Perrins sale occurred at a physical ebb in my life. I sometimes think the excitement of those sales kept me alive. At the rate I was spending, most people felt I had written myself off as doomed and wanted to go out with a bang. The fact is that, in sickness or in health, such opportunities are not to be missed by anyone as devoted to manuscripts as I am. Bookmen from all parts of the globe flocked to London. I went, leaving Hanni behind to manage the business. Sotheby's was jammed. Flashbulbs popped as, one after another, the little army of aristocratic volumes came to the rostrum: books under wraps for half a century now unfurled their colors as proudly as peacocks. The quiet moments at most sales, when inconsequential lots are being sold and the chance comes to make notes or gather one's thoughts, did not occur at the Perrins auctions. With nearly every lot, thousand- and multi-thousand-pound bids came from every part of the room.

On that first day I returned to my hotel happy, with the two things I most coveted: the best manuscript, the *Helmarshausen Gospels*, and international publicity. Once again, as with Dr. Rosenbach's exploits at the Britwell sales, a New Yorker had gotten the spoils and was going to take them across the sea.

The *Helmarshausen Gospels*, unquestionably the finest manuscript I had owned up to then, cost £39,000, about $110,000. I had no commission, not even a client who expressed mild interest. But I never doubted the rightness of buying it. For such a fabulous piece of art, price did not seem to matter.

Immediately after the sale, James J. Rorimer, then director of the Metropolitan Museum, called my New York office seeking to buy the *Helmarshausen Gospels*. He had been underbidder on this outstanding

12th-century codex with beautiful pictures. Hanni came to the telephone. She knew nothing of the day's events, since I had had no chance to inform her because of the time difference between London and New York. So Hanni had to call me in London. It was, and still is, my policy to charge customers 10 percent if asked to bid for them at a sale. If I buy an item at my own risk and someone wants it immediately afterward, I charge more. Therefore I told Hanni to ask 20 percent. Rorimer was angry and decided not to buy. This was a mistake on my part, as I soon realized. As long as Rorimer was alive I could never do business with the Metropolitan Museum.

This contretemps did not dampen our spirits. We were on top of the world, with news of the sale reported everywhere, magazine articles, interviews, television appearances, and new friends (and potential clients). Collectors back in New York congratulated me. There, as in London, more interviews, more pictures, more personal appearances. Never had 46th Street seen so much activity. Never had I been so busy. Too busy, for that time in my life. I was unwell and grew worse after returning to New York. In the midst of the excitement, and with scores of people waiting to see me, I had to go to Flower and Fifth Avenue Hospital with ulcerative colitis.

My family knew I was seriously ill, but became truly apprehensive when the Perrins purchases arrived and I did not even want to look at them. When a bookman cannot be aroused by the books he loves, medical science stands little chance. Still, I had business to tend to. Even in the hospital, flat on my back, I sold the *Helmarshausen Gospels*, a transaction described in Chapter 40.

Sotheby's let a whole year pass between the first and second Perrins sales. By December, 1959, my health had improved, some of the previous year's acquisitions were sold, and I was ready—financially, morally, and physically—for more.

As things turned out, the first sale was pale compared to the second, with higher prices and more excitement. Once more I was the largest single purchaser, against furious competition that included every major name in the book world. The gallery comprised a Who's Who of dealers from Europe and America. The big book this time, and the monetary highlight of the whole Perrins series, was an English manuscript of about 1250 called the *St. Albans Apocalypse*. It was obvious to me that, to maintain the reputation I had established, I had to buy it. I had to have it against all competition, with no flinching at the price, even if it might rest on my shelves unsold for years. (This, incidentally, is not entirely so frightening as it might seem; one's cash may be tied up in an unsold book, but the book generally increases in value while cash decreases through inflation.)

The *St. Albans Apocalypse* ranked as the most significant English manuscript to be sold in years. The work of monks at St. Albans Abbey (the same St. Albans of the anonymous "schoolmaster" printer in the 15th century), it contained no less than 82 miniatures, all of them half-page in size. Only a few such manuscripts were written in mediaeval England and most of them had found permanent homes in museums and institutional libraries.

I had studied the catalogue as soon as it arrived, about a month prior to the sale, and my eyes kept returning to Lot 58, *the* manuscript. It thoroughly captivated and seduced me. A non-collector would fail to understand my passion. But who could be unmoved by such a volume, its bright rich colors and its forceful figures? As an example of English mediaeval art it could be matched only by the country's old cathedrals, which fall outside the collector's realm. The mediaeval English, unlike most continental Europeans, did no altarpiece or panel painting and virtually no fresco painting. Their painting was confined to manuscripts, but in this medium their virtuosity was not surpassed.

Two weeks before the sale, while I was still without a potential customer for the book but still resolved to buy it, the phone rang. It was William S. Glazier, about whom I have written in Chapter 29.

"What do you think about the Perrins Apocalypse?" he asked.

"A great manuscript," I replied.

"Yes. But the price? What will it bring?"

"At least forty-five thousand pounds," I said, basing my estimate on the price levels of the first sale.

"Well, in my opinion it'll go for less. Would you take my bid for £32,000?"

"Yes," I agreed, "if you don't object to me bidding for myself if it goes beyond £32,000."

"Okay, but call me after the sale and give me first refusal at the price you paid plus 10 percent."

This suited me, though of course I failed to share Glazier's optimism about a low price. Businessmen tend to make that mistake about rare books.

The Apocalypse came up early in the sale; it was lot 58, but Sotheby's had continued the numbering of lots from the first sale. If I had had to wait longer, I would have burst. The tension, built up for weeks, ran high. The room was ghostly quiet. Here was the moment.

For some reason the bidding started at only £8,000. Gradually, more slowly than expected, it climbed, at first by bids of a thousand pounds, then two and a half, then five. Glazier's limit of £32,000 was soon eclipsed. At £40,000 I was still bidding and thought I'd won. There was a brief pause, the kind that comes when everybody stops bidding. False alarm! Instead of being over, the bidding was raised by £20,000. "Sixty thousand," came a near-whisper.

"Sixty-five," I called back.

When somebody raises a bid by £20,000, he expects to shock the competition into silence. By showing I was not discouraged I stopped him—whoever he was—and he bid no more. Nor did anyone else. It was mine at sixty-five.

Suddenly I realized I had bought the most expensive book ever sold. Sixty-five thousand pounds translated into about $182,000.

The sale touched off a global storm of publicity. My first order of business was to make the promised call to Glazier. As he had bid less than half the price I doubted he would be interested, but one never knows. The prospect of losing a book can be far more upsetting than paying a price for it that is higher than anticipated.

"Sorry, no," came the voice 3,000 miles away. "Too rich for my blood."

And he meant it.

It wasn't a serious setback. I had other manuscript buyers among my clientele. There were the museums. And—who knows?—the publicity might generate new customers.

While still in England, I and my precious manuscript were put on television, on the "Tonight" show, not be confused with the American program of the same name. I had only a few hours to prepare. An urgent call went to Sotheby's, to have the manuscript removed from its vault and delivered to my hotel room. It arrived late, at 6 P.M., just before the deadline to leave for the studio and too late to get insurance. So I was obliged to transport a book worth nearly $200,000 after dark, without insurance. A big book cannot be discreetly hidden. To make matters worse, my picture, with the book, was in all the British papers. I would be recognized, and it would not be hard to guess the contents of my parcel.

The car sent by BBC to take us to the studio arrived on time. That raised my spirits somewhat, until I saw the car. I expected something like a Rolls or a Bentley. What pulled up looked more like a tired old refugee from a taxi fleet. Nor did its cockney-speaking driver inspire any great confidence.

With considerable reluctance, Hanni, I, and the book got in.

Our destination was the BBC studio in Shepherd's Bush. I had no idea whether it was around the corner or ten miles away.

"How long a drive is it?" I inquired anxiously.

"Arf an hour in clear weather," he replied. "More in fog."

Apparently the latter applied, as we saw nothing from the windows but clouds of white soupy mist rolling by. It was an authentic, Dickensian London fog, with just an occasional streak of light visible from other vehicles.

There we were, somewhere in the midst of a strange city, in the hands of a cabbie who looked like Fagin in *Oliver Twist*, surrounded by fog, with a $182,000 book on my lap. To make matters worse, we had seen the Hitchcock film *North by Northwest* the previous evening. It was all coming true. Cary Grant couldn't have felt any worse in our predicament, even if we had no planes dive-bombing us.

The atmosphere got to Hanni. "How do you know the driver and car are from the BBC?" she asked anxiously.

How indeed?

We had taken his word for it. He might just as well be taking us to a robbers' roost. The real BBC driver was undoubtedly bound and gagged in the car's trunk. Or floating down the Thames.

"How long?" I asked again. And again.

Each time the answer came back, "Don't know. Tell ya when we get there."

Fearing that each minute might be our last, Hanni and I discussed (in German, which we felt pretty confident our captor did not speak) our options. They included physical violence, giving up without a struggle, offering ransom, and leaping out of the car. But suppose our apprehensions proved unfounded? None of these would look well in the press.

We sat back and waited.

Instead of highwaymen, the BBC studio came into view, bathed in light. To us it looked like the promised land. We got out, visibly shaken, and I'm sure that the cabbie went away thinking it sure takes all kinds to make a world.

Despite the trip, the show was a success. Afterward I was told that an audience of millions had watched it and seen the Apocalypse. It was even said that I had a certain theatrical flair and might try acting. No thanks. I was living a real drama; I didn't need to act.

For my performance the BBC gave me a check for one pound. That confirmed my decision against an acting career. But I was told that the Queen gets the same wages whenever she appears on television.

American TV also wanted me and the Apocalypse. My "secret" on "I've Got a Secret" was, "I have a book backstage worth $182,000." This had to be solved by the panelists by asking questions in turn. After the game had ended, Garry Moore, the show's host, interviewed me briefly and seemed genuinely interested in the book.

"Do you intend to keep this book or to sell it?" he asked.

"I am a bookseller, not a bookkeeper," was my answer. It drew some laughs.

Then he wanted to know, "If someone offered you a 10 percent profit, what would you say?"

"No thank you."

I never had stage-fright on television. The only thing that bothered me on this occasion was Mr. Moore's habit of leaning on the open book with his elbow.

The next year brought the third and final Perrins sale. This time the stellar item was a German Psalter attributed to the Black Forest monastery, St. Blasien, and dating from the pinnacle of German manuscript illumination, the late Romanesque age. In its way it was just as significant as either the *Helmarshausen Gospels* or the *St. Albans Apocalypse* and there was no doubt it would go high. The geographical attribution, unconfirmed at the time of the sale, was later established by the learned Dr. Harry Bober, who wrote a valuable monograph on the book. (*The St. Blasien Psalter*, "Rare Books Monogrphs Series" vol. III.)

Perrins sales and my ill health seemed to coincide. I was again troubled with colitis attacks. Hanni accompanied me to London, not just to act as a nurse but also as a sobering influence to restrain me from spending too wildly. But regardless of my health, I would not be talked out of the *St. Blasien Psalter*. Its purchase would give me the equivalent of a "grand slam," having bought the best book at each Perrins sale.

For reasons not clear to me Sotheby's estimate was low—perhaps because it wasn't of English origin and bidders at the previous two sales seemed most interested in English manuscripts. From the outset, I doubted that it could possibly sell so low; a dozen bidders would jump for the bargain, bid against each other and drive up the price to twice the estimate at least. Anyway I was anxious to see it. On arriving at New Bond Street for the pre-sale exhibition I discovered it had already become the center of attention. It was receiving a more-than-casual inspection by the librarian of the Landesbibliothek in Stuttgart and from my old friend, the Munich dealer Helmuth Domizlaff. Without having to be told, I guessed what was going on. The Landesbibliothek wanted to buy it and was entrusting its bid to Domizlaff. That meant formidable competition. German libraries could afford to spend heavily then, backed up by funds from corporations like Volkswagen, Thyssen, and the national lotteries.

Of course, the book was everything and more than I expected, the kind that causes a manuscript lover's fingers to tremble as he touches the pages. What would it fetch? If the Landesbibliothek was bidding, the Staatsbibliothek in Munich might also, and other German libraries, as well as any number of foreign institutions. To any of them, fifty or even a hundred thousand pounds would not be too high.

I awoke on sale day determined to pay up to $300,000, or about £120,000. Admittedly this was not the way to marital harmony. So I told Hanni my limit was $100,000 (about £40,000.) This still sounded too high to her, battle-weary as she was from previous Perrins sales and with so many unsold Perrins books on our shelves.

"Who would buy it from you?" she asked.

"I never think of that. The main thing is that I like it. I want to have it. It's a great manuscript."

Because of the low estimate, bidding started at only £10,000. At £20,000, which was my bid, I seemed to have it. Then, just as had happened earlier, the pause turned out to be a false alarm. A new bidder with a German accent—Domizlaff—went up to £25,000. I raised five, he raised five. We were locked in battle, just the two of us, the whole room watching. At £40,000, Hanni kicked my shin. "Enough is enough," she admonished. My supposed limit of $100,000 had been reached. But I couldn't stop, and had no intention of doing so. We got to £50,000 at which point I thought the bid was mine, but apparently the auctioneer picked up my adversary's bid before mine.

"It is not yours," said the auctioneer.

Quickly I called out 55, despite another kick. Domizlaff, fighting valiantly, went to 60. I said 62, and it was over. Dejected, the Stuttgart librarian and Domizlaff left the hall. I stayed and spent more. Why rest on one's laurels?

"I was ready to pay £100,000," I told reporters, and it was the absolute truth. "Maybe I would have gone even higher, in the heat of competition."

Another round of whirlwind publicity followed, with both our pictures (and the book's, of course, it being the real star) in the press, interviews, dinners, television. No longer did we flinch at the mention of the BBC. We were becoming veterans. My only problem was a black-and-blue shin, from all that kicking.

Never had I been so satisfied with a purchase. Never for an instant did I have second thoughts or regrets. But I must say that Hanni's doubts about finding a buyer proved prophetic. The *St. Blasien Psalter* remained in my possession for a dozen years, until it was sold to a collector in Stuttgart for about 20 percent above cost. Of course there was no profit at all. When a book is held that long, it must be sold for twice the purchase price or more to show a profit. But great books of great prices cannot al-

THE BATTLES OF THREE AUCTIONS 267

ways find buyers easily. Sometimes the seller must forget about profits and even be willing to suffer an occasional loss. That is why I never feel guilty when making a large profit.

Thus ended the Perrins sales, not soon to be forgotten. They stand as a landmark in book-auction history and are certain to be looked back on for generations. Perrins, if he had viewed the proceedings from above the clouds, must have been blissfully happy. His books were scattered to the far corners of the earth, but their prices confirmed his faith in the importance of illuminated manuscripts. For me the sales were equally epochal.

In addition to the above-mentioned manuscripts, which comprised the cream of the Perrins collection, I also bought a number of others, any one of which would rank as the chief attraction in a sale of lesser magnitude. A 13th-century Bestiary, for which I paid £36,500. (See Chapter 45.) For £26,000 I bought the *Psalter of King Wenceslas* of Hungary and Bohemia, about 1260, the "good king" of the famous Christmas carol. And I paid £25,000 for the *Gilles Li Muisis* Codex of French poetry, executed at Tournai in 1351.

Fig. 16. The origin of the Perrins fortune.

I cannot resist relating the final act of the Perrins sale. The last day of the third sale Mrs. Perrins (or was it Sotheby?) gave a luncheon at Claridges to celebrate the great financial success. Members of the staff of Sotheby who were active at the sale were invited, and also all the chief buyers, myself included. It was a festive event, well arranged, and at the end Mrs. Perrins gave a very charming address of thanks. "And as a token of my appreciation, I have prepared a gift for every member of Sotheby's in this room." At a sign, waiters entered carrying cases of the famous Lea & Perrins Worcestershire Sauce. I believe that every Sotheby member was well-provided for life.

Like all great sales, the Perrins auctions continued to cause reverberations in the book trade after they were over. Marlborough, the London art dealers, for some reason had bought five high-quality manuscripts at the sales, each of them against me. No bookseller likes to be outbid, but losing illuminated manuscripts to a firm whose major business is in Rouault and Rothko rubbed salt in my wounds. I presumed Marlborough had commissions, which seemed the only logical explanation. Such was not the case. They were buying for stock, and they lived to regret it.

An art dealer trying to sell rare books is comparable to my dabbling in paintings. I have tried this occasionally over the years and always with disappointing results. The people who buy paintings may be the same ones who buy rare books, but they prefer to buy each from a specialist.

Marlborough had about £100,000 tied up in these books, plus another £32,000, an astronomical sum for them to spend, in a manuscript known as the *Llangattock Hours*. This, though not a Perrins manuscript, was of Perrins quality, coming from a Christie's sale in 1958. For the art of 15th-century Flanders, the *Llangattock Hours*—so called after its only known owner—represents one of the most important single manuscript discoveries of our time. The two chief miniaturists drew their inspiration from Jan van Eyck's *Turin Hours* and Petrus Christus. I had wanted it and made a high bid, but Marlborough topped me. The manuscript had fourteen full-page miniatures of great beauty in a contemporary binding signed by Lievin Stuvaert.

The books bought by Marlborough at the Perrins sale were a Gratianus manuscript of about 1175 with Romanesque miniatures; a Vidal commentary on the laws of Aragon, written at the Royal Scriptorium in Barcelona about 1260, with ten large and 146 smaller miniatures showing secular subjects, such as various trades; a 14th-century text manuscript of Dante written for Juan de Borgia with three miniatures, bound in a spectacular mudéjar binding; a *Histoire de Thèbes* executed at Lille in 1469 with 128 pen and ink drawings, lightly colored by the Wavrin master; and the very attractive *Gualenghi Hours* with 21 miniatures by Taddeo Crivelli. When none had been sold after three years, Marlborough began to get tired.

While vacationing in Villars, Switzerland, in 1961, I was suffering

THE BATTLES OF THREE AUCTIONS 269

from another bad attack of colitis. But, as I knew from past experience, the phone rings in sickness and in health, and it is almost impossible to vacation incognito. This time Mr. Fischer from Marlborough called from London. Would I be interested in the six manuscripts at 20 percent above cost? That came to about $400,000. Such a large expenditure in my precarious state of health was unwise, but it seemed a good opportunity. The Perrins sales had raised the selling appeal of the *Llangattock Hours* considerably over Marlborough's cost; and regarding the five Perrins manuscripts, I had been willing at the 1958 sale to pay just slightly less for each manuscript than Marlborough had paid. So I said yes.

There was no joy after closing the deal, but plenty of worries. I had acted irresponsibly as a husband and father of five children. My good wife was terribly disturbed. I was aware that I had a very serious ailment and possibly had to face surgery. I felt the danger and realized the risks for my family if I should die. I also knew the difficulty of selling high-priced manuscripts. But then it was too late for reproaches.

The manuscripts were mine. That was my consolation. I recovered my old energy and went back to New York and into feverish action. Even my health had somehow improved. I pushed through the publication of my Catalogue 100 which contained these manuscripts as well as many others, mostly from the Perrins sale. With the assistance of Lehmann-Haupt, Kebabian, and Bober I often worked late into the night. The result was spectacular. Within a few months we had our magnum opus, a folio volume with many color plates: a dazzling array of precious manuscripts. It also contained, in a rear pocket, a brochure of photos and information on me, my family, my staff, and the house on 46th Street, celebrating my 30th year in business. This catalogue has itself become a collector's item.

I might also add that Catalogue 100 sold better than our wildest expectations. Many of the manuscripts found buyers, including the more expensive ones. This catalogue dispelled the general notion that I had bought at the Perrins sale only as agent for someone else, as George D. Smith, Rosenbach, Quaritch, and other big dealers had previously done.

That summer my daughters Mary Ann and Barbara took an art course in Brussels under Harry Bober and Dorothy Miner. The main subjects of their studies were the illuminated manuscripts in the Bibliothèque Royale of Brussels. When Herman Liebaers, director of the Bibliothèque Royale, ordered the *Llangattock Hours* on approval I took the book myself to Brussels to deliver it and to visit my daughters. In honor of the participants of the art course I gave a dinner to which I invited Mr. Liebaers and other members of the library staff. After some toasts Liebaers got up to make an important announcement: it had been decided to buy the *Llangattock Hours* for the Bibliothèque Royale. I was elated, everyone congratulated me, and I went happily to Klosters, Switzerland for a vacation. There a letter from Liebaers was waiting: the deal had to be canceled due to opposition from a senior staff member. I took it rather poorly. First up in heaven, then down to earth. Hanni was brave and cheered me up: "I'm sure someone else will buy this great manuscript." And so it was. By the end of the summer most of the expensive manuscripts were sold to Dr. Ludwig, Dr. Martin Bodmer, and other collectors. What a relief! I owed it to my crazy courage and unbelievable luck. Filled with fresh confidence I was ready for new adventures.

CHAPTER 37

The Collector *Par Excellence*

THE FOLLOWING NOTES can hardly do justice to the 20th-century prince of bibliophiles; the story of Dr. Martin Bodmer (1899–1971) and his library actually deserves a book in itself. He was a patrician and a scholar, the scion of a great Swiss family which made a name for itself in the world of industry and banking. Originally from Zurich, he settled later in the vicinity of Geneva and became a vice president of the International Red Cross. A man of great wealth, he applied his money judiciously to his collection, exercising a polished taste for rare books and related materials.

Bodmer, tall and gaunt with large friendly eyes, was fundamentally shy by nature. Only after a few years of acquaintance did he drop his reserve and show a warmer and more humorous side. Of all collectors I have known, and they are many, I can think of only two or three who were as human and lovable; Dr. Bodmer was a kind and amiable friend. Otto Schäfer, the great collector of Schweinfurt, said of him in his memorial address: "None who knew Martin Bodmer can ever forget that eminent and upright figure. It is no exaggeration that he was renowned the world over, not only among book lovers and collectors but all those concerned with arts and literature. In forming this admirable collection which bears his name, this highly perceptive man was not only concerned with acquisitions of works of art, and of precious manuscripts and books, but wanted to provide an epitome of the story of the human spirit, in accordance with the plan drawn up by him and described in his writings [on world literature]."

His library, at the time of his death, amounted to over 150,000 items: Sumerian tablets of the third millennium, Babylonian cylinders, Books of the Dead, Greek papyri, mediaeval manuscripts, incunabula, first editions up to the present day, autographs, and musical scores. Twelve days before he died he created the Martin Bodmer Foundation, given to the City of Geneva for the benefit of the scholarly world.

Dr. Bodmer rose to the first rank of collectors in 1931 when he bought a Gutenberg Bible for a price rumored to be £30,000—not the inflation-riddled, devalued pound of today but the old prewar value of $5, thus making it the highest price paid for a printed book up to that time. It came from the Russian Czarist treasures liquidated by the Communists. With this purchase Bodmer became, though it could hardly be suspected then, the last European collector to buy a Gutenberg Bible. Thereafter he went on to build a magnificent library, diverse in scope, based loosely on "World Literature" but extending out beyond all formal guidelines. It was Goethe who, in 1827, framed the concept of World Literature (*Kunst und Altertum,* Vol. 6, pt. 1). Bodmer published two important philosophical works on the subject with the following titles: *Eine Bibliothek der Weltliteratur* (Zurich, 1947) and *Variationen zum Thema Weltliteratur* (Frankfurt, 1956). There are many interpretations of the concept of *Weltliteratur,* the broadest of which comprises the totality of the literary production of all peoples of the world at all times. For practical reasons, Bodmer limited the scope of his library to the first editions of great works and ideas.

It might fairly be stated that he assembled the finest rare-book collection that could be gathered during his lifetime, in the light of availability, prices, and competition. His success was due in part to the very event which spelled disaster for so many collectors: the Great Depression. Of all banking nations of the world, Switzerland suffered least; the Swiss franc remained strong. With prices tumbling elsewhere, Bodmer could buy books in New York, London, Paris, and Brussels for a fraction of what they had brought a few years earlier. At auctions, Bodmer had little competition during the worst of the depression. He acquired many of his finest books in that period and lived to see them rise 10, 20 and, in some instances, 50 times in value.

Bodmer showed great shrewdness and levelheadedness in book buying. Cost-conscious, he possessed that ingredient so often missing in collectors, patience. He could say no and mean it. He could wait for a better copy, or for one to come along at a better price. The greatness of a book did not guarantee a sale to Bodmer. Complaining of high prices, he wrote to Rosenbach, who offered a 1459 Durandus for £14,000, that a copy of the same book could be had in Germany for considerably less—£4,000 (this was nearly 50 years ago). He had a great skill in negotiating and was not too proud to plead poverty on occasion in the hope of getting a discount; his purchase from Rosenbach for $46,500 of a manuscript of *The Canterbury Tales* in an original monastic binding, priced in the catalogue at $85,000, was a classic example. In selling he drove just as hard a bargain. He could have become a successful dealer, I think, had he been inclined in that direction.

I sold great books to Bodmer and bought equally great ones from him. My association with him began inauspiciously. As a young dealer in Vienna in 1935 I received a postal card from Bodmer ordering several books from one of my catalogues. At that time I was unfamiliar with the name, otherwise I would have been honored to sell books to the owner of a Gutenberg Bible. Instead I looked upon the card with some doubt. He was ordering the most expensive items in the catalogue, listing them by numbers only as if in haste, without supplying titles or prices. Perhaps he intended to order from the previous catalogue, I concluded. In that case the books would be of much lower price. A letter of inquiry was sent, and I received back an almost immediate reply: there was no mistake. The combined amount was 25,000 Swiss francs or in that neighborhood. I inquired at my bank about his credit and discovered he was good not just for 25,000 francs but for 250,000 or even for two and a half million. I mailed off the books and was paid promptly. For the next 20 years (not including the war years of course) I sold Bodmer books by mail from my catalogues, a few choice ones here and there. But I did not meet him until 1956.

In that year I was invited to see his new library, a marvelous building overlooking Lake Geneva, in nearby Cologny. The taxi driver, unfamiliar with the area, left me off at the wrong address. Trudging along with a heavy suitcase filled with books in which I hoped he might be interested, I encountered a man similarly burdened. He carried a large and apparently very heavy book in a parcel. This turned out to be Dr. Bodmer. The book, he explained, had just arrived from London on approval. I was curious about it, but he volunteered no information beyond the fact that it was expensive.

"I want very much to buy it," he said, "so I'm afraid I can't afford anything from you right now." That was Bodmer's way, to set limits for himself, to enjoy one acquisition fully before passing on to another. The precious volumes in my valise returned with me to New York.

Following my old principle, "When you cannot sell, buy," I asked, rather timidly, if there might be any books in his collection that he would consider selling. I had not, up to then, bought anything from him, and he did not have a reputation for selling. But this was the right moment;

he needed a large sum to buy the book he had received on approval, and would rather pay for it with another book than with cash. He showed me a small manuscript prayerbook in German containing attractive miniatures of the 15th century. The artistic quality was, to my then untrained eye, above average and I did not hesitate an instant to buy it for his price of $23,500. It seemed modest. I imagine he charged me the amount due on his newly arrived and apparently very costly book.

Anyone who deals in manuscripts is foolish to sell without making some effort to identify the artist or school, or to learn something about the origin. But on this occasion I was impatient to sell this little book. Having come a long distance without making a sale, I wanted to turn over this purchase and at least finance my trip. Next morning I called on the great collector Mlle. Edmée Maus at Geneva, showed her the volume, and asked a modest profit. Luckily for me she turned it down. Though enchanted by the miniatures, as any manuscript lover had to be, this confirmed collector of French books regarded it as "too German."

Sometimes the best sales are the ones that do not materialize. Research subsequently showed it to be more than just a pretty example of late mediaeval illumination. It was the famous Prayer Book painted by Simon Bening, last of the major Flemish miniaturists, produced for the equally noteworthy Cardinal Albrecht von Brandenburg, Archbishop of Mainz. It was he who gave the license to Johann Tetzel for selling indulgences and, in a roundabout way, sparked the Reformation by incurring Martin Luther's wrath. The worldly Cardinal, a man of some reputation as an art connoisseur, delighted no less in the temporal glories of illuminated prayerbooks than in the sacred thoughts they inspired; he commissioned a whole series of them, for his own library, of which three are known to have survived. Despite being "late," they represent miniature painting and manuscript decoration at the height of achievement.

Dorothy Miner of Baltimore's Walters Art Gallery, a well-known specialist, not only identified its background but was sufficiently fascinated by the find to give a lecture with slides before invited guests at 46th Street. The discovery of this great manuscript became sensational news in the book world. Nevertheless, the volume remained unsold much longer than it deserved to be, thanks to the recession in the book market. The few U.S. libraries to which I offered the manuscript failed to grasp its significance, replying that they already owned a representative number of Books of Hours by Simon Bening. Finally in 1960 Dr. Ludwig bought it. No further manuscripts decorated and signed by Bening came to light until recently (see Chapter 43). Miss Miner's research showed that it was actually signed by Bening and is the only recorded manuscript carrying his name. We learned subsequently that it came from the Rothschild family before reaching Bodmer. Did he regret giving it up? One does not ask such questions. He was not a specialist in manuscripts by any means but, had he known it to be a Bening, he might have chosen to keep it.

One of the more exotic sales I made to Bodmer was a papyrus Book of the Dead of late dynastic Egypt (715–525 B.C.). In ancient Egypt these collections of prayers went into the tombs of the deceased, along with the usual food, clothing, and household furnishings; hence the name.

In 1960 I bought this fine example from Dr. Otto Fischer of Detroit, who passed away shortly thereafter. He acquired the papyrus as a tightly rolled scroll and took the gamble (which I chose not to take with the Dead Sea Scrolls) to have it unrolled by an expert. After successful performance of that operation, Dr. Fischer decided to have its 32 feet 7 inches separated into eight portions of fairly equal length and mounted between panes of glass in wooden frames. It was written in clear and attractive hieroglyphs in black ink, with the text reading from right to left and arranged in narrow vertical columns. All told, it contained 132 colored miniature paintings, one of them of uncharacteristically large size (560 × 228 mm) depicting the judgment of the soul of Amun Hor, a priest and the individual for whom the scroll was prepared. The large miniature was in itself a major work of Egyptian art.

Dr. Fischer had placed the papyrus on loan with the University Art Museum in Ann Arbor, in the hope of selling it to that institution. The museum was interested but, despite the reasonable price, failed to buy, so Dr. Fischer sold it to me. It was the earliest "illuminated manuscript" I ever owned. I featured it in Catalogue 95, accompanied by illustrations in color and monochrome, and awaited public reaction.

Nobody expressed interest. After a year I still had it, with a pricetag of $50,000. Then, while in Zurich, I visited a loan exhibition of Egyptian art at the Museum. Along with the usual mummy cases and sculptures were a few Book of the Dead fragments, much smaller than mine and with uncolored drawings only. The label indicated they were lent by a private collector in Switzerland. It must, I assumed, be Bodmer; and if Bodmer was interested in the Book of the Dead, he was not the kind of collector to stop at second best.

I lost no time calling on him, armed with my catalogue.

"Is it possible," I boldly asked, "that you own no better examples of the Book of the Dead than the mediocre ones shown in Zurich?"

He was surprised. "How do you know where they come from?"

"Who else in this country would have them?"

"You are right. They are mediocre. But where can a better example be found?"

I showed him the much finer one in my catalogue and he bought it without hesitation.

I now faced the challenge of transporting these fragile items to Europe. Lehmann-Haupt went with them to Geneva. To the great relief of all parties they arrived unhurt. But the drama did not end there. In examining them, the eagle-eyed Bodmer discovered tiny dots of mildew, or what he feared to be mildew, under the glass. This is of course always a danger with papyrus, textiles, and other fragile archaeological items. Mildew can begin innocently, microscopically, then grow like a cancer and destroy the whole surface in time (a very long time, usually, but that provides little solace to the owner). Bodmer showed it to restoration experts from the local museum; they shook their heads in despair. With great presence of mind Lehmann-Haupt thought to lift the glass and, using a soft brush, whisked away the spots. They were on the glass, not on the papyrus. The surface was not harmed. Bodmer was happy, I was happy, and Lehmann-Haupt, saved from the task of bringing them back to New York, was infinitely more so.

It may seem an irony, but here I have to mention that Bodmer had been sent—more than a year before my visit—a copy of Catalogue 95 describing and illustrating the Fischer papyrus. Presumably he had read it. Yet he failed to order. In Chapter 49, I speak at greater length on this phenomenon of collectors failing to notice or appreciate what is offered in catalogues.

Later I came into possession of a large, valuable collection of Greek and Coptic papyri assembled by a well-known collector. Along with it came a remarkable object, a silver dedicatory plate or plaque from the foundation of the Serapeum. This was the second building of the famous Alexandrian Library. Dating from the reign of Ptolemy III (246–221 B.C.), it bore a Greek inscription composed of dots punched into metal with an awl-like tool, reading as follows:

ΒΑΣΙΛΕΥΣΠΤΟΛΕΜΑΙΟΣΠΤΟΛΕΜΑΙΟΥΚΑΙ
ΑΡΣΙΝΟΗΣΘΕΩΝΑΔΕΛΦΩΝΣΑΡΑΠΙΕΙ
ΤΟΝΝΑΟΝΚΑΤΑΠΡΟΣΤΑΓΜΑ

KING PTOLEMY [SON] OF PTOLEMY AND
ARSINOE THE SIBLING GODS TO SERAPIS
[DEDICATES] THE TEMPLE BY ORDER [OF THE GOD]

THE COLLECTOR *PAR EXCELLENCE* 277

Not being an authority on antiquities, I called on experts at the Brooklyn Museum for their opinion. Their verdict was: genuine but not unique. Excavations in Egypt during World War II, while Rommel's and Montgomery's tanks battled not far away, resulted in the discovery of ten such plaques, one each in gold, silver, bronze, faience, and Nile mud, and five in glass. It seemed likely that my specimen was the only one on the market, the others having, so far as could be determined, gone into museums. It seemed to me that no more appropriate place could be found for a relic of the ancient world's most famous library than one of the greatest of modern times, the Bodmeriana. Though he chose not to install the plaque in the cornerstone of his new library building, Bodmer recognized that such an item belonged in his collection.

Bodmer, it must be remarked, never balked at anything because it was unusual or unlike material already in his collection, in contrast to many collectors, even some great ones, who lack the capacity to appreciate an item outside the sphere of their particular specialty.

Another of my important sales to Bodmer was Schopenhauer's *Die Welt als Wille und Vorstellung*, one of the most influential philosophical works, in its first three editions, a total of six volumes, each heavily annotated and corrected in the author's hand, the most desirable copies of these volumes in existence. I acquired them in 1964 for the high price of 180,000 marks (then about $45,000) at a Hauswedell auction in Hamburg. Before the sale I brought them to the attention of Fritz Liebert of Yale's Beinecke Library. Fritz expressed interest but funds happened to be low at the time, so we worked out an arrangement. I would buy the volumes and give Yale first refusal, without obligation. After examining them, the library reached a negative decision. Since most of the corrections and additions were incorporated in a later edition, they represented no fresh thought and therefore could be deemed only of "sentimental" value, for which Yale was in no mood to spend a lavish sum of money. I had had similar experiences in the past with other clients and ought to have anticipated it; still it came as rather a surprise. Invariably the "sure buyer" one has in mind for a book fails to buy.

What does one do in such situations? Sell to someone else. The someone else this time was Bodmer, who needed no urging. He would have bid for them at the auction, he told me, but missed the sale (in light of his cursory reading of *my* catalogues I did not find this hard to believe). It came to his attention only afterward and he tried to learn the buyer's name in case a dealer had bought for stock, but as usual with continental auctions my name was not revealed. On learning I was the owner he was overjoyed. Later he called the volumes one of the highlights of his collection.

Bodmer only selected such manuscripts as fitted into the scope of his library of world literature. It is, therefore, understandable that he excluded Books of Hours, Breviaries, Missals, and other works of religious devotion. In a few instances, however, he broke this self-imposed rule and indulged in buying first-class and very expensive manuscripts of this type. He was, after all, a lover of art and could not resist acquiring books with miniatures by great masters. Later he regretted his "sins" and sold some manuscripts to clear his conscience. For many years I was the happy recipient. I bought the *Brandenburg Hours*, the *Psalter of Bonne de Luxembourg*, Duchess of Normandy; the *Mainz Missal* from the Arenberg Library, and finally the Prayer Book with miniatures by Michelino da Besozzo. This last one had a fairy-book story behind it.

In 1949, while visiting Milan, I was taken by Professor Armani, manager of Hoepli's Antiquarian Department, to call upon a collector who had books to sell. I bought a superb 15th-century Book of Hours in a three-way partnership with Hoepli and my traveling companion Schab. At the time of purchase no research had been done and the artist's identity was yet to be learned. Still, it contained superb miniatures and, at $3,000, it was an investment that required no deliberation. On getting the book back to my hotel and examining it more thoroughly I became convinced that it was really of greater importance than we had imagined. I called on Schab and persuaded him that we should buy out Hoepli at $1,500—that is, the $1,000 he had put up plus a $500 profit. Not expecting so rapid a return on his investment, Hoepli was satisfied. We subsequently offered the manuscript to Bodmer, who bought it for $12,000, still with no information about the artist. Bodmer, to his credit, never allowed such considerations to dampen his natural lust for beautiful books. It proved to be one of his best buys. A few years later Dr. Rosy Schilling, the art historian, published a study of the manuscript in the *Wallraf-Richartz-Jahrbuch*. She recognized the hand as that of Michelino Molinari da Besozzo, a High Renaissance master well known for altarpieces and other paintings.

Had I known the artist's identity I might have asked a much larger amount. After reading Dr. Schilling's article I began plotting to buy back the manuscript. On each succeeding visit to Bodmer—I saw him usually once a year—I brought up the subject, insisting that a Prayer Book did not belong in a collection of world literature. After a time it became almost an obsession to repurchase this treasure. I was angry at myself for selling it so quickly, without the pleasure of owning it and studying it for a while. My offer rose each year but Bodmer persisted in his refusal. Finally, after having kept me dangling like a fish on a hook for 15 years, he relented and sold it to me a few years before his death, at a very imposing figure considering the low purchase price.

This brings up an interesting question, one I have often asked myself after buying from men like Bodmer, James F. Bell, Arthur Houghton, or Alastair Bradley Martin. Why do wealthy collectors sell books from their libraries, books that they once wanted badly? These are all very rich men. What would the money mean to them? They could easily raise as much, and more if necessary, in other ways, without disturbing their collections.

I think a variety of factors is behind sales by wealthy collectors. First, of course, is the undeniable change of heart which any collector, poor or rich, may experience. Tastes can change; one who begins as a collector of English literature may gradually—or abruptly—switch to French illustrated books or sporting volumes. Then, too, some collectors buy rather impulsively and acquire, over the years, a number of books which do not fit their collections and can be pruned out. There is also something else: insecurity. Often these people are very much concerned, despite their wealth (or maybe because of it), about getting their money's worth in every purchase. They become curious to know if the money being spent on rare books is holding up as well as other investments, so they make test sales once in a while. If the sale shows a big profit they go out and buy more heavily than ever. The collector is thereby vindicated in the eyes of his family, who may have chided him for putting so much money into books. This is just my theory, but the more I observe wealthy collectors and their ways, the more I am convinced of it.

But to return to the Michelino Book of Hours; finally repurchased and safely arrived in New York, it became one of the star attractions in my exhibit of illuminated manuscripts held in January 1970. For this show, staged in our Tudor Room on 46th Street, I assembled the best manuscripts then in stock without regard to age, place of origin or other considerations. I can say without boasting that it was at that time the greatest array of manuscripts in a dealer's hands anywhere in the world. Opening night served as the occasion for a gala party, attended not only by book collectors and librarians, but also by prominent figures from the art world. More than the usual number were in town, attracted by the Metropolitan Museum's "Year 1200" exhibition, to which I had contributed seven manuscripts; seldom have there been two such opportunities to indulge a taste for mediaeval art, within 35 blocks of each other. A number of Morgan Library trustees came: Charles Morgan,

Miss Alice Tully, and others. The Michelino Book of Hours was, of course, prominently displayed.

The following May, while Hanni and I were in Munich with the Grolier Club, a cable arrived informing us that the Morgan Library wished to buy the Michelino. This came as somewhat of a surprise since it had not previously expressed interest. At dinner that night, Mary Hyde—widow of Donald F. Hyde, Johnsonian collector and herself an avid bibliophile—gave me an all-knowing smile. She already knew more of the affair than either of us, thanks to a phone conversation that day with Charles A. Ryskamp, the Morgan Library's director. The party on opening night of our manuscript show had been the scene of a Morgan Library plot. Its trustees came not for our hospitality, nor to regale themselves in the glories of mediaeval and Renaissance book painting, but to study the Michelino Book of Hours for possible acquisition. They arranged in their clever way to study it one at a time, lest I should suspect them of wanting to buy it. I knew nothing of it until the news arrived. As often before, the Library paid in cash and duplicates. This time I got three choice volumes including the first English book printed by Caxton at Bruges. All this for an original investment on my part (though later substantially increased) of $3,000.

The *Juengere Titurel* by Albrecht von Scharfenberg, an important literary manuscript of the Middle High German era with 85 beautiful miniatures produced in South Germany in the early 15th century, was one of my most important acquisitions of the early postwar period. I purchased it from Count Wilczek, the father-in-law of Prince Franz Josef von Liechtenstein. The price asked was modest. *Titurel* is a romance of the Arthurian cycle, one of the many variations on the search for the Holy Grail. As a text it fitted perfectly into the Bodmeriana. There were no long negotiations; Bodmer readily bought the manuscript. I was satisfied, he was satisfied. A few weeks later, as luck would have it, Bodmer played bridge with Count Wilczek and told him proudly that he was now the owner of the *Titurel*. Wilczek told Bodmer how much he had sold it for and Bodmer told Wilczek how much he had paid. So all hell broke loose. My position was correct and could not legally be contested. I had paid the price asked and did not bargain. Still, Bodmer was outraged and wrote me an indignant letter. To stay in his good graces I paid half my profit to Wilczek and both were appeased. This I never regretted because it led to important transactions with Bodner in later years, including my repurchase of the *Titurel* for ten times the amount Bodmer had paid. The manuscript is described in my exhibition catalogue:

Monumenta Codicum Manu Scriptorum, No. 34. It found its final home at the Bayerische Staatsbibliothek in Munich.

The greatness of books sold to Bodmer over the years can be equaled only by the greatness of books bought from him. The volumes I succeeded in purchasing from Bodmer were, to put it mildly, of fabulous beauty and importance.

In 1968 business boomed. In October I sold Ed Beinecke a group of illuminated manuscripts for Yale for $450,000. A few weeks later the money came in especially handy, as I was able to buy from Bodmer for a large six-figure amount the famous *Psalter of Bonne de Luxembourg* from the Horace de Landau collection.

I believe it will interest my readers to learn about my relations with this collection, one of the famous private libraries in Florence. It was in 1946 that I learned it was for sale. Baron Landau (1824-1903) was one of the very rich entrepreneurs of the 19th century. He was a director of the Vienna House of Rothschild. I was told the following story about the origin of his wealth: in the middle of the 19th century while traveling on business by stagecoach from Zurich to Bern, Landau was sitting next to a gentleman who was bitterly complaining about the inconvenience and delay in traveling by coach; Landau told the gentleman about the railroad the Rothschilds had built from Vienna to Trieste. It turned out that his traveling companion was the head of the Swiss government and soon Landau brought home to Rothschild the contract to build the Swiss Railroad. I don't know to what extent Landau participated, but he became a very rich man. Later in his life he settled in Florence, where he lived in a palace. There was housed his precious library described in the privately printed two-volume catalogue of 1885-90. He left his palazzo and the library to his niece, Mrs. Hugo Finaly, and after her death her grandson inherited it.

At that time (1946) I had already acquired the confidence and trust of Ernest Zucker (my wife's uncle) and he promised to lend me up to $200,000 if I could acquire this library. The grandson of Mrs. Finaly, M. René Le Bret, who was the executor of the estate, wrote me from Paris that "the library collected by my family during the last century is very important as it amounts to 80,000 volumes. All selected by the great collector Baron Horace de Landau, our great-great uncle, and by my grandmother, Mrs. Hugo Finaly. We will sell in accordance with the wish expressed in her will by Mrs. Hugo Finaly: on that account we mean to proceed only by private sales without resorting to auction sales." In March 1947 I received a letter from Tammaro de Marinis, the book dealer from Florence, on a letterhead: "Liquidation des Biens . . . de la succession Finaly" to advise me that he was in charge of the sale of the library. De Marinis even arranged for the auction sale at Sotheby although Le Bret did not anticipate this, according to his letter. The sale took place on July 13, 1949. Martin Bodmer bought there the famous *Psalter of Bonne de Luxembourg* with wonderful miniatures from the atelier of Jean Pucelle, one of the greatest miniature painters of the 14th century. He paid £16,000, a very large amount, worth at that time about $64,000. I bought it in 1968 from Bodmer and sold it to the Metropolitan Museum of Art (the Cloisters) on May 7, 1969, the day I was—fortunately—unsuccessful in buying the first edition of the Declaration of Independence at auction in Philadelphia. (See Chapter 44.)

For a long time Bodmer regretted selling this manuscript. Many collectors miss their books once sold; Bodmer was one of them. Though hundreds of manuscripts remained to fill the void, he mourned for the Luxembourg Psalter. To lift his spirits I sold him a large folio copy of Redouté's *Roses* with plates in two states, colored and uncolored.

In 1968 or 1969 the late Harry H. Ransom, then Chancellor of the University of Texas at Austin, approached me with the suggestion of trying to purchase the entire Bodmer Library, with backing from the university's oil-rich benefactors. This would have been the biggest transaction ever in the rare-book business, making the famous sale of Lord Spencer's library to Mrs. John Rylands seem paltry. An offer of sixty million dollars was made in a letter from me to Bodmer, received in time for his 70th birthday celebration. At the party that evening in Rome he took out the letter with a flourish and read it aloud to the members of his family. Flattered and impressed, he nevertheless answered no.

"Kraus, you are a devil of a fellow," was his formal reply.

Ransom was disappointed. But the rightness of this collection remaining in Geneva, as the Morgan has remained in New York and the Huntington in California, was unarguable.

In May 1970, I was in Geneva with the Grolier Club. Bodmer showed his collection to the club members, then met me the next day and explained his intentions. He had decided to leave his library as a public foundation. A man of grand design, he had doubtless had this in mind for years. Two to three million dollars would have to be raised, he explained, to establish an endowment. I had been repeatedly trying to buy from Bodmer over the years and he had repeatedly declined, except in the few instances mentioned earlier. So, selling a number of his books to me was, he felt, not only an act of business but of friendship, giving me the long-denied chance to make a selection from his shelves.

Some years ago I read in the Rosenbach book (*Rosenbach, A Biography,* by E. Wolf, 2nd, with John Fleming, 1966) with great envy about the treasures of the Holford purchase in 1925. I asked myself: "Will it ever be possible for me to make a coup like that?" I welcomed the opportunity, but having just bought Arthur Houghton's Gutenberg Bible and having made other large purchases, a sum of that size sounded chilling. "Money, money, money!" I wrote in my diary. "Where are you? Where is all the money I need and where are all the clients to buy these treasures?" Of course I plunged ahead; Hanni put some of her own money into the project.

On June 20 I returned to Geneva and began going through the library. I was very familiar with it; many of the books had been bought from me and even those acquired elsewhere had become known to me from prior visits and the generous hospitality of their owner. Now I approached the shelves not merely with curiosity and awe but the practical consideration of what would be most desirable to own and (hopefully) most salable. Bodmer had not by any means given me carte blanche. He would sell only what he chose to. Many volumes I wanted he would not release at any price. But by making generous offers I succeeded in purchasing a number of books that he was at first unwilling to sell. "Kraus, you are destroying my library," he moaned.

"I bring you money," I answered.

"You have succeeded in denuding me," was his comment after we had finished.

"You have succeeded in making me broke," I retorted, which was closer to the truth.

My purchases from Bodmer are certainly among the most notable transactions ever to take place in the book trade. They far outclassed the famous Holford purchase, both in the sums of money involved ($500,000 for the Holford books, several millions for the Bodmer deal), and in the intrinsic importance of the materials.

The Bodmer purchases covered a great range in time—from the Adler papyri of the 2nd century B.C., to the Molière *Oeuvres* of 1682 (one of three recorded copies of the uncensored first state)—and in value— from the Arenberg Missal of the 11th century to a collection of little poetical tracts of the cobbler-poet Hans Sachs, the "Master-Singer of Nuremberg." The vast range of the collection is a reflection of Dr. Bodmer's all-encompassing interests; the books he sold me came from every corner of his library.

In English literature I obtained from Bodmer some of the "Crown jewels" in the field. The first edition of *King Lear*, 1608; the first edition of *Lucrece*, 1594 (both of them from the Holford Collection); the first edition of John Bunyan's *Pilgrim's Progress*, 1678; all three "high spots," and all three of fabulous rarity. Certainly as rare, certainly even more expensive was the truly immaculate copy of *Reynart the Foxe*, Caxton's own translation, printed by him in 1481. A Coverdale Bible of 1535 (the first edition in English) was imperfect, like all the known copies, but it was nevertheless practically snatched from my hands to fill a gap in the collections of the Beinecke Library at Yale, which also bought the *King Lear* and the *Pilgrim's Progress*. Another Caxton was the first military book in the English language, Christine de Pisane's *Fayttes of Armes*, 1489, one of the few extant complete copies.

These printed books, fine as they are, hardly stand comparison with the manuscripts of English origin or authorship which also came from the Bodmeriana. In date, two leaves in Anglo-Saxon script come first (8th or 9th century); they are from a Bible made for Salisbury Cathedral, where several other fragments of this codex still remain. The *Ecclesiastical History of the English People*, by the Venerable Bede, a Latin manuscript, dated from the early 9th century. Passing to the post-Conquest period, there was a beautiful codex of the *Lumiere as Lais*, a long poem in Anglo-Norman French. The Middle English period supplied three gems, *The Regiment of Princes* by Thomas Hoccleve, a younger contemporary of Chaucer; an English translation of the New Testament, in the version prepared by Wycliffe and his disciples; and a codex containing three Arthurian romances, this manuscript being the sole source for most of their texts.

The early printed books from Bodmer were copies such as will probably never be seen again on the market. They included a complete blockbook, the unique Basel *Planetenbuch* of about 1465; the Balbus *Catholicon* of 1460, probably the last book from Gutenberg's press; the Bible printed by Gutenberg's successors, Fust and Schoeffer, in 1462; and the Lactantius printed at Subiaco, near Rome, in 1465. The Poggio *Facetiae* of about 1470 is the predecessor of a long line of joke books—the earliest one and the rarest, and still one of the funniest. The German Bible of 1475 has the distinction of being the first illustrated edition of this text, and along with it came the 1477 edition, the second to be illustrated. The first engraved maps ever made were in a copy of the 1477 Ptolemy printed in Bologna, a copy in a truly gorgeous contemporary binding, made for the physician Hieronymous Muenzer. The Dante *Commedia* of 1481, with engravings by Botticelli, is one of the few to contain 20 engravings (most copies only have 19, and some copies contain only three or four). There was also a 1472 Dante, the Venice edition, one of three to be printed in that year. Books of the post-incunabula period included the Aldus Vergil of 1501, and the first edition of Ariosto's *Orlando Furioso*, 1516, one of the classics of Renaissance literature, one of perhaps ten extant copies.

Fig. 17. Four famous firsts. (Martin Bodmer Collection.)

But the crowning glory of the Bodmer purchase was the group of manuscripts. The principal one was the Arenberg Missal, notable both for its binding in high-relief silver and enamel plaques from the Mosan region of Belgium, and for its seven full-page miniature paintings of the Ottonian school of Germany. Such a manuscript is just "unfindable" for any price these days. But there were even more: an 8th-century manuscript containing the records of the early Christian church councils; a *Historiae Romanorum* by the Lombardic author Paulus Diaconus (Paul the Deacon), of the 9th or early 10th century, the earliest manuscript of this text known. German literature was represented by three "black tulips": a universal or world history by Rudolf von Ems, of the 13th century; another work by the same author, *Barlaam und Josaphat*, a richly illustrated 15th-century codex; and, as mentioned earlier, the *Titurel* by Albrecht von Scharfenberg.

In addition to all these outstanding books and manuscripts, there were a great number of volumes in the range between $50 and $500, all easily sold.

I considered these acquisitions a personal triumph but the highlights proved more difficult to sell than I had anticipated. It was not the fault of the books but circumstance, or rather a combination of circumstances. These purchases occurred in 1970, with the stock market going down. Paul Mellon, normally an active client, was not buying. The same was true of Yale. Their great benefactor, Ed Beinecke, had died and this had cast a pall over their rare-book collecting (see Chapter 39). At the same time Harry Ransom resigned as Chancellor of the University of Texas at Austin; the new regime took a conservative line toward big purchases, content to bask in the glories of the previous 15 to 20 years. For a while I envisioned myself as another Gabriel Wells or Rosenbach, who often were obliged to search 20 years for buyers of their greatest treasures. But I never doubted the rightness of buying the Bodmer books, come what may.

Bodmer's collection of Shakespeare was renowned as the finest in private hands. The works of Britain's chief dramatist had long appealed to him and he succeeded, over the years, in making a number of important acquisitions. Then in 1951 came the much-heralded purchase by Bodmer of Rosenbach's Shakespeare collection, the "million-dollar collection," that Bodmer, thanks to his negotiating abilities and circumstances (the Rosenbach brothers were advanced in age, unwell, and no other customer could be found for the collection), bought for $330,000 plus a trade of Bodmer's very choice duplicates—he had a fine set of the Four Folios plus some Quartos. The Folios, though desirable, are of only moderate rarity. They can be obtained whenever one is able to pay the price. To buy Shakespeare Quartos, those fragile little publications sold

THE COLLECTOR *PAR EXCELLENCE* 287

originally for a shilling outside the theater, is quite another matter. In a whole career a dealer is unlikely to own even one in the first edition. Even the second quarto edition of *King Lear* is very rare. Here was the first.

Never in my fondest dreams had I hoped to possess it. For me it carried a special significance, too. Twenty years earlier I delighted in telling the story of King Lear to my three daughters (Susi and Johnny had not yet arrived), how he too had three daughters—Goneril, Regan, and Cordelia—and how much they loved him. The king's daughters had different temperaments; Goneril and Regan assured him of their love, while Cordelia remained silent, believing it unnecessary for a daughter to proclaim her love of her father. Because of her silence she received nothing when the king divided his kingdom. Half went to Goneril, half to Regan. But it proved to be Cordelia, the silent, whose love was strongest. When Lear came seeking shelter in old age, his fortune gone, both other daughters turned him away. When I asked my daughters who would be Goneril or Regan, none chose those roles; all were Cordelias.

Having purchased these precious books, I wanted to be certain of getting them home safely. I decided, because of their small size and light weight, to send the Shakespeare Quartos, *King Lear* and the *Rape of Lucrece*, from Geneva to New York by airmail. I made a single parcel of them, very neatly wrapped (I congratulated myself, having been out of practice for 30 or more years, on being able to pack so professionally), and sent it by registered mail, first class, special delivery. The value was $200,000 and I was certain that my insurance covered parcels up to that amount. A week later, when I arrived home, the package had not yet been received. Looking at the post office receipt, I found it did not indicate airmail. Had I overlooked to tell the clerk at the post office to send it by air? This meant a long wait and more chance of mishap. Then I checked my insurance policy. Instead of $200,000 the limit was only $50,000; the parcel was under-insured by $150,000. Should it be lost, this amount would be unrecoverable. If any employee had done such a thing, I would not have hesitated to fire him. But I had made the error myself. Rather than being fired, I received my punishment in another way, by enduring the agonizing wait, not knowing whether my books were safe or lost. After three weeks I became truly desperate; my Swiss agent inquired at the Geneva post office and was told that a surface parcel to New York could not take any longer. Four, five, six weeks passed. I was furious about my stupidity and gave up the books for lost. Then one day, in the midst of my afternoon nap on the third floor, the phone rang. Annoyed at being disturbed, I grunted into the phone, "What is it?"

My secretary was on the line from downstairs.

"Your wife told me to wake you up. They're here!"

"Who is here?" I asked, not expecting any special callers that day.

"The Shakespeares. The package has come."

I rushed down and kissed the books. Not only had they arrived but survived their journey in good condition.

After so much worry about getting my hands on these books, I felt unwilling at first to part with them. In pricing them I set very high figures, almost hoping that nobody would want to pay that much. After four years Yale bought the *Lear*. At this writing, the *Lucrece* is still mine.

CHAPTER 38

In Noble Company

ROTHSCHILD IS A NAME of great magic. When Mayer Amschel set up as a moneylender at Frankfurt late in the 18th century, doing business at the sign of the Red Shield (Rothschild), the family assumed that name.

Since then, the name has become a synonym for wealth, ability, power, and quality. It means many things to many people. To the banker it suggests international loans by which nations survive or fall, and daily meetings at which the world price of gold is set. To the gourmet it prompts a debate about the virtues of Château Mouton-Rothschild and Château Lafite-Rothschild, and their years.

To me, the name means illuminated manuscripts.

The Rothschilds were one of the families of great book collectors of all times. For over a hundred years, various members formed extraordinary libraries, the most recent being that of 18th-century English literature assembled by Baron Victor Rothschild, who is also (such are the diverse abilities and interests of the family) a distinguished biologist at Cambridge University. The libraries of Baron James (1844–81) and Baron Henri, his son, are now part of the treasures of the Bibliothèque Nationale.

Most of the Rothschilds rarely discuss or reveal their book treasures, so that many of them are virtually unknown even to determined scholars. How important these possessions can be was disclosed when a catalogue of twelve illuminated manuscripts was issued for a sale to be held in Paris on June 24, 1968. The catalogue was a sensation. The tradition with French sales is for little advance fanfare, and the catalogues are circulated only one or two weeks beforehand. Nobody in the U.S. expected that such choice manuscripts were to be sold; many were unaware of the sale until after it had taken place. My Paris agent saw to it that I had a copy on time. When I arrived in Paris two days before the sale, I had been able to study the manuscripts carefully.

The catalogue gave no indication of the owner, but it soon became known by the book-world grapevine (an efficient system of communication) that they were the property of a member of the Rothschild family. One rumor connected them with the late Baroness Alice Charlotte of Waddesdon Manor (Buckinghamshire, England), a huge house built in the style of a French château by Ferdinand de Rothschild in 1880.

Like many rumors, this was not correct. The manuscripts were, in fact, part of a collection begun by James Mayer Rothschild, youngest son of the founder, Mayer Amschel, and enlarged by his youngest son, Edmond James, at whose death in 1934 the collection was divided among his three children. One son's portion was bequeathed to the British National Trust. His brother, Maurice, later added to his original share the manuscripts that had been left to his sister, Miriam, and the whole passed, on Maurice's death in 1957, to his son, Edmond Adolphe. From this source came the manuscripts to be auctioned at Paris, as well as a few others that were sold privately.

The manuscripts were the choicest of the choice—real Rothschild quality. They were unknown to modern scholars, only a few of them having been briefly mentioned in obscure notes between 1853 and 1904.

The sale began very quietly, in the large, elegant hall of the Palais Galliera which is reserved for auctions of distinction. The little group of books sparkled. No Renaissance prince could have had handsomer volumes. I bought the first item with little opposition. It was a 13th-century commentary on the Bible with 69 full-page miniatures and 200 smaller paintings, of most unusual mystical subjects. It was later sold to Edwin J. Beinecke for presentation to Yale.

The second item was the finest in the sale: a 13th-century manuscript of the Apocalypse, with 72 large paintings, again in a very unusual manner (see Plate 15). It was comparable to the more famous Dyson Perrins Apocalypse I had bought a decade earlier (see Chapter 36). The keeper of manuscripts at the Bibliothèque Nationale, Marcel Thomas, was sitting near me, and I imagined that his expression was menacing. The bidding began at a relatively low level and climbed slowly, with an occasional bid from me. At 600,000 francs (about $120,000) there was a pause. It was not my bid, and I saw Thomas smile as if he had the bird already in hand. Everyone looked at me, expecting that I would yield.

"*Un million,*" I shouted, standing up in my excitement. (The equivalent in dollars was more than $221,000.)

There was great commotion in the gallery, after which the auctioneer resumed his ritual. "*Un million j'adjuge . . . j'adjuge . . . j'adjuge . . . Monsieur Kraus!*"

The spontaneous applause was sweet to my ears, as was next day's headline in the *Figaro*, for it signaled that I owned one of the world's finest manuscripts.

"Why did Kraus jump from 600,000 to a million?" everyone asked. "He could have had it cheaper."

I looked at the sad face of Thomas, and I knew what others had forgotten: that at a lower price, he would have exercised his right of preemption, that is, the right of the French Government to purchase the item at the hammer price and thus supersede the accepted bid.

Of the remaining ten manuscripts I bought five well within my limits for them. It had been a memorable afternoon.

Next day I called on Thomas to arrange export licenses for my Rothschild manuscripts. He was very kind and said how sorry he was that the Library had not been able to meet the price on the Apocalypse.

There was, however, just another little matter. . . . Even if the government could not meet the auction price it could still, with an item of first importance for art and culture, refuse an export license. It was regrettable, but. . . .

My joy dissolved into ashes. It was of no use to me to own a manuscript, however beautiful, if it had to remain in France. The lawyers I consulted were of little help.

After long and rather emotional negotiations, the export license was finally granted, and all my Rothschild manuscripts were shipped to New York.

I called on Thomas again and offered, as a mark of my gratitude, to give to the Bibliothèque Nationale a 7th-century Merovingian manuscript, partly on papyrus and partly on vellum, which was of great importance for French history, palaeography, and linguistics. Not only was my offer accepted with Gallic grace, but in 1975 a learned study by Pierre Gasnault with reproductions of these early fragments appeared in *Collection de Documents inédits sur l'Histoire de France*.

Once I had the Rothschild manuscripts on my table in New York, I began trying to find my way through the mazes of this family of collectors, to trace their provenance. I did not then know what has been said above about their source. Each of my manuscripts, I noticed, had a number written in pencil on the flyleaf, evidently a shelf mark, indicating where they had stood on the shelf in the same library.

I remembered that the Morgan Library had recently acquired one part of the Book of Hours of Catherine of Cleves, which had also come from one of the Rothschild collections. I went to the Morgan Library. Yes, on the flyleaf of the Cleves manuscript was a penciled number just like those in my manuscripts. Perhaps these were the marks of the library at Waddesdon, from which rumor suggested they had come.

I was discussing the problem in the reading room with Fred Adams, who sensibly suggested that a list of Rothschild manuscripts with the same pencil shelf mark, if circulated among other libraries, might help to establish their source. At this point, a scholar working next to us in the reading room politely joined our conversation.

"Gentlemen," he said, "I think I can save you some trouble. Here is a list of the manuscripts at Waddesdon, on which I am working."

I was speechless. As Adams said afterward, "Such things can only happen at the Morgan Library." It was clear that the manuscripts sold at Paris had not come from Waddesdon, and the scholar, Mr. James Marrow, later helped to establish, from his knowledge of the Rothschild collections, the true provenance which I have given above.

A short time afterward, I had a telephone call from a New York attorney inviting me to examine some illuminated manuscripts. His office was nearby and in a few minutes I had in my hands two very fine manuscripts, a *Chronicles* of Froissart with splendid miniatures by the Master of Edward IV, and the *Book of Hours of Queen Claude*, wife of François I of France, the work of the celebrated scribe Geoffrey Tory and with exquisite miniatures. (See *The Master of Claude, Queen of France,* by Charles Sterling, "Rare Books Monographs Series," Vol. 5, 1975.) From the pencil marks on the flyleaves it was plain that they came from the same collection as those sold in Paris.

"Of course, these are Rothschild manuscripts," I said quietly.

His jaw dropped. "I am instructed to keep the ownership strictly secret," he said with great embarrassment.

I decided immediately to buy these two manuscripts, for more than $200,000. Now the lawyer was astonished all over again.

"I have never made such a quick deal. In a matter as big as this, people go away and think it over for weeks." The importance of the manuscripts makes it clear why I did not hesitate.

Now I had bought nine and was still the owner of eight great Rothschild manuscripts, at a cost of considerably over a million dollars. One of them had caught the discriminating eye of Edwin J. Beinecke, and I had bought it on his order for presentation to Yale. It was a prose work,

Le Livre des Trois Virtus, by Christine de Pisan, whose poetry has been extensively studied and published but whose other writings have received little attention. It was illuminated with four large paintings of high quality executed in the 1460s and judged of sufficient importance so that one was reproduced in color on the cover of the Paris sale catalogue. Later, Beinecke also bought for Yale a 13th-century Bible commentary, as mentioned above, and an exquisite little Paris Book of Hours of about 1510, with 15 large and 15 small miniatures in grisaille and gold and the text written in calligraphy so fine as to resemble print.

After the three Beinecke purchases I still had six of the Rothschild manuscripts in stock, including the million-franc Apocalypse. Where were the buyers?

Three months after the auction, Hanni and I attended the opening of the exhibition of Italian frescos at the Metropolitan Museum. My diary for the next few days records how, for the Apocalypse at least, I soon had a surfeit of buyers.

At the buffet stood the director of the Metropolitan Museum, Thomas Hoving. Young, energetic, tall, and good-looking, he had been previously the director of the Cloisters collection of mediaeval art.

Frankly I had not considered the Metropolitan Museum a potential customer for any of the Rothschild manuscripts. It rarely had large sums to spend on illuminated manuscripts. There were of course the two great ones purchased from Baron Maurice de Rothschild in 1953, the *Hours of Jeanne d'Evereux* of 1325, with miniatures by Jean Pucelle, and the *Belles Heures de Jean de Berry* of 1413 with miniatures by the Limbourg brothers. But since then there had been no major purchases. Still, Hoving was known to be a devotee of mediaeval art. No harm could be done, I thought, in bringing the Rothschild manuscripts to his attention.

I knew him but was reluctant to greet him. "He will not know who I am," I said to Hanni. I took a drink and waited until he was, for a moment, by himself, then I introduced myself: "I am Hans Kraus."

Since my name is often misunderstood, I was prepared to spell it, but he greeted me with friendly cordiality. I told him I had some of the finest Rothschild manuscripts, including the Apocalypse.

"I will come to see them next Monday morning," he replied.

I was skeptical. Such visits are more often promised than made. But on Monday he came, accompanied by Theodore Rousseau, Jr., the Museum's curator of paintings. They looked at the manuscripts, took descriptions and photographs, and departed.

The following day, Dr. Ludwig dropped in. He saw the Apocalypse and was immediately enchanted.

"I must have it! How much is it?"

"$750,000." I had quoted the same to Hoving.

I had not specifically promised Hoving that I would hold the manuscript for him, and was unsure of my position, so I called Rousseau to say that I had another buyer. Ludwig stood next to me at the telephone where he could hear the conversation. Rousseau asserted that they were seriously considering the Apocalypse and would give me an answer within two days.

For two days I stayed home at Ridgefield horseback riding. When I returned to the house I found that the phone had been busy. Both Hoving and Rousseau had called and left messages that the Museum would buy the Apocalypse. I reached Ludwig and finally persuaded him to let it go. It does not happen often that a bookseller has to talk a client out of spending $750,000. The Museum was in fact so proud of this new acquisition that a fine facsimile edition was published. Such is the luck, the unpredictability, and the drama of the rare-book business.

CHAPTER 39

Yale and Beinecke

FEW OF MY COLLECTOR FRIENDS made such a deep impression on me as Edwin J. Beinecke. His love for Yale University was contagious. Here was a man who valued that institution of learning as one of the most important pillars of our civilization and who backed his opinion with his money. He ranks high among great American collectors.

The eldest of three sons of a prosperous German family, he entered Yale with the class of 1907, but did not graduate. He was put to work for a construction company that was then erecting the Plaza Hotel, and he had many good stories about life on the work crew. When his two younger brothers married the daughters of one of the founders of the Sperry and Hutchinson Company, he joined them in the business of selling the familiar S&H green trading stamps, which he headed from 1923 until 1967, presiding over its remarkable growth.

Devoted as he was to the company, he was equally ardent in pursuit of his hobbies. One was early German glass, of which he formed the finest collection, now at the Corning Glass Museum by his gift. He also collected fine china, especially Meissen figurines. He decorated his Greenwich estate with wide plantings of daffodils, azaleas, and rhododendrons, adding new strains every year. But his first love was books.

He spent many years and constant attention in assembling the books, manuscripts, and letters of Robert Louis Stevenson, and when, toward the end of his life, he printed a catalogue of his collection, it occupied six large volumes.

His interest in the Yale University Library was first aroused by Chauncey Brewster Tinker and was extended by James T. Babb, Yale's librarian. In the late fifties, when Yale's rare-book collection was overflowing its quarters in the main Sterling Library building, he undertook, with his brothers and other members of his family, to build a separate rare book library at Yale. The Beinecke Library, one of the largest buildings in the world devoted to rare books, was opened in 1963 and is notable for its architecture, its collections (including his Stevensons), and the generous endowment provided by the Beinecke family. He continued to take an active interest in the library, presenting to it many papyri, early printed books, and illuminated manuscripts until his death in 1970.

Such an account might be written about many collectors and benefactors, but it gives no feeling for the man. He was a person of extraordinary natural gifts, not literary or artistic in the academic sense, but with a native sense of taste and recognition of quality that were unerring.

I met Ed Beinecke late in his life. He used to come to my shop several times a year, often with Fritz Liebert, the first librarian of the Beinecke Library, to see (as he put it) "if there was anything worth buying." And there always was.

These visits were remarkable. I would show him incunabula or exquisite illuminated manuscripts, which he would look at while he listened to my descriptions of them. Then he would reach out and put two or three to one side; these were the ones he would buy for Yale, and they were unfailingly those of the very highest quality among what he had seen. He did not know the details of the author's or printer's significance, or the miniature-painter's skill, but he instinctively knew something more important: the best.

Nor was he afraid to think big. In 1961 I issued a catalogue of very fine classical papyri containing 140 items. Liebert was anxious to secure three of the principal items, and called them to Mr. Beinecke's attention. Beinecke telephoned in reply and asked, "Aren't the rest of the papyri any good?" Fritz assured him that they were. "See how much Kraus wants for the whole catalogue," said Mr. Beinecke, and later that day the whole collection was Yale's.

Liebert, a scholar of wide learning and the most active librarian I have ever met, has an insatiable love of great books and Beinecke was fortunate to have him as advisor. His independent judgment could never be influenced, and his taste is impeccable. He knows what is good.

Once Beinecke said to me: "I want to give a good Caxton to Yale. It must be complete and a very important text, one which is not in the Mellon collection. Do you know of any?"

After a short reflection I told him: "Yes I know of one in a private collection; give me a day or two."

The next day I telephoned Martin Bodmer in Switzerland and I asked if he would consider selling me his *Reynart the Foxe* of 1481, a Caxton of the greatest importance, a fine complete copy.

Bodmer said: "If you really want it you have to pay a huge price." The figure was $250,000.

I called Beinecke; the amount did not frighten him.

"Let me see it. If it is really fine, I will take it."

I went to Geneva and bought the Caxton. When I came back Beinecke was dead, and I still can admire the beauty of *Reynart the Foxe* on my shelves.

Like most big men, he was not reluctant to speak his mind. In the sunken courtyard in front of the Beinecke Library, the architect had placed three pieces of contemporary abstract sculpture, which Beinecke did not admire. Leaving the library one day, he saw a family looking at the sculpture and, as he passed, he heard the father say, "I wonder what damn fool paid for those." Fritz turned pale, but Beinecke walked over and said, "I want to shake your hand. I'm the damn fool who paid for those."

Among the many great collectors who have been my customers, there is none with whom it was a greater pleasure to do business. Mr. Beinecke knew his own mind, he knew quality when he saw it, and he was ready to act on his judgment. Among the many items he bought for Yale I remember these especially:

A handsome copy of the first edition of St. Augustine's *De civitate Dei* (Subiaco), 1467, one of the four books (all of great rarity) printed by Sweynheym and Pannartz, Italy's first printers, before they moved to Rome.

The *Bedford Book of Hours*, written at Paris about 1425, with 16 full-page miniatures of which 11 are attributed to the "Master of the Bedford Hours" who painted the Book of Hours for John of Lancaster, Duke of Bedford, now in the British Museum. The painter is often regarded as the leading miniature artist in the second quarter of the 15th century.

A 15th century illuminated Missal, in French (see Chapter 16).

An illuminated and signed manuscript of Dante's *Divina Commedia*, written by the Dominican scribe Franciscus at Florence late in the 14th century.

The *Savoy Hours*, made between 1307 and 1348 for Blanche de Bourgogne, Countess of Savoy, and later the property of King Charles V. It is one of the finest surviving examples of 14th-century illumination. Most of the manuscript was destroyed by a fire at the University of Turin library, but these 56 leaves were later found in an English library, and their 48 miniatures are specimens of mediaeval painting of the highest quality.

An illuminated manuscript containing the *Canticles of the Virgin* and other mystical texts, written in the Netherlands about 1325. It contains 46 full-page miniatures, 23 full-page wash drawings, 200 smaller miniatures, and over 500 marginal drolleries.

The *Capitularies*, or edicts, of Charlemagne, his son Louis the Pious, and his grandson Charles the Bold, written in northern France in the third quarter of the 9th century, with 11 large colored initials.

One of the most beautiful manuscripts I have ever possessed, the Bible written in northern Italy for Cardinal Niccolò Albergati and finished on August 13, 1428. Written on the finest vellum, every one of its 682 leaves (except for four blanks) is decorated and the principal pages have miniatures on so delicate a scale as to defy appreciation without a glass. It has been called "one of the finest of all Italian late Gothic illuminated manuscripts." It was among the last of his gifts that Mr. Beinecke lived to see, and it delighted him.

For these eight items, Mr. Beinecke paid over $1,100,000. The pleasure that he showed in the beauty of these treasures made it evident that he was sure he had gotten his money's worth.

Large as his expenditures were, money was never better spent. Not only are treasures such as he bought available today only at many times what he paid for them, but his library and its contents have made the name of his family famous in the wide world of books. Every time I visit the Beinecke Library and see the inscription on the bronze plaque opposite the front door, "May this library . . . serve as a source of learning and as an inspiration to all who enter," I am glad to think that Mr. Beinecke's wish has been realized.

Under Beinecke's influence I made up my mind to imitate him in a way befitting my smaller resources, and I contributed to the rare-book collection at Yale substantial gifts like the Cipher manuscript about which I speak in Chapter 31. Through him, and the many members of Yale's faculty and library staff, I became enamored of this great University which I think of privately as my Alma Mater; I who never had the luck to graduate from any university.

I cannot resist the temptation to add to this chapter the story of the Robert Sterling Clark Collection on Horses and Military History which I presented to Yale in 1961.

My friends in the trade know my passion for horses and riding. Therefore it was not surprising when, in 1960, a Parisian bookseller who ran a small shop asked whether I would like to buy a collection of books on horses. I was taken to a garage in the suburbs, which was rather dirty and oppressively humid, but stacked with books in piles, six to seven feet high. At first glance they made a poor impression. I wanted to leave without wasting more time.

"Please," the dealer begged, "look and see if there is anything of value."

I did.

To my surprise a number of imprints of the 16th and 17th centuries emerged from beneath the dust and spiderwebs. The collection was being sold as a lot only, and had to be removed within a week. Because of this stipulation, the price was quite low. I bought the books and had them shipped to New York.

"Who was the owner?" I wanted to know.

The answer was vague. "I don't know his name. I learned that he was an American turfman who had been living for many years in Paris. Ten years ago he sold his house, went back to the U.S., and the books were sold to me."

At 46th Street we cleaned and shelved the books. Loosely inserted in some were bills, by which we discovered the owner's identity: Robert Sterling Clark. A man of substantial wealth, he had died in December 1956 at age 79, and had left an estate reported by the *New York Times* to be worth around $84 million. Well-known as an art collector and international sportsman (his horse, Never Say Die, won Britain's Derby in 1954), he was a benefactor of Williams College in Williamstown, Massachusetts. He came from the famous art-collecting Clark family of Cooperstown, New York, which owns a large share of the Singer Sewing Machine Co. (his grandfather, Edward Clark, having become in 1851 an equal partner with the founder, Isaac M. Singer, and becoming president of the company after Singer's death in 1875).

With his wife he founded the Sterling and Francine Clark Art Institute in 1951, near the campus of Williams College, at a cost of about $9 million. It could hardly be believed that his library met such an ignoble fate, to lie in jumbled stacks in a garage. *Habent sua fata libelli.* (Books have their own destiny).

To break up such a collection seemed a pity, considering the lifelong effort that must have gone into assembling it. I resisted all attempts by various clients to buy single volumes or groups. By the end of 1961 I knew that the only possibility of keeping the Clark books together was by the gift of it to an institution. Yale University, with its active interest in and large collection of sporting books, was the obvious recipient. Formal presentation was made on November 16, 1961. I said on that occasion:

Fig. 18. Bookplate made for the Clark Collection. (Yale University.)

I would like to say to you a few words about a bookseller who makes a donation of books—an act completely contrary to his *raison d'être* and to his philosophy of business. All my life as a bookseller, I have been occupied with the buying and selling of books. One of my ideals in this profession is to bring the right book to the right place. Unfortunately, this ideal is rarely realized. When I buy a book, I immediately visualize the collector or collection where it should find its permanent home. Usually—and I know this from long experience—the book ends up somewhere else, much to my disappointment. I cannot prevent this if I want to stay in business.

When I acquired the Robert Sterling Clark collection of horse books, I thought immediately of the perfect home for it. Of course, as usual, this did not work out. However, there was the thought of another home where this collection would fit in very nicely. The Yale University Library with its already distinguished collection of horse books would undoubtedly appreciate and cherish the Clark books. I did not dare risk a refusal by suggesting that it should purchase this collection. So I offered the books as a gift. Now, with the Wagstaff and other collections already at Yale, that library's holdings of sporting books will be unsurpassed.

Mr. Clark managed to bring together no less than 800 books and over 600 pamphlets dealing with all aspects of horsemanship. I think that such an accumulation represents an extraordinary achievement, considering the fact that books on horsemanship were usually not collecting dust on the shelves of some library but were constantly consulted by their owners for practical purposes and were often worn out by daily use. Nowadays it would be impossible to duplicate such a collection, even without regard to cost.

Of course, this giving away of books should not become a habit. After all, a bookseller should sell books, and I do not suggest that other booksellers should follow my evil example. But I believe one should combine some idealism with business.

Yale was grateful and had a suitable bookplate designed, here reproduced, which appears in every volume.

CHAPTER 40

The Great Collector of Aachen

HEAVYSET, six feet tall, Dr. Peter Ludwig looks today the same as when I first met him 20 years ago. He was then just 32 years old, but already an avid collector. He studied art history, and art in all its forms—from pre-Columbian and mediaeval to American Pop Art—is his joy and obsession. I could never understand how a lover of illuminated manuscripts could find equal delight in the works of Andy Warhol, but such are the all-encompassing interests of this extraordinary man. His collecting activity also covers mediaeval ivory, silver, porcelain, and possibly other subjects unknown to me.

Of course, I am best familiar with his collection of illuminated manuscripts, most of which he has purchased from me. With unerring flair he selects the most superb examples from various periods and schools. His decision to buy or not to buy is made quickly. After a few minutes of studying some miniatures he says, "Beautiful, I'll take them." If he says nothing, that means rejection. Despite his wealth, the price always counts with Ludwig. Besides being a connoisseur, he is a skilled businessman who knows the best way to use his resources. His wife, Irene, a very attractive lady, is also an art historian, and participates in his collecting activities with enthusiasm. She is a member of the Mohnheim family that owns the largest chocolate firm in Europe. Founded in 1857, it is still a family business.

Ludwig is "Honorar" Professor at the University of Cologne, and he and Mrs. Ludwig are big benefactors to the Museums of Aachen and Cologne. A large part of their precious collections belongs now to these museums. We at 46th Street conferred on him the pseudonym "Charlie," so we could talk freely about him in front of other dealers. Nearly every one of our major clients has a code name: Pumpkin for Mellon, Bally for Schäfer, Waldy for Rosenwald.

Ludwig and I met quite by chance. In 1957 we had a very unusual window display on 46th Street. We showed a huge collection of 3,500 paper soldiers representing French and German troops of Napoleon III's time, manufactured by Silbermann of Strassbourg. We arranged them neatly in battle formation: infantry, cavalry, artillery, camps. It drew a crowd. One day a young couple came in and asked the price of the collection. Luckily I was there. We talked and I discovered that they were collectors from Germany. They did not buy the soldiers but asked to see illuminated manuscripts. This was my introduction to Ludwig and his wife.

I had no idea of their wealth or love of art, but even at that first chance meeting they impressed me as the sort who could become important customers. Shortly thereafter my belief was confirmed when Ludwig bought a number of valuable manuscripts from Catalogue 88. Most of his purchases were of the Arnhold manuscripts, the great prewar collection from Dresden. With his appetite thus whetted, he sought to acquire more. Only when sufficient material is available does a collector have the urge to indulge himself. The big opportunity for Ludwig was the Perrins sales of 1958–60; many of the manuscripts I had bought were later sold to him.

The main manuscript I purchased at the first sale was the 12th-century Latin Gospels from the Imperial Abbey of Helmarshausen founded by Emperor Otto III in 997. In the 12th century the Abbey was one of the leading centers of German book illumination, its most famous product being the Evangeliary of Henry the Lion. The Gospels contain miniature paintings which could rightly be called the glory of the Middle Ages, magnificent initials and the portraits of the four evangelists painted in gold and colors, all in dazzling condition.

When I arrived home from the first Perrins sale in December 1958, I was seriously ill and went to the hospital in New York. A phone call from Germany, from the Mayor of Helmarshausen, gave me some pleasure. He wanted to buy my best purchase of the sale, the *Helmarshausen Gospels*, in exchange for a Rubens painting. I politely declined. Next day another call came from Germany. It was Ludwig from Aachen. Two needles were sticking in my veins, one for blood transfusions, the other for intravenous feeding. I could not move my arms; a nurse held the phone to my ear. In this condition I learned that he wanted to buy the

Helmarshausen Gospels. No better moment could have been chosen. In such a miserable state I would have sold even at cost, but I got a 20 percent profit.

That hospital-bed sale was physically the most uncomfortable I ever made. It was also the largest of a single book up to then. Opportunity knocks when least expected, and often when one is least equipped to be appreciative.

Later I bought back some of Ludwig's important manuscripts at high prices, when he needed money in a hurry to buy Pop Art. Several years after that, when his taste swung back to illuminated manuscripts, he repurchased some of these very same volumes, at still higher prices. We both are bibliophile nuts and react rather unreasonably at the sight of great books. This now happens to me more than ever, a constant source of worry to Hanni, my reasonable wife.

It would be difficult and redundant to list even the most important manuscripts I sold to Ludwig, many of which are mentioned in other chapters of this book. One of the jewels in his collection is the *Life of St. Hedwig,* the story of which is worth telling here.

My Catalogue 100 was issued in a limited edition and copies were for sale at $35. It must have been the most expensive bookseller's catalogue up to then (1962). Because of its 41 color plates, it cost around $50 a copy to produce, and, I might add, it sells today for considerably more as an out-of-print reference work on illuminated manuscripts. As usual when a catalogue is advertised for sale, many orders come from people unknown to us. Rather than being potential customers, most of these people just want the catalogue and have no intention of buying anything from it. (Some, I think, clip out the color plates for framing.)

My staff handles these orders routinely, without calling them to my attention. Only when someone makes an inquiry about a specific item do I hear about it. So it was no surprise that the arrival of a $35 check from a man in Vancouver, British Columbia, ordering Catalogue 100, received no special notice. Riffling through some papers, I happened to come across the invoice. Without that incident, one of my biggest manuscript purchases might never have occurred.

The name on the invoice was Rudolf von Gutmann—Baron Rudolf von Gutmann. This rang a bell. Gutmann had spent 50 years of his life collecting prints and books; he came from Vienna to Vancouver, about as far on the North American continent as one could possibly get away from Hitler.

In partnership with Rothschild of Vienna, Gutmann had owned the steel and coal works at Witkowice in Czechoslovakia, the largest in the Austro-Hungarian monarchy. I remember that he once came to my shop in Vienna to buy a book for about 100 schillings (around $4). He, one of the richest men in Vienna, complained: "This is an excessive price." I felt obliged to allow him a discount of 10 percent and he was happy. Later I realized that his complaint was only a *façon de parler*.

Gutmann's most celebrated acquisition, the manuscript of the *Hedwig Legend*, was made in the early 1900s. For more than half a century the story of this book and of how the Baron came to possess it flourished among bibliophilic folklore.

Along with the price list to Catalogue 100, printed on a separate sheet, I enclosed a letter sending my greetings and asking if he still owned his Hedwig manuscript. It was not just an effort at smalltalk; I thought that he might have sold it, or that it was confiscated, during the war.

"Yes, I have it," came the answer.

Now my emotions changed gears, from curiosity to a burning desire for possession. I was familiar with the manuscript.

A luxuriously illuminated life of St. Hedwig, it was Silesian, dated 1353, and carried an impressive provenance: First it was owned by Duke Ludwig I of Liegnitz (d. 1398), then reposed for many years in the Piarist Monastery of Schlackenwerth near Karlsbad in Bohemia. In 1876 the monastery was secularized and its possessions taken over by the town. Not long thereafter, local officials decided to lay a new water main. Looking for a way to finance it, they remembered the monastery library. It was sold en bloc to the Viennese firm of Gilhofer & Ranschburg, its first large purchase.

It could hardly be termed an exciting library. It did not contain many rarities. Mostly it consisted of printed religious texts which lodged in Gilhofer & Ranschburg's stock for years and gained very little in value. But one item, the Hedwig manuscript, made the deal sweet indeed. When Heinrich Ranschburg, father of my friend Otto Ranschburg, sold it to Gutmann, he was rumored to have recovered the cost of the whole monastery purchase. Just what the price was nobody could learn. Undoubtedly it was a manuscript sale that made history in the rare-book trade and received great publicity.

Baron Gutmann fortunately fared better than the manuscript during World War II. In 1938 it was seized as valuable property by the Nazis and deposited in the Austrian National Library. During the war, for reasons of safety, it and most of the library's other treasures went into a salt mine near Alt-Aussee, out of the way of aerial bombardment. Much luckier than many collectors, who never saw their books again after the war, Gutmann was given back the manuscript in 1947. But, he explained, it never made the journey to Vancouver. It was in the vault of New York's Warburg Bank—very near my office.

Gutmann was old and, with the manuscript not at his fingertips to enjoy, I wondered if he might be persuaded to sell it.

After lengthy correspondence, I was invited to inspect the manuscript at the bank. It proved to be everything that I had hoped and more. What a book! What illuminations, capturing the heart and soul of mediaeval art! I had never seen anything of such beauty.

Gutmann was willing to sell and quoted a price of $200,000. This was a great deal of money. I hadn't spent that much on any of my Perrins manuscripts, bought in open competition against very strong bidding. Such a price would leave no room for profit.

I called Vancouver. Gutmann was not at home. His wife spoke to me.

I offered 200,000 Canadian dollars. Surely, I explained, this was what the Baron had meant. The Canadian dollar had been falling sharply. After being worth $1.04 in 1958 it was down to around 90 cents. If this proposal was accepted I would save $20,000, amounting to a 10 percent discount. Even then I would be paying generously. Should the Baron try his fortune in the auction rooms he might fare much worse and stood only a slim chance of doing better.

The Baroness had no immediate reply. She would confer with her husband and report back.

When a transaction this big hangs in the balance it does neither digestion nor temper any good. I sulked. I fretted. I pleaded with the phone to ring.

Silence on the part of a seller often is a bad sign. A silent buyer could be trying to raise cash to complete a deal, but silent sellers are generally shopping around, getting other offers.

After a week, my nerves were worn to a frazzle.

To make another call seemed inadvisable; instead I sent a wire. It must have struck the proper chord; 24 hours later the reply arrived. Yes, the Baron would take $200,000 in Canadian dollars, but extension of credit—even to a dealer of international reputation—was out of the question. Only after payment in full would Gutmann release the book to me. He drove a hard bargain, but I saw no reason why the game should not be played his way. I had the money and I knew he had the book.

My bank was instructed to transfer $200,000 Canadian by telegraph to Gutmann's bank in Victoria.

This was toward the end of January 1963. A week later I was scheduled for a vacation in Jamaica. Hopefully, Gutmann would let me know by then—the wire must have reached him within hours—and I would go to the bank and collect the book before my departure.

But once again Gutmann fell silent. This was getting under my skin. A delay was unjustified, with the deal closed and the money paid.

I called Vancouver and got the news: Gutmann was ill, perhaps seriously. He had been taken to a hospital. At his age, 85 or beyond, any illness was dangerous. I figured that in the event of his death, the manuscript could be tied up in the estate for ages. I would then have to sue the estate for delivery, and the result of all this would be very unpredictable.

Two days later the Baroness called—the first time *she* had called *me*. Like the Delivering Angel she took me out of my misery. She had spoken to Warburg's and they were instructed to release the book.

Mary Ann and I rushed to the bank. Next morning I went on vacation. Jamaica never looked so good.

Meanwhile, Dr. Harry Bober and my staff gave the manuscript a thorough going-over, studying it more carefully than it had ever been studied. I anxiously awaited their findings.

To my disappointment, Bober failed to share my enthusiasm for it. The *Hedwig* manuscript is only culturally and historically important, he concluded. Artistically it could only be called ordinary, nothing of great merit. Miniatures just as good could be found in many other manuscripts of the period.

I was hurt both in pride and in purse. Illuminated manuscripts sell on account of their art. If customers agreed with Bober, I could not even hope to recover my cost, much less realize any profit.

A year later, after we had made photos of some pages, I showed them to Ludwig. This was done very informally, in my hotel room in Zurich. He asked the price. When I said $285,000 he accepted without hesitation. For Ludwig to pay the asking price, it took an extraordinary book. Nobody doubts today that he got a good buy. In 1972 a splendid facsimile of the *Hedwig* manuscript was published.

CHAPTER 41

The Bibliophile of Schweinfurt

A PRIVATE TRAIN was waiting for members of the Grolier Club in Munich in May 1970. The happy group of book lovers was in high spirits. After three weeks of viewing some of Germany's and Switzerland's finest libraries—in museums, castles, and private homes—the trip's high spot awaited them: the library of Otto Schäfer of Schweinfurt, Germany. Few of us had ever traveled in a private deluxe train. Delicious food and the best German wine regaled us. After a few hours we arrived at the small industrial town and were greeted by Mr. Schäfer and his wife, Ida.

To me they were old friends. I am proud to say that many of Schäfer's best books came from me. His chief field of collecting, great illustrated books, is the same as Lessing Rosenwald's. Both are great human beings and both enjoy seeing beautiful books.

Showing Schäfer a valuable book is a pleasure. Even when choosing not to buy, he is full of admiration and enthusiasm. Schäfer treats us warmly, inviting Hanni and me to his beautiful house overnight. There we discuss business and personal affairs.

To Schäfer's great advantage, Rosenwald ceased buying a few years ago. Without major competition, Schäfer was rapidly able to build a fabulous collection of graphic arts and of illustrated books of the 15th to 19th centuries from such collections as Loncle, Gillet, Bodmer, and others. Many opportunities arose to acquire fine volumes, and Schäfer missed few of them. He enjoys the rare luck to be married to a beautiful and exceptionally charming lady who encourages his collecting. Wives of some collectors consider the hobby a more than eccentric folly.

I met Schäfer for the first time in 1952, when he bought the marvelous copy of the first edition of Columna's *Hypnerotomachia,* Venice, 1499, from the Gotha Library (see Chapter 17); a few months later he bought the Cusanus Map of Germany, Basel, 1530 (Catalogue 69, item 37) for $3,250 (see Chapter 15), quite a high price at that time. The first engraved map of Germany, it was perhaps originally published at Rome in 1464 and reissued at Eichstatt in 1491. Of these two editions no copy is known. The plate was preserved and another edition published at Basel in 1530. This monument of cartography appealed to Schäfer, possibly because of his love for early engravings.

In his early years of collecting he moved slowly, even when prices were very low. At first he missed many opportunities; but within a few years he became an expert and made up by spectacular purchases more than he had missed earlier. The higher prices brought top material to the market and Schäfer took full advantage.

A major acquisition in 1962 was a group of illustrated books from the collection of Maître Maurice Loncle of Paris. Schäfer did not want to buy the whole collection. Therefore we agreed that I should buy it and let him have first choice of single items. Many famous illustrated books of the 15th century found their way to Schweinfurt, most of them in flawless condition. Loncle had the discriminating taste typical of French collectors. I cannot resist mentioning Petrarch's *Historia Griseldis* (Ulm, 1473–74); Boccaccio's *De claris mulieribus,* Ulm, 1473; *Mer des histoires,* two volumes, Paris, 1488–89; Jean d'Arras' *La Melusine* (Lyon, 1477–81), and several Grolier bindings in pristine condition.

One of the jewels in the Schäfer collection is his copy of Boccaccio's *De la Ruine des Nobles Hommes et Femmes,* Bruges, 1476, printed by Colard Mansion. This copy has all nine engravings pasted in, unlike my Arenberg copy (see Chapter 25) without the engravings.

This later copy, which had so enthralled me, drew mixed reactions from my clients. Its lack of the pasted-in engravings made the volume undesirable, despite the unlikelihood of finding a complete copy. I had, it seemed, placed too much confidence in the book by paying $35,000 for it. After having it in stock more than a year, during which it was featured in my Catalogue 80, Mlle. E. Maus of Geneva bought it for $40,000—a very modest profit, but I was glad to make the sale. After her death the volume was sold to the Morgan Library at a considerably higher price. Among those who had read the catalogue description were librarians at the University of Göttingen, Germany, who recognized in it and the accompanying illustrations a book that they also owned, but to which they had never attached any special importance. The University's library possessed a copy of the Boccaccio with *all* the engravings. So startled were they to discover the value that it became a news item and appeared in the German press. Immediately I wrote and asked if they might consider selling their copy; I offered to pay the price in the catalogue, $40,000. As usual in these situations, the correspondence went slowly. After months the University agreed to accept my offer, subject to approval of the Ministry of Education. More delays. I heard nothing at all. After my patience had been stretched to the limit, I placed a call to Göttingen and asked for the library's director, Professor Hartmann, with whom I had been negotiating. I was told, to my great regret, that he had retired. After a few seconds of silence while I collected my thoughts, I asked to speak with his successor. This was a gentleman named Dr. Luther. "I will have to explain everything from the beginning," I thought. But Dr. Luther was well informed on the matter.

"Mr. Kraus," he exclaimed, "I am glad to inform you that our Ministry of Education and Finance has consented to the sale."

Not long thereafter the book arrived. It was as beautiful and in as good a condition as I had hoped. That evening my four girls joined in the celebration; caught up in the excitement, they chanted the following verses as I entered:

> This was another most glorious day
> In the annals of H.P.K.

"Now I own it," I cried, with sublime satisfaction. Long waiting and uncertainty had made victory even sweeter.

The Boccaccio printed by Colard Mansion in 1476 is one of the most important illustrated books of the 15th century. There is only one copy in America, the Marquess of Lothian copy, now at the Museum of Fine Arts in Boston. This copy, in which all the engravings are colored (a state not pleasing to a print collector), fetched in the depression year of 1932 the sensational price of $32,000 at Anderson Galleries. Book prices were then at a very low level.

My first impulse was to keep it for myself. Hanni was less than enthusiastic over that prospect. Soon I became convinced that it should be sold, and anticipated no difficulty in finding a buyer. Nobody could turn down this copy on grounds of incompleteness.

It was unquestionably Lessing Rosenwald's kind of book, but the nation's leading buyer of illustrated incunabula said no when I offered it to him. Perhaps the timing was wrong. My next move was to offer it to the

Fig. 19.   Basel Planetenbuch.   (Schäfer Collection.)

Morgan Library, at what I considered a very fair price. Adams was interested, but after thinking and talking the matter over with the trustees he also declined. Other prospective clients likewise turned it down. When Mr. and Mrs. Schäfer called at my office, I beamingly showed them the volume, saying, "This will be the prize of your collection." Schäfer might have bought it, but his wife discouraged him. The illustrations of killings and other foul deeds offended her.

So it seemed that I would remain the happy owner of the book.

Long after I had stopped trying to sell it, Schäfer asked if it was still available.

"Yes," I replied, "but what about your wife? Has she changed her mind about the pictures?"

"I don't think so. I hope she won't be too angry with me."

So the Boccaccio again crossed the seas, to settle in Schweinfurt. In the space of a few years I had sold two copies of one of the great rarities of early printing.

Soon after this, Arthur Rau and I stepped into a treasure trove. Rau was the great friend of Charles Gillet, the noted collector of Lausanne (formerly of Lyons), who began to sell early French books from the C. Fairfax Murray collection, which he owned in its entirety. This matchless library, well known to the book world from the sumptuous catalogue prepared by H. W. Davies in 1910, had for 50 years been the envy of bibliophiles all over the world. Once again the best of the best, mostly French incunabula, went to Schweinfurt. A unique copy of the Gouda edition of the *Chevalier délibéré* and the Vérard edition of the same book, with different woodcuts, were among the treasures.

Who among private collectors, with the exception of Rosenwald, owns five or six blockbooks? The best of them, the unique copy of the *Basel Planetenbuch* (mid-15th-century) came from the Bodmer collection, and I had the great satisfaction of supplying it to Schäfer. (See Fig. 19.) So, in the third quarter of the twentieth century, a magnificent book collection came into being. To see it grow was thrilling and rewarding both for its owner and for me.

Schäfer's modesty is remarkable. Though the head of one of Germany's leading industrial enterprises, he apparently enjoys being humble. In 1965 he asked me how to become a member of the Grolier Club. I told him it was simple, that a collector of his stature and reputation should have no difficulty gaining acceptance, and that I would gladly place his name in nomination.

"Don't forget," he said, "I own only four Grolier bindings. Is that enough?" I assured him, without hesitation, "That is enough."

CHAPTER 42

Three Generations of Collectors

ON MARCH 5, 1948, I offered to William (Bill) H. Scheide, the son of the great collector John H. Scheide of Titusville, Pennsylvania, some books of possible interest for his library. I wrote that I understood that he was continuing the collection of his father. Scheide's answer was negative. He wrote on April 5, 1948: "For your information I may say that my present life brings me more into touch with the musical world and that I do not have the time or the means available to pursue book collecting with any intensity." In 1954, however, Scheide bought the first edition of the New Testament in French, Lyons, about 1476, and the Durandus *Rationale Divinorum Officiorum*, (Mainz), 1459, printed on vellum, the Duke of Gotha copy (see Chapter 17).

This taught me that one cannot trust negative answers from a potential collector. Usually and fortunately the bug of bibliomania comes to the surface after all. Scheide is now one of my best clients and a good friend. He never wakes me at three in the morning to complain about a price he paid, as others have. Even more: he is grateful for the opportunity to buy important books. Of course he gets the best of the best and he knows it. He has a great advantage in his librarian, Mrs. Mina Bryan, a lady of great knowledge and experience, who watches his collecting like a guardian angel. She was the elder Scheide's librarian and has seen this fabulous collection grow to its present size.

I also sold him a manuscript of top importance: the complete *Gospel of St. Matthew* in Coptic on vellum from the 4th or 5th century, in a hand similar to the *Codex Sinaiticus*. It also contains the Great Doxology in two

313

languages, Greek and Coptic, the earliest manuscript of this text. I remarked recently that this is certainly the greatest book in his collection. With this he did not agree and answered with his typical and disarming modesty: "The manuscript you sold me is quite a good one, but don't forget that I have a few other books which are not bad, such as a Gutenberg Bible, the *Blickling Homilies,* an Anglo-Saxon manuscript dated 971, a Cambridge Platform, Cambridge, Massachusetts, 1649, and a Declaration of Independence."

His library, a treasure house *par excellence,* was started by his grandfather at a time when prices and taxes were extremely low. It is a great satisfaction to me that I have been able to add a few jewels to this great library and to watch Scheide's growing interest in and dedication to his collection.

Among the treasures of the Scheide library are two early Psalters. Printed at Mainz with Gutenberg's equipment (which Fust obtained in a 1456 lawsuit, after Gutenberg defaulted on a loan), they are typographical landmarks of hardly less magnitude than the 42-line Bible. They are also considerably more rare. Compared to the 48 recorded copies of the Gutenberg Bible, there are ten of the 1457 Psalter and 13 of the 1459. That of 1457 is an especially noteworthy production, the first book with a printed date and the first to identify its printer and place of publication in the colophon. The Gutenberg Bible has no colophon. The 1457 Psalter was also the first book printed in more than one color; it has large initials in red and blue. (See Figs. 20 and 21.)

The story of my purchase of these books is one of the most incredible episodes in my career, or indeed in the career of any bookman. Even to dream of owning such works was foolish. They could not be had at any price.

While reading Seymour de Ricci's Census of the Mainz presses, at least half a century old but never superseded as the standard work of reference, I discovered something I had not known; the Bibliothèque Nationale of Paris owned two copies of the 1457 and 1459 Psalters, the only institution in the world with duplicates of these books. This was electrifying news. I had, in the past, succeeded in obtaining fine books from libraries which had duplicates. Never had they been of this stature, but I saw no reason not to try.

Next day I wrote to Marcel Thomas, at the Bibliothèque Nationale, proposing to trade several important illuminated manuscripts for some of its duplicate printed books. I listed the two Psalters, together with several other titles. There was no point in offering to trade printed books with a library as well endowed as the Bibliothèque Nationale. It already has virtually every important European printed book ever published. Its

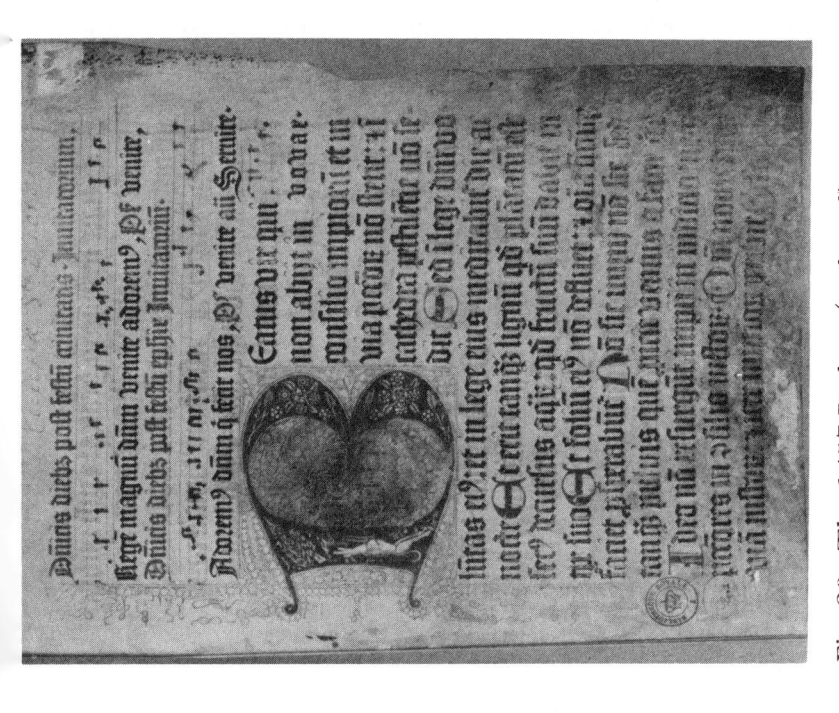

Fig. 20. The 1457 Psalter (reduced). (Scheide Collection.)

Fig. 21. The 1459 Psalter (reduced). (Scheide Collection.)

shelves are no less rich in manuscripts, but I had some extraordinary items which I hoped it would find irresistible.

Later that year, in October 1969, I met Thomas at the International Congress of Bibliophiles in Vienna. Nothing was mentioned about my letter, but as usual we talked shop and the conversation eventually got around to a magnificent illuminated *Speculum Historiale* from the library of the Duc de Berry, which I had bought at the Chester Beatty sale a year earlier. It had been the object of Thomas' affections ever since the sale, at which the Bibliothèque Nationale was, unknown to me at the time, the underbidder. He explained sadly that the library lacked funds to buy it, but left no doubt that the administration would do almost anything to acquire it. That was just what I wanted to hear.

The Bibliothèque Nationale could have the manuscript, I said, if it were willing to trade some of its important duplicates of printed books. I mentioned, casually, the titles that had been listed in my letter. Yes, Thomas replied, the possibility was already under discussion. Julien Cain, the library's Administrateur Général, thought favorably of such an exchange. Cain and I, both ex-inmates of Buchenwald, had known each other for many years. It was arranged that I could examine some of the duplicates in Paris on my way back to New York.

I was ushered into the "Réserve" of the Bibliothèque Nationale and a bibliophilic feast was placed before me. It was one of the exhilarating moments of my career. Millions of dollars in books lay on the table.

My first act was to collate both Psalters to determine or rather to verify their physical condition. I was not, of course, the first to do this, but one can never be certain that a book collated 40 or 50 years ago is still in the same state. They passed this inspection, and the excitement of handling them—the 500-year-old vellum still fresh and crackling—only increased my wish to own them. The two Psalters were, of all the books before me, those I chiefly wanted, because the chance to obtain copies elsewhere was absolutely nil. Yet I realized that, together, their value was several times that of the *Speculum*, for which I had paid $200,000—a matter of public record. I had to offer something more in trade.

One year earlier Marcel Thomas had visited New York and had seen several of our superb illuminated manuscripts. When I mentioned them, he was more than willing to discuss a trade involving some of the manuscripts. As it finally worked out, I received the two Psalters, and the following four major mediaeval manuscripts went to the Bibliothèque Nationale in exchange:

Vincent of Beauvais, *Speculum Historiale*. Two volumes. With 708 miniatures. From the libraries of Charles V of France; Jean, Duc de Berry, and Sir Alfred Chester Beattie. Paris ca. 1370.

Life of Christ. A manuscript of 87 full page miniatures. From the Carnot collection. 13th century.

Livy, Third Decade. With miniatures of the Master of the Maréchal de Boucicault. Phillipps 2924. Paris about 1410.

Missale Parisiense. Written for the Cathedral of Notre Dame. With 16 miniatures. From the Bourbon-Parma Library. Paris, early 14th century.

These four manuscripts represented a substantial sum of money, even at my cost, let alone the prices at which I had hoped to sell them. But it was an entirely fair exchange, great books for great books, both lots really worth more than any sum of cash could express. The transaction had to be approved by the French Ministry of Education, which controls the nation's libraries. This arrived in January 1970. Hanni and I were in Washington to attend the luncheon given in our honor by the Library of Congress to celebrate our gift of Latin American documents (see Chapter 50). I was chatting with Frederick R. Goff in his office and asked if I could use his phone to call New York. Then I heard the news that official approval had arrived.

"Wonderful, wonderful!" I shouted into the phone, as a surprised Hanni and Goff stood by. After hanging up I explained, "This is the coup of my life. I have achieved the impossible. I have gotten some precious duplicates out of the Bibliothèque Nationale."

But I named no titles until the volumes were safely in my hands. I was afraid this could bring bad luck, especially with so many formalities yet to be concluded. It was a number of months before the trade was completed.

On May 20, in the evening, Kebabian flew to Paris carrying one of the four manuscripts, the *Life of Christ.* The other three had been shipped by air freight the previous week, to arrive before my emissary. Kebabian was given the two Psalters and brought them back in person, returning to Kennedy Airport the same day. Together they must have weighed about 25 pounds; vellum leaves are heavier than paper, and these were big books. Customs officials had been alerted beforehand to expect a man carrying two old books worth something in the vicinity of a million dollars. I was there waiting to meet Kebabian and I finally held the two Psalters in my hands. I was elated.

I now had on my shelves a Gutenberg Bible, and the two Mainz Psalters, all acquired within several months. No bookseller has ever had these three works at the same time, not even in the distant past when prices were low.

But of course in the business of bookselling, successful acquisitions must be balanced by equally successful sales. After a full year, I still had all three books, at a cost of more than three million dollars. Feldman had canceled his purchase of the Gutenberg Bible and nobody had shown interest in the Psalters. All three were listed and described at length in my Catalogue 131, *Monumenta Xylographica et Typographica*, the most outstanding incunabula catalogue published in this century, but it brought no orders. The catalogue received glowing comments. It was even reviewed as a book, but nobody was in a buying mood. When Scheide asked about the Psalters, I let them go at cost.

CHAPTER 43

One Manuscript for $750,000

MOST GREAT BOOKS that reach the auction rooms come from great or at least known collections. Even when auctioneers resort to veiling the consignor's name ("the property of a gentleman" or "the property of a lady of title"), the owner's identity is usually well known within the trade. Only on the rarest of occasions does a great book fall from the sky, its provenance a mystery to all.

A Book of Hours, one of the finest illuminated manuscripts sold since World War II, which brought the highest price ever (it fetched five times more than any Dyson Perrins manuscript), came to the salesrooms without the blare of trumpets. The story as given by Sotheby's was that the seller arrived one day at its Munich office and walked in unannounced with the book under his arm. Unknown as a collector or descendant of a titled family, he was thought to be acting as an agent. The manuscript was of extraordinary artistic appeal, matched by few in public institutions and by none in the hands of dealers. Where it came from or how it got to Sotheby's seemed to matter little; this is not to say that prospective buyers could totally stifle curiosity. We exchanged theories, made guesses. As the manuscript appeared never to have been recorded in the whole annals of book auctions, nor any mention made of it in the literature of book illumination, the most logical conclusion was that it came from an old family library, perhaps a family of royal blood, to which scholars had never had access.

This manuscript was to be sold on July 5, 1976. It was not, like so many outstanding manuscripts, high-priced merely because it dated from an early era—Carolingian or Ottonian—or contained the earliest appearance of a text of great importance. In fact it happens to be a common sort of book, a Flemish Book of Hours of the late Gothic era, such as were produced in the thousands and still exist today in plentiful numbers. Its great value lay entirely in the artwork, in large numbers of gemlike miniatures and ornamentation of the highest possible beauty. Its artists were three of Flanders' most renowned miniaturists: Sanders Bening and his son Simon, and Gerard Horenbout. As miniature painters these men won reputations comparable to those of Van der Weyden or Van Eyck for altarpieces. In this book they created their masterpiece. Here the art of illuminating rivaled even that of easel paintings. Obviously it was executed for a noble family, at a noble price. No ordinary person could have owned such a book. Page after page displays the work of months, perhaps even years, of toil. Those familiar with the beauty of ordinary Flemish Books of Hours will find it really breathtaking.

I studied the manuscript carefully a month before the auction and decided to bid in person, to take no chances. On July 2, a Friday, Hanni and I arrived in London. The sale was scheduled for the following Monday, which meant we had a weekend to prepare, to figure out a price limit, and to get nervous. The excitement preceding a big sale—or, in this case, an essentially minor one featuring only one big item—never dulls, no matter how many you've attended or how old you get. Each is different. Each is uncertain. Unexpected things, sometimes disastrous things, can happen. You never know who the competition will be, or how far they're prepared to go. With an item in this price range, a bid can rise $50,000 in half a second.

Sotheby's placed an estimate of £100,000 to £150,000, or roughly $180,000 to $270,000 on the manuscript. With the exchange rate fluctuating daily, the translation into dollars was tentative, on top of which there were rumors of a sterling devaluation. This could have saved me a considerable sum but did not materialize.

"How far shall I go?" I asked Hanni.

Above the estimate?

Double?

Hanni, who in our leaner days scolded me for overspending, suggested double the estimate: £300,000, or more than half a million dollars (considerably more, in fact, after Sotheby's tacked on its annoying "buyer's premium" of 10 percent). For a dealer who spent seven figures on a Gutenberg Bible, $500,000 to $600,000 might not seem large, but that Gutenberg Bible was still in stock after more than six years. Would we have the manuscript for six years or longer? Could we continue tying up large capital, not getting a penny of return on the investment?

With all of this going through our minds, Hanni, I, and our son John, then 18, arrived at Sotheby's on the morning of the day of the sale. It was 10 o' clock, the sale was set for 11. Again we looked at the manuscript, admired it, and exchanged words of counsel.

"Don't go overboard," advised Hanni. I didn't ask what overboard meant.

"Buy it, Dad, buy it," urged John, who did not have to worry about unsold stock.

As the clock reached 10:30 and the room filled, I went round and spoke briefly to everyone whom I thought might be a competitor. They would undoubtedly be bidding for a client whereas I had no buyer. Still I wanted to feel them out and get, if possible, some indication of how high they might go.

The low estimate worked in my favor. If an institution gave one of my competitors a bid, it was not likely to be much above the estimate. Many institutions allow themselves to be guided closely by the estimates, not realizing that these represent just educated guesses or, in the case of rarely sold material, wild guesses.

Everyone agreed about the manuscript's importance and said the estimate was low, but I found no one willing to admit he would pay more. This was encouraging. Sometimes a bidder will try to scare off others by threatening to buy at any price.

Still, one never knows. Maybe the big bidding would come from someone unexpected. Maybe the auctioneer had a substantial desk bid.

I was seated near a window flanked by Hanni and John. London was roasting in a hitherto unknown July heatwave and so was the auction room; the old building had atmosphere and charm but no air-conditioning. In deference to the occasion's solemnity, nobody removed jacket or tie. What with the heat and several wide-awake nights thanks to the book's haunting my dreams, I began to doze. In what seemed like 30 seconds later, but must have been a lot longer, John was elbowing me. Bidding on the manuscript had begun and was already at £100,000!

Hands were going up all over the room.

Within a few moments the estimate of £150,000 was eclipsed, then £200,000, £225,000, £250,000. It was incredible!

At £250,000 I grabbed Hanni's hand. The bid was against me. Two seventy, I answered. Back came the competitor (now down to one), three hundred. Lord John Kerr, conducting the sale, looked around for another bid. Three hundred thousand was supposed to be our limit, to preserve both domestic felicity and financial solvency. But who cares about limits at a time like this? I looked at Hanni, looked at John, and said three ten.

It wasn't enough. By advances of ten thousand, the bidding went on. We were getting close to the equivalent of three quarters of a million dollars, I told myself. Still I could not, would not, allow myself to be defeated on a manuscript that I very passionately wanted.

At £370,000 my competitor went silent. Lord John banged his gavel and the book was mine.

Victory! And never sweeter. It was my most rewarding auction-room triumph in years—since the Perrins sales.

Hanni kissed me. There was commotion in the room and it was several minutes before the auction could resume. For once, Hanni made no "Hans-you're-driving-us-to-the-poorhouse" remarks. I think she wanted me to buy the manuscript as much as I did.

Within a few hours, Reuter's and the Associated Press had the story on the ticker and were sending it all over the world. WORLD RECORD PAID FOR A MANUSCRIPT, read the headlines. THE HIGHEST PRICE FOR A MANUSCRIPT IN THE SALES ROOM. The ticker carried the story to thousands of newspapers throughout the world. I had figured the publicity value in the price I paid.

As expected, a cascade of letters from newspaper readers arrived shortly thereafter at 46th Street. The news of an old religious book bringing $750,000 prompted raids upon attics and cellars. Usually such a letter starts: "Dear Sir, I own a manuscript at least a hundred years old which I want to sell for less than you paid in London." Still, as a result I got a few good buys that never would have found their way to me.

The manuscript was in an armorial binding of the 18th century, whose owner Sotheby's could not identify. As soon as it arrived at 46th Street we began to research the arms, hoping that they might hold the key to its origin or at least its later provenance. Over the weekend we scanned the huge work of Rietstap, *Armorial général*, a voluminous set with 110,000 illustrations of coats of arms. We were ready to give up when I heard the shout, "I have it!" It was Hertha Bauer, our reference librarian. The coat of arms was that of the Spinola family of Genoa, whose members were prominent in war and politics through centuries. Many were art collectors. One of the Spinolas, the Spanish General Ambrogio (1569–1630) captured Breda in the Netherlands in 1625, an important victory celebrated by Velasquez in the famous painting at the Prado in Madrid.

Later in September we attended the Congress celebrating the 500th anniversary of the introduction of printing in England by William Caxton. I was proud to have identified the Spinola arms and told this to Anthony Hobson, the eminent bookman. His eyes lit up when he heard "Spinola." The same family had owned the *Très Riches Heures du Duc de Berry* in Chantilly, and the same coat of arms was on the binding of that famous manuscript. This was electrifying news. My manuscript must have the same provenance as this world-famous manuscript. I was happy that Sotheby's had missed the identification of the previous owner. It might have resulted in an even higher price.

A short time later Dr. Ludwig saw the manuscript and bought it without any hesitation.

CHAPTER 44

A Constitution Bought, a Declaration Lost

OVER THE YEARS my reputation has been built on European books: illuminated manuscripts, incunabula, early science, medicine, and geographical works. I have been content to leave important Americana in the English language to specialists. But buying any big book at auction, regardless of subject, gradually became a sort of obsession. I wanted to be known as a buyer of great books in all fields. Such is the appetite of an ambitious bibliophile.

I have always dealt in early Americana, primarily those relating to the discovery of America, but when I started to buy expensive English Americana at auction, everyone (including the auctioneers) assumed I must be acting as agent for some client. They found it hard to believe that I was buying for stock, so atypical were my purchases of English Americana. It seemed rash for the leading dealer in rare European books to enter a new terrtory after 30 or 35 years, one in which he had limited knowledge and no established customers. I can say now, looking back over those eight or nine years, that no better decision could have been made. I have had good success with Americana of this kind and will continue dealing in them.

My first major purchase in this field was the General Rochambeau Archives, which contained 79 autograph letters of Washington to Rochambeau (see Chapter 22). They are now in the collection of Paul Mellon.

The next excursion into this field came on April 15, 1969, when a copy of the first printing of the U.S. Constitution came up for auction at

Parke-Bernet. Here I faced the competition of the experienced and seasoned Americana trade, challenged by me, the newcomer. Eight copies were known out of 60 printed. The copy offered had belonged to Pierce Butler, delegate from South Carolina, and bore his manuscript annotations and signature. The estimate by Parke-Bernet was $30,000, but I was driven up to $155,000. This established a record at the time for any printed Americana, surpassing the $151,000 paid in 1947 for the Bay Psalm Book bought by Rosenbach and now at Yale. I had no interest in setting a record that day; I merely fell victim to auction-room fever. I had the urge to outbid everyone. On sober reflection afterward, it seemed an outrageous price, much more than I could ever hope to get back. Once again I had tied up a large sum of money without the prospect of a willing buyer. This time, unbelievable luck was on my side. A few weeks later I got a call from a well-known Chicago dealer.

"Is the Constitution still available?" I was asked.

With a certain hesitation I said: "Yes, you can buy it. I'll take 20 percent above the purchase price."

The voice at the telephone said: "I'll take it. Send it along."

I asked myself: Was the price I paid still unreasonable?

In May of that same year, a highly publicized sale occurred at Samuel Freeman & Co. of Philadelphia. Leary's Book Store of that city, one of the nation's largest and oldest secondhand bookshops, had shut down and its stock of about half a million volumes was consigned to Freeman's for liquidation. It was a bulk sale, the kind Parke-Bernet would conduct by sealed bid. Nine-tenths of the books, if not more, comprised quite commonplace volumes that retailed at a few dollars. They were to be sold in cartons, several hundred books per lot, according to subjects (300 mysteries, 400 travel, and the like). Obviously, such a sale is of interest only to dealers in this kind of cheap material. The rare-book trade paid little attention to the whole affair. Then, a few weeks before the sale, came sensational news. It was announced that employees working in Leary's had opened a crate and discovered a copy of the first printing of the Declaration of Independence, one of 16 copies known. (See Fig. 22.) How it got there no one could learn. Apparently the crate had been unopened since about 1911 and nobody connected with the shop in those days was still living. Whoever had handled this precious relic of American history did so carelessly; it was unevenly folded in half, then folded five times laterally down to roughly postcard size, and put into a scrapbook. Its condition, however, was otherwise good, without the usual stains, tears, or worming. It was at once compared with the American Philosophical Society copy in Philadelphia and pronounced genuine by

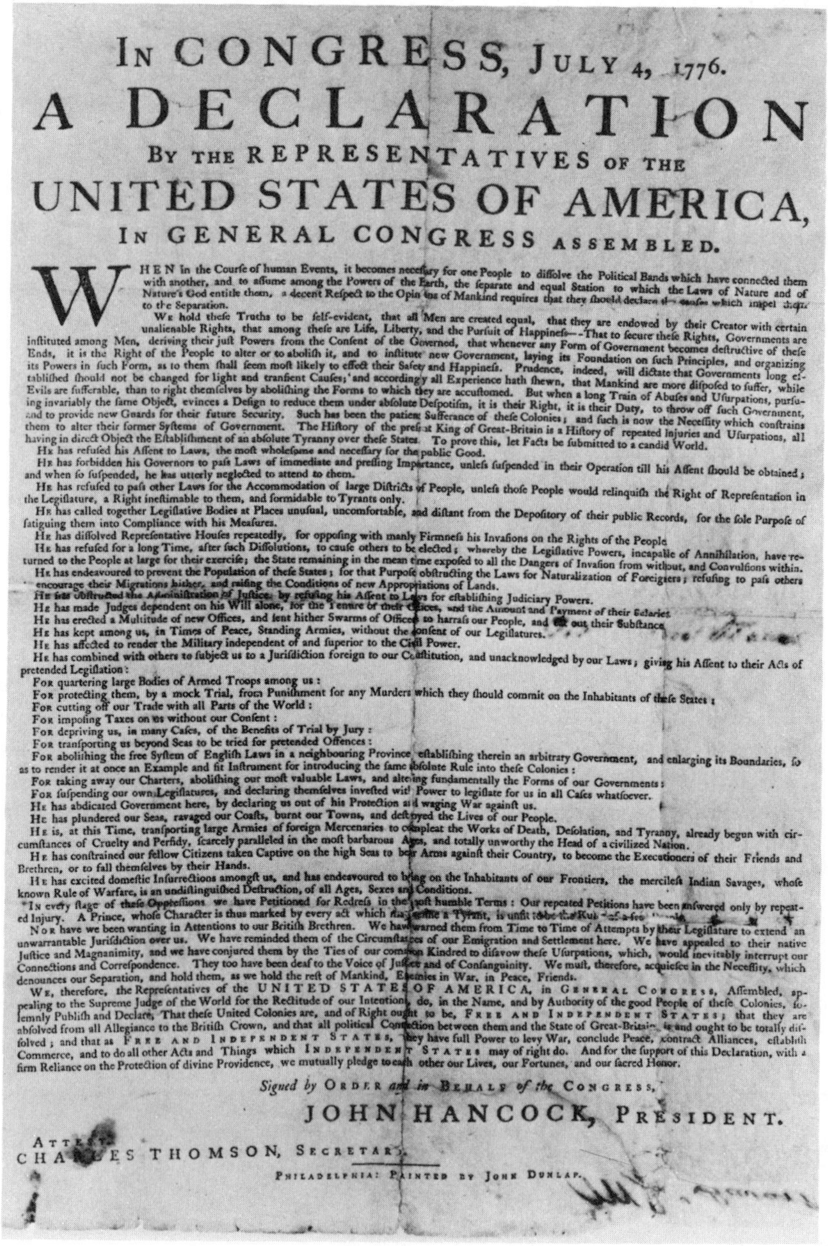

IN CONGRESS, JULY 4, 1776.

A DECLARATION

BY THE REPRESENTATIVES OF THE

UNITED STATES OF AMERICA,

IN GENERAL CONGRESS ASSEMBLED.

WHEN in the Course of human Events, it becomes necessary for one People to dissolve the Political Bands which have connected them with another, and to assume among the Powers of the Earth, the separate and equal Station to which the Laws of Nature and of Nature's God entitle them, a decent Respect to the Opinions of Mankind requires that they should declare the causes which impel them to the Separation.

WE hold these Truths to be self-evident, that all Men are created equal, that they are endowed by their Creator with certain unalienable Rights, that among these are Life, Liberty, and the Pursuit of Happiness—That to secure these Rights, Governments are instituted among Men, deriving their just Powers from the Consent of the Governed, that whenever any Form of Government becomes destructive of these Ends, it is the Right of the People to alter or to abolish it, and to institute new Government, laying its Foundation on such Principles, and organizing its Powers in such Form, as to them shall seem most likely to effect their Safety and Happiness. Prudence, indeed, will dictate that Governments long established should not be changed for light and transient Causes; and accordingly all Experience hath shewn, that Mankind are more disposed to suffer, while Evils are sufferable, than to right themselves by abolishing the Forms to which they are accustomed. But when a long Train of Abuses and Usurpations, pursuing invariably the same Object, evinces a Design to reduce them under absolute Despotism, it is their Right, it is their Duty, to throw off such Government, and to provide new Guards for their future Security. Such has been the patient Sufferance of these Colonies; and such is now the Necessity which constrains them to alter their former Systems of Government. The History of the present King of Great-Britain is a History of repeated Injuries and Usurpations, all having in direct Object the Establishment of an absolute Tyranny over these States. To prove this, let Facts be submitted to a candid World.

HE has refused his Assent to Laws, the most wholesome and necessary for the public Good.

HE has forbidden his Governors to pass Laws of immediate and pressing Importance, unless suspended in their Operation till his Assent should be obtained; and when so suspended, he has utterly neglected to attend to them.

HE has refused to pass other Laws for the Accommodation of large Districts of People, unless those People would relinquish the Right of Representation in the Legislature, a Right inestimable to them, and formidable to Tyrants only.

HE has called together Legislative Bodies at Places unusual, uncomfortable, and distant from the Depository of their public Records, for the sole Purpose of fatiguing them into Compliance with his Measures.

HE has dissolved Representative Houses repeatedly, for opposing with manly Firmness his Invasions on the Rights of the People.

HE has refused for a long Time, after such Dissolutions, to cause others to be elected; whereby the Legislative Powers, incapable of Annihilation, have returned to the People at large for their exercise; the State remaining in the mean time exposed to all the Dangers of Invasion from without, and Convulsions within.

HE has endeavoured to prevent the Population of these States; for that Purpose obstructing the Laws for Naturalization of Foreigners; refusing to pass others to encourage their Migrations hither, and raising the Conditions of new Appropriations of Lands.

HE has obstructed the Administration of Justice, by refusing his Assent to Laws for establishing Judiciary Powers.

HE has made Judges dependent on his Will alone, for the Tenure of their Offices, and the Amount and Payment of their Salaries.

HE has erected a Multitude of new Offices, and sent hither Swarms of Officers to harrass our People, and eat out their Substance.

HE has kept among us, in Times of Peace, Standing Armies, without the Consent of our Legislatures.

HE has affected to render the Military independent of and superior to the Civil Power.

HE has combined with others to subject us to a Jurisdiction foreign to our Constitution, and unacknowledged by our Laws; giving his Assent to their Acts of pretended Legislation:

FOR quartering large Bodies of Armed Troops among us:

FOR protecting them, by a mock Trial, from Punishment for any Murders which they should commit on the Inhabitants of these States:

FOR cutting off our Trade with all Parts of the World:

FOR imposing Taxes on us without our Consent:

FOR depriving us, in many Cases, of the Benefits of Trial by Jury:

FOR transporting us beyond Seas to be tried for pretended Offences:

FOR abolishing the free System of English Laws in a neighbouring Province, establishing therein an arbitrary Government, and enlarging its Boundaries, so as to render it at once an Example and fit Instrument for introducing the same absolute Rule into these Colonies:

FOR taking away our Charters, abolishing our most valuable Laws, and altering fundamentally the Forms of our Governments:

FOR suspending our own Legislatures, and declaring themselves invested with Power to legislate for us in all Cases whatsoever.

HE has abdicated Government here, by declaring us out of his Protection and waging War against us.

HE has plundered our Seas, ravaged our Coasts, burnt our Towns, and destroyed the Lives of our People.

HE is, at this Time, transporting large Armies of foreign Mercenaries to compleat the Works of Death, Desolation, and Tyranny, already begun with circumstances of Cruelty and Perfidy, scarcely paralleled in the most barbarous Ages, and totally unworthy the Head of a civilized Nation.

HE has constrained our fellow Citizens taken Captive on the high Seas to bear Arms against their Country, to become the Executioners of their Friends and Brethren, or to fall themselves by their Hands.

HE has excited domestic Insurrections amongst us, and has endeavoured to bring on the Inhabitants of our Frontiers, the merciless Indian Savages, whose known Rule of Warfare, is an undistinguished Destruction, of all Ages, Sexes and Conditions.

IN every stage of these Oppressions we have Petitioned for Redress in the most humble Terms: Our repeated Petitions have been answered only by repeated Injury. A Prince, whose Character is thus marked by every act which may define a Tyrant, is unfit to be the Ruler of a free People.

NOR have we been wanting in Attentions to our British Brethren. We have warned them from Time to Time of Attempts by their Legislature to extend an unwarrantable Jurisdiction over us. We have reminded them of the Circumstances of our Emigration and Settlement here. We have appealed to their native Justice and Magnanimity, and we have conjured them by the Ties of our common Kindred to disavow these Usurpations, which, would inevitably interrupt our Connections and Correspondence. They too have been deaf to the Voice of Justice and of Consanguinity. We must, therefore, acquiesce in the Necessity, which denounces our Separation, and hold them, as we hold the rest of Mankind, Enemies in War, in Peace, Friends.

WE, therefore, the Representatives of the UNITED STATES OF AMERICA, in GENERAL CONGRESS, Assembled, appealing to the Supreme Judge of the World for the Rectitude of our Intentions, do, in the Name, and by Authority of the good People of these Colonies, solemnly Publish and Declare, That these United Colonies are, and of Right ought to be, FREE AND INDEPENDENT STATES; that they are absolved from all Allegiance to the British Crown, and that all political Connection between them and the State of Great-Britain, is and ought to be totally dissolved; and that as FREE AND INDEPENDENT STATES, they have full Power to levy War, conclude Peace, contract Alliances, establish Commerce, and to do all other Acts and Things which INDEPENDENT STATES may of right do. And for the support of this Declaration, with a firm Reliance on the Protection of divine Providence, we mutually pledge to each other our Lives, our Fortunes, and our sacred Honor.

Signed by ORDER *and in* BEHALF *of the* CONGRESS,

JOHN HANCOCK, PRESIDENT.

ATTEST.
CHARLES THOMSON, SECRETARY.

PHILADELPHIA: PRINTED BY JOHN DUNLAP.

Fig. 22. Declaration of Independence.

A CONSTITUTION BOUGHT, A DECLARATION LOST

the librarian, Dr. Bell. It was later examined by Goff, who concurred in the opinion that it was authentic and this view was subsequently supported by all experts who inspected it.

Rather than sell such a fabulous item in the Leary sale, amid tons of trivia, it was pulled out and scheduled for inclusion in a mixed-properties auction five months later. Also in that sale, in addition to material from other owners, were some further surprises from the Leary stock, mostly 18th-century broadsides.

This was an opportunity not to be missed. Would the chance ever again occur to own a first printing of the Declaration of Independence? Only one other copy was known to be in private hands, in the possession of William H. Scheide; all the rest were institutionally owned and would not come on the market, or so I thought. A few years later I knew better. Furthermore, the approaching Bicentennial would enhance the sales potential of such an item, even if it had to be held several years before finding a buyer.

I resolved to buy it, or at least make the effort.

Kebabian, and I went to Philadelphia to bid in person. Most other prominent dealers were also there. I wondered how many had bids from clients. Guesses about the price varied widely. Some expected a record, others hoped for a bargain. The opening bid, $100,000, was made by Lew Feldman. It advanced in increments of $25,000 at first, then more slowly by $10,000. Only four or five bidders remained. At $180,000 Mabel Zahn of Sessler's dropped out and I was bidding against a stranger. We kept at it, for what seemed an hour, until $400,000 was reached. No one had counted on anything like this. It was a stupendous sum, the highest auction price for any book or related item up to that time, American or otherwise. I knew it was too high, that resale would be impossible at such a price, yet the drama of competition led me to continue bidding. Finally Kebabian kicked my shin and I got the message. I stopped bidding and my competitor bought the document for $404,000. Everyone in the room jumped up and applauded. I felt relieved to have saved nearly half a million dollars.

I also saw a possibility of turning the afternoon to my advantage.

Leaving the room, I went to a phone and called Sanka Knox of the *New York Times*. I told her what had happened and the next day a story on the sale ran on page one, across two columns. "A collector beginning at the top defeated a veteran to take the prize," it proclaimed. The collector was Ira Corn of Dallas, a 48-year-old executive, who bought the document in partnership with a business associate. He was quoted as saying, "It was an exhilarating experience. I've always been interested in American history. I couldn't resist it." I was asked to comment and said,

"If you fight with a Texan, you have a fight on your hands." Hanni was quoted by the *Times* as having said to me before I left for Philadelphia: "Don't come home if you have to pay more than $250,000." So it amounted to good publicity all around. The story linked my name with valuable Americana and showed that I was willing to pay a higher price than any dealer.

Arriving back from Philadelphia, I received some very welcome news: Thomas Hoving had called to confirm purchase of a manuscript we had reserved for the Metropolitan Museum, the *Psalter of Bonne de Luxembourg* with miniatures from the Pucelle atelier, at nearly the same price at which the Declaration of Independence sold.

A few years later another copy of the Declaration of Independence was offered at Parke-Bernet and reached only $120,000, less than a third of the Philadelphia copy. Again I was the underbidder. But in July 1975 I bought another copy of this great document at Christie's in partnership with Kenneth Nebenzahl of Chicago, the dealer in Americana and maps. With each successive sale the price dropped; it was now £40,000, less than a hundred thousand dollars. But we sold it very successfully a few weeks thereafter, for $180,000.

Habent sua pretia libelli. (Every book has its own price.)

CHAPTER 45

Bestiaries

During my early years in New York I did considerable business with Dawson's Bookshop of Los Angeles. Ernest Dawson came East every few months, searching the shops for books with West Coast appeal and occasionally bringing items to sell. In 1941 he showed me a small illuminated manuscript of the 13th century with pictures of animals. I was permitted to keep it on approval for several days.

My curiosity had been greatly aroused by this delicate, attractive little manuscript, but at that time I could do no more than guess about its origin, rarity, or the artistic quality of the miniatures, having had practically no experience with illuminated manuscripts. I handed it to a pair of Columbia University scholars, Dr. Hellmut Lehmann-Haupt and Dr. Samuel A. Ives (both of whom later became trusted associates of mine for many years), so that they might examine it. It impressed them and they judged it to be of English workmanship, quite unusual, and of considerable artistic excellence. Their opinion was that I should buy it. Sadly, Dawson, an experienced bookman who knew a treasure when he had one, asked a high price, more than I could safely afford. The depression's gloom, coupled with the war in Europe, had so weakened the rare-book market that even dealers with ample capital hesitated to buy expensive books.

Attempts to negotiate the price failed.

"Give me a bit more time," I asked.

Finally I found what I was looking for: a good argument for a discount.

In closely examining the paintings I noticed pin holes around the outlines of each animal. "This will surely be considered a detraction," I pointed out, "by anyone who may be interested in buying it."

In light of this "fault," Dawson agreed to a lower price, and I bought it.

Lehmann-Haupt could hardly believe his eyes. "Of course, I should have noticed this at first glance," he exclaimed, slapping his forehead. "These pin pricks are the unmistakable evidence of a model book. The pictures were intended to be copied; it's the oldest way of transferring drawings."

By placing a sheet of paper or vellum under each picture, and gently inserting a pin into each hole, the basic design was outlined on the new sheet. The artist then filled in the outline, much like the children's game of "connect the dots."

What I took for a defect proved to be an unexpected bonus.

The discovery was important enough to call for an analytical study in print. Lehmann-Haupt and Ives undertook it, and I published it in 1942 under the title *An English 13th-Century Bestiary* as the first of my "Rare Books Monographs Series." Here I incurred an additional expense, but not without a good return. The publication created great interest and soon the entire edition sold out. It stands today as a respected contribution to the very sparse literature on model books.

As to the manuscript, Philip Hofer of Harvard University bought it for $3,500, a price that has looked smaller and smaller with the passing of each of these nearly 40 years. Today I would gladly buy it back at ten times as much. The chance to acquire another fine model book will not be likely to occur again. In 1955 it was featured in the Fogg Museum's big exhibition of illuminated manuscripts and received much attention.

Not only did this manuscript excite my interest in model books but in Bestiaries as well, a class of books obtainable but not plentiful. Ives wrote the following about them:

> For fully fifteen hundred years following the date of its composition the recognized authority in the field of natural history was the great encyclopedia of the elder Pliny. However, for the unscientific-minded layman there had come into being, probably in second-century Alexandria, a work aimed to teach theological doctrine by way of animal legend and story. This book, originating in the schools of Christian Egypt where Greco-Roman culture was strongly imbued with and influenced by Oriental ideas and ideals, came to be known by the title of its anonymous author, Physiologus, or "The Natural Historian," while in later times it went simply under the name *Bestiarium*, or "Animal Book." Its content consists of a series of brief descriptions of animals, birds, fish and stones. These descriptions frequent-

Fig. 23. English Bestiary. 13th Century.

ly commence with a verse of Scripture relating to the natural object. Following this comes the statement: "Physiologus says . . . ," as if quoting the scientific authority of the ambiguous Physiologus concerning certain characteristics of the object, and thereafter drawing analogies, however farfetched, wherein Christian doctrine and ethics are taught.

My next Bestiary was written and illuminated with 32 lovely colored drawings in the early 12th century at the Austrian monastery of Göttweig. It was to me a familiar name. While living in Austria before the war, I visited this monastery in search of great books. (See Chapter 6.) When the manuscript was offered to me in New York I was unable to resist purchasing this fine Bestiary. Soon after buying it, I sold it to the Morgan Library, where it became manuscript M 832 and received a glowing description in the library's first annual report, that for 1950.

From the collection of Sir Sydney Cockerell, I acquired another noteworthy specimen in 1956. This was of 14th-century origin, slightly later than the others, executed probably at Fountains Abbey in Yorkshire, the Cistercian house from which came many remarkable manuscripts. Since the 16th century, when Henry VIII dissolved the monasteries and most of their contents were scattered, it was owned by the Yorkshire family of Ingilby at Ripley Castle. Sir Sydney acquired it in 1920. It contained no less than 102 curious and beautiful uncolored line drawings of animals. I sold it to the American collector Alastair B. Martin, who in turn presented it to the Morgan Library, where it joined one of the finest Bestiary collections in America. It is now Morgan manuscript M 890.

Several years later one of the outstanding Bestiaries in private hands reached the salesroom, from the Perrins collection. Like almost everything else in that auction, it went for what appeared to be quite a high price at the time, £36,500. Today that figure also seems low. Richly illuminated in northwest France in the second half of the 13th century, the Bestiary had an imposing provenance. Apparently made for King Louis IX and Blanche of Castile, whose arms appear in two of the miniatures, it later belonged to Joseph Barrois of Lille. Eventually it came to the renowned Ashburnham collection, in the sale of which in 1901 it brought the formidable price of £325 (at $5 to the pound). Fairfax Murray acquired it, and it went to Perrins in 1906. The manuscript is now in the library of Dr. Ludwig. This three-part work of 102 vellum leaves, containing 68 miniatures and numerous initials in red and blue penwork, was illuminated by an English artist, despite its French origin. This has been deduced from the guide letters, still visible beneath the initials, which followed the English language: R for Rose, G for Green, W for White, and so forth.

Printed Bestiaries are, of course, quite another category. The most spectacular of several that I have owned was the *Dialogus Creaturarum Moralisatus* printed at Gouda by Maynus de Mayneriis in 1480, the first edition of one of the most beautiful woodcut books, with 122 illustrations of vitality and humor—the latter arising to a great extent not from any conscious effort in that direction, but from the artist's lack of knowledge of animal anatomy. It was a fine copy from the famous library of Richard Heber; I sold it to the Bayerische Staatsbibliothek in Munich.

Numerous other animal books, not strictly in the class of Bestiaries, in print and manuscript, have passed through my hands. Among them was a mid-15th-century German manuscript of Aesop's fables in Latin, with 163 spirited drawings in pen and watercolor. This was another prize from the Perrins collection and went also into the library of Dr. Ludwig.

One rarely thinks of important animal books in terms of modern works, but I once had such a volume, a set of original etchings by Picasso for Buffon's *Natural History*. A series of 31 very free interpretations in typical Picasso manner, they were bound with an extra suite of proofs and a brilliant original drawing of a cock, one of only five copies on nacre Japan paper. Published in Paris in 1942 by Fabiani (Picasso had begun work on the series in 1936 for Vollard, who died before its completion), this was a signed presentation copy in a mosaic binding by Jacques Anthoine Legrain. Paul Mellon now owns it.

In the last 36 years I have owned four illuminated Bestiaries of the Middle Ages, all that were offered for sale during that period. I could therefore not believe my eyes when a Sotheby catalogue arrived announcing a sale of books and manuscripts from the Sion College Library to be held on June 13, 1977. It listed one of the most famous Bestiaries, the one owned by Humphrey, Duke of Gloucester (1391–1447), brother of King Henry V and a great bibliophile. His library had gone to the University of Oxford, in several portions, between 1411 and 1447, when he died. Unfortunately it was dispersed in the days of Edward VI and only three volumes now remain in the Bodleian Library. Seven volumes are in the British Library; others exist in various colleges, including Sion. With 105 miniatures, this Bestiary is the most splendid of its kind. It was made in Northern France in the 13th century and came to England at a very early date. I knew I had to buy it, and I believe the price of £97,000 I had to pay was reasonable.

CHAPTER 46

My Lifelong Romance with Cartography

MY FASCINATION WITH MAPS, atlases, globes, and the science of cosmography as a whole began as a youth, long before I began to deal in books. That Mercator atlas, found in an Austrian villager's attic (as related in Chapter 2), proved to be a catalyst.

Early atlases are often incomplete, though perhaps I should not say "early" because this is true of Carey atlases as well as Mercators and Blaeus. The original owners thought of them not as books but as collections of maps, from which any needed map could be removed. Few dealers specialized in cartography during my early years, in spite of opportunities to buy cheaply. Dealing in atlases and maps on a large scale calls for intimate knowledge and patience; one is always collating, checking, and rechecking. There is nothing easy about it, and there are many disappointments. I suppose that was enough to discourage the trade. Atlases and maps were also looked on as unprofitable, since they took up a great deal of space and moved slowly. But now interest in this subject has very markedly increased.

One of the "finds" I made in Europe in those prewar days was the Lafreri Atlas from the monastery of Wilhering in Austria, the story of which is told in Chapter 6.

Together with Schab I bought one of the finest copies in existence of the *Atlantic Neptune* by Desbarres. It was bound in contemporary calf with blue silk doublures and came from the family of Eugène Beauharnais, Duke of Leuchtenberg, son of Josephine Beauharnais, first wife of Napoleon I. This is a collection of nautical charts of the eastern American coastline, including many views of harbor towns. Over the years it has been collected by atlas specialists as well as by those interested in early American views. Each copy differs somewhat in the number of plates and it is seldom complete. The rarest plate is the so-called "Wooded Heights" view of New York, of which Phelps Stokes could trace only four copies in his monumental *Iconography of Manhattan Island*. In addition to the above, I succeeded in turning up a sixth, now the property of the New York Historical Society.

This herculean work was normally bound in four or five volumes of moderately large folio size, with the maps folded down the center. Ours, however, had been made into a single volume, measuring about 34 by 25 inches, nearly as big as the Audubon double elephant folio. The knowledge that we probably owned the only copy with unfolded plates provided little consolation for the agony of dragging it about. When we came to New York in 1939 we anticipated a rush of eager buyers for this item, whose like had not been seen in America. It did not materialize. Nobody wanted a book that required a windlass to lift. It remained unsold for a year, until my good friend and later associate Roland Tree, then one of the few experts on American maps, sold it to a Philadelphia collector for $3,600. This fortunate customer got a good bargain. We ought to have charged by the pound, we told ourselves later. Such a volume, clumsiness and all, would easily realize fifty thousand dollars today.

The map hunter stands a better chance of making discoveries than the collector of, say, first editions of Melville or Shelley. In the shop of a Swiss dealer I made one of my best cartographical finds, a manuscript parchment map of Palestine, dating obviously from an early period. It showed rivers, mountains, and cities painted over a net of squares, a grid foreshadowing Mercator's projections. Later investigation ascribed it to the Venetian Pietro Vesconte and placed the date at about 1300. It was the prototype of the map in Marino Sanudo's *Liber secretorum fidelium crucis* or "secret book" of the early 14th century, and the first postclassical map of a specific country rather than of the world or Europe, which mediaeval maps generally showed. It is now at the Morgan Library as M 877. Fred Adams referred to it as "a significant landmark in the development of working maps . . . which may indeed be the earliest to portray with a conscientious attempt at accuracy the geography of a particular country."

My first large-scale acquisition of maps, which not only provided me with a big stock but also added great impetus to my private collecting, occurred in 1949. This was the Prince Liechtenstein Collection. I had, a few months earlier, purchased the major portion of this notable library, comprising the small but choice group of illuminated manuscripts and the huge quantity of printed books of the 16th through the 18th century. (See Chapter 18.) But the map collection, housed separately in an outbuilding behind the Prince's castle, was not included in that transaction. Without exaggeration it could be called the largest, finest collection of maps in private hands at that time. I wanted very much to buy it. This was no mere portfolio but a whole room of maps, thousands of them, many of great rarity and beauty. Included were the gores of the first Waldseemüller globe of 1507, in which the name America appears for the first time on any map or globe, down to important works of the 17th century.

The Prince was prepared to sell, but only on his own terms. He held out for an exorbitant sum. I went to Vaduz to carry on the negotiations in person, accompanied by William Schwitzer, my Paris agent (a former associate of my father-in-law). The Prince was represented by his director, Dr. Wilhelm. After four weeks of discussions, offers, and counteroffers, we had gotten virtually nowhere.

Finally in order to speed up negotiations, I arranged with Schwitzer that he was to act as if he were my valet and I told Dr. Wilhelm, "This is my last day in Vaduz, and I have made my best offer." When he turned it down, I called Schwitzer at the hotel: "Schwitzer, pack my luggage." As I turned to leave, Dr. Wilhelm weakened. He suggested that a compromise might be achieved. Again I called: "Schwitzer, unpack."

His compromise was a small one and now it was my turn to decline. Another call: "Schwitzer, pack again."

As I went to leave the second time, Dr. Wilhelm knew I was not acting and yielded. He accepted my offer, which was fair, and the collection was mine. It was almost all mine, I should say, because the star attractions, the Waldseemüller gores, the only specimens then known, were not included.

A year later these precious gores became the cause of controversy. As a result of my having tried to purchase them, I knew (as not many other people did) that they were repaired. Several tears had been mended expertly by a restorer. When they came up for auction at Parke-Bernet in 1950 and failed to reach the reserve of $50,000, the Prince's agent charged me with spreading rumors to hurt the sale. Accusations, denials, and counter-accusations flew back and forth. Fortunately the matter was settled out of court. The gores are now in the James Ford Bell collection at the University of Minnesota Library. Proof that the $50,000 reserve was high, and that no rumors were needed to keep them from attaining that price, was provided in 1960 when a newly discovered set sold at

Sotheby's for £12,500. I was the purchaser and still own them. (See Fig. 24.) I rather hope that a third specimen is not discovered. It is really extraordinary that the only two recorded copies are owned in America.

I ought to explain for the benefit of noncollectors just what a gore is. The early cartographers devised a method of printing almost oval-shaped map sections, called gores, and applied them to a globe, usually a wooden ball. This required very precise drafting, so that the gores would fit properly and the printed matter would be aligned. The gores were printed on ordinary sheets and then cut out for gluing. Occasionally one finds them uncut in sheets.

I also succeeded in getting from the Prince Liechtenstein Collection the famous Brixen globes of 1522, now owned by Paul Mellon. These are hollow wooden globes with painted terrestrial and celestial gores, bearing a presentation inscription dated 1522, to Sebastianus Sperancius, Bishop of Brixen. They are believed to have been made by Johann Schoener, the well-known cartographer. The terrestrial Brixen globe is designed after the Waldseemüller map of 1507, then only 15 years old and the most reliable available. The celestial globe is especially interesting, as it incorporates constellation figures after Dürer.

We included some of the major Liechtenstein maps in a special Catalogue, No. 56. Without doubt this was the most noteworthy catalogue of maps issued up to that time by an American dealer. Assuming that many recipients of the catalogue would come to see the maps, we displayed them at 46th Street. It made quite an impressive show, especially the wall maps of the world by Vopell, Venice, 1558, and Rosaccio, Venice, 1597, and the epochal Vespucci world map of 1524. Before anyone else had a chance, Curt Reisinger, of the Anheuser-Busch family, bought the whole collection for Harvard University. The price of $35,000, which seemed high for maps then, would not buy many of the individual items today, much less the whole lot. On the present market, that collection has a value of around half a million dollars but in practical terms is priceless as it would be virtually impossible to duplicate. Some of its prominent pieces were featured in a Walters Art Gallery (Baltimore) exhibition, "The World Encompassed," arranged by Dorothy Miner in 1952.

The science of cartography, like many others, had its roots in the ancient world. Under the Greeks it progressed far, reaching the point of spherical celestial globes. Greek teachings remained the substance of cartographical and geographical knowledge during the Middle Ages and into the Age of Exploration. Notable among the ancient maps were those of Claudius Ptolemaeus (or Ptolemy). The 15th century, with its rebirth of interest in science, witnessed an outpouring of editions of Ptolemy's writings, first in manuscript and then in the new medium of

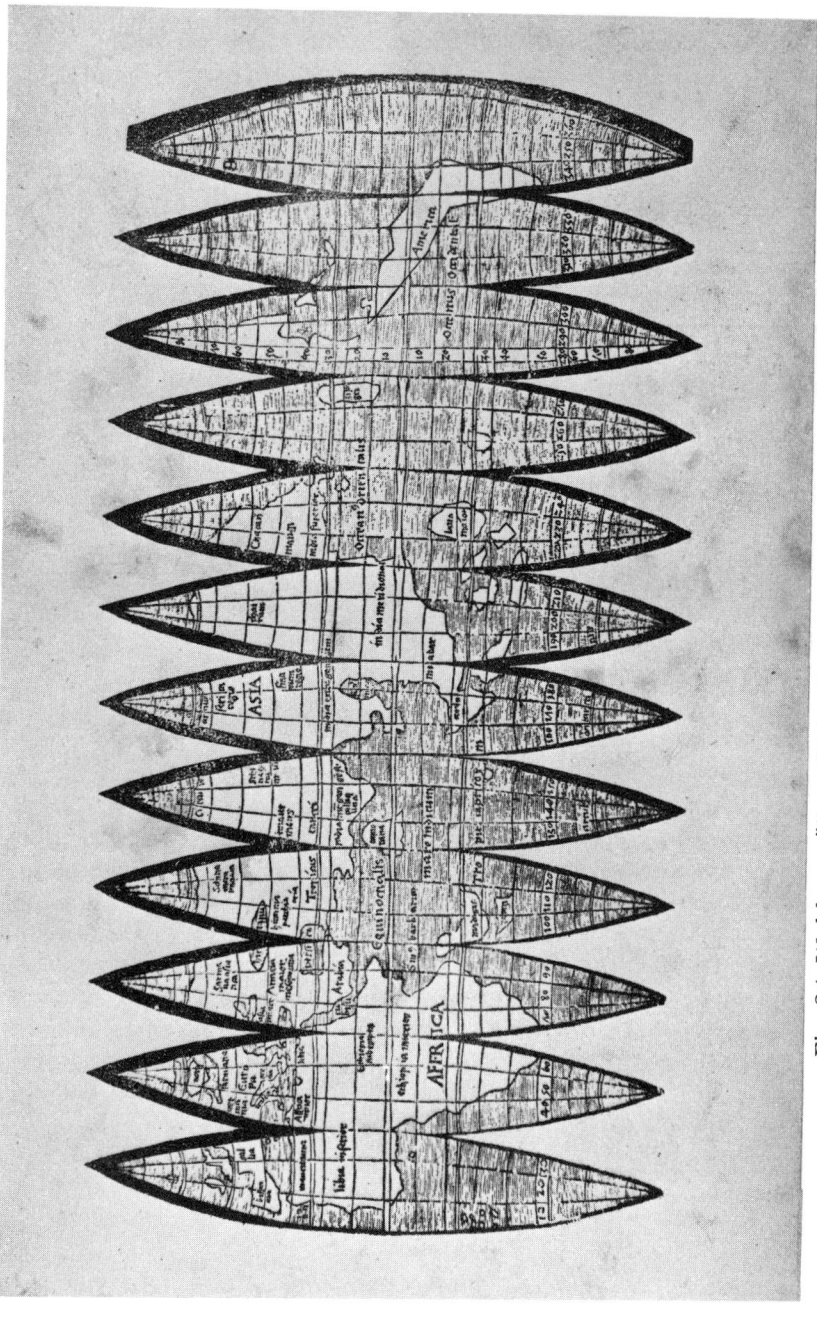

Fig. 24. Waldseemüller, Globe Gores, 1507—one of two copies known. (H. P. Kraus Collection.)

print. As an ardent collector of cartography, I had to get as many of these as I could, as well as important 16th-century editions. I have owned, at one time or other, at least one specimen of each major edition as follows:

1. The Wilczek Manuscript of 13 Ptolemaic maps, drawn in Italy in the 15th century (in the John Carter Brown Library, Providence, Rhode Island).

2–3. The Bologna edition of 1477, with engraved maps by Crivelli, in its first issue (from the Beans collection, now Schäfer), and its second issue, a complete and beautiful copy, owned by Hieronymus Muenzer (from the Bodmer collection).

4. The Rome edition of 1478 (Rosenwald Collection).

Of the subsequent editions I have owned several copies, so that no locations are given:

5. Berlinghieri's Ptolemy in Italian terza rima, Florence, 1482.
6–7. The Ulm editions of 1482 (Holle) and 1486 (Reger).
8. The Rome edition of 1490.
9. The Rome edition of 1508, with the Ruysch world map.
10. The Venice edition of 1511 by Sylvanus of Eboli.
11–12. The Strassbourg editions of 1513 and 1520, based on Waldseemüller.
13. The first Pirckheimer edition, Strassbourg, 1525.
14. The first Servetus edition, Lyons, 1535.

Also of interest to me are portolans: navigational charts made by and for seamen in the 15th and 16th centuries. Entirely hand-drawn, they present a picture of the world as seen by those who sailed the high seas. They often differed considerably from printed maps of the same era. These are the most immediate, tangible relics of the age of nautical adventure. I used to pore over them for hours. One can almost see the level of knowledge grow, year by year, in comparing charts made just a few years apart. On the other hand, some serious blunders remained uncorrected until very late. Many navigational charts show California as an island in the maps of the 17th and 18th centuries, though it had been represented as a peninsula in the 16th century.

Important early navigational charts are becoming very difficult to get. I remember with pride some of the more spectacular ones that went through my hands, never again, in most instances, to be seen on the market:

1. Franciscus Becharius' manuscript portolan chart on parchment of the Mediterranean and Black Sea and the Atlantic coasts of Europe and

Africa, Savona, 1403. This is the earliest sea chart in America and a document of first importance in the history of navigation. (Yale.)

2. Grazioso Benincasa's manuscript portolan atlas on vellum, with seven double-page charts, Venice, 1468.

3. The first recorded Jewish cartographer, Jehuda Ben Zara's manuscript portolan chart on parchment of the coasts of Europe, North Africa, the Asiatic coasts of the Mediterranean and the Black Sea, Alexandria, Egypt, 1500. (Yale.)

4. Battista Agnese's manuscript portolan atlas on vellum, of ten charts (Italy, circa 1542). (Private collection, Japan.)

5. Francesco Ghisolfi's manuscript portolan atlas on vellum, with 14 double-page charts, maps, and gores; splendidly bound for Francesco de' Medici and Joan of Austria (North Italy, after 1565). (Albert Ehrman collection, Bodleian Library, Oxford.)

6. The Mallorcan Jaume Olives' unrecorded manuscript portolan chart on vellum of the Mediterranean and Black Sea and the Atlantic coasts of Europe, Africa, and America (Barcelona, 1571). (Private collection, Spain.)

7. Hercules Doria's (O'Doran) manuscript portolan atlas, Marseilles, 1592. The only other extant work of this Irish cartographer is a single chart. (John Carter Brown Library, Providence, Rhode Island.)

This is just a partial list. A full one would occupy many pages.

Among other valuable cartographical items that I once owned was an unrecorded and unpublished manuscript on cosmography by Pedro de Medina (c. 1493–1567), the first writer to specialize in the art of navigation. The manuscript was dated 1543 and is believed (though this is difficult to confirm) to be in his holograph. It is now part of one of the great collections, that of Henry Taylor at Yale.

There was also a collection of ten manuscript maps and plans by Jehan Bourdon (1602–68), engineer, cartographer, and explorer, who held several government posts after settling in Canada in 1634. These plans proved sensational, being the first to depict French settlements and forts in Canada. They date from 1635 to 1642, earlier than any previously recorded. They also added to our knowledge of Bourdon, of whom only four maps and plans were known. They found a home at McGill University.

And then there was a large collection of terrestrial and celestial globes, dating from the 16th to 18th centuries, which I built up over a number of years, which found a buyer in Japan—my first major sale to that country. Western globes are comparatively rare in the Orient; the Chinese and Japanese exported quantities of their manufactured goods westward in those centuries, but very little European handiwork found its way into the Orient. Later I had another collection, consisting of globes and maps, on which my Catalogue 124, *Monumenta Cartographica*, was based. This too was sold as a collection. The buyer was the University of Texas at Austin. Among the items it acquired with this purchase was a magnificent pair of the large terrestrial and celestial globes by the 17th-century Venetian cosmographer Vincenzo Maria Coronelli. However, another copy of this terrestrial globe, in the original wooden stand which I found in an antique shop in Florence, has a story of its own (see Chapter 35). Besides the globe collection there were outstanding maps: a set of Gastaldi's wall maps of the four continents, published in Venice in the later 16th century, which I got about 20 years earlier from Hoepli of Milan thrown in as part of a large mixed lot of Italian books (see Chapter 12). Then there was Blaeu's giant wall map of the world, Amsterdam, 1648, in the first state.

My interest in cartography spills over into town views and plans, a specialized branch of the mapmaker's art. Very likely the most beautiful and spectacular of all city plans is Jacopo de Barbari's six-sheet woodcut of Venice in a bird's-eye view, painstakingly designed to show every street and building in the city in fairly good detail. I once owned a specimen in the rare first state of 1500, now at the Boston Museum of Fine Arts, and two in the even rarer second state: one went to Lessing Rosenwald, the other to the University of Texas.

There is still much to be learned of the history of cartography and cosmography. I trust that my catalogues on the subject, with extensively researched descriptions, have aided in that direction.

CHAPTER 47

I am Also a Collector

FOR A BOOKSELLER who is not merely a merchant, but who takes an interest and delight in books, the temptation is great to form his own collection from the precious and unusual material that passes through his hands. In France this is not uncommon. French dealers are well known for making their private collections. In America it has been less generally the case.

A large part of my success I owe to our reference library. To me it is like a fine piano that never fails to respond to the proper touch of its masters (and I am a good pianist). Even with a lot of experience, one cannot know the answers to all the questions posed by books and manuscripts. In most instances, however, it is possible to find the answers quickly with the help of good bibliographies and reference books and the knowledge of how to use them. We have therefore built a very large collection, perhaps the most extensive in private hands, of more than 30,000 volumes and about 20,000 selected dealers' and auction catalogues, located on three floors of the 46th Street building. I stand before these walls of volumes and ask questions. Here is the accumulated knowledge of all branches of human endeavor, in many languages. First and foremost, of course, are materials on the history and art of the book, thousands of volumes on incunabula, early manuscripts, bookbindings, and related subjects. In addition there are works in the fields of history, literature, classical studies, sciences, medicine, art, etc. With such a library one can usually identify the author of an anonymous piece of writing, the printer of an anonymously published book, or the binder in whose shop a binding was fashioned. Or, when this is not possible, the proper research may at least provide the basis for making educated guesses.

Then: How many copies are recorded? What is the value? Catalogues and the various magazines must be consulted. Prices fetched at auction sales and those charged by other dealers serve as guides, to be amended, of course, depending on the condition of the present copy. These and many more questions I ask my reference library. Most of the time I get answers. I can hardly call it work; it is rather a stimulating game and I most intensely enjoy it. To answer a vexing question and, with that answer, to make a bibliographical discovery of lasting importance, are enough to satisfy my pride.

To play my game of bibliography I have accumulated even at home some 15,000 volumes—duplicates of those at 46th Street—so that I can research in the evenings and during weekends. Also at home is my collection of rare early reference works printed before 1800. To indicate the scope of this collection, I reproduce the title pages of a few highlights. (See Figs. 25, 26, 27.)

It is never easy to part with certain beautiful and rare books. Especially dear to my heart are illuminated manuscripts. To collect them, however, would be extremely costly and I could not afford it. One of my basic rules of business is to keep a large amount of cash constantly available, and to have both is impossible. Yet, living in a world where many of the great collectors bought some of their treasures from me, I felt somehow left out. I could not help but think, sometimes, that it was they, rather than I, who enjoy the fruits of my labors. I have tried to start a few collections of my own, but have usually been persuaded to sell them.

One collection which I have succeeded in holding, despite many offers from would-be buyers, relates to Sir Francis Drake. This unique collection has grown over the years to a quite substantial size. It began in an unusual, unexpected way. The late James Ford Bell, chairman of General Mills of Minneapolis, a wealthy man and renowned bibliophile, was for years among my best clients. Many of the important books in his library, now at the University of Minnesota, I had sold to him. His collection is one of the largest on trade routes and expeditions for commercial purposes up to 1800. The fortune-seekers of old, and their exploits, appealed to this captain of industry. "They were motivated to risk their lives in the hope of making huge profits," he explained. Columbus discovered America only accidentally; he too was profit-motivated, having set out in quest of a westward route to the rich Spice Islands.

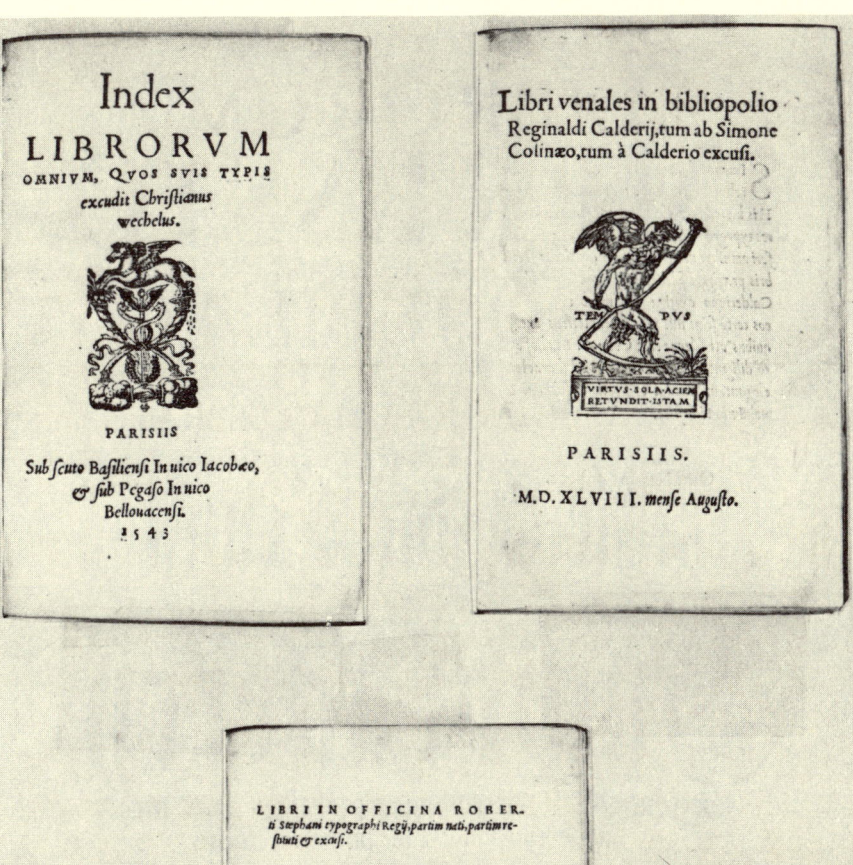

Fig. 25. Three famous Early Book Catalogues.
(H.P. Kraus Collection.)

EXPRESSA LIBRORUM IMPRESSIO,
CORONATAQUE ANNO JUBILÆO TERTIO
PRAGÆ BOHEMORUM CELEBRATO.

Das ist:

Die Edle-Kunst
Der
Buchdruckerey,

Gecrönt mit Dritten-hundert-jährigen, und mehr,
als drey Hundert Reym gebundenen
(was sag ich)
vielmehr froh und freyen

Jubel-Geschrey,

Wie solches Jubel-Fest in Prag ward celebriret,
Hat dieses Freuds-Format (unform zwar formiret,
Mit wenig Nachdruck auch) in Druck gegeben aus
JOSEPHUS FRANCISCUS ANTONIUS KRAUS,
Nat. Bohem. (p. t.) Jun. Com. Præf.

Samt Anhang Erster Kunst-Genossen,
Wie solche nach und nach vom Anfang her entsprossen,
Bis sie zu höchster Kunst-Vollkommenheit gelanget,
Mit Privilegien und vieler Freyheit pranget.

Gedruckt in der Königl. Alten-Stadt Prag, bey Wentzel Urban Suchy.

Fig. 26. J.F.A. Kraus, Celebration of 300 years of printing.
(H.P. Kraus Collection.)

SPECIMEN

OF

PRINTING TYPES,

FROM THE

FOUNDERY

OF

Binny & Ronaldson.

PHILADELPHIA.

———•••●●●••———

FRY AND KAMMERER, PRINTERS.
1812.

Fig. 27. First American Type-Specimen Book.
(H.P. Kraus Collection.)

On one occasion Mr. Bell asked me to buy for him at auction a rare edition of an early book of voyages, a lovely copy in fine contemporary binding.

"Allow me to bid up to $1,000," I asked, knowing that Bell wanted it badly.

He agreed and gave me the order. But the unexpected occurred. As can happen at auction, the book went for much less than anticipated, for only $200. Naturally I imagined Bell would be happy to have a good bargain. Quite the contrary.

"Now you see how wrong you are with your prices," he complained. "If you owned this book, you would have charged me a thousand dollars and it's worth only $200."

I insisted that it would still be a bargain even at a thousand dollars.

"All right," he replied, "would you give me $1,000 for it?"

I could do nothing but pay up.

"I hope you are pleased," I remarked. "Five hundred percent is a nice profit."

After a few moments of musing—while mathematical figures, I suppose, clicked in his brain—he said, "Did you know that Sir Francis Drake and Queen Elizabeth made a 5,000 percent profit out of his circumnavigation of the world?"

I knew nothing of the kind, but it seemed interesting. Here was a part of history not often related in the encyclopedias. I began to study Drake's life. His story, as told by numerous authors, began to fascinate me. A man of humble birth, he became the national hero of Elizabeth I's hierarchical England.

At home I talked a lot about Drake. My children enjoyed listening to my hero's romantic adventures. One of my daughters even composed a limerick about him, which for the sake of posterity I here inscribe:

> There was a young fellow of Devon,
> He sailed the seas all seven.
> He singed Philip's beard,
> Spain's glory he smeared,
> This brave Francis Drake out of Devon.

I had not realized how difficult it would be to build up a Drake collection. I wanted to gather only original and contemporary materials, in printed books, manuscripts, letters, maps, portraits, and medals. The motive for my collection was to learn about Drake the same way his contemporaries, not only in England but in Spain, Germany, Italy, and elsewhere, learned about him. I hoped to feel their admiration or dread of him. This was a beautiful concept but so little was available that at times I felt inclined to abandon the whole plan. Strangely enough, very little about Drake's exploits appeared in print during his lifetime. Until his raid on Cadiz, England and Spain were officially (though perhaps not emotionally) at peace. His earlier piracies at the expense of Spanish merchants and Spanish finances were officially condemned by Queen Elizabeth, despite her sharing in the booty.

When my interest in Drake became known, a trickle of offers began to arrive. I was able to acquire many prime Drake items within 15 years. Prices, unfortunately, went up and up. This forced me to suspend all purchases in order to keep values within bounds. After two years prices slipped somewhat, as I had hoped, and I could buy at more modest figures.

In 1965 I started to write a biography of Drake based on the materials in my collection. After a year I had made good progress and invited Lt. Commander David N. Waters to come and live with us in Ridgefield in the summer of 1966 to give editorial assistance. The Curator of Navigation and Astronomy at the Greenwich (England) National Maritime Museum, he took a keen interest in the collection and was of immense help. Later his assistant, Dr. Richard Boulind, came and finally the first 100 copies of the finished book arrived on January 23, 1970. As one can see, this was no overnight production, but well worth the time, effort, and cost: a richly illustrated folio volume, a most beautiful piece of printing, and a book that highlights Drake as seen in contemporary sources.

Several reviews appeared after my book came out, and I was asked by the University of Minnesota to give a lecture on my Drake collection. After this I had to repeat it in Chicago, Ridgefield, and other places. I enjoyed being a lecturer. I am sorry that Mr. Bell, who was no longer alive when my interest in Drake began, was not there to listen.

The year 1977 marked the 400th anniversary of Drake's departure from Plymouth (December 13, 1577) to circumnavigate the globe. Three star items from my collection were featured in the British Library's Drake exhibition:

1. Nicholas Breton's *Discourse in commendation of . . . Drake,* London, 1581. The only copy known of a little book celebrating his safe return from his voyage around the world, the first after Magellan.

2. The medal struck in commemoration of Drake's circumnavigation, the famous "Silver Map." It is the specimen bearing the date 1589 and signature of Michael Mercator, grandson of Gerard Mercator, the celebrated cartographer; it is the only copy known in this state.

3. View and ground plan of San Juan de Ulúa by Christobel de Eraso, drawn on vellum, about 1570, the earliest view of this key fortress of Latin America, where Drake battled with the Spaniards.

I cannot resist telling about another collection which has grown within 12 years to formidable proportions. In January 1967, I stumbled by chance into an exhibition of Persian illuminated manuscripts at Sotheby's. It was the sale of part of the stock of Hagop Kervorkian, a well-known American dealer. To me it was a new world: miniatures in brilliant colors illustrating the famous epic *Shah-Nama* by the Persian poet Firdawsi, manuscripts from the 14th to 17th centuries. Despite their lack of knowledge of linear perspective, or perhaps because of it, their painters' work has a fascinating beauty.

This started a new adventure for me. I spent about £60,000 at the sale and began learning about the different schools of Iranian painting. As usual when I delve into a new field, I quickly built up a reference library. Within a year I was well versed in the subject and bought extensively whenever choice material reached the market. Dr. Ernst J. Grube, former director of the Islamic Department of New York's Metropolitan Museum, advised me, and I will always be grateful for his aid. It followed quite naturally that he compiled the catalogue of my collection, a substantial folio volume with 54 color plates and 252 monochrome illustrations which will serve as a lasting work of reference. My friends were surprised at my switch from my old love—European manuscripts—to Persian miniature paintings. My explanation: *Variatio delectat.* (Variety is delightful.)

These two examples may serve to show that even now, at this late date, a major collection can still be built around a special subject.

CHAPTER 48

Why I Will be Remembered

ON A SHELF IN MY OFFICE stands a row of old soldiers, some of them a bit shabby from years of service, but still (I like to think) noble; personal copies of my 150 catalogues issued over 45 years as a book dealer. They begin with small, modest ones, hardly bigger than pamphlets. My first 50 catalogues make up only two moderately sized bound volumes. Since the 1950s, however, I have published catalogues many of which are more lavish than those of any other book dealer. Often they are of folio size, bound in cloth and filled with color plates, fully the equal of art books in layout, production, and overall appearance.

Book catalogues have, of course, as their first purpose the selling of books, to customers near and far. Beyond this they may—if competently prepared and especially if they deal with some special subject—become useful reference tools. I never tire of reading catalogues of other book dealers old and new. Old catalogues, though generally lacking the thorough descriptions and scholarly notes expected today, vividly reflect activities in the book market of yesteryear, though one may weep at the low prices for which brilliant volumes could be bought in those days, compared to perhaps ten, fifty, or a hundred times as much today. It is sometimes possible to trace the provenance of a particular copy through old catalogues. This is why most dealers, even those who take no personal pleasure in reading catalogues of a generation or two ago, maintain a file of them. So far as recent catalogues are concerned, they are the means of replenishing one's stock or just keeping posted on what the trade has to offer and at what prices. Dealers obviously base their prices to some extent on what is being asked by other booksellers for the same titles.

My own experience with catalogues as a selling tool is rather mixed. Librarians, dealers, and scholars make a practice of reading them diligently, and order according to their needs and means. With other collectors it is often quite different. I have found time and again that they may compliment me on the splendor of a handsome catalogue filled with precious items but, being for the most part busy executives always pressed for time, they give the contents little more than a brief appreciative glance before the catalogue is filed or discarded. They do not take the opportunity to read a catalogue and perhaps place an order from it—yet these are the wealthy individuals upon whom a dealer must depend as customers for valuable books. It is a deep disappointment, considering the efforts and expense that go into making a good catalogue. Many items which I bring to the attention of clients later on, and which they are eager to buy, could have been ordered from one of my catalogues years earlier, and often at lower prices. Such is the penalty for not reading catalogues. Another common failing among collectors is their assumption that everything from a catalogue has been sold within a month or two, and the catalogue is thereafter obsolete. If this were only so!

I usually say about my catalogues, "Everybody admires them, nobody reads them!"

The catalogues evolved from very small lists (I hesitate to bestow even the name of catalogues upon them) in Vienna in 1932 and 1933. Gradually, as my staff grew and business increased, the descriptions became more detailed and scholarly, based on bibliographical research. My first illustrated Catalogue, No. 8, offered manuscripts and incunabula from the library of Dr. Eduard Langer (1852–1914) of Braunau in Bohemia, an expert on the history of printing in Austria and an important collector of his era. In the quality and nature of its content this catalogue served as a precursor of the more elaborate ones I would issue later in New York. It was prepared by Felix Grafe, poet and translator and a bibliophile in his own right. He became a good friend and I was horrified to learn of his murder by the Nazis in 1942. The Langer books sold out within a few months, thanks in a measure to Grafe's descriptions.

My tenth catalogue, issued in 1936, was the most ambitious up to then. Among other items it featured a number of treasures I had purchased from Austrian monasteries and the editio princeps of Harvey's *De motu cordis*, 1628, purchased from Domizlaff, the story of which is told in Chapter 6. I made a substantial profit by selling it at 7,500 Swiss francs, then about $2,800. In 1974 another copy of this rarity of rarities—so flimsy and fragile that only a few specimens have survived—brought $55,000. The next 40 years may well see a comparable rise in its price.

Unlike some other booksellers who came from Europe to America, I decided to continue the numerical sequence of my catalogues rather than starting over again. Thus, since I had issued 18 catalogues from Vienna, prior to my arrest by the Nazis and the loss of my business, my first in New York bore the number 19. It was prepared with the assistance of my future wife, who has worked with me and our staff on all catalogues ever since.

Despite our efforts and high expectations, my first American catalogue met a cold response. It was, in fact, a total failure. The war's gloom hung heavily over the book trade; with business slow even for the old, well-established dealers, newcomers without an American clientele fared badly indeed. The star piece, the Verardus Columbus letter of 1494, at the low price of $2,250, remained unsold for two whole years. It finally went to the collector and Yale benefactor Henry Taylor. Fortunately, my later catalogues did better. The war's end brought not only a resumption of book collecting activity in this country but the transatlantic buying and selling so necessary to the book market, which had been suspended for six years.

Up to 1977 we have published 150 catalogues. These are not, however, all devoted to rare books and manuscripts. (The early catalogues of our periodical branch were numbered in the same series.) On the other hand, there have been many additional rare book catalogues published outside the numerical sequence (Special Subject Bulletins, Bi-Weekly Bulletins, and Lists). As the descriptions became better researched and lengthier, and the books more precious, we took pains to have the catalogues well printed and suitably illustrated. Until 1969, when he was named Professor of Bibliography at the University of Missouri, Dr. Hellmut Lehmann-Haupt, distinguished as an art historian as well as an authority on books, designed each of the major catalogues and also supervised the actual printing. All credit for layout and typography belongs to him. Some catalogues ranked as masterpieces of modern bookmaking and accordingly won honors as "one of the fifty best-designed" books of that year. The makeup of title pages and covers was the result of many hours of discussion over, and selection from, Lehmann-Haupt's suggestions.

Our catalogues are printed in relatively small editions, from 800 to 1,500 copies, and have an international circulation among collectors, librarians, and other interested parties. The more elaborate ones are also

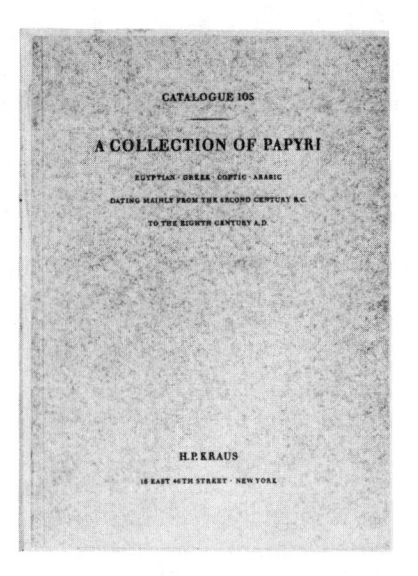

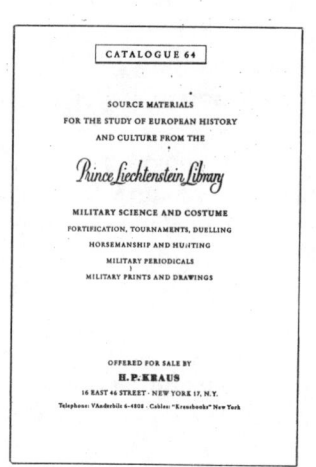

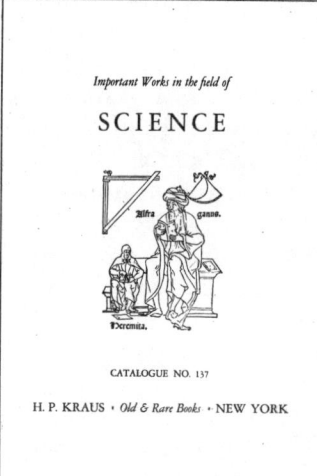

Fig. 28. Some Catalogues issued 1932–1975.

Fig. 28. Some Catalogues issued 1932–1975.

made available to the general public at a nominal price. Many have become collector's items in themselves, and have taken their places on the reference shelves of some libraries.

As I said, these deluxe catalogues, however sumptuous and seductive, for all the high-quality volumes they picture and describe, seldom elicit a strong response from customers. One often has to wait for months until the first order arrives. Sometimes there are exceptions: the Perrins manuscripts in my Catalogue 100 drew more orders in a shorter length of time than expected. Another exception was Catalogue 105, with its collection of Greek and Coptic papyri. This, the first important catalogue of papyri issued by a bookseller, was prepared by Father Theodore Petersen of St. Paul's College in Washington, an authority on Coptic texts. Among its highlights was a fragment of a 6th-to-7th century magical text bearing what is believed to be the earliest reference to December 25 as the date of Christ's birth. It seemed at the time rather daring to devote a whole catalogue, and the time and expense necessary for its preparation, to such material, for which there were few potential customers. To my surprise the collection was bought en bloc by Yale. The *New York Times* carried a story of the sale, published the morning of my surgery in Mt. Sinai Hospital. Again a few years later, very unexpectedly, the University of Texas in Austin purchased the contents of catalogue 124, *Monumenta Cartographica*. It thereby acquired in a single transaction one of the finest collections of antique maps and globes in America, probably finer than could ever again be offered by a dealer. I kept for myself, however, the Waldseemüller gores of 1507 (see Fig. 24 and Catalogue 124, Suppl. No. I) as well as the terrestrial Coronelli globe of 1688 in its original stand (see Catalogue 124, Suppl. No. V). (See Plate 16b.)

I could also name catalogues whose items took a long while to find buyers. When issuing an important catalogue, one must be prepared for this. Why, then, go on publishing them, and incurring enormous expense? At heart I am a collector. I sell only because, as a businessman, it would be impossible to do otherwise. Nevertheless I regret when a precious volume, one whose acquisition may have been the object of lengthy negotiations or high-tension drama, leaves my hands. By placing my cherished books in our catalogues, I can remember them and feel that they have never left, though they may be now in worthier homes. The catalogues serve, too, as a record of my achievements in bringing together collections of important books and manuscripts; I survey them with pride.

In addition to the catalogues there are also the introductory essays to many of them, which I call "Rare Book Notes." One catalogue, No. 38, *Sidelights on the Renaissance*, carried no less than 20 essays, all written by

Samuel A. Ives, giving the historical and cultural background of the books described. The early death of Ives was a great loss to me.

Besides catalogues we also publish a series entitled "Rare Books Monographs Series" at irregular intervals, whenever we find a subject that merits research in depth. They are written at my request by scholars in the respective fields and contain discussions of new discoveries or attributions, providing a fresh impetus for further investigation.

I am confident that our catalogues will retain their value as reference works and, as they have already done, contribute to the sum of bibliographical knowledge. After 50 or 100 years my name will have been forgotten except by those who will use my catalogues, still preserved on library shelves.

I believe this is the proper place to thank the staff who have worked with me for all these many years. In the first 20 years, there were the late Dr. Hans Nachod, the eminent humanist and Petrarch scholar, and Lehmann-Haupt who are mentioned earlier. Later, there were John (Jack) S. Kebabian, Dr. Lotte Labus, Jens Christoffersen, and Dr. Roland Folter; they all helped to create beautiful catalogues and researched and described the great books. To all of them go my heartfelt thanks.

CHAPTER 49

The Elegant Bookman

MY TASTE IN BOOKS has always run toward volumes of historical significance: mediaeval manuscripts, incunabula, early works in science, old atlases. I also was fond of 17th- and 18th-century illustrated books, depending on subject and quality of illustration, and even of French books of the 1800s adorned with wood engravings. These, however, were the most recent books to which my interest extended. For books of the late 19th and especially for those of the 20th century, I failed to feel any emotion. They seemed too new, too much a product of our own age; they could hardly be termed "rare" nor did they seem "fine" when compared to books of an earlier period, despite the efforts and skills of some of their designers. So prejudiced was I against modern "fine" books that I could not be induced even to look at them. Then, in a single afternoon, my point of view changed.

In the early 1960s I visited Colonel Daniel Sickles in Paris, where he was living with his aging mother in a lovely house on Avenue Frédéric le Play. A collector of international renown, Sickles specialized in modern French illustrated books. These limited editions, printed on fine paper, containing original etchings or lithographs by 20th-century French artists, signed by the artists, and often in bizarre, imaginative bindings, had always found an enthusiastic market on the continent. Only on occasion had I examined such books. I welcomed the opportunity to see this collection, but little suspected that the books would prove to be of more than passing interest to me.

Included in the Sickles library were works illustrated by such masters as Manet, Redon, Matisse, Derain, Picasso, Braque, Léger, Bonnard, and many others. I was at first impressed by the monumental size of the books, and their unique bindings, bold and colorful, not at all inspired by classic designs but entirely a product of their times. Here was work by Paul Bonet, Creuzevault, Legrain, and others, wild swirls of color, fantastic motifs, kaleidoscopic patterns composed from inlays of different leathers in various colors. Inside I discovered the fine handmade paper, wide-spaced type, ample margins, and other touches reminiscent of the days of elegant printing. The illustrations, the most important feature of these books, were represented, usually with one or more extra suites of the plates in different states or as proofs. Original drawings were sometimes added as well, rendering each volume unique in its way.

Daniel Sickles, an American in Paris, a man of the world, tall, good-looking, elegant, is the grandson of Daniel Edgar Sickles (1825–1914), Congressman from New York, Union General in the Civil War, who as a young man had killed, in a fit of jealousy, Philip Barton Key, son of Francis Scott Key, of "Star-Spangled Banner" fame. In Paris, Sickles had opportunities to acquire modern French illustrated books that could be matched nowhere. There was little doubt that his collection, both in overall size and in quality, surpassed all others in its field. Though not assembled as an investment, it had served excellently in that regard as well; the rise in value of these artists' paintings brought increased demand, and higher prices, for the books they illustrated. Sickles and I became good friends. Thanks to him and his collection I learned to see the beauty of modern fine books. I went away not only with admiration and a new-found interest, but with books; for a huge six-figure sum I bought highlights from the collection and featured many of them in my Catalogue 103. It was a new venture for me, and I went into it in a big way.

Some of the great books I acquired from Sickles have to be mentioned. There was a marvelous copy of Petronius's *Satyricon*, with 38 drawings by André Derain; a complete set of Picasso's *Saltimbanques* in the 1913 edition (the principal engraving, "Le Repas Frugal" in the first state, I purchased only later); Verlaine's *Parallèlement* proof sheets with Bonnard's original charcoal drawings.

These few examples should give some idea of the wealth of my purchases.

I got hold of all the available literature on modern French illustrated books and within a short time did enough reading to compensate for my years of neglect.

My purchase of his great copies of the "Livres d'Artistes" as they were called (plus three auctions in which he disposed of others in this line) did not terminate Sickles' collecting activities. The proceeds helped him to expand his existing collection of 19th- and 20th-century French literature and to create the greatest collection of this subject in private hands: first editions in the most perfect state of preservation, special copies on large or Japan paper, many inscribed by the authors. The highlights of the collection are autograph manuscripts of literary works. His librarian stated proudly: *"Il y a déjà plus de 30,000 fiches."*

If this little story has a moral, it must be that a collector is never safe in presuming what kinds of books will or will not appeal to him, until the opportunity has been given to meet them "in person." I had a similar experience in 1957, where at Sotheby's Kevorkian sale, I became enamored with the strange beauty of Islamic miniatures.

CHAPTER 50

Thank You, Uncle Sam

THE EXCITEMENT OF THE NEWS of a new world on the western side of the Atlantic, which spread through Europe in the late 15th and early 16th centuries, continues nearly 500 years later to inspire interest in the rare books and manuscripts that record one of the greatest events in human history.

The various editions of the letter of Columbus which in 1493 first told of the unknown other half of the globe, and all of the later publications that expanded his fragmentary view, have led many collectors to try to assemble the printed history of the exploration, settlement, and early administration of the Western Hemisphere.

But behind all those books there were always manuscripts, many of them written by the men who had actually been there when it was happening. Such manuscript material is (compared with printed items) of a more spontaneous nature and of fabulous rarity.

My interest in cartography spilled over into the field of travel and exploration, and from there to early Americana. The term "early Americana" signifies to many people colonial broadsides and old almanacs, but there are far earlier and, in my opinion, more thrilling, Americana to be collected: the letters, diaries, charts, and other writings of the first explorers, settlers, and missionaries.

A large quantity of such material once existed. From the era of Columbus up through the 16th century, observations on America and the continent's exploration poured from the pens of writers in both the Old World and the New. Woodcutters and engravers produced illustrations

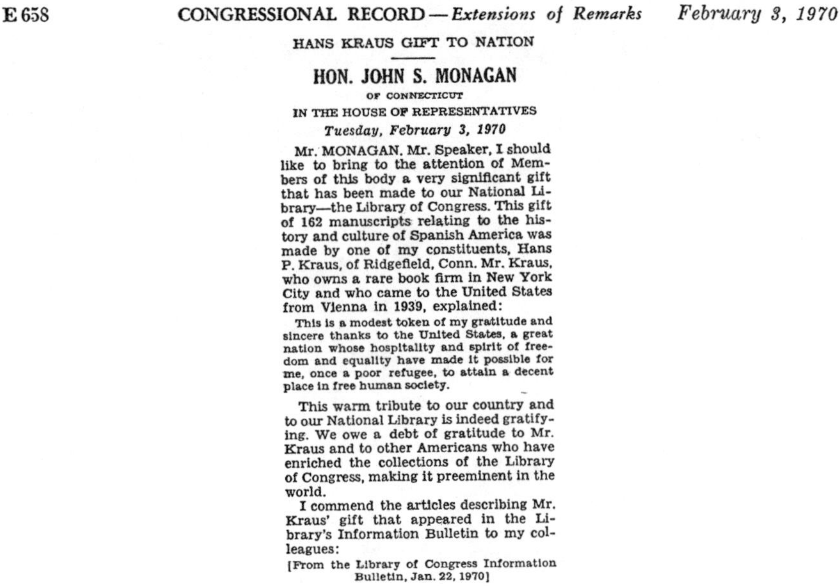

CONGRESSIONAL RECORD — *Extensions of Remarks*   *February 3, 1970*

HANS KRAUS GIFT TO NATION

HON. JOHN S. MONAGAN
OF CONNECTICUT
IN THE HOUSE OF REPRESENTATIVES
Tuesday, February 3, 1970

Mr. MONAGAN. Mr. Speaker, I should like to bring to the attention of Members of this body a very significant gift that has been made to our National Library—the Library of Congress. This gift of 162 manuscripts relating to the history and culture of Spanish America was made by one of my constituents, Hans P. Kraus, of Ridgefield, Conn. Mr. Kraus, who owns a rare book firm in New York City and who came to the United States from Vienna in 1939, explained:

This is a modest token of my gratitude and sincere thanks to the United States, a great nation whose hospitality and spirit of freedom and equality have made it possible for me, once a poor refugee, to attain a decent place in free human society.

This warm tribute to our country and to our National Library is indeed gratifying. We owe a debt of gratitude to Mr. Kraus and to other Americans who have enriched the collections of the Library of Congress, making it preeminent in the world.

I commend the articles describing Mr. Kraus' gift that appeared in the Library's Information Bulletin to my colleagues:

[From the Library of Congress Information Bulletin, Jan. 22, 1970]

Fig. 29. Gift to the Library of Congress, 1970.

(mostly fanciful) of the new land; mapmakers turned their attention to it. America became the subject of hope, debate, and controversy. Gradually the sum of knowledge increased. Today the collector of this kind of early Americana faces a formidable challenge. During more than 400 years, most of it has disappeared, either physically or (amounting to just about the same for potential collectors) into institutional libraries and museums.

From the earliest years of my career I have bought manuscripts and printed books dealing with early America. The European market yielded some attractive finds of this kind in the 1940s, sometimes at reasonable prices because the owners failed to realize their significance. After three decades of buying—never acquiring a single large collection, because none was available, but adding one item to another—I had assembled probably the largest collection in private hands and without doubt the largest owned by a dealer. My intention was to issue a spectacular catalogue.

I said to Hanni how sad it was to think that all the important manuscripts should be dispersed among various libraries and collectors. As so often, my wife had the right answer: "The only way to keep this collection together is to make a gift of it to one library that already has similar material." It was the kind of gesture every bibliophile would like to make, devoting his carefully selected treasures to the public good.

It did not take me long to decide. I knew the Library of Congress had strong holdings in this field and an entire department of Latin American studies, with a staff of specialists.

I spoke to Fred Goff, at the Library of Congress, who assured me that such a gift would be welcome. We commissioned Dr. Richard M. Boulind, a specialist in Latin American history, to make a short-title catalogue of the material, and in December 1969 the collection and its catalogue were delivered to the Library of Congress.

Experienced donors are accustomed to receiving a polite letter of acknowledgment and to wonder a little at the subsequent silence. It was an agreeable surprise, therefore, on January 10, 1970, to find my own face—opposite a portrait of Amerigo Vespucci—on the front page of the *New York Times,* as part of a long story about my gift. (See Fig. 30.)

The reaction was phenomenal. Reports on this gift were not limited to the American press. Even Alistair Cooke wrote about it in the *Manchester Guardian*. On February 3, 1970, the "Hans Kraus Gift to the Nation" was entered in the Congressional Record, quoting the appreciative acknowledgment in the *Library of Congress Information Bulletin* of January 22 as well as the Henry Raymont article in the *New York Times* of January 10, 1970. Strangers wrote us letters, thanking us for "our gift to the nation."

The *Times* story described the 162 manuscripts in the collection, especially a contemporary copy of a 17-page letter from Amerigo Vespucci to Piero Soderini, head of the short-lived Florentine Republic. This was the *Amoretti Codex* (see Fig. 31), so named after its owner in the early 19th century, Padre Antonio Amoretti of Rome. The codex was long believed to be lost, when—to my surprise—I came across a photocopy of it in the *Mostra Vespucciana* which was held in the Palazzo Vecchio in Florence in 1954 in celebration of the 500th anniversary of the birth of Vespucci, one of the great citizens of that town. I admired all the original documents brought together in this magnificent exhibit; at the same time, I deeply regretted that there was no way for me ever to possess any of them. Coming to the photo-reproduction of the *Amoretti Codex,* I was stunned by the tantalizing news that the original was owned by a Swiss private collector. Here was my chance!

After good detective work and with the help of a local antiquarian bookseller, I found out the owner's identity and finally succeeded in buying the codex. For almost two decades I enjoyed owning this authentic account of the four Vespucci voyages, written on September 10, 1504. It

The New York Times

1970 The New York Times Company. NEW YORK, SATURDAY, JANUARY 10, 1970

Vespucci MS. Given to U.S. Library

By HENRY RAYMONT

A narrative by Amerigo Vespucci of his four voyages to America between 1497 and 1502 has been donated to the Library of Congress as part of a collection of 162 historical documents spanning 300 years of colonial Spanish America.

The collection, donated by Hans P. Kraus, a leading New York dealer in rare books, also includes letters from Emperor Charles V, his daughter Princess Joanna and King Philip II of Spain.

Although some of the material is known to scholars, a number of the original manuscripts have never been published.

In an announcement to be made in Washington today, by L. Quincy Mumford, the Librarian of Congress, the documents are characterized as "the most important acquisition of Hispanic materials" since the late Edward P. Harkness, the philanthropist, gave his collection to the library in 1929.

Dr. Richard H. Boulind, a Cambridge University specialist in Latin-American history who catalogued the collection, said here yesterday: "As a whole, the documents offer a fresh and vivid picture of the Spanish Court's administration of mainland America from the time of the conquest of Mexico by Hernán Cortés in the decade of the fifteen-twenties to the decline in 1819.

"Specifically, it details some of the less known controversies between the court and the Viceroys over the living conditions of the Indians and the conduct of the Catholic Church."

One of the earliest documents is a contemporary copy of a 17-page letter by Vespucci, the Italian navigator whose first name, Amerigo, was given to the continent of America. The letter, dated Sept. 10, 1504, was written to Piero Soderini, the gonfaloniere (president) of Florence, describing all four of Vespucci's voyages to the New World.

The letter, which was believed lost for several centuries, was obtained by Mr. Kraus from a Swiss dealer in 1955 after secret negotiations

Continued on Page 25, Column 3

A portrait of Vespucci by Botticelli, a contemporary.

Hans P. Kraus — The New York Times

Fig. 30. *New York Times*, January 10, 1970. (Front page.)

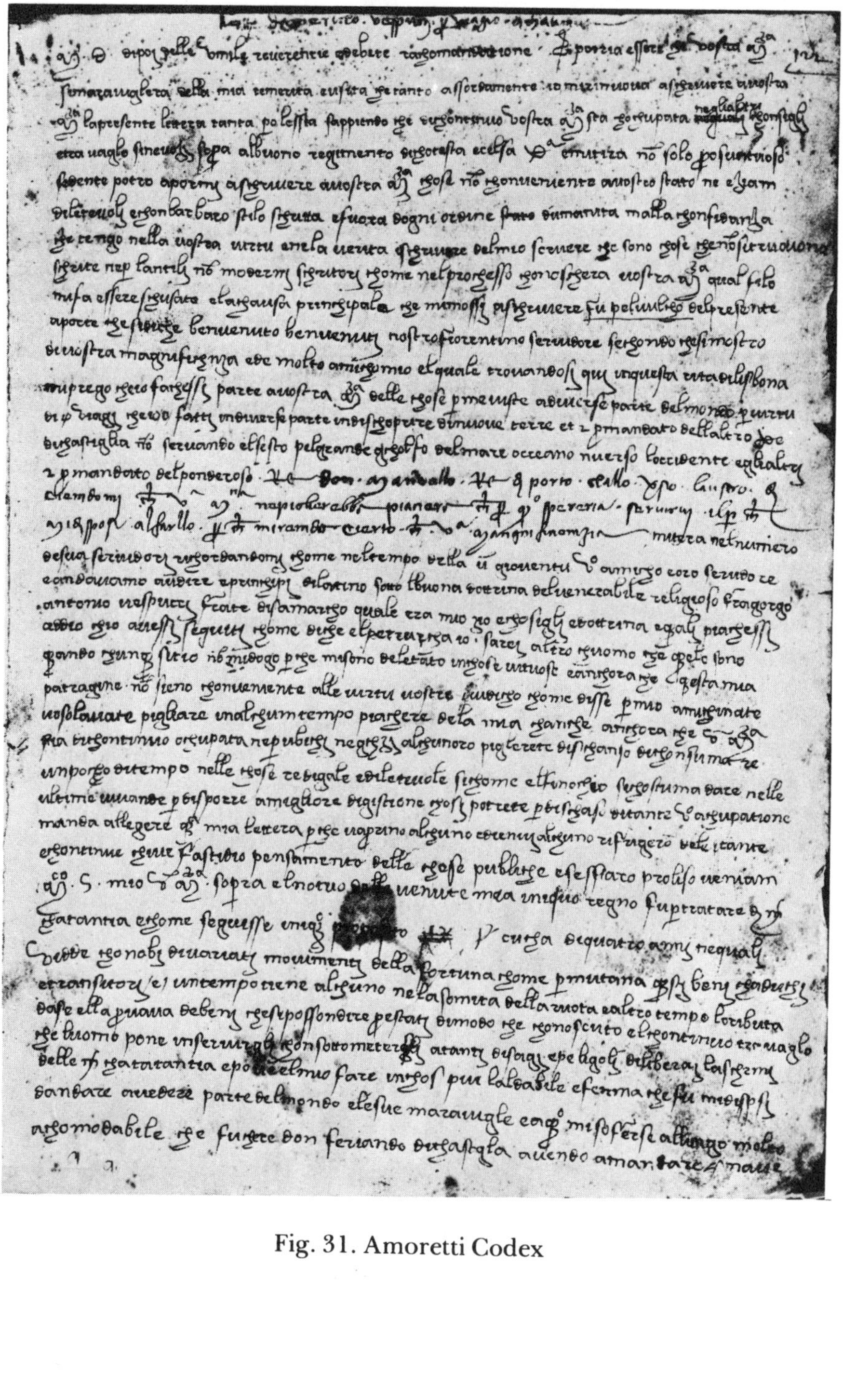

Fig. 31. Amoretti Codex

contains many unpublished passages differing from the printed text and thereby confirms the veracity of Vespucci's account, which had been questioned by modern historians.

Also in the collection were letters from the Emperor Charles V, his daughter Joanna, Princess of Spain and Portugal, and King Philip II of Spain, all concerning conditions in the Americas, especially protests about unjust treatment of the Indians, and manuscripts concerning the explorations of Cabeza de Vaca and Verrazzano.

The star piece in the collection was the "Royal File on the Indies," the actual portfolio of papers used by Emperor Charles in connection with the New Laws and the revocation of the Law of Inheritance. It was also used by King Philip II in his decision to sell the perpetual rights to the Peruvian encomiendas. The file consists of 17 original documents including an eight-page Las Casas holograph relating to the deplorable plight of the Indians.

L. Quincy Mumford, then Librarian of Congress, characterized the collection, whose value was estimated at one million dollars, as "the most important acquisition of Hispanic material" since the late Edward P. Harkness gave his collection, relating mainly to Peru, to the library in 1929. Our collection's contents are extensively described in a handsome catalogue published by the Library of Congress in 1975.

The feelings with which this collection was given to the country were summed up in a sentence I wrote in the letter presenting it, which the *Times* printed as its Quotation of the Day on January 10, 1970: "This is a modest token of my gratitude and sincere thanks to the United States, a great nation whose hospitality and spirit of freedom and equality have made it possible for me, once a poor refugee, to attain a decent place in a free human society."

Or, more briefly, "Thank you, Uncle Sam."

CHAPTER 51

The Great Transaction

BY 1957 OUR BUSINESS in periodicals and scholarly books had flourished for eleven years (see Chapter 11). In time we realized that we received multiple orders for the same journals, which we were unable to fill, titles that were out of print, or nearly so, and we started to entertain the idea of reprinting the most desirable ones.

The reprint business, so widespread and successful today, was little known before World War II, although it is of relatively early origin. The traditional reprint usually was a deluxe publication, in which an effort was made to duplicate the original in quality of paper and binding, not just in text and illustrations. To enhance its bibliophilic appeal it was often issued in a limited edition, designed to be a collector's item.

I realized the difficulties of this new business. Technical knowhow, capital, and a large staff would be essential. The details of enlarging the business occupied us day and night. The planned reprint business would place within the reach of libraries entire sets or runs of out-of-print periodicals. They had to be more durable than the original, of which the paper often had become brittle and the bindings had frequently fallen apart. We found that the only way to prepare a reprint edition economically was to have photo-offset printing plates made by photographing each of the original pages.

Our entry into reprint publishing began innocently enough with my acquisition in 1957 of a copy of Bishop John Wilkins' *A Discourse Concerning a New World & Another Planet* (London, 1640). This forerunner of science fiction was virtually unknown as literature, though book collectors were familiar with it and appreciated its scarcity and significance. Among Wilkins' prophetic "propositions," laid out like Biblical commandments, was the following:

". . . that tis possible for some of our posteritie to find a conveyance to this other world."

That was one of the earliest speculations on space travel. It must have meant very little to anybody. People at that time were far more concerned with the troubles between Stuarts and Puritans.

In preparing a description of the book I checked its not-very-extensive bibliography and found it mentioned in the first issue of *Jet Propulsion*, the Journal of the American Rocket Society. Begun as a mimeographed bulletin in 1930, with the appearance of a fan-club newsletter, this journal grew steadily in circulation, stature, and size. The first issues, when the organization called itself the American Interplanetary Society, were of only about 100 copies and survived in far fewer numbers. Not many libraries had any of the early issues, nor was there any way to get them. I felt that, with rockets and missiles so much in the news, libraries would try to improve their holdings in this field and would want complete sets of all relevant periodicals. We quickly acquired the reprint rights for the full run of *Jet Propulsion* and its English counterpart, the *Journal of the British Interplanetary Society*, begun in 1934.

Nothing could have been timelier. We were closer to the Space Age than I thought.

On October 4, 1957, the Soviet Union announced the launching of the world's first space satellite. This was not a manned flight, or moon probe; a little piece of machinery, not much bigger than a soccer ball, called Sputnik I, was sent into space and orbited the earth. This was epochal news. The newspapers were filled with reports of it, and with articles speculating on how soon the U.S. might attempt a similar feat. Everywhere there were discussions on flights to the moon, Mars, and on other possibilities of space travel.

Next morning I called together my periodicals staff, led by Fred Altman, for a strategy session. We must reprint *Jet Propulsion* and the *Journal of the British Interplanetary Society* as soon as possible, I told them, to capitalize on developments. Together we worked out details. Our meeting reminded me of the Bosch painting, "The Blind Leading the Blind." None of us knew anything about reprint publishing. Within a short time we succeeded in acquiring the essential ingredient, a complete file of the original issues of both publications. Two weeks after Sputnik's launching we had a prospectus in the mail to 10,000 libraries in all parts of the world, announcing the project and soliciting orders. We could only guess at the timetable and production cost; we had to set a retail price long before knowing our actual expense.

Within two months we had our two reprints ready for shipment. The volume of orders was sufficient to keep us working overtime. All of us, including Hanni and my mother, threw our energies into it. The effort was well invested. It proved to be a very successful undertaking. Any library that needed sets of these periodicals did not hesitate to order.

Without ever entertaining thoughts of abandoning or cutting back on our rare-book or periodicals activities, we began to divert capital into the reprint business. Here we were on the ground floor and could build and enlarge this business before other publishers came into the market with reprints of their own. We wanted to move quickly, to select titles worth printing, and to secure exclusive reprint rights. Thus we forestalled all competition, and achieved what amounted to a virtual monopoly.

We established certain criteria to govern our choice of materials to be reprinted:

The work had to be in permanent or at any rate long-term demand, rather than on a subject in which interest might be short-lived. Because another U.S. firm began to specialize in reprints in the field of medicine and exact sciences, we decided against competing in these subjects. Instead we would concentrate on the humanities, where practically no large-scale reprinting had been done: biographical and bibliographical sets, multivolume scholarly classics like the *Monumenta Germaniae Historica*, periodicals in history, art, linguistics, archaeology, economics, historical-society journals, museum and society publications, and the like. The potential was unlimited. Journals such as the *Philosophical Transactions of the Royal Society* and *Economic History Review*, to name two out of hundreds, are vast storehouses of knowledge. The reprint publisher, in addition to turning a profit, performs a service to mankind, one whose future impact will be even greater than at present. The time may well come when originals are no longer in existence, deteriorated by the crumbling of their poor paper, leaving the reprints as the only records of their content.

Ambitious though our program seemed at the time, it was modest compared to what we have accomplished over the years. In twenty years our firm has issued reprint editions of more than 30,000 volumes, with new titles added constantly. Our publications have gone into libraries all over the world.

The mid-1950s presented opportunities for this venture that may not occur again. European libraries damaged in the war were rebuilding. Rare books, stored underground by most libraries during the war or sent to neutral zones, escaped wholesale destruction but sets of periodicals fared very badly, not just from bomb damage but also from water damage in fighting fires after bombing. In addition there were new libraries starting up, in Europe and America, which had no periodical collections at all and needed the serials we were making available. Without reprints, some would still today be vainly seeking to complete files of certain periodicals and scholarly works. Our only challenger for reprint rights in the U.S.—not an arch-rival because our subject territories seldom collided—was Walter Johnson, a personal friend of prewar times.

In 1959, just two years after our first reprint, we also founded a reprint division in our Liechtenstein operation which had been in the periodical business since 1956. E. V. D. Wight was appointed manager there and assembled an efficient staff.

In 1963 when Congress made extensive revisions in the tax law in regard to foreign companies owned by Americans, our lawyers advised us to divest ourselves of 51 percent of the Liechtenstein business and to find a European buyer. We began with the reprint business. Morgan et Cie., the Paris branch of Morgan Guaranty Trust, our New York bankers, advised us to sell the shares privately rather than using a broker. So the summer of 1963 found me in Paris, accompanied by balance sheets, sales records, high expectations, and my very able financial advisor, Maxwell B. Fields. For two weeks we talked to French businessmen and investors, ate with them, drank wine with them, passed endless hours in cafés with them, and accomplished nothing. They were interested in acquiring our business but only on their own terms, which I found impossible to accept.

I left Paris without making a sale. I had lost time but learned at first hand about the mechanics of selling a company: it was far more difficult than founding one.

There was nothing to do but wait for another opportunity. Rushing into a transaction seemed inadvisable and the possibility always existed, though slim, that Congress would not pass the proposed legislation.

One day news came from S. M. Warburg, the London investment bankers, that a client had been found for 51 percent of the Kraus Reprint shares, but with a condition. The interested party not only wanted 51 percent of the Liechtenstein shares, which we were offering, but 51 percent of the New York reprint company as well. I had not intended to relinquish control of domestic operations, but if this was the only way to settle matters, it had to be seriously considered. The prospective buyer was a man I had known only by reputation, Roy H. Thomson. Canadian-born, he lived in England and headed a conglomerate of firms in the field of communications. His company owned over 270 newspapers throughout the world, including the London *Sunday Times*, and many radio and television stations; later he became owner of the most respected and venerable London daily *Times*. He had just recently been created a baron and took the title Lord Thomson of Fleet. Past 70, he was apparently still seeking new worlds to conquer.

THE GREAT TRANSACTION 371

A meeting was arranged and I flew to London, accompanied by Fields.

Lord Thomson was a living legend. He had flair and charm. At our first meeting we were soon talking like old friends. "Call me Roy," were his first words on being introduced. But we did little talking about business. Lord Thomson had a deputy to handle such details, Gordon Brunton, who later became chief executive of the Thomson English empire. He was equally friendly and we had several days of what I thought to be productive conferences. Hanni, active in the reprint business since its inception, was able to help greatly in these negotiations. Having kept a running account of sales of all titles since the start of business, she was able to provide much-needed information in a four-hour transatlantic phone marathon with Fields in London. Hanni also kept all royalty accountings on her own, until the firm was large enough for a computer to take her place.

I was summoned to a meeting at Lord Thomson's office, attended by executives of his various corporations and the Warburg bankers. Though I knew nothing of Thomson's method of business procedure, I assumed that some kind of decision had been reached and would be announced.

I arrived half-drugged, having had to consume large doses of painkiller to quiet another attack of colitis, nearly as bad as that which plagued me at the Perrins sales. Lord Thomson opened the session with a rather impassioned address, pointing out the advantages to us of joining his organization. This lifted my spirits, although I had the feeling that nothing was yet decided. It turned out that these negotiations had also failed.

When I returned to New York, Hanni thought I should have closed the deal, in spite of the unattractive terms, because of my poor health.

Six months later, after I had undergone surgery to correct my ailment, a familiar but unexpected figure appeared on 46th Street: Gordon Brunton came to reopen negotiations. Lord Thomson was still interested.

I was invited to London again to meet with Thomson and arrived on February 17, 1965. There was no conference-hall meeting, no bankers or board members. He and I met and talked things over in the Caprice Restaurant. By the time dessert arrived we had placed our initials on a preliminary agreement. There was no bargaining.

Drawing up the formal contract consumed five months and reams of paper, not to mention a series of transatlantic calls and meetings of attorneys for both parties. On July 30, 1965, the deal was closed in New York. Assembled at our lawyer's office to sign or witness the signing of the 600-page document were myself, Hanni, our two older daughters, Mary Ann and Barbara, attorneys, and my colleagues Altman and Fields. Thomson was represented by his son, Kenneth. The lawyers took us to lunch and afterward I invited my party to return to 46th Street by subway, the way Hanni and I had traveled after our marriage 25 years earlier. Now, however, the fare was 20 cents instead of 5 cents, the cars a little shabbier, but our spirits no less high.

Visions of Polycrates haunted my sleep that night; the old pagan gods, if they still existed, would not allow such overabundance of good luck to go unbalanced by bad. I wondered what all the money would do to us. After all, this was a multimillion-dollar transaction. Looking back now, at a distance of thirteen years, I can see that my fears were unfounded. The gods chose to contain their wrath, and instead of evil and misfortune, the money brought us more success. It gave us the necessary capital to increase our buying of rare books, and to purchase many of the finest illuminated manuscripts, early printed books, maps, and other rarities on the auction market. This after all, was the most exciting and rewarding phase of the business. Reprint publishing made large profits, was more dependable than dealing in old and rare books, but offered comparatively little adventure.

As for Lord Thomson, he did well and knew it. Nobody of his long experience in publishing would have entered into such a transaction without being confident of its prospect.

But one problem remained to be solved.

The same tax law would also affect our periodicals business, since part of it was in Europe. My lawyers advised me to do the same with it as with the reprint business; to find a European buyer for a 51-percent controlling interest. The obvious buyer was Lord Thomson and he was willing.

We agreed to meet again in June 1967, and the deal was closed soon thereafter.

Thus was born the Kraus-Thomson Organization, Ltd., one of the largest firms in its field. Of such importance was the news of this transaction to the business community that it appeared in all the English and American newspapers.

Once again we put most of the profits into the rare-book business, still privately owned by Hanni and me.

Altman retired as President in 1976 after 30 years of ably leading our firm, and our son-in-law, Herbert W. Gstalder (husband of our second daughter Barbara) has taken over this position, running the business in his quiet and competent way. I am chairman of the board and Hanni a director. But we both cannot help but be proud of what has become of the small business we started over 30 years ago. (See Plates 10 and 11.)

Epilogue

READERS MAY UNDERSTANDABLY get the impression that I am interested only in making money.

It is clear that this has been one of the motivating forces of all my activities. Having had to start twice in my life without a penny, I was anxious to achieve financial independence. When I had independence, I wanted wealth. For me, money's principal use has always been to spend it, on more precious books, more beautiful manuscripts, more and more and more. It has become a kind of obsession. Perhaps money cannot buy happiness, but, as the saying goes, "with money one can have plenty of pleasure."

Friends who know me as an ardent book lover often ask: "How can you bring yourself to sell these objects of your love?"

I have spent many hours of reflection seeking to frame an answer. It is this:

Early printed books and manuscripts can for me be divided into two groups: those which I am glad to sell and those which, as a collector, I hope to keep. The first group comprises the beautiful ones which appear from time to time in the salesrooms at high prices, like the Audubon *Birds* in giant folio, and those printed and illustrated by the masters of all periods. I usually fight to buy them, and then I am willing to let them go—at a price. Here I am like Don Juan, who loses interest in a maiden once he has possessed her.

The other group consists of the great or unique books and manuscripts that can be had once in a lifetime which I feel are too good to be sold. My reasonable wife often admonishes me: "Hans, you are a bookseller and not a bookkeeper!" And so I unfortunately do not follow the example of my French colleagues and keep the best books for myself, but unhappily say good-bye to these most beloved treasures. They live now, for my consolation, in libraries, museums, and private collections more worthy than mine, but I still consider them my children. Sometimes, a certain nostalgia drives me to visit them wherever they are, and in this I find consolation.

In the course of history, great libraries have been created by the wealth or power of their founders, kings and nobles, bankers and industrialists. These shrines of learning are pillars of our civilization; in them scholars work for the benefit of posterity. My contribution to the growth of these storehouses of knowledge through the acquisition of rare books and manuscripts, reprints and periodicals has given me great satisfaction and happiness, as, I hope, it will continue to do in the years to come.

What the future holds, of course, no one knows. But I do know that there are still great books and manuscripts to come on the market, some of them hitherto unknown; there will be new collectors, one hopes as ardent (and as wealthy) as those I have mentioned in these pages. There are still many opportunities for a dealer in this field, and I look forward to each new day with enthusiasm and curiosity as to what it will bring. This is how my life has been, and I would have it no other way.

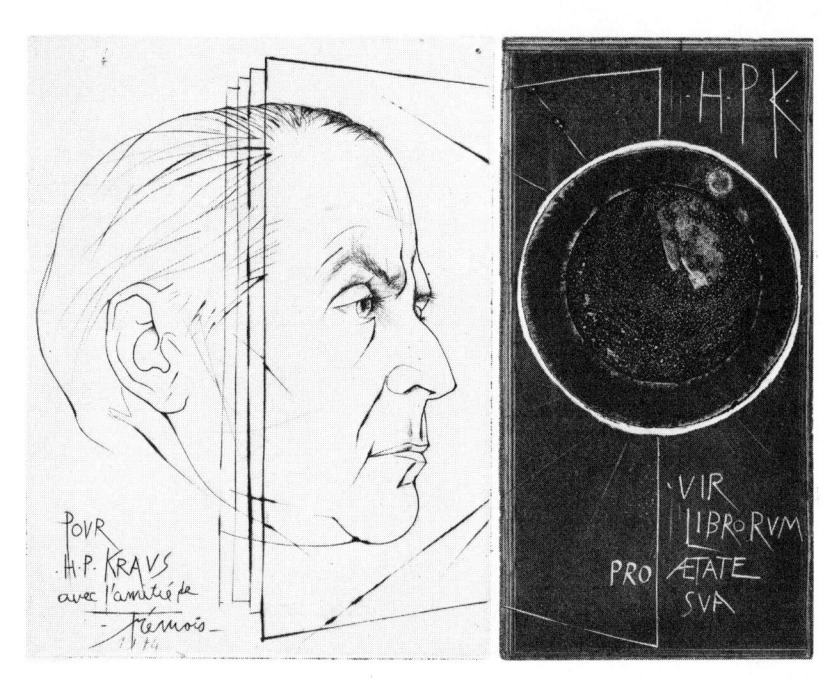

Etching by Yves Tremois

INDEX

Index

Acosta, José, 181
Acts of the Apostles, 214
Adams, Frederic B., Jr., 159 ff, 230, 233, 292, 336
Adler Papyri, 283
Admont Abbey, 52
Aeneas Sylvius see Pius II
Aeschlimann, Erardo, 107
Aesop, 149, 333
Alba, Duke of, 168 ff
Albergati Bible, 298
Albrecht von Brandenburg, 274
Alexandrian Library, Serapeum, 276
Altman, Frederick, 102, 368, 371, 372
Amoretti Codex, 363
Andreas, Father, 229 ff
Angelico, Fra Giovanni, 203
Anhalt-Dessau, Dukes of, Library, 139
Anhalt Gospels (Ms), 139–141
Apocalypse *see* Bible
Arenberg, Duke of, 191 ff
Arenberg, Grandes Heures d' (Ms), 192; Missal (Ms), 278, 283, 286
Ariosto, Lodovico, 284
Armani, Mario, 133, 278
Arnhold Collection (Mss), 303

Ars Memorandi, 122, 217
Ashburnham, Earl of, 248
Atlantic Neptune, 172, 335
Atlases: *Atlantic Neptune*, 172, 335; Lafreri, 51, 335; Mercator, 14, 16, 19, 335; Ptolemy, 122, 284, 338, 340
Augsburg Stadtbibliothek, 234
Augustine, St., 106, 297
Austrian Ministry of War Library, 41
Austrian National Library, 17, 52 ff

Babb, James T., 296
Bacon, Roger *see* Cipher Ms
Baer, Joseph, 37
Balbus, Johannes, 241, 284
Barbari, Jacopo de, 342
Bartel, Casimir (Prime Minister of Poland), 31
Barthou, Jean-Louis, 48, 254
Bauer, Hertha, 322
Bayerische Staatsbibliothek, Munich, 229, 266, 281, 333
Beans, George H., Collection, 340
Beatty, Sir A. Chester, 205 ff
Beatty Library, 209
Bede, Venerable, 284

378 INDEX

Bedford Book of Hours (Ms), 297
Beinecke, Edwin J., 142, 281, 290 ff, 295 ff
Beinecke family, 296
Bell, James F., 178, 190, 344, 348; Collection, 337
Bening, Sanders, 192, 320
Bening, Simon, 182, 274 ff, 320
Bennett, Richard, 248
Bergbau-Museum, Essen, 177
Beristayn, Ingrid, 147 ff
Beristayn, Jorge, 144 ff
Berlinghieri, Francesco, 340
Berners, Dame Juliana, 185
Berry, Jean, Duc de, 316; (Ms), 293
Bestiaries: 329 ff; *Fountains Abbey,* (Ms), 203, 332; 12th cent., Göttweig, (Ms), 332; 13th cent., Engl. (Ms), 329 ff; Sion College (Ms), 333
Bible: *Albergati* (Ms), 298; *Coverdale,* 284; Fust & Schoeffer, 284; German, 1475, 284; German, 1477, 284; *Giant Admont* (Ms), 52 ff; *Giant Mainz* (Ms), 122 ff; Gutenberg see below; New Testament, 1476, 313; Ostrog, 91; *Sarezzano* (Ms), 132 ff; *Shah Abbas* (Ms), 203; *Wycliffe* (Ms), 284. *Acts of the Apostles* (Ms), 214. Apocalypse: *Rothschild,* 290 ff; *St. Albans,* 212, 261 ff. Commentary (Ms), 290, 293: Gospels. *Anhalt* (Ms), 139 ff; *Helmarshausen* (Ms), 260 ff; 303; St. Matthew (Ms), 313. Psalter: *Bonne de Luxembourg* (Ms), 278 ff, 328; Psalter, 1457, 185, 227 ff, 314 ff; Psalter, 1459, 227 ff, 314 ff; *St. Blasien* (Ms), 265 ff; *King Wenceslas* (Ms), 267
Bible, Gutenberg (42-line-Mazarin): 50, 123; Bodmer, 236, 238, 272 ff; General Theological Seminary, 241; Immenhausen, 143; Pforzheimer, 236, 238; proof-sheet, 185; Scheide, 314 ff; Shuckburgh-Houghton, 193, 227 ff, 283, 318
Bibliotheca Lindesiana *see* Crawford

Bibliothèque Nationale, Paris, 111, 181, 203, 314 ff
Bibliothèque Royale, Brussels, 182, 269 ff
Bick, Anton, 53 ff
Birley, Sir Robert, 240
Blaeu Maps, 342
Blickling Homilies, 314
Bloch, Karl E., 41 ff, 72
Block Books: *Ars Memorandi,* 122, 217; *Doctrina Christiana,* 181; *Planetenbuch,* 284, 312
Bober, Harry, 213, 269, 307; *The St. Blasien Psalter,* 265
Boccaccio, Giovanni, 191, 309 ff
Bodega y Quadra, Francisco de la, 170
Bodleian Library, 341
Bodmer, Martin, 49, 55, 138, 236, 238, 270 ff, 297, 308, 312, 340
Bolan, Simeon, 90 ff, 99
Bonnard, Pierre, 359
Bonne de Luxembourg Psalter (Ms), 278, 281, 328
Bonnecroy, Jean Baptiste, 194
Book of Hours: *Arenberg* (Ms), 192; *Bedford* (Ms), 297; *Brandenburg* (Ms), 274; *Catherine of Cleves* (Ms), 192, 292; Flemish *(Spinola* Ms), 319 ff; *Gualenghi* (Ms), 268; *Jean de Berry* (Ms), 293; *Jeanne d'Evreux,* 293; *Llangattock* (Ms), 268 ff; *Michelino da Besozzo* (Ms), 193, 248, 278 ff; Paris (Ms), 293; *Philippe of Cleves* (Ms), 192; *Queen Claude* (Ms), 292; *Savoy* (Ms), 297
Book of the Dead, 275
Botticelli, Alessandro, 284
Botto, Padre Domenico (Dean of Sarezzano), 133
Boulind, Richard M., 349, 363
Bourdon, Jehan, 341
Brahe, Tycho, 221
Brandenburg Hours, 274
Breslauer, Bernard, 209 ff
Breslauer, Martin, 42, 47
Breton, Nicholas, 349

INDEX

Breviary: *Monte Cassino* (Ms), 196 ff; Spanish (Ms), 86 ff
British Library, 349
British Museum, 138
Brixen globes, 338
Brown, John Carter, Library, Brown University, 340 ff
Brown, Mrs. John Nicholas, 155
Brumbaugh, Robert S., 219
Bryan, Mina, 238, 313
Buchenwald Concentration Camp, 56–72 passim, 316
Buffon, Georges-Louis, 333
Bühler, Curt F., 231, 240
Bunyan, John, 283 ff
Butler, Pierce, Collection, 89
Butler, Pierce (Constitution), 325

Cabeza de Vaca, Alvar Nuñez, 366
Cain, Julien, 316
Cambridge Platform, 314
Cambridge University Library, 246, 248
Canticles of the Virgin (Ms), 298
Carnot Manuscript, 317
Carter, John, 237; *Operation Shuckburgh*, 237, 241
Catherine of Cleves Hours (Ms), 192 ff, 292
Caxton, William, 118, 173 ff, 185 ff, 233, 241, 244 ff, 280, 284, 297
Chadenat, C.H., 172
Chamonal, Maurice, 171 ff, 212
Charlemagne Capitularies (Ms), 298
Charles IV, King of France, 210
Charles V, Emperor, 366
Charles VI Missal (Ms), 139 ff, 297
Chaucer, Geoffrey, 185 ff, 204, 233, 246
Chelles, Abbey of Notre Dame de, 213
Chelles Sacramentary (Ms), 212
Chevalier délibéré, 312
Chicago, University of, Library, 91
Christie, Manson & Woods, Ltd., 241, 328
Christine de Pisan, 241, 250, 284, 293

Christofferson, Jens, 357
Christus, Petrus, 268
Cicero, 241
Cipher Manuscript, 218 ff, 298
Clark, Robert Sterling, 299
Claude, Queen of France, Hours (Ms), 210, 292
Cleveland Public Library, 102
Cockerell, Sir Sydney, 201 ff, 258, 332
Collegium Romanum, 218
Collijn, Isaak, 71 ff
Colombe, Jean, 140
Columbia University, Butler Library, 79 ff
Columbus, Christopher, 72 ff, 178, 353
Columna, Franciscus, 147 ff, 309
Columna, Guido de, 212
Communist Manifesto, 160
Concordantia Caritatis (Ms), 152 ff
Constance Missal, 166, 196, 228 ff, 235
Conway, G.R.G., 174 ff
Coptic Manuscript, 214
Corn, Ira, 327
Coronelli Globe, 252 ff, 342, 356
Cortez, Hernando, 174 ff
Coverdale Bible, 284
Crawford, David, Earl of, 134 ff
Creswick, Richard, 246
Crivelli, Taddeo, 268
Cusanus, Nicolaus, Cardinal, 128 ff; map, 128, 185 ff, 309

Dachau Concentration Camp, 56–72 passim, 96
Dante Alighieri, 132 ff; (Ms), 268; 284; (Ms), 297
Dawson, Ernest, 329 ff
Dead Sea Scrolls, 127 ff
Dechert, Robert, 178
Declaration of Independence, 282, 314, 325 ff
Dee, Arthur, 222
Dee, John, 221 ff
De Golyer, Everett, 176
Demby, Stefan, 32, 44

INDEX

Demidoff, Prince Anatole, 254
Des Barres, 335
Deutsche Staatsbibliothek, East Berlin, 159
Dietrichstein Collection, 43
Doctrina Christiana, 181
Dodgson, Campbell, 121 ff
Domizlaff, Helmuth, 45 ff, 55, 229, 265 ff, 352
Drake, Sir Francis, 344 ff
Droz, Eugenie, 110 ff
Durandus, G., 145 ff, 313
Duvet, Jean, 122

Eames, Wilberforce, 88 ff, 110
Eismann, Father, 129 ff
Eton College, 240
Eugene of Savoy, Prince, 53 ff
Eyck, Jan van, 268

Feldman, Lew D., 240, 317, 327
Fenwick family, 223 ff
Ferdinand III, King of Bohemia, 221
Fields, Maxwell B., 370 ff
Figdor Collection, 42
Finaly, Mrs. Hugo, 281
Fischer, Otto, 216, 275
Fleming, John F., 100
Florentine pictorial chronicle (Ms), 203
Fock, Gustav, 48 ff
Foligno *see* Dante
Folter, Roland, 357
Fountains Abbey Bestiary (Ms), 203, 332
Fouquet, Jean, 140, 203
Franz Ferdinand, Archduke of Austria, 4 ff
Free Library of Philadelphia, 93
Freeman, Samuel, & Co., 325
Friedman, W.F., 219
Froissart, Jean, (Ms), 292
Fuchs, Abbot, 54
Fust and Schoeffer, 71, 121, 144, 227 ff, 314

Galanti, Blasio, 180 ff
Gargantua, 154

Gastaldi, Giacomo, 51, 108, 342
General Theological Seminary, 241
Ghisolfi, 253, 341
Gilcrease, Thomas, 174 ff
Gilhofer & Ranschburg, 17, 46, 54, 305
Gilles Li Muisis Codex (Ms), 267
Gillet, Charles, 208, 312
Gimbel's, 86 ff
Glazier, William S., 211 ff, 262 ff
Globes: Brixen, 338; Coronelli, 252 ff, 342, 356; Waldseemüller, 337
Goff, Frederick R., 111, 240, 317, 327, 363
Golden Fleece Armorial (Ms), 182
Gospels *see* Bible
Gotha, Dukes of, Library, 122, 147, 217, 309, 313
Göttingen, University of, 309
Göttweig Abbey, 51 ff, 332
Gower, John, 248
Grafe, Felix, 352
Gratianus (Ms), 268
Greene, Belle da Costa, 87 ff, 132, 140 ff
Greenwich National Maritime Museum, 52, 349
Grimm, Brothers, 49
Grinnell, Julius S., 160, 163
Grolier Club, 159, 197 ff, 214, 282, 308 ff
Grube, E.J., *Islamic Paintings,* 350
Gstalder, Herbert W., 372
Gualenghi Hours (Ms), 268
Gutenberg, Johann, 228 ff, 241 ff; *see also* Balbus and Bible
Gutenberg Museum, Mainz, 241
Gutman, Baron Rudolf von, 304 ff
Gutman, Baroness von, 306 ff

Habsburg, Fidei-Kommiss-Bibliothek, 53
Hachette, André, Sale, 212
Halbey, Hans, 241
Hale, Herbert Z. *see* Zucker
Hanes, James G., 248
Hardt, Baron Kurt, 178

INDEX

Harper, Lathrop C., 78, 92, 95, 107, 179
Harrsen, Meta, 132
Harvard University, Houghton Library, 87, 93 ff, 224, 338
Harvey, William, 54 ff, 217, 352
Hauslab, Franz von, 152
Hauswedell Auction, 277
Hayes, R.J., 209
Haymarket Collection, 160 ff
Hayward, John, 241 ff
Hearst, William Randolph, Collection, 86
Hedwig, St. (Ms), 304 ff
Helmarshausen Gospels (Ms), 260 ff, 303
Hermentrude, Queen of France, 213
Hertzen, Alexander, 159, 164
Hess, Julius, 49
Hibbert, George, 248
Hiersemann, Karl W., 36 ff
Hispanic Society of America, 37, 86
Histoire de Thèbes (Ms), 268
Hobson, Anthony, 203, 323
Hoccleve, Thomas, 284
Hoepli, Ulrico, 107 ff, 133, 252, 278, 342,
Hofer, Philip, 87 ff, 330
Homage to a Bookman (H.P.K. Festschrift), 214
Horblit, Harrison, 122, 226
Horenbout, Gerard, 320
Hořeys, 46 ff
Houghton, Arthur A., Jr., 187, 193, 234 ff, 279, 283
Hoving, Thomas, Jr., 293 ff, 328
Hull, Cordell, 80
Humphrey, Duke of Gloucester, 333
Huntington, Archer M., 37, 86
Huntington, Henry, 95, 258
Hupp, Otto, 228 ff
Hyde, Mary (Mrs. Donald F.), 280

Indiana University, Bloomington, Lilly Library, 179, 188, 246
Ingold, 120
Ives, Samuel A., 329 ff, 357 and Hellmut Lehmann-Haupt, *An*

English 13th Cent. Bestiary, 330

Jackson, William A., 93 ff, 224
Jakobson, Roman, 91
James, Montague R., 258
Jeanne d'Evreux (Ms), 293
Jefferson, Thomas, 216
Jesuit Relations, 177 ff
Joachim of Floris (Ms), 203
Joanna, Princess of Spain and Portugal, 366
John Rylands Library, 135
Johnson, Walter, 370
Jolowicz, Leo, 49

Karl, Emperor of Austria, 6 ff
Karl-Marx-Haus, Trier, 159
Kebabian, John S. (Jack), 160, 216, 238 ff, 269, 317, 327, 357
Keim, Anton, 241
Kelmscott Press, 201 ff
Kent, Roland G., 219
Kepler, Johannes, 221
Kern, Jerome, Sale, 84
Kerr, Lord John, 321
Kervorkian, Hagop, 350
Kircher, Athanasius, 221
Koehler's Antiquarium, 48 ff, 54, 58
Kotula, Rudolf, 31
Koziebrodzki, Count, 183 ff
Kraus, Dr. Emil, 1–25 passim
Kraus, Hanni (Zucker), Chapter 9 et seq.
Kraus, Hilda (Rix), 1–72 passim, 85, 113 ff
Kraus, Dr. Ignatius, 2
Kraus children: Mary Ann *see* Mitchell; Barbara (Mrs. Gstalder), 112; Eveline (Mrs. Rauber), 112; Susan (Mrs. Nakamura), 112; Hans P., Jr. (John), 112, 321 ff
Kraus firms: H.P. Kraus, 77 et seq.; Kraus Periodicals, Inc., 102; Back Issues Corp., 103; Kraus Reprint Corp., 370 ff; Kraus-Thomson Org., Ltd., 372
Kredit-Anstalt, Vienna, 36 ff

Kress, Rush, 156
Kress von Kressenstein, 155 ff
Kundig, William S., 140 ff
Kunze, Horst, 159

Labus, Lotte, 357
Lactantius, 284
Lafayette, Marquis de, 173
La Fontaine, Jean de, 48
Lafreri Atlas, 51, 335
Landau, Horace de, Collection, 281
Landesbibliothek, Stuttgart, 265 ff
Langer, Eduard, 352
Lardanchet, Paul, 105 ff, 111
Las Casas, Bartolome de, 366
Leary's Book Store, 325 ff
Le Bret, René, 281 ff
Lechner's Universitätsbuchhandlung, 22 ff, 39
Leclerc, Victor Emmanuel, 172
Leclerc-Rochambeau Papers, 174
Le Fèvre, Raoul, 246, 248
Legrain, J.A., 333
Lehman Brothers, 211
Lehman, Emanuel, 100
Lehman, Philip, 100
Lehman-Haupt, Hellmut, 123, 185, 233, 269, 276, 329 ff, 353, 357; *Gutenberg and the Master of the Playing Cards*, 125; see also Ives
Lenin, Vladimir I., 158 ff
Lenin Library, Moscow, 165
Library of Congress, 111, 117, 126, 181, 236, 317, 363
Liebaers, Herman, 269 ff
Liebert, Herman W. (Fritz), 142, 277, 296
Liechtenstein, Hartmann, II, 152
Liechtenstein, Prince Franz Josef II, 152, 280; Library, 151 ff, 176; Map Collection, 336 ff
Lilly, J.K., Collection, 178 ff, 246
Limbourg Brothers, 293
Livius (Ms), 317
Llangattock Hours (Ms), 268 ff
Lobo, Julio, 174
Login, B., & Son, 103

Loncle, Maurice, 308 ff
Lothian, Marquess of, 310
Louisiana Purchase, 216
Luce, Henry R., 113
Ludd, Gualther, 77
Ludwig, Irene (Mrs. Peter), 302
Ludwig, Peter, 199, 203, 213, 243, 270, 274, 293, 302 ff, 323, 332
Lumiere as Lais (Ms), 284
Luther, Martin, 136
Lwów Polytechnic Institute, 31
Lwów University Library, 31

Maggs Brothers, 137 ff, 210, 236
Maisonneuve, 105
Mansion, Colard, 191, 309 ff
Maps: Blaeu, 342; Bourdon, 341; Cusanus, 128, 185 ff, 309; Gastaldi, 51, 108, 342; Liechtenstein Collection, 336 ff; Montresor, 47; Palestine (Ms), 336; Pedro de Medina (Ms), 341; "Silver Map," 349; Vespucci, 338; see also Portolan charts
Marcus, Joannes M., 221 ff
Marinis, Tamaro de, 281 ff
Marlborough Fine Arts, 268 ff
Marot, Clément, 111
Marrow, James, 292
Martens, *Recueil*, 48
Martin, Alastair Bradley, 192 ff, 332
Martin, Major Nigel, 242 ff
Martini, Giuseppe, 108 ff
Marx-Engels, *Communist Manifesto*, 160
Master of the Playing Cards, 123
Maus, Edmée, 274, 309
Mazarin Bible see Bible, Gutenberg
McCoy, James C., 177 ff
McGill University, Montreal, 341
Mears, Captain John, 170
Medina, Pedro de (Ms), 341
Mehltretter, Hans, 229 ff
Melk Abbey, 50
Mellon, Paul, 173, 189, 246, 254, 286, 333
Melusine, 309

INDEX

Mendel, Bernardo, 179
Mer des histoires, 309
Mercator, Gerard, 14 ff, 335, 349
Mercator, Michael, 349
Merton, Wilfred, 209
Metropolitan Museum of Art, New York, 260 ff, 279, 282, 293, 328
Michelino da Besozzo (Ms), 193, 248, 278 ff
Middle Hill Press, 224 ff
Miner, Dorothy, 269, 274, 338
Mining Book of Schwaz (Ms), 176 ff
Minnesota, University of, 337, 344
Missals: *Arenberg* (Ms), 278 ff, 283, 286; *Charles VI* (Ms), 139 ff, 297; *Constance,* 166, 196, 228 ff, 235; *Paris* (Ms), 317
Mitchell, Mary Ann, 85, 112 ff, 194, 197
Molière, Jean-Baptiste, 283
Mondragone Library, 218
Mongan, Elisabeth, 125
Monte Cassino, Monastery, 196 ff
Monte Cassino Codex (Ms), 196 ff
Montresor Map, 47
Monumenta Germaniae Historica, 48
Morgan, Charles, 279
Morgan, J.P., 95, 203, 258 ff
Morgan, Junius S., 233
Morgan Library *see* Pierpont Morgan Library
Muenzer, Hieronymous, 284, 340
Mumford, L. Quincy, 366
Munby, A.N.L., 226
Münster University Library, 195
Murray, Charles Fairfax, 259, 312
Museum of Fine Arts, Boston, 310, 342
Myrror of the World, 233

Nachod, Hans, 99, 123, 146 ff, 185, 215 ff, 357
Nakayama, Shozen, Shimbashira of Tenrikyo University, 251
National Gallery of Art, Washington, 117
Nebenzahl, Kenneth, 328

New-York Historical Society, 336
New York Public Library, 77
Newberry Library, Chicago, 89, 91, 217
Newbold, Wm. R., 219
Newton, A. Edward, 84
Nicolajewski, Colonel, 90
Nijhoff, Martinus, 108
Nikolaus of Bruenn, 153
Nill, Ann, 219 ff
Nordkirchen Archives, 195
Norman, Don Cleveland, 236
North Carolina, University of, 248

Oettingen-Wallerstein Collection, 129
Olschki, Leo, 107
Orbis Terrarum, 27
Orsetti Library, 108
Ostrog Bible, 91

Palestine map (Ms), 336
Papyri, 356
Parke-Bernet Galleries, 76 ff, 246, 325, 327
Patetta, Senator, Collection, 107
Paul, Prince, of Yugoslavia, 253 ff
Paulus Diaconus (Ms), 286
Peck, Clara, 153
Pellechet, Marie, 111
Perlstein, Israel, 90 ff
Perrins, C.W. Dyson, 81, 212, 241, 257 ff, 303
Perrins, Mrs., 267
Perrins Sale, 257 ff
Petersen, Father Theodore, 356
Petrarca, Francesco, 309
Petronius, 359
Pfister, Albrecht, 145 ff, 150, 185, 242
Pforzheimer Collection, 236 ff
Philip II, King of Spain, 366
Philippe of Cleves Hours, 192
Phillipps, Sir Thomas, Collection, 138, 203, 213, 223 ff, 333
Philobiblon, A.G., 42
Picasso, Pablo, 333, 359
Piekarski, Kazimierz, 32, 43 ff

INDEX

Pierpont Morgan Library, 86 ff, 92, 99, 132 ff, 140 ff, 153, 193 ff, 211, 217, 230 ff, 246 ff, 279 ff, 292, 309, 311, 332, 336
Pius II, 93
Planetenbuch, 284, 312
Poggio Bracciolini, 284
Polain, Louis, 110 ff
Poole, George A., III, 179, 186 ff, 246
Portolan Charts, 340 ff
Prague, Ministry of War Library, 41
Prague, University Library, 44
Proksch, Josef, 49 ff
Psalters *see* Bible
Ptolemy *see* Atlases
Pucelle, Jean de, 293; Atelier of, 282
Pynson, Richard, 248

Quaritch, Bernard, 135, 234, 237

Rabelais, François, 154
Rabinovitz, Louis M., 246
Raffet, Denis, 254
Randall, David A., 233
Ranschburg, Heinrich, 305
Ranschburg, Otto, 46, 78, 82, 179, 305
Ransom, Harry H., 282, 286
Raspe, Rudolph E., 173
Rau, Arthur, 177 ff, 212, 312
Redouté, P.J., 282
Reisinger, Curt, 338
Revilla-Gigedo, Count, 169 ff
Reynart the Foxe, 248 ff, 284, 297
Ricci, Seymour de, 314
Ripon Cathedral Library, 246
Ritter, François, 166 ff
Rix, Dr. Adalbert, (great-grandfather), 2
Rix, Anton, (grandfather), 2
Rix, Hermine, (grandmother), 3
Robinson brothers (Lionel, Philip), 210, 224 ff
Rochambeau, Général (Conte de Vimeur), 172
Rochambeau, Maréchal (Vicomte de Vimeur), 172 ff
Romont Monastery, 229 ff

Rona, Lilly, 74
Ronsard, Pierre de, 48
Roosevelt, Franklin D., 80
Rorimer, James J., 260 ff
Rosen, Gerd, 39
Rosenbach, A.S.W., 76, 79, 84, 92 ff, 100, 190, 286
Rosenthal, Edwin, 51
Rosenthal, Jacques, 37, 51
Rosenthal, Ludwig, 229
Rosenwald, Julius, 117
Rosenwald, Lessing, 85, 106, 117 ff, 181, 185, 308, 340, 342
Rothschild Apocalypse (Ms), 290 ff
Rothschild Collections, 193, 274, 289 ff
Rousseau, Theodore, Jr., 293 ff
Roxburghe, Duke of, 248
Royal Library, Stockholm, 71
Rubakin, N.A., 164 ff
Rudolf von Ems (Mss), 286
Rudolph II, Emperor, 221
Ruysschaert, Monsignor José, 222
Ryan, Clendening, 173, 188 ff

Sachs, Hans, 283
Sacramentary, Chelles (Ms), 212
St. Albans Apocalypse (Ms), 212, 261 ff
St. Blasien Psalter (Ms), 265 ff
St. Paul's Monastery, 50
St. Peter's Abbey, 51, 71
St. Vincent College, Latrobe, Pa., 246
Samuels, Howard, 189
Sarezzano Purple Bible (Ms), 132 ff
Savoy Hours (Ms), 297
Schab, Wm. H., 54, 74 ff, 104 ff, 122, 152, 171 ff, 180 ff, 191 ff, 202 ff, 231, 278, 335
Schäfer, Ida (Mrs. Otto), 308 ff
Schäfer, Otto, 129, 150, 186, 217, 250, 288, 308 ff, 340
Scharfenberg, Albrecht von (Ms), 280, 286
Schedel, Hartmann, 33 ff
Scheide, John H., 236, 313

INDEX

Scheide, William H., 150, 238, 313 ff, 327
Scheler, Lucien, 48, 110 ff
Schembart Books, 154
Schiele, Egon, 24
Schilling, Rosy, 278
Schirach, Baldur von, 58
Schirach, Helene von, 58
Schlackenwerth Monastery, 305
Schopenhauer, Arthur, 277
Schuschnigg, Kurt, (Chancellor of Austria), 57, 59
Schwitzer, William, 337
Scribner's Book Store, 237
Seligman, Germain, 191
Seligman, Jesse, 100
Sessler's, Charles, 327
Shah Abbas (Ms), 203
Shakespeare, William, 190, 283 ff
Shuckburgh Library, 236 ff, 241 ff
Sickles, Daniel, 358 ff
Sigenulfus Codex, 196 ff
Silver, Louis H., 215 ff
"Silver Map," 349
Sion College Library, 333 ff
Smetana, Fredrich, 49 ff
Sotheby & Co., 47, 135, 138, 203, 209, 217, 246, 250, 257 ff, 282, 316, 319 ff, 332 ff, 350
Spanish Breviary (Ms), 86 ff
Spanish Forger, 87
Speculum Historiale (Ms), 316
Spencer, Earl, 248
Sperancius, Sebastian, Bishop of Brixen, 338
Stalin, Joseph V., 163
Sterling, Charles: *Master of Claude, Queen of France*, 292
Stevens, Henry, Son & Stiles, 172
Stonehill, Charles, 223 ff
Strachwitz, Arthur, Count, 152
Strahm, Hans, 163 ff
Streeter, Thomas, 178
Strickland, Father J., 218
Strong, Patrick, 240
Stuvaert, Lievin, 268

Suida, William, 155 ff
Sukenik, Eleazar Lipa, 127 ff
Sweynheym and Pannartz, 297

Taylor, Henry C., 178, 341, 353
Texas, University of (Austin), 108, 217, 237, 282, 286, 342, 356
Teyler Endowment Library, Haarlem, 108
Theatrum Sanitatis (Ms), 153
Thomas, Marcel, 290 ff, 314 ff
Thomas Aquinas (Ms), 153
Thomson, Kenneth (Lord Thomson of Fleet), 372
Thomson, Roy H. (Lord Thomson of Fleet), 224, 370 ff
Thun-Hohenstein Library, 45 ff
Tinker, Chauncey Brewster, 296
Titurel (Ms), 280, 286
Tory, Geofroy, 292
Tree, Roland, 171 ff, 188, 336
Trier, Stadtbibliothek, 237
Trotsky, Leon D., 158 ff, 163
Tully, Alice, 280

United States Constitution, 324 ff
Universum Co., 103

Valturius, 122, 218
Vatican Library, 222
Verardus, 72 ff, 353
Verlain, Paul, 359
Verrazzano, Giovanni da, 366
Vescomte, Pietro, 336
Vespucci, Amerigo, 363 ff
Vespucci Map, 338
Vidal (Ms), 268
Vincent of Beauvais, 316
Virgil, 284
Vocabulary (Caxton), 246 ff
Voigts, Landrat, 123
Vopell Map, 338
Voynich, Ethel (Boole), 219, 222
Voynich, Wilfred Michael, 122, 218 ff
Vrelant, Willem, 192

Wagstaff Collection, 300
Waldseemüller Globe, 337
Waldseemüller Gores, 356
Walla, H., 12 ff
Walters Art Gallery, Baltimore, 274, 338
Warburg, S.M., 224, 370 ff
Warner, Sir George, 258
Warsaw National Library, 32, 43
Washington, George, 173
Washington-Rochambeau Papers, 173 ff, 188 ff
Wasmuth Verlag, 26–40 passim
Waters, David N., 349
Wavrin Master, 268
Weelan, J.E., 172
Weiller, Paul Louis, 141
Wells, Gabriel, 84, 92 ff, 139 ff
Wenceslas Psalter (Ms), 267
Wien, Rudolf, 121
Wight, E.V.D., Jr., 152 ff, 370
Wilczek, Count, 280, 340
Wilhelm, H., 337

Wilhering Monastery, 51, 335
Wilkins, Bishop John, 367
William the Affable of Austria (Ms), 153
William the Conqueror, 137 ff
Williams College, 299
Wilson, H.W., Co., 103
Wolf, Alfred, 39, 57 ff, 70
Worde, Wynkyn de, 241

Yale Center for British Art, 174
Yale University, Beinecke Rare Book & Manuscript Library, 142, 222, 277, 284, 295 ff, 341, 356; Sterling Memorial Library, 89, 295 ff

Zahn, Mabel, 327
Zink, Karel, 46
Zucker, Alois, 46
Zucker, Ernest, 98, 224, 259, 281
Zucker-Hale, Herbert, 80 ff, 98, 104 ff, 231
Zurich, Zentralbibliothek, 233

B KRAUS, H.
Kraus, Hans Peter, 1907-
A rare book saga : the
autobiography of H. P.
Kraus.

		DATE DUE